Shifting to DIGITAL

A Guide to Engaging, Teaching, & Assessing Remote Learners

James A.
BELLANCA

Gwendolyn Battle
LAVERT

Kate
BELLANCA

Solution Tree | Press
a division of
Solution Tree

Copyright © 2022 by Solution Tree Press

Materials appearing here are copyrighted. With one exception, all rights are reserved. Readers may reproduce only those pages marked "Reproducible." Otherwise, no part of this book may be reproduced or transmitted in any form or by any means (electronic, photocopying, recording, or otherwise) without prior written permission of the publisher.

555 North Morton Street
Bloomington, IN 47404
800.733.6786 (toll free) / 812.336.7700
FAX: 812.336.7790
email: info@SolutionTree.com
SolutionTree.com

Visit **go.SolutionTree.com/technology** to download the free reproducibles in this book.

Printed in the United States of America

Library of Congress Cataloging-in-Publication Data

Names: Bellanca, James A., 1937- author. | Battle-Lavert, Gwendolyn, author. | Bellanca, Kate, author.
Title: Shifting to digital : a guide to engaging, teaching, and assessing remote learners / James A. Bellanca, Gwendolyn Battle Lavert, Kate Bellanca.
Description: Bloomington, IN : Solution Tree Press, 2021. | Includes bibliographical references and index.
Identifiers: LCCN 2021034020 (print) | LCCN 2021034021 (ebook) | ISBN 9781952812217 (paperback) | ISBN 9781952812224 (ebook)
Subjects: LCSH: Web-based instruction--Planning. | Web-based instruction--Evaluation. | Lesson planning. | Educational tests and measurements. | Internet in education.
Classification: LCC LB1044.87 .B426 2021 (print) | LCC LB1044.87 (ebook) | DDC 371.33/44678--dc23
LC record available at https://lccn.loc.gov/2021034020
LC ebook record available at https://lccn.loc.gov/2021034021

Solution Tree

Jeffrey C. Jones, CEO
Edmund M. Ackerman, President

Solution Tree Press

President and Publisher: Douglas M. Rife
Associate Publisher: Sarah Payne-Mills
Managing Production Editor: Kendra Slayton
Editorial Director: Todd Brakke
Art Director: Rian Anderson
Copy Chief: Jessi Finn
Senior Production Editor: Tonya Maddox Cupp
Content Development Specialist: Amy Rubenstein
Acquisitions Editor: Sarah Jubar
Copy Editors: Mark Hain and Jessi Finn
Proofreader: Kate St. Ives
Text and Cover Designer: Abigail Bowen
Editorial Assistants: Charlotte Jones, Sarah Ludwig, and Elijah Oates

ACKNOWLEDGMENTS

We wish to thank those teachers, administrators, parents, and students who contributed ideas to these pages and gave constructive feedback. These include Sophie, Elise, and Anna Kahler and their mother, Carla; Elias, Jo, and Holger Dulin; Leo and Vivi Bellanca; and others whose quotes we acknowledge throughout the chapters.

More directly, thanks go to key Solution Tree Press staff who helped frame the content and prepare it for publication. We appreciate our editor Tonya Cupp's talent and her ability to ask just the right questions and to make the exact suggestion to clarify meaning and ensure that text says what was truly meant, getting every nuance just right. Thanks to the Solution Tree design team for inviting us to collaborate in the cover and internal designs.

Solution Tree Press would like to thank the following reviewers:

Tonya Alexander
English Teacher (NBCT)
Owego Free Academy
Owego, New York

Aaron Cass
English Teacher
Sanborn Regional High School
Kingston, New Hampshire

Eric Lindblad
English Teacher
Andover High School
Andover, Minnesota

Christina Takach
History and Social Studies Teacher
Glasgow Middle School
Alexandria, Virginia

Visit **go.SolutionTree.com/technology** to download the free reproducibles in this book.

TABLE OF CONTENTS

Reproducible pages are in italics.

ABOUT THE AUTHORS ix

INTRODUCTION 1
    The Paradigm's New Path 3
    Teachers' Needs to Know 9
    This Book's Organization 10
    Where to Start 11
    Guiding Questions 13
    Instruction Idea Gathering 15
    Connecting Dots Between Experience and Inexperience 16
    Brainstorming Chart 18

Chapter 1
THE TECHNOLOGY TO MASTER 19
    What Do I Need to Know About My School's Learning Management System? 19
    What Do I Need to Know About My School's Video Conference System? 20
    Which Video Conference System Might Work Best for My Sessions? 25
    How Should Students and I Set Up Workspaces in Preparation for a VCS? 26
    How Do I Introduce Students to the Technology I Have Available? 28
    How Do I Initiate Student Engagement Using a Video Conference System? 32
    How Do I Expand Students' Digital Skills? 34
    What If the Video Conference System Crashes? 35
    How Can I Help Students Who Have Too Little or No Internet Access? 36
    Conclusion 38
    My Takeaways 39
    Students' Digital Skills 40

Chapter 2
INSTRUCTIONAL DESIGN FOR VIRTUAL LEARNING 41
    How Do I Use Design Thinking to Adapt My Given Curriculum to Online
        Lessons and Projects? 42

How Do I Balance the Technology, Documents, Activities, Feedback, and
Assessment in Online Lessons? 46

What Research-Based Practices Work Best for Online Instruction?. 46

How Do I Ensure Deeper Learning Outcomes? 48

What Evidence-Based Methods Promote Cognitive and Affective Online Engagement? 51

What Other Digital Tools and Strategies Stimulate Collaborative Discussions? 62

How Do I Add Project-Based Deeper Learning Units to My Instructional Options? 65

How Do I Design Game-Based Learning in Online Instruction? 68

How Can Flipping My Online Classroom Help? 72

How Do I Engage English Learners With Online Instruction? 72

How Do I Make Up for Online Learning Losses?. 73

Conclusion 75

My Takeaways 75

Resources, Activities, Support, and Evaluation Planning and Assessment 76

Chapter 3
DIGITAL DOCUMENTS 81

How Do I Create Digital Documents to Organize Workflow? 81

How Do I Organize Digital Documents? 84

How Do E-Portfolios Help My E-Classroom Organization? 85

Where Can I Find an Effective Portfolio System for My Students? 86

What Entries Most Enrich E-Portfolios? 87

How Do Students and I Manage E-Portfolios? 90

What If Students Lack the Technology Needed for Electronic Portfolios? 97

How Do I Safeguard Students' Portfolio Privacy? 100

What Should I Know About My Teacher Portfolio? 100

Conclusion 101

My Takeaways 101

Chapter 4
MINDFUL ENGAGEMENT IN DIGITAL CLASSROOMS. 103

How Do I Increase Student Engagement by Building Autonomy? 105

How Do I Engage Students in Goal Setting? 106

How Do I Build Community to Enrich Online Learning Time? 110

How Do I Stimulate Mindful Online Reflections? 117

How Do I Create Community in Hybrid Classes in Split Locations? 128

Conclusion 131

My Takeaways 131

Chapter 5
POSITIVE INTERACTION AND SOCIAL-EMOTIONAL LEARNING ... 133

- How Do I Develop Students' Social-Emotional Skills? ... 134
- How Do I Engage Students in Prosocial Behavior? ... 139
- How Do I Address Distractive or Dysfunctional Behaviors? ... 147
- How Do I Address Failure to Adhere to Prior Agreements or a Major Dysfunctional Behavior? ... 152
- How Do I Deal With Student Stress, Anxiety, and Depression? ... 154
- Conclusion ... 158
- My Takeaways ... 159

Chapter 6
FEEDBACK ... 161

- What Does Effective Feedback Look Like in a Virtual Classroom? ... 162
- What Are Online Feedback Best Practices? ... 166
- How Can Students Give Me Feedback? ... 170
- How Can Students Give Effective Two-Way Peer Feedback? ... 172
- How Do I Engage Students in Peer-to-Peer Feedback? ... 174
- How Do I Keep Track of the Correspondence Generated by Two-Way Feedback? ... 177
- Conclusion ... 178
- My Takeaways ... 179

Chapter 7
ASSESSMENT IN A DIGITAL ENVIRONMENT ... 181

- How Can Technology Enhance the Assessment Process? ... 182
- How Do I Assess Student Learning in a Digitally Rich Learning Environment? ... 186
- Can I Abandon Assessment in Certain Situations? ... 187
- How Can I Address Cheating in Distance Learning? ... 187
- How Do I Assess Online Cooperative Learning? ... 188
- How Do I Assess Project-Based Deeper Learning in a Digital Environment? ... 192
- How Do I Assess Engagement? ... 193
- Conclusion ... 194
- My Takeaways ... 195

Chapter 8
STUDENTS WITH SPECIAL NEEDS ... 197

- What Challenges Occur While Teaching Students With Special Needs? ... 197
- What Transferable Skills Benefit Students With Special Needs When Online? ... 201

How Do I Differentiate Instruction for Special Needs Students?. 202

How Do I Ensure Compliance With the Americans With Disabilities Act?. 203

Conclusion 203

My Takeaways 204

Chapter 9
COMMUNICATION *WITH* PARENTS AND GUARDIANS 205

What Resources Help Parents and Guardians Communicate High Expectations
for Digital Learning? 206

What Activities Help Parents and Guardians Communicate High Expectations?. 210

How Can I Support Parents and Guardians as They Show High Expectations?. 212

What Is the Parent's or Guardian's Role in Student Assessment?. 213

How Do I Help Families With Primary-Grade Digital Learners?. 215

What Should I Be Aware of Regarding Parental Consent, Law, and Student Privacy? . . . 215

Conclusion 218

My Takeaways 218

REFERENCES AND RESOURCES 219

INDEX 245

ABOUT THE AUTHORS

James A. Bellanca is internationally recognized as a practical innovator who provides teachers and administrators with the how-to knowledge to make abstract ideas concrete and ready to go on the next school day. He is a senior fellow with the Partnership for 21st Century Learning and was founding editor of its innovative online publication, *P21 Blogazine*. He is the 2013 recipient of the Malcolm Knowles Award for lifetime contributions to the field of self-directed learning from the International Society for Self-Directed Learning.

With his extensive experience as a classroom English and language arts teacher, alternative school director, professional developer, intermediate service center director, business owner, and not-for-profit executive, Jim has developed expertise for transforming mandates, such as the Common Core State Standards, into practical classroom tools that enrich instruction and engage students.

He is past president of the Illinois Consortium for 21st Century Schools and lead trainer for MindQuest: Project-Based Learning in the 21st Century Classroom, which helps schools with large English-learner populations and students of color and poverty adopt the project-based learning model of instruction. Jim has worked with educational leaders in the United States, Australia, New Zealand, Norway, and Israel. His specialty is the application of group investigation and inquiry models of learning as the primary methods for helping school leaders and teachers adopt 21st century models of instruction. His aim is to help school districts design, implement, and assess programs that promote 21st century skills to increase academic performance among all students, including high-risk populations.

Jim works closely with Solution Tree Press to identify emerging authors who address the themes and practices that define and describe 21st century learning. He has authored or coauthored multiple Solution Tree Press how-to books about thinking in the Common Core, enriched learning projects, and leadership for the Common Core. He coedited *21st Century Skills: Rethinking How Students Learn* with Ron Brandt and edited *Deeper Learning: Beyond 21st Century Skills* and *Connecting the Dots: Teacher Effectiveness and Deeper Professional Learning*, all part of the *Leading Edge* series. In 2020, he added *Personalized Deeper Learning: Blueprints for Teaching Complex Cognitive, Social-Emotional, and Digital Skills* to his list of many prior publications with Solution Tree Press.

Jim earned his master's degree in English from the University of Illinois, Urbana-Champaign.

Gwendolyn Battle Lavert, PhD, is an international literacy specialist. She is a former elementary principal of Frances Slocum Elementary in Marion, Indiana. She provided school leadership and literacy development in the Middle East, where she led curricular improvement and professional development initiatives. Gwen has been an educator since 1974, with a background as a teacher, district literacy specialist, and district administrator in a variety of school settings. Her experiences range from working in a predominantly low-income minority school to some of the most affluent and high-performing schools, including Highland Park Elementary School in Texarkana, Texas. She has been an assistant professor at the College of Education at Indiana Wesleyan University, where she taught foundations of early literacy and literacy in the content areas. She also taught graduate courses in leadership and led several masters' cohort groups.

Gwen is a member of the Indiana Administration Association and is the Indiana Department of Education lead for literacy. Her strong belief in developing highly effective schools that are responsive to students' cultural learning and cognitive styles has resulted in marked improvement in various schools. She has presented throughout the United States on topics ranging from developing a culture of high expectations to implementing support systems for students who are struggling academically and behaviorally, and worked with educational leaders to make curricula more relevant to minority students.

Gwen received a bachelor's degree in elementary education and a master's degree in literacy from Texas A&M University. Her doctorate in education leadership is from Indiana State University.

Kate Bellanca has twenty years of experience working directly and digitally with districts, schools, families, and fellow professionals to improve learning outcomes through professional development. Her aim is to ready educators to increase student achievement, cognitive and digital skills, and social-emotional learning outcomes. Long before COVID-19 arrived, Kate was providing online instruction for educators and showing them how to adapt common digital tools for communicating with distant students and parents.

Kate has overseen the development and distribution of statewide practical graduate-level courses for Illinois educators in a professional development framework and customized school change models for districts around the country. Her collaborative work style always includes up-to-date, practical-to-implement, research-strong strategies and the digital tools necessary to improve instruction. In her face-to-face and online collaborations with schools in the United States, Canada, Europe, and the Middle East, her passion to help teachers enhance every student's learning potential shows through. Having completed a rigorous three-year apprenticeship with Nobel Prize nominee Dr. Reuven Feuerstein, she brings special insights into the value of his groundbreaking practices and their adoption for helping any student who struggles to learn. She works for one of largest privately held companies as a senior learning strategist and instructional designer.

Kate graduated with a bachelor's degree in psychology from DePaul University and holds post-graduate certificates in instructional design and user experience design.

To book James A. Bellanca, Gwendolyn Battle Lavert, or Kate Bellanca for professional development, contact pd@SolutionTree.com.

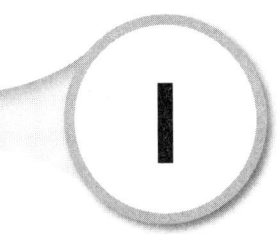

Introduction

We need to bring learning to people instead of people to learning.
—**Elliott Masie**

The year 2020 will stand out as a watershed year in the history of education. For the first time ever, schools were challenged to bring learning to *every* student via technology. Few educators were prepared. Few parents were ready. Few knew the best way forward in the overnight paradigm shift that not only moved learning almost totally into a virtual world but also portended technology's ubiquitous saturation wherever students might be located.

Early in the hunkering-down days of the COVID-19 pandemic, educators, students, and parents alike were caught up in the novel effects of its day-to-day, pervasive presence. Sarah Parcak (as cited in Torres, 2020), professor of anthropology at the University of Alabama at Birmingham, a 2020 Guggenheim Fellow, 2016 TED Prize winner, National Geographic Explorer, and author of *Archaeology From Space: How the Future Shapes Our Past* (2019), announced that she was removing her first-grade son from the online learning that started as a result of the pandemic's imposition of digital learning every day, all day: "It's 100% not OK that every single parent I know is struggling and is 100% miserable." Acknowledging her family's advantages, Parcak's words summarized the struggles most families faced:

> We obviously have enormous privilege to make this decision. We have jobs, a garden/yard, Wi-Fi, good books and learning materials, and our son has already been all over the world. So many families are struggling with job loss, food insecurity, illness, no internet . . . and school is where their children may get their only two meals of the day. (as cited in Torres, 2020)

She added that her son's teacher was very kind and understood that Parcak needed to do what was best for her family (as cited in Torres, 2020).

Further, long after the first month of universal online learning (also known as digital, virtual, or remote learning) closed in-person classrooms, parents, teachers, and community leaders celebrated teachers' service. One parent we know noted, "I will never, ever say a bad thing about teachers," adding, "I can't imagine how they do it. I'm trying to juggle my job and three kids trapped under one roof" (A. Mazorowski, personal communication, April 5, 2020).

In the meantime, teachers struggled:

- "Virtual learning? What a joke. I can tell that fewer than half my kids are online" (T. Constance, personal communication, February 10, 2020).

- "I thought I was tech savvy. My principal told me I was a standout digital native. I'm all thumbs trying to organize my kids' home study" (S. More, personal communication, March 3, 2020).
- "When I'm in front of the classroom, I get to interact with the content. . . . In a Zoom meeting, you don't have that option. Either you're the focus or the content is the focus. When you switch over to screen share, you disappear, and you lose the ability to make eye contact" (Jamie Ewing, as cited in LaBarre, 2020).

Students struggled:

- "Real school is easier because you can ask for help, and you don't have to figure things out alone" (Lilah, a seven-year-old student, as cited in Golinkoff & Halperin, 2020).
- "[Virtual school] doesn't really work. My teachers think I can read six books a week and answer a hundred questions to send in" (M. Roberts, personal communication, June 2, 2020).
- "We miss our friends. It's soooo boring at home" (S. Kahler & E. Kahler, personal communication, October 27, 2020).

Parents struggled:

- "I have a master's degree in communications. I have no idea how to help [my daughter] with calculus" (D. Blodget, personal communication, September 2010).
- "I'm already working two jobs. I can try to help but I am not her teacher" (M. Orbess, personal communication, January 12, 2021).

Understanding that decisions about when and where students would attend online school were in the hands of school boards and local elected officials, we, as the authors of this book, chose to address the immediate concerns centered around what was and was not happening day to day during limited instructional time and what these changes meant for teaching and learning for the coming years.

As our team's—Jim, Gwen, and Kate—research progressed, it became clear that distance learning was not here just for the time being but for the long haul. A U.S.-wide survey revealed the following:

> 1 in 5 districts are considering, planning to adopt or have already adopted a fully online school in future years. One in 10 has adopted blended or hybrid instruction, or plans to. Of all the pandemic-driven changes in public education, the creation of virtual schools was the change that the greatest number of district leaders anticipated would continue into the future. (Schwartz & Hill, 2021)

This makes sense. There are many other reasons forecasting the growing need for classroom-free learning. Shifting to digital minimizes the need to rely solely on large, dedicated physical spaces with learning limited to classrooms within school walls. In addition to the pandemic, issues unrelated to COVID-19 are forcing changes in living and learning for large swaths of students. In 2019, for instance, 23.9 million children and adults internationally were displaced due to weather-related disasters (Internal Displacement Monitoring Centre [IDMC], 2020).

We understood that we needed to go beyond the immediate challenges and address how learning best happens when students and teachers are *also* learning the ever-developing digital tools, methods, and other factors being added to daily instruction wherever students might be: sometimes in a remote learning space, sometimes face-to-face in a walled classroom, and sometimes in both. We grasped the idea that incremental, on-the-side instruction that *occasionally* included digital communication and collaboration in daily lessons was fast fading into the sunset. The pandemic forced educators to reexamine the place of digital teaching and learning and discover the need to prepare for more seismic shifts in where, when, and how near and far future instruction would occur. We knew we were looking to a long-term future with the understanding that this paradigm shift toward the full dedication of anywhere, anytime, digitally enabled teaching and learning was shifting from part-time to full-time, from one location to any space, from an option for some to a prerogative for *all*.

The Paradigm's New Path

As technology grows and grows in its saturation of everyday life, it will increase more learning experiences in the K–12 classroom as well. Teachers already are no longer the most efficient or effective information gatherers or data storehouses. But teachers will not disappear. They are becoming all the more effective and ever more in demand as coaches who guide each student's personal learning journey.

As an example, compare the teaching of reading in past years with today's evidence-based, digitally enhanced methods. Increasingly, teaching students how to read will look more and more personal, like the scene of a young reader in a learning cubicle trying to make sense of a story she is reading as she wears earbuds. For instance, today's teachers are able to apply evidence-based research to increasing student competence as they learn to read. That research tells them that the amount of reading young students experience is the number-one factor affecting their success.

In Francis Slocum Elementary School in Indiana, early-grade teachers apply that research by increasing the class time given to read-alouds followed by another evidence tactic: feedback from a coach. In a like manner, with the help of technology, teachers of early reading can expand students' directed reading thinking activity (DRTA) time, encouraging students to be engaged, thoughtful readers by asking questions, making predictions, and then finding evidence of them in text. The array of free, culturally relevant materials to select grows daily with audiobooks and stories—sometimes accompanied with video and music, digitally stored guiding questions to prompt students' recorded answers, guiding rubrics with student playbooks, online reading games, and personalized learning plans to help even the youngest students read. Students can set personal goals and track their own progress. When adopted, this digital cornucopia extends the time a teacher can spend kneeling to talk as a coach with each child, bringing the vision of individualization closer to full implementation. With digitized personalized learning plans, teachers now have the capability to prepare, manage implementation, coach, and assess each student's progress through each lesson, unit and semester, store and share those records for immediate access, and communicate progress to parents.

The teaching community sits on the cusp of e-promise. Propelled by the pandemic, more educators are taking small steps at a time, shifting away from pencil-and-paper, teacher-centered talk and assessment-driven instruction. They are shifting their instruction into the digital domain. Here they not only can call on digital tools and methods to engage students with deeper dives to understand, transfer what and how students are learning, expand students' capabilities for deeper learning, and increase achievement results but can also ready students for living and working in their future world as productive citizens. It's possible that these small steps, such as with DRTA, will turn into giant steps that impact even the most impoverished, so far digitally denied classrooms and free those students to access the equitable outcomes necessary for succeeding in society.

What other innovations can teachers expect as research catches up to practice and informs the learning community with a long list of evidence-based best practices that result in 21st century outcomes? How long will it be before digital innovations saturate every classroom similar to what technology innovators, such as Jim Bentley, a veteran grades 5–6 teacher in California's Elk Grove Unified School District (personal communication, January 3, 2021), has done? When Jim grew dissatisfied with his students' slow pace and low test scores, he turned to filmmaking as a way to motivate his students to master the three Rs, reading, writing, and arithmetic. He transformed his classroom into a digital workshop with students learning the three Rs and science by developing 21st century skills in public works–commissioned public service announcements. When this technology-centered approach drove his class's test performance to the top of the district charts, he didn't stop. He examined how online videos from National Geographic Kids (https://kids.nationalgeographic.com/videos) and other digital innovations could lead him to teach all subjects in an integrated, project-based learning style.

We hold that future learning will occur through such intensely personalized, student-centered, and digitally derived interactions.

- Teachers and students will interact more often with each other through and with digital devices in amounts of time, tasks to be done, and intensity of learning.
- Schools may give up seat time requirements, and attendance policies may go out the window as students spend more time at home or other locations other than sitting in a classroom with a teacher (Schwartz & Hill, 2021).
- As tools for accessing online information increase in number and variety, teachers will call on their own unique abilities as coaches on the side. By helping students figure out evermore complex problems as their students spend more time on self-managed schoolwork, teachers will become less and less the purveyors of information (U.S. Department of Education, n.d.).
- As world populations continue to expand (Worldometer, n.d.) and an increasing number of discombobulating events occur like the COVID-19 pandemic, Australian and North American fires, and other weather-related disasters, brick-and-mortar schoolhouses will disappear in favor of increased remote, at-home learning.
- Improved technologies will accelerate the spread of knowledge to remote learners as teachers become more familiar with its capacity.

In short, the future will also increase demand for teachers to enable students sitting wherever they may be to learn how to access internet data (or whatever its future versions may be) so students can figure out how to solve problems anyone in the world has yet to experience.

In this context, what does research say about best practices for universal online K–12 instruction? A 2010 meta-analysis was the first comprehensive study seeding the investigation of this question (Means, Toyama, Murphy, Bakia, & Jones, 2010). It reported mixed results. Online practices examined in the early 2000s had nothing to say about universal remote learning practices.

The study gave a tangential nod to remote learning as learning by mailed packets. For the very few K–12 virtual learning schools, it identified the need to blend some form of machine learning with face-to-face instruction. The authors had no reason to even think about universal virtual learning throughout the United States and world.

Another pre-pandemic study conducted by Susanna Loeb (2020), director of the Annenberg Institute for School Reform, still limited virtual instruction with the statement: "Online courses are generally not as effective as in-person classes, but they are certainly better than no classes."

However, due to COVID-19, virtual learning became the quintessential teaching paradigm. Schools shifted from classroom carts of laptops and notebooks to digital learning tools that not only allowed one-to-one experiences but also led to a learning day that embraced e-learning anywhere, anytime, and with everyone. To uncover some of the most compelling reasons for this shift, examine this sample of studies, which tout learning benefits gained from digital instruction.

- There's more opportunity for teachers to focus on social-emotional learning (SEL) and improved awareness about mental health (Ellerbeck, n.d.).
- Tutoring is more available to students outside a four-walled classroom, especially for those who cannot receive before- or after-school help because of transportation issues (Matusek, 2021).
- It brings diverse and advanced coursework to students in isolated communities (U.S. Department of Education, n.d.).
- In times of crisis (like the pandemic), distance learning via digital tools is a physically safer approach for teachers and older students.

Countering these statements announcing the benefits of remote learning, critics emerged to say "Hold on, not so fast. Kids belong in four-walled classrooms." This much-voiced concern stirred up a bees nest of no votes for remote learning. Opposition blogs and articles used shortcomings, such as students' increased feelings of isolation, the large number of students of color living in poverty without internet access and basic cell phones, the number of students in isolated rural communities also lacking internet connections, teachers unready and ill-equipped for digital instruction, costs to add or upgrade digital infrastructure, the challenges of students with special needs, the difficulty for English learners (ELs) and young children to manage digital tools, and increased home supervision for working parents (especially single parents), to declare that remote learning was bad. Indeed, some 2020 studies declared remote learning had already put students years behind expected grade-level performance norms:

> The damage to the future workforce will be far worse. Students denied in-person education will suffer permanent learning loss that will degrade their skills for decades to come. One estimate by the OECD roughly pegs the long-term cost in foregone productivity to the United States at around $15 trillion. (Chait, 2020)

There is little doubt that the COVID-19 pandemic caused the issue of technology in classrooms to spring forward faster than most schools were ready or willing to acknowledge. Many schools have long lagged in their efforts to make digital learning anywhere close to matching what has long been its integration into 21st century homes, entertainment, and workplaces. Technology is everywhere in our students' lives, except in many classrooms where minimal time and effort are given to teaching digital natives how to become digital learners or making all lessons digitally driven. As the pandemic-inspired switch to remote learning demonstrated, this shortfall documented predictable negative effects on student achievement as well as other aspects important to their success in school.

1. Students immersed in distance learning feel increased isolation that has led to increased feelings of anxiety and depression (Curtis, 2020).

2. Students of poverty fare less well with more limited access to digital tools for remote learning. Students in poverty and those in rural areas are most likely to lack at-home internet access. According to UNICEF (2020), two-thirds of school-age children across the world lack internet access at home. This is true in many countries, including the United States, Australia, and Indonesia (Jalli, 2020; McCutcheon, 2020; USA Facts, 2020).

3. Students with disabilities, English learners, and students experiencing homelessness struggle to learn via remote media alone. Educational inequities are highlighted with online instruction and continue to happen to students who already experience those inequities (Kamenetz, 2021).

4. The large numbers of children in homes with working parents make parent inclusion in the learning process difficult.

5. Teachers may lack the background to integrate social-emotional skills, metacognition, and know-how with digital tool operation (Bellanca, 2021).

6. Districts expect teachers to duplicate the communication modality of face-to-face instruction and fail to provide teachers with the professional preparation to adapt teaching style to remote media. Teachers are navigating new expectations, contending with loss of socialization (their own and students'), contacting parents, and upgrading technology skills (their own and students') (Welcomer, 2020).

7. Young children and students with special needs, ELs, and students of poverty require more explicit support than may be possible online. In addition to common difficulties with learning reading, writing, and arithmetic, with shorter attention spans, impulsivity, and episodic thinking, early elementary students are likely to be at a loss when technical glitches pop up. These issues lead to other problems not easily noticed (Feuerstein & Behnam, 2012).

As valid as these concerns are, when properly used, technology should assist students in acquiring the skills they need to thrive in the complex, highly technological knowledge-based economy in which they already find themselves. Selected and skillfully used, technology tools that seasoned educators identify to enhance teaching and enrich learning have powerful potential to expand and deepen student learning outcomes. The application of these tools to solve real-world and academic problems, deepen understanding, and prepare students for living and working in society has already proven valuable as students learn how to navigate technologies that are already everyday staples outside school walls. Just as education served its young in the 20th century to live and work in a manufacturing world, today's schools must face up to the challenge of preparing students for the future—a future that is already here.

The more technologically prepared K–12 students are to navigate the omnipresent goods and bads of their technologically saturated world, the more they will be able to navigate that world. Those who want to decry remote learning by caving to negatives, which sidestep the unique potential of students becoming as well-versed in applying digital skills as they are in learning the basics of reading, writing, arithmetic, science, history, and the arts, miss the central, most salient point. It's about preparation. We must do more to prepare tomorrow's citizens and leaders for the next pandemic, dramatic climate shifts that shut down schools, or other possible future disasters.

In this context, transforming digital natives to digital learners will mean more than a laissez-faire free-for-all that trusts all will do what it takes to self-direct their personal and individual digital skills development. It is also more than offering a coding or programming class for gifted students. It will mean a full, all-hands-on deck response. This response needs to include a K–12 curriculum emphasizing digital skills with daily integration. It will mean the abolition of pencil-and-paper writing tasks in favor of digital communication skills. It will mean active engagement of students' complex cognition, collaboration in teams, and frequent teacher-student and student-student interactions with constructive feedback that prepares students for their work and home lives as 21st century citizens. Soon-to-be obsolete debates do little to advance what's most important to know: How can research inform my decisions about delivering the curriculum and measuring my course outcomes, aided in the best ways possible by technology so all my students are prepared to be effective digital learners?

Although critics of remote learning, especially those who prefer having students back in school for social reasons alone, express skepticism of remote learning's positive effects (Hill, 2020), there is an emerging list of evidence-based counterarguments. Of course, research time is needed to determine the evidence-based achievement results for digital learning. However, the debate does make it clear that it is time to think deeply about, embrace, and improve virtual learning as a different way of teaching and learning for all students (Dorn, Hancock, Sarakatsannis, & Viruleg, 2020; Lockee, 2021). There are emergent trends indicating that remote learning may not be the disaster that many naysayers, who don't have to undergo the rigor necessary to prove outcomes, are touting. Consider the following.

- **Engagement:** For those who believe learning is not just about earning high grades with content recall or academic achievement, a study investigating how technology use, self-directed learning, student engagement, and academic performance interrelate notes a direct positive relationship with students' engagement and self-directed learning to academic performance (Rashid & Asgar, 2016).
- **Complex thinking:** Even in the earlier days of online instruction, researchers defined its quality by how well it balances improvement in academic performance with metacognition, higher-order thinking, and collaboration (O'Dowd & Aguilar-Roca, 2009).
- **Facilitating competence:** The teacher's competence in facilitating online learning plays a major role in students' satisfaction. Facilitation involves how well the teacher brought diverse student thinking into the discussion (Gray & DiLoreto, 2016).
- **Tutoring:** Dorn and colleagues (2021) report that personalized tutoring and other evidence-based acceleration methods help students of poverty overcome losses caused by limited access to online learning.
- **Project- and problem-based deeper learning (PBL and PBDL):** Research has suggested that technology-enabled project learning has the greatest benefits when the projects allow students to be intellectually challenged while providing them with a realistic snapshot of what real-world problems look like (Terada, 2020).

- **Differentiated instruction:** Technology makes it easier for teachers to differentiate instruction. It encourages educators to adopt different ways to reach different types of learners and assess student understanding through multiple means (Mahoney & Hall, 2017).
- **Expanded resources:** With technology, teachers and students can increase the variety of learning tools and materials at their fingertips. Teachers can adopt whiteboards and integrate them into digital interactions with students, interact in digital breakout rooms with small groups working at the same time or asynchronously, and share e-portfolios for giving and getting feedback and assessing student productivity. Students can work alone or in groups, find more information on one topic than can be delivered in a lecture, play learning games, communicate with peers, find online print resources, and use digital devices to communicate through podcasts, shareware, video streams, and more.
- **Research skills:** ELA standards call for students to learn research skills at a young age. With internet access, students have no reason to depend solely on teachers to learn course content. They can learn to search on their own. When students learn how to research online, they free teachers to coach on the side (Bellanca, 2021).
- **Specific subject-matter achievement:**
    - *Mathematics*—As happens with offline manipulatives, using free virtual manipulatives improves understanding of mathematics concepts and attitudes toward mathematics.
    - *Science*—Technology can improve inquiry science by allowing students to conduct virtual experiments using dynamic simulations of difficult-to-see scientific phenomena via well-researched science aids, generate and test models of complex data, and collect and analyze data to test predictions.
    - *ELA*—Technology can enhance students' ELA writing achievement. In addition to motivating student interest in writing, timing writing to supplement teacher instruction with feedback increases student achievement. The structured practice is especially helpful for students who struggle to organize follow-up writing time (Graham, 2019).
- **Synchronous, asynchronous, and polysynchronous learning times:** A skillful blending of synchronous (happening at the same time), asynchronous (not occurring at the same time), and polysynchronous time (a mixture of face-to-face and online synchronous and online asynchronous instruction) allows teachers to differentiate instruction and expand student agency (Dalgarno, 2014).
- **Flipped classrooms:** When students watch tutorial videos as asynchronous homework and discuss with teachers in synchronous time, they can increase their achievement in a variety of subjects (Cheung & Slavin, 2016).
- **Brain-based instruction:** Using brain-based learning strategies, teachers can deepen engagement, participation, and results.
- **Correct usage:** To ensure students' readiness for achieving lesson outcomes, learning goals and instructional plans optimize how best to use digital tools. Teachers should be partners and coaches with students. Never are teachers to leave students alone to figure out what to do with their devices.

Our limited meta-analysis through doing professional learning examines the effects of technology on student learning. We reinforced our own, colleagues', and teachers' experienced-based hypothesis that digital tools can be a significant addition when engaging today's students in what and how they learn and how they can increase academic performance DNA, improve critical thinking, and develop better attitudes toward learning (Chaplin, 2009; Freeman et al., 2007; Hake, 1998; Knight & Wood, 2005; Michael, 2006; O'Dowd & Aguilar-Roca, 2009).

A RAND Corporation survey of school leaders highlights virtual learning policy changes intended to expand flexible staffing, student schedules, class sizes, and virtual professional learning communities (Schwartz, Grant, Diliberti, Hunter, & Setodji, 2020). As is the case with future college students, more secondary students are likely to choose learning online as they take advantage of specialty dual credit or Advanced Placement (AP) science, technology, engineering, mathematics, and language course offerings not previously available at their isolated schools. The RAND Corporation survey reports that more districts are looking to include digital skills in their curricula, as "about one in five [school leaders] anticipated that a fully remote learning option will be a permanent public school offering in the years ahead" (Schwartz et al., 2020, p. 18). This shift to more ubiquitous virtual learning could mean that cash-strapped rural and urban K–12 schools would be able to provide students with virtual field trips to science, history, and art museums, make classroom connections across state and international borders, offer virtual computer camps in which students learn to program and design apps and games, and offer advanced informational technology studies at partner trade schools, community colleges, and universities.

Teachers' Needs to Know

In our experience and conversations with educators, teachers need the most help making remote learning appealing enough to catch and keep students' attention without depending on increasingly overwhelmed parents. In addition, our interviews uncovered feelings regarding hybrid practice and the future of remote learning (personal communications, January 2021). Their needs for help with remote learning, now morphed into hybrid learning, had not changed. They requested increased time to plan for the shifts back and forth between full remote and different forms of hybrid classes, and they wanted to know the core digital outcomes that would fit any of the three modalities: (1) all remote, (2) hybrid, and (3) blended. Given their time constraints while planning, teachers want to know how to prepare students for digital lessons wherever and whenever everyone might be. With that information, they could prepare to develop methods for each of the three modalities. Beginning with the highest priority concern our interviewees expressed, the following list indicates what teachers wanted to know and do.

- How to engage and manage multiple students online at one time
- How to design lessons and projects that will engage virtual students
- How to assess online learning and students' digital skills
- How to give feedback when students are on a digital device
- How to personalize digital learning for diverse populations
- How to devise activities that will engage students as they work offline
- How to incorporate digital skills into project-based deeper learning lessons and units
- How to help students who lack digital resources and tools for online learning

- How to engage parents to help their children with digital assignments
- How to help students collaborate with peers online
- How to address the learning needs of their students with special needs, ELs, and students who could not afford digital tools, including at-home internet

This Book's Organization

We have framed this book to respond to nascent research and our own investigation into evidence-based best practice in a digital learning environment. We intertwined evidence, teacher ideas and requests, and our own experiences as teachers and professional learning developers to respond to the question of *How?* from teachers: "How can research inform my decisions about delivering the curriculum and measuring my course outcomes, aided in the best ways possible by technology so all my students are prepared to be effective digital learners?" This theme is woven throughout the chapters.

Following each chapter's conclusion, we provide a recurring feature called My Takeaways, in which we encourage you to write what you find most pertinent in the chapter's content. Chapters offer tools that make digital instruction possible. We follow with a series of topics that address what teachers who are shifting to digital teaching and learning need to know. These are set so you can pick your entry point based on your need to know, or you can follow the sequence.

- Chapter 1, "The Technology to Master," addresses some things you need to know about your school or district's learning management system (LMS) and video conference system (VCS). This chapter also explores ways of communicating to students about technology and best circumventing students' lack of laptops, broadband service, or reliable Wi-Fi access.

- Chapter 2, "Instructional Design for Virtual Learning," lists lesson-design ingredients dictated by researched best practices for virtual learning, including, but not limited to, bigger concepts like cooperative learning, project-based learning, and games.

- Chapter 3, "Digital Documents," gives you some ideas for organizing links and documents, and helps you see how to engage and inform students by using portfolios for their work.

- Chapter 4, "Mindful Engagement in Digital Classrooms," helps you foster community among your students and move into cooperative learning and goal setting for high student agency.

- Chapter 5, "Positive Interaction and Social-Emotional Learning," offers ideas for engaging students in prosocial behavior online, incorporating social-emotional learning (SEL) into lessons, and dealing with distracting or dysfunctional behaviors.

- Chapter 6, "Feedback," tackles the various methods and technologies you can use to offer individual or whole-class feedback, both synchronously and asynchronously, and how to engage students in two-way peer-to-peer feedback.

- Chapter 7, "Assessment in a Digital Environment," discusses lesson-embedded formative assessments and assessing gamified instruction.

- Chapter 8, "Students With Special Needs," explains how you can differentiate and deliver instruction to work better for learners with various kinds of needs, as well as the considerations to make regarding requirements for the Americans With Disabilities Act (1990).

- Chapter 9, "Communication With Parents and Guardians," explains how you can link with parents and guardians to let them know not only what is happening in class but how it is happening and how they can help.

We offer digital information without giving app or website-specific instructions to avoid resulting in an obsolete set of steps, as you might find online or in platform- or program-specific books. To learn how to best use any technological feature, search the manufacturer's website for help or try finding instructional videos on online resources such as YouTube.

As you read through the chapters, refer to the reproducibles "Guiding Questions" (page 13), "Instruction Idea Gathering" (page 15), "Connecting Dots Between Experience and Inexperience" (page 16), and "Brainstorming Chart" (page 18) as you think critically about your classroom, your students' needs, and your own needs and resources.

Where to Start

As you gather information from our book, we encourage you start with the driving question from teachers who helped frame this book's content: "How can research inform my decisions about delivering the curriculum and measuring my course outcomes, aided in the best ways possible by technology so all my students are prepared to be effective digital learners?" As you answer this question, bring the best of what you have learned well from teaching with digital tools in your classroom experiences. We urge you to stay grounded in what you have already learned to do well and then add new ideas and polish your efforts with this book's ideas so you can more adroitly engage your students in meaningful digitally enhanced learning, be it in your walled classroom or at a distance. Then, we urge you to make a priority list, put those bits of new or reinforced ideas into an action plan, try that plan, and assess which digital strategies you will add to your instructional toolkit for next year.

We are certain that the increased challenges of increasingly universal virtual learning will not deter you and your colleagues from adding new digital tools and ways of blending virtual instruction across the K–12 curriculum. As educators always do, you will undoubtedly put on your problem-solving hat, adjust the brim, and go to work. As you do so, we encourage you to record what digital instruction you know has worked for you and your students, both inside the walls of your real-time face-to-face classroom as well as in your experiences with remote and hybrid instruction. Your first list might include evidence-based instructional strategies like:

- Cooperative learning that works well in all environments
- A solid scope-and-sequence digital curriculum following the International Society for Technology in Education (ISTE) standards
- Emerging 21st century topics like coding or nanotechnology that have proven to be highly engaging for students
- New ways to relate with students by adapting familiar apps, such as Instagram and TikTok
- Ways to build in district-, state-, province-, or nationwide mandates that bring increased digital instruction into the classroom

Your next list should include what you need to know about emerging technology so you can improve your e-teaching repertoire and students' learning in a fully digital classroom, or one that supports blended or hybrid instruction. Piece by piece, idea by idea, you can look for where you need help connecting the new digital dots, collaborate with colleagues to create new digital lessons, and transform your intuitive digital natives into strong digital learners and citizens. You can create these lists on the reproducible "Connecting Dots Between Experience and Inexperience" (page 16).

We want you to take away helpful answers to your needs-to-know questions. We want those answers to include personalized, practical, and effective ideas that give you new options, whether you are teaching in a room with students present, in a room by yourself while talking to students who appear on your computer screen, switching between these configurations, or talking to students in your physical classroom and online simultaneously. We also want to assure you that all the ideas we present, including examples given in a directive tone, are an invitation. The choices are yours to design, implement, and assess.

Whether you are looking to improve digital instruction in a completely remote scenario or a part-time or full-time hybrid or blended scenario, the strategies in this book will work for you. The *where* is secondary in importance. We have endeavored to give you information so that you can adapt your instruction *wherever* and *whenever* you are able to connect with students. Once you have mastered the big tools such as your school's LMS, what matters most is the quality of the connection so that students learn not only what you have to teach at a given moment but also how to become more digitally efficient for the days and years to come. As you make your shift to digital, know that your design cycle lets you hypothesize what might work best to help you achieve both immediate and long-term outcomes. By selecting digital tools that accomplish a given outcome, and empowering students to master those tools, you give them the gift of learning that goes deeper than a test. You prepare them to manage the shift to digital for a lifetime.

Guiding Questions

In each row, write in an idea that responds to each chapter's topic.

Driving Questions	Possible Answers
How do I use technology to teach students? (Chapter 1, page 19)	
How do I adapt my curriculum to work online? (Chapter 2, page 41)	
How do I integrate documents into online lessons? (Chapter 3, page 81)	
How do I foster mindful engagement in online students? (Chapter 4, page 103)	

Shifting to Digital © 2022 Solution Tree Press • SolutionTree.com
Visit **go.SolutionTree.com/technology** to download this page.

How do I encourage positive interactions and teach social-emotional skills to students online? (Chapter 5, page 133)	
How do I provide feedback to distance learners? (Chapter 6, page 161)	
How do I use assessment when teaching online? (Chapter 7, page 181)	
How do I accommodate online students with special needs? (Chapter 8, page 197)	
How do I communicate with parents and guardians? (Chapter 9, page 205)	

Instruction Idea Gathering

Print or copy a separate version of this form, or fill it in here as you read each chapter. When an idea strikes you as useful, record it on this form.

Idea and Page Number in the Chapter	How I Can Use This Idea	How I Think This Will Promote Engagement	Any Concerns I Have About Adopting This Idea

Connecting Dots Between Experience and Inexperience

List what has worked for you, both in your face-to-face classroom and in remote instruction.

Area	What I Know Works
Instructional strategies	
Curriculum	
Engaging topics or approaches	
Strategies for relating with students	
District, state, provincial, or federal mandates	
Technology	
Other:	
Other:	
Other:	

Shifting to Digital © 2022 Solution Tree Press • SolutionTree.com
Visit **go.SolutionTree.com/technology** to download this page.

Now list what you need to know to improve online learning. Piece by piece, look for where you need help connecting the dots.

Area	What I Need to Know More About
Instructional strategies	
Curriculum	
Engaging topics or approaches	
Strategies for relating with students	
District, state, provincial, or federal mandates	
Technology	
Other:	
Other:	
Other:	

Brainstorming Chart

Complete the chart to brainstorm what you know works, what you need to learn more about, and your next steps.

1. In the What Works column, write in the ideas that you will target to work on first based on what you know works.

2. Modify those ideas to fit into your instruction, specifically addressing your students' needs (for example, "Learn to use grid on Skype for asynchronous groups").

3. Identify what you still need to know in the What I Need to Know column. Note where in the book you may find the answers (for example, "I want to see other options for managing many groups from my screen during async time," chapter 1). Or, identify where you might go outside the book (for example, "I am going to ask my teammates how they do it").

4. Test your ideas, and assess how well they worked for you. Think about any refinements that will make the next use better. Go on to the next idea, and repeat the process. One step at a time is fine.

5. In the My Next Steps column, add information you gathered and how you intend to use it (for example, "I learned I am OK with Skype").

What Works	What I Need to Know	My Next Steps

Shifting to Digital © 2022 Solution Tree Press • SolutionTree.com
Visit **go.SolutionTree.com/technology** to download this page.

The Technology to Master

We are hard-wired to engage with those we trust, and this hard-wiring has led to a constant push for greater interaction and connection on the Web.
—**David Amerland**

For all concerned, including students, parents, teachers, administrators, and staff, catching up, keeping up, and putting up with fast-moving, computer-based technology have complicated daily teacher-student interaction. Every educator now has the added responsibility of being technologically literate. Distance learning itself depends on this literacy. Teachers must add new technology fairly consistently because of its quick evolution. Not only do teachers need to know about laptops, notebooks, Chromebooks, LMSs, smartphones, and PCs, they must be well versed in using the internet, printers, scanners, USB drives, digital recorders, microphones, and sometimes (still) even DVD players. In addition, educators benefit by knowing how to use a variety of even more specialized tools that increase student engagement, including apps and video players, as well as desktop video conference systems like the ubiquitous Zoom.

In this first chapter, you will continue on your remote learning journey. You will cover aspects of what you need to know about LMSs and video conference software, two technologies that distance learning relies heavily on. We also offer ideas on how to organize technological tools, such as apps and bots, communicate to students about the technology they will use, expand students' digital skills, devise contingency plans for technical glitches, and help students who don't have the technology that some people take for granted when it comes to distance learning.

What Do I Need to Know About My School's Learning Management System?

Your school probably uses an LMS to track student grades, attendance, and other data. Beyond those functions, most LMSs allow you to share files and connect online with students, communicating by way of discussion boards, video conferences, and chat rooms. It is important to know your LMS's general capabilities.

In terms of teaching online, the following LMS capabilities are helpful.

- **Access to materials at all times:** Teachers can modify the content, and students can see the updated material. If a teacher sets up an interactive template, students can fill it in whenever and wherever.

- **More options for assessment:** Students can access a rubric to self-assess; teacher and students can give, receive, and save feedback; and teachers can review the formative feedback and complete an assessment.

- **Support for teacher-facilitated collaborative learning:** This can be a good place to start with videoconferencing for feedback and collaborative learning if you're just getting started or haven't vetted what platform works best for your class.

If you haven't done so already, check what features your LMS has so that you can immerse yourself in the big and little tools that will help you manage your digital instruction. To assess your school's LMS features, go to its manufacturer website. For example, some do not enable the videoconferencing option. If you are comparing LMS options because you can choose one yourself, make sure you know the pros, cons, limitations, and capabilities of each.

With the understanding that districts and schools typically decide which LMS to use, the following are common and highly rated by *PC Magazine* (Fenton, 2018).

- Blackboard at www.blackboard.com/teaching-learning/learning-management
- Canvas at www.instructure.com/canvas
- Edmodo at https://new.edmodo.com
- Google Workspace (also known as Google Classroom or, formerly, G Suite) at https://workspace.google.com
- Moodle at https://moodle.org
- Schoology at www.schoology.com
- Gradecraft (for those who want to gamify their courses) at www.gradecraft.com

What Do I Need to Know About My School's Video Conference System?

Video conference systems (VCSs) are where a majority of teachers conduct online classes, with discussions, shared videos and slides, collaboration in different sized groups, and chatting with students and parents. Educators can teach lessons with all students sitting in the same "room" in a hybrid schedule (students spending some time in the physical classroom and some time online) in a blended configuration (students in the physical classroom and students online simultaneously), or in a fully remote configuration with all students at a distance. In any of these arrangements, VCSs make it possible for a teacher to lecture, guide an activity, demonstrate an experiment, show videos to an entire class, create small groups, play games, or instruct and confer with one student, one family, or a whole class. Many popular video conference systems work on smartphones as well as on computers, which is something to keep in mind for equity's sake (when, for example, your district can't offer laptops).

Just like the LMS, VCSs have different features such as chat, screen sharing, breakout rooms, and gallery view. Which system you use is likely dictated by your district, determining which features you'll be able to use. The following sections cover these features.

- Registration
- Waiting room entrances
- Screen sharing
- Chat rooms
- Breakout rooms
- Apps and bots
- Websites

Registration

After you receive your class roster, enter it on your computer via the registration feature of the VCS. This function will let you track attendance and make group assignments. Some VCSs will let you track completed assignments and other data. Use your roster to set up the master gallery grid on your device's screen. The grid is a feature in your VCS that allows you to divide your screen into many small squares, to see all students at once.

In addition to each student's name on a grid space, you might assign team names and roles for collaborative work. This helps you facilitate group work in both asynchronous and synchronous time. On the first day of class, invite students to share their names, a talent, hobby, or special interest, email addresses, and home phones.

Waiting Room Entrances

Ensuring that students can access your virtual classroom is a critical early step. Send an invitation to each student (if teaching secondary school) or to parents (if teaching elementary school) with instructions for direct entry to the master screen.

Figure 1.1 is an example of the written instructions you would give to students to enter a Zoom waiting room. You would also create a video of yourself giving these instructions aloud. Share it for students to store in a designated section of their portfolio or for young students' parents to keep on hand. Note that each VCS will have its own sign-in procedures.

When joining our online class, here are the steps you need to follow.

1. Sign in to your account in the web portal and access the Settings tab.
2. Click the In Meeting (Advanced) option.
3. Search or scroll to find the Waiting Room option.
4. Click the button next to the Waiting Room to enable this feature.
5. Arrive five minutes early so you can prepare for class. Check your homework, have all materials ready, and review our class norms.
6. Wait for me to let you into class.

Thank you. If it doesn't work the first time, log off and try again. If that doesn't fix it, visit www.contigencyplan.lms.edu for our contingency plan. You should have the hard copy with you.

FIGURE 1.1: Student directions for waiting room procedure.

Screen Sharing

Videoconferencing is not just about talking heads. You have the opportunity to increase that intuitive engagement with tactics that intensify what comes naturally for them.

With many of the popular VCSs, you can share your screen to show yourself and whatever is on your screen simultaneously: slides, videos, graphic organizers, rubrics, playlists, photographs of sample student work, and more. For example, if your microscope is equipped with a camera, you can broadcast microscopic slides, too. As you share, you can keep your image onscreen, use a digital pointer, guide students to complete a template, and so on.

Chat Rooms

While in a whole-class setting or in breakout rooms, encourage students to ask questions and communicate with you and other students. Figure 1.2 has instructions that encourage students to participate during chats through your VCS. This example is based on Canvas.

> Welcome to our chat room. You are encouraged to be an active participant in all chats scheduled for our whole class or by your team. Ask your questions, share your ideas, and when asked, give feedback.
>
> You will receive alerts for upcoming meetings. To check for alerts, click the New Message Alerts button. If this option is turned on, you will receive alerts. If your chat is open in Canvas, but your browser window is minimized or you are viewing another browser tab, Canvas will warn you. Canvas will not send you alerts if you leave chat to view another area in Canvas.
>
> Open the chat page with the button on your Canvas screen. The chat page will open in the content window with your name and avatar.
>
> When you open the chat page, you immediately join the chat. You can enter your comments or send an emoji.
>
> If you want to chat just with me or your team, please send us an email.
>
> Remember to follow the positive interaction protocols we have discussed. They apply here as well.

FIGURE 1.2: Student chat room directions.

Breakout Rooms

Breakout rooms may be the most important feature you have for promoting student engagement. They are your avenue to small-group tasks, workshops, and tutors. They are spaces that allow teachers to set up, observe, or join remote students, allowing students to collaborate, dialogue, create community, and problem solve. These rooms, controlled from your computer screen, allow you to engage students in deeper learning more readily than on your master screen. Once you have a VCS set up for synchronous use as a whole classroom, you can set it up for students to use breakout rooms asynchronously. Prepare students for breakout rooms and share different instructions for each of the following situations.

- **Team synchronous time (students all online with the teacher at the same time):** Set up and label groups to show on your master grid. You can observe each group to field and ask questions and give feedback. In a given lesson, you can move from one group to another. Or if you choose, you can schedule a single time for one student group to meet with you. For this, follow your system's instructions. It is best to start teamwork in synchronous time in the first quarter of your school year. Observe and give feedback to increase their team skills. By the second quarter, introduce the teams to asynchronous meetings with you gradually fading to the background. Be sure to include instruction, coaching, and feedback each step of the way.

- **Team asynchronous time (students learning online without the teacher present):** After students show they have learned to work together without your oversight, you can prepare each team that's ready to work on its own to manage the task and when they work together. Your VCS should allow you to set up at least half as many breakout rooms as you have teams in your largest class. This will allow every student to be placed in a pair as well as team-to-team asynchronous communication.

- **Solo synchronous time:** During a whole-class session, you can break the class into one room per student. (Some systems do have a maximum number of available rooms.) When you need to meet with students one to one, it may be better to access the student by email, FaceTime, or another option. However, if you must do so on your VCS, and it allows the confidentiality you need, follow the directions for doing this based on your system.
- **Solo asynchronous time:** At times when all students are offline, you can meet with any student or family. Get off the VCS if possible and rely on alternate means such as email or texts.

Give access to students in each room full audio, video, and requests for help. You can give students access to screen sharing so they can do appropriate visual work during asynchronous team time, for presentations to the whole class, or in a private conference with you and parents. Once students have their team-management skills in place, you can add asynchronous team time to your class schedule, which boosts autonomy and doesn't require as much bandwidth. Whatever tools your VCS provides for visual sharing, be sure to teach students how to use each properly before setting them on a task.

Apps and Bots

Apps and bots enhance screen organization and provide specialized services.

- An *app*, or *application*, is another technological tool that works when attached to a VCS. Apps help you and students share information, communicate, build a classroom learning community, and create a culture of equitable inclusion. You might hear students refer to apps they use, like Snapchat, TikTok, and Instagram. Google Apps and Google Podcasts are resources to help you with digital lesson designs.
- A *bot* is a software application that performs repetitive or automated tasks, such as setting an alarm, giving a weather report, or searching content on the internet. Apple's Siri, Amazon's Alexa, and Google Assistant are all voice-activated bots.

Websites

You can post website links in your LMS and share the sites on students' screens via VCS as appropriate to your goals. Some websites, such as the award-winning science sites PhET (https://phet.colorado.edu) and the groundbreaking Khan Academy (www.khanacademy.org), let you flip daily lessons without charge. Flipped classrooms allow students to complete assignments prior to coming to class, so teachers can coach and ask questions during class; flipped instruction fits well with breakout rooms, especially when differentiating instruction. During online learning, you can direct students to sites to learn a lesson solo in asynchronous time before coming to a synchronous time slot for whole-class or team discussions. Showing students how to download and complete lessons from sites will build their ability for self-managing their offline learning experiences.

Table 1.1 (page 24) offers examples of apps, bots, and websites, most of which will come with embedded instructions.

TABLE 1.1: Student-Friendly Apps, Bots, and Websites

Grade Level	Name	App, Bot, or Website	Content Area or Topic
Grades preK–2	ABCmouse	www.abcmouse.com/abc	Reading and language arts, mathematics, science, social studies, and art
Grades preK–2	BedTimeMath	https://bedtimemath.org	Mathematics
Grades preK–2	E-Learning for Kids	www.e-learningforkids.org	Mathematics, science
Grades preK–3	Little Pim	www.littlepim.com	ELA, EL
Grades preK–5	Epic!	www.getepic.com	Reading
Grades preK–8	Khan Academy Kids	www.khanacademy.org	Math, science, and ELA flipped lessons
Grades preK–8	National Geographic Kids	https://ngkidsubs.nationalgeographic.com	Science
Grades preK–12	Illuminations	https://illuminations.nctm.org	Mathematics lessons and plans
Grades preK–12	IXL	www.ixl.com	Personalized learning
Grades preK–12	National Library of Virtual Manipulatives	http://nlvm.usu.edu	Mathematics
Grades preK–12	Nova	www.pbs.org/wgbh/nova	Science
Grades preK–12	Readwritethink	www.readwritethink.org	ELA
Grades K–6	Tang Math	https://tangmath.com	Mathematics
Grades K–12	GeoGebra	www.geogebra.org	Mathematics (free graphing calculator)
Grades 2–3	Factile	www.playfactile.com	Reading and language arts, mathematics, science, and social studies
Grades 2–12	1Password	https://1password.com	Password storage
Grades 2–12	CodaKid	https://codakid.com	21st century skills, coding
Grades 2–12	Edpuzzle	https://edpuzzle.com	Self-paced learning interactive video
Grades 2–12	Flipgrid	https://info.flipgrid.com	Discussion board with interactive video
Grades 3–8	English Grammar 101	www.englishgrammar101.com	Grammar
Grades 3–12	Dropbox	www.dropbox.com	Storage
Grades 3–12	Grammarly	www.grammarly.com	Interactive grammar checker and coach
Grades 3–12	iBrainstorm	www.ibrainstormapp.com	Concept mapping
Grades 3–12	iMovie	www.movavi.com	Video making
Grades 3–12	Notability	www.gingerlabs.com	Mapping
Grades 3–12	Smart Word Cloud	shorturl.at/aoE29 for Android; https://apple.co/34gmO66 for Apple	Reading and language arts
Grades 3–12	Zinn Education Project	www.zinnedproject.org	History
Grades 4–12	TED Ed	https://ed.ted.com	Video talks
Grades 6–8	Coursera	www.coursera.org	Various
Grades 6–8	Desmos	www.desmos.com	Mathematics
Grades 6–12	Dotstorming	https://dotstorming.com	Brainstorming, organization

Which Video Conference System Might Work Best for My Sessions?

The list of guiding questions in figure 1.3 is not meant to recommend any specific system. This review will help you start a selection process or decide what additions you can make to your school's existing system. After you finish this book, start a list of your online instructional wants and needs. If you are looking ahead to replace a current VCS for a more robust model, keep a running list with you and your colleagues' ideas. Use the form in the figure to record answers to some questions to consider as you seek details and compare systems. You will find this chart helpful when you are involved in the system's selection process for your school.

How much will the system cost, and can the school budget afford it?	
How much bandwidth will it need?	
What functions are necessary?	
What functions are nice to have?	
What level of complexity can I handle?	
What level of complexity do I think students can handle?	
Do I want video and screen sharing only, or do I need more specific features like chat and breakout rooms?	
What apps or websites do I want to be able to use with this software?	

FIGURE 1.3: Video conference system detail collection form.

*Visit **go.SolutionTree.com/technology** for a free reproducible version of this figure.*

The following list indicates some of the more popular video conference system, which all have both important features and notable flaws. Don't plan on finding any flaws revealed on the creators' websites. However, each site directs you to detailed instructions for various functions.

- Google Hangouts (https://hangouts.google.com)
- Microsoft Teams (www.microsoft.com/en-us/microsoft-teams/group-chat-software)
- Skype (www.skype.com)
- Zoom (https://zoom.us)

How Should Students and I Set Up Workspaces in Preparation for a VCS?

Facing a scarcity of research that informs educators about best instructional practices with VCSs, we found helpful guidance in turning to brain and health research for ideas about teaching through a VCS and setting up your work.

- Brain studies describing the effects of videoconferencing's close cousin, TV viewing, offer some assistance. Brain researchers reveal that extended TV screen time is detrimental to children's and adolescents' brain development. Noting that TV watching is mostly a passive, solitary activity, there is a strong suggestion that extensive daily screen exposure may stunt verbal proficiency, reasoning, and social skills development, increase fatigue, and incite anxiety and depression. Consider this research as you plan your digitally enriched classroom. Because classroom time isn't passive, video conference systems make it easy for teachers to avoid sit-and-get instruction and continue or heighten students' brain activity.

- Health research details the detrimental physical effects that sitting at a screen without moving can have. Correct your posture and move around and stretch during long sessions. Brain breaks are the perfect time to do this.

- Jeremy N. Bailenson (2021), director of Stanford University's Virtual Human Interaction Lab, presents four reasons for what those who spend lots of time on a VCS call *Zoom fatigue*. Those reasons include "excessive amounts of close-up eye gaze, cognitive load, increased self-evaluation from staring at video of oneself, and constraints on physical mobility" (Bailenson, 2021). Table 1.2 points out the problems and offers possible solutions for each. Share these with students as well.

Stuck with video screens and microphones as the predominant technology tools, what can you do to minimize negative effects and maximize learning outcomes? The applicable TV research suggests that students who spend long amounts of time in front of screens would benefit from teaching methods that pull them out of passive watching and engage them with peers and teachers and in mind- and body-engaging activities off screen. How you choose to activate students' minds, hearts, and muscles—and yours as well—even as instructional time takes place predominantly on screens, begins with workstations.

Your Workstation

You and students will do best with private, comfortable spaces that allow for screen breaks and movement. The ideal space minimizes distracting sounds and sights but is set up for all

TABLE 1.2: How to Mitigate Video Conference Fatigue

Problem	Solution
Videoconferencing involves excessive, highly intense amounts of close-up eye contact with people onscreen.	Don't maximize your screen. Instead, make the VCS screen smaller so students' faces are smaller. Use an external keyboard (instead of the one on a laptop, for example) to put some distance between you and their faces.
Videoconferencing demands more from our brains to process.	During long classes, go audio only so your brain doesn't also have to interpret visual information. Turn off video and turn away from your screen.
Videoconferencing requires that users see themselves onscreen almost constantly in real time.	Hide your own image during class. How you do this depends on your VCS; try right-clicking your image.
Videoconferencing can reduce a user's mobility drastically.	Again, an external keyboard is helpful so you have a little more room to move. If you can set up an external camera (instead of relying on your webcam), you also can move around more.

Source: Adapted from Bailenson, 2021; Ramachandran, 2021.

active teaching and learning techniques and healthy breaks for the brain and body (Weslake & Christian, 2005). Active teaching may call for you to sing, act as a historic or literary character, stretch and exercise with students, conduct scavenger hunts, or play games. Active learning calls for a space where students can respond to your calls to sing along or move and play games. This boosted mobility will help reduce VCS fatigue (Bailenson, 2021). In addition, be sure you have a good microphone, headphones, and speakers. A comfortable plug-in combination headset-microphone is a worthwhile investment for you.

Your teaching station is your control tower from which you manage distant students. Before you go online with students, use the checklist in figure 1.4 (page 28) to ensure that your own workstation is ready to enhance your and your students' remote learning experience.

Student Workstations

In addition to having your own workstation fully operational, it's important to help students set up their home stations before your first online session. For all grades, any operational-procedural communication you make with students necessitates a copy to parents. Procedural communications for elementary and middle school students, starting with home workspace recommendations, should go through parents. Secondary students can directly receive these communications, though following up with parents is a good idea. Whether your class is 100 percent face to face, blended, hybrid, or fully remote, information about a learning workspace outside class (which can be at home if possible, or in a public library or café) informs everyone that learning is important. It may be necessary to make first contact to introduce yourself and offer workstation guidelines with everyone via paper or by phone. Put a copy of this communication and all future communication to parents in a central online location, and share your email address and other means of confidential communication you prefer.

☐ I have sufficient bandwidth for my VCS and apps.
☐ I know the capabilities and limits of my LMS.
☐ I know the capabilities and limits of my VCS.
☐ I have tested my VCS.
☐ I have a second screen.
☐ I have a device with a large screen, microphone, headphones, and a camera.
☐ I have a separate smartphone at my desk.
☐ I have tested all the digital device components I will use to teach (including whiteboard, asynchronous grid, chat function, and discussion board).
☐ I have a workspace with room for light movement.
☐ I have a professional-looking background (preferably where I display student work or materials needed for my lessons) behind my chair.
☐ I have a workspace with a comfortable chair.
☐ My desk height and equipment allow for good posture.
☐ I have a workspace with food, water, and special teaching aids in arm's reach.
☐ I have desk space in which to organize materials.
☐ I have the materials I will read or refer to during a lesson.
☐ I have lighting on my face instead of behind me.
☐ I have a door to close and a Do Not Disturb sign to hang on it.

FIGURE 1.4: Teaching workstation checklist.

*Visit **go.SolutionTree.com/technology** for a free reproducible version of this figure.*

Figure 1.5 is a checklist students, parents, and guardians can use for setting up students' workstations. Give K–3 parents and students an onscreen reminder to check their audio and video setup while waiting to come online.

You can review students' checklists and decide how to work with parents to address inadequacies. As you consider how you will design online lessons (chapter 2, page 41), make sure you address these needs.

How Do I Introduce Students to the Technology I Have Available?

Don't assume students are familiar with any of the tools you plan to use. Start each semester with a thorough checkup when students check in, and share a list of procedures you expect to be followed. Review the procedures in figure 1.6 (page 30), and check for understanding.

As you review the most important features for your LMS, VCS, apps, websites, and other tools, it is important to prepare for safe and secure use and teach students the procedures necessary for them to assume responsibility for managing each feature. Check to see early in your course the degree to

Dear _____,	
Here is a checklist for setting up your learning workstation.	
Please send an email to me at _____ if you have any difficulty or questions about the setup. You may not have everything that is mentioned in this checklist. Please write *N/A* (not applicable) on those lines so I know what changes to make. Please click this hyperlink ∞ with the chain-link icon, and enter your email address. Thank you.	

All information in this document is private. It is not to be shared with anyone other than the following people.

Student	
Parent	
Teacher	
Date	

Workstation Setup

- ☐ I have as much privacy and quiet as possible.
- ☐ I have some space to get out of my seat and move my arms.
- ☐ I made a Do Not Disturb sign.
- ☐ I have a flat surface and a chair.
- ☐ I set the volume for my microphone and laptop.

Joining Class

- ☐ I can mute and unmute my sound.
- ☐ I can turn my video on and off.
- ☐ I share and stop sharing my screen.
- ☐ I can use the LMS chat function.
- ☐ I can use the VCS chat function.
- ☐ I can send a document.
- ☐ My face is centered on my screen.
- ☐ The light is in front of me instead of behind me.
- ☐ I put up my Do Not Disturb sign.
- ☐ My space is clear for my work and lets me focus on learning.
- ☐ I have a plan for my brain and body breaks.
- ☐ I have a timer or clock to help me remember to take brain and body breaks.
- ☐ I have all the materials I need for class.
- ☐ My completed work is ready.
- ☐ I have reviewed the class norms.
- ☐ I am ready to join class when asked.
- ☐ I know what is expected of me when I interact with others.

My email is:	
My phone number is:	
Teacher email	
Teacher phone	

FIGURE 1.5: Workstation checklist for students.

*Visit **go.SolutionTree.com/technology** for a free reproducible version of this figure.*

Dear _____,	
Here is a checklist to ensure you're ready for class. The Joining Class section has a checklist for you to use before trying to join any video session.	
Please send an email to me at _____ if you have any difficulty or questions about the setup. You may not have everything that is mentioned in this checklist. Please write *N/A* (not applicable) on those lines so I know what changes to make. Please click this hyperlink ⌁ with the chain-link icon, and enter your email address. Thank you.	
All information in this document is private. It is not to be shared with anyone other than the following people.	
Student	
Parent	
Teacher	
Date	
Joining Class	
☐ I can mute and unmute my sound.	
☐ I can turn my video on and off.	
☐ I share and stop sharing my screen.	
☐ I can use the LMS chat function.	
☐ I can use the VCS chat function.	
☐ I can send a document.	
☐ My face is centered on my screen.	
☐ The light is in front of me instead of behind me.	
☐ I put up my Do Not Disturb sign.	
☐ My space is clear for my work and lets me focus on learning.	
☐ I have a plan for my brain and body breaks.	
☐ I have a timer or clock to help me remember to take brain and body breaks.	
☐ I have all the materials I need for class.	
☐ My completed work is ready.	
☐ I have reviewed the class norms.	
☐ I am ready to join class when asked.	
☐ I know what is expected of me when I interact with others.	
My email is:	
My phone number is:	
Teacher email	
Teacher phone	

FIGURE 1.6: Joining class checklist for students.

*Visit **go.SolutionTree.com/technology** for a free reproducible version of this figure.*

which students can already manage a feature. If they don't yet have the skills, schedule a tutorial on what you need them to know and teach them how (or use online video tutorials instead).

By translating procedures and skills into observable behaviors, you are able to infer a student's ability to follow the steps to complete a procedure until he or she can do so independently and automatically. Every student in every digital classroom needs skills to perform the procedures in the checklist automatically. They also need automaticity with these procedures.

The checklists for students to set up their workstations and join class will also give you information about what they know how to do with your shared technology tools. Be sure they send answers back to you. With the data you receive, preferably before the first day of class, you can decide how much whole-class, small-group, or individual time you must schedule in the first week so that all students are able to handle the class communication tools from the start. Before you begin using a new tool that may be unfamiliar to most students, schedule time to teach its correct-use procedure. Then, follow up with coaching opportunities so that everyone is sufficiently prepared to connect with you and each other on both synchronous and asynchronous schedules.

Follow the checklist with activities during the first week that engage and excite students about your class and what they will learn.

- Invite students to meet each other with an online people search or other activity adapted to a whole-class screen.
- Conduct a more complete, age-appropriate digital tool needs assessment. Which students need to know what information about the conference system, its buttons, norms, and other functions? Who knows what? If you can, let those students who already have the needed skills coach those who are still learning how to use the technology. This peer-to-peer coaching could be as complex as pairing a more-skilled student with a still-learning student for personalized coaching, or as simple as two students partnering in a think-pair-share.
- Ask students to "answer a question about the syllabus or to list two goals for their learning in the course. Reply with a short personal greeting so they know you received the message and are available to help" (Darby, 2019).
- Have students convert a photo of their handwritten work into a PDF and submit it as an assignment. You can share instructions for how to do so with students (Darby, 2019).
- After show-and-tell, follow up with the activities given in the Entry Activity section (chapter 5, page 133) to make students comfortable with the technology, you, and each other. Be aware of including students with special needs (chapter 9, page 205).
- Discuss the value of brain and body breaks, including reduced stress, increased productivity, brain health, and improved learning (Terada & Merrill, 2020). Hold a whole-class brainstorm of what students can do every ten or twenty minutes when working alone to move and engage other parts of their brains.
- Have students meet with you one to one so you can share brief tours of each other's workstations. This way you can learn about each other, and you can see how students have their workstations set up. If everyone privately agrees to share with the whole class, use an "on the grid" round-robin to ask each student to share what he or she does or does not like about his or her space. Positively remark on whatever a student may have in place and

make a private note for any improvement ideas. Model the most appropriate response, such as an all-class hurrah perhaps with an emoji. ("Raymundo, I really like that you have a plant in your space. I'm giving you a thumbs-up!")

After the first technology introduction, blend in your class norms, form teams, set up portfolios, and get ready for the first lesson or project. The following list offers tips so that your VCS can bolster communication among everyone.

- Set up and share your contingency strategies in anticipation of technical glitches.
- Let students who are already skilled with technology present a show-and-tell for peers who need to know more about a digital procedure. Formalize peer help. For example, at Katherine Smith Elementary School in San Jose, California, students who are so-called *tech geniuses* help students with technology issues as part of project-based learning (Brengard, 2015). You can have the same system as part of formal authentic learning experiences with deliverables (also known as *artifacts*) and identified skills. Identify potential tech geniuses. Invite your candidates to a first-week needs-to-know lab, where students (or you) have indicated they need coaching on a specific topic: identify responsibilities, norms for helping, and their digital skill base.
- Check in with students regularly about the LMS and VCS operations. How adept are they with getting into the waiting room? Raising a hand? Chatting?
- Introduce pacing charts (figure 2.6, page 60), instructions for teams in synchronous and asynchronous times, and different communication modes.
- Be present in discussion forums. Guide these discussion forums, and ask a volunteer or chose a student to be a moderator. This role would also be a formal project-based learning role with identified skills and deliverables. For preK–2 students, students with special needs, and ELs, it often helps to include audio instructions about how to work in pairs, give recorded answers, draw, work with tutors, and confer with the teacher one to one.
- Plan to integrate formative assessment using quizzes, discussion boards, or synchronous signals (such as emoji, hands up, thumbs-up, or other symbolic indicators available) to supplement the formal assessment process that relies on guiding rubrics. See chapter 7 (page 181) for more about guiding rubrics.
- Provide "'timely, actionable, and substantive" feedback (Martin, Budhrani, Kumar, & Ritzhaupt, 2019). This can be formal, with guiding rubrics, or informal, with typed comments in documents or in chat rooms, and so on. Be sure to teach students how to give *warm feedback* (positive) and *cool feedback* (noting places for improvement) starting with prompts (table 6.1, page 164).

How Do I Initiate Student Engagement Using a Video Conference System?

Students can take charge of their own learning. For instance, a team of secondary principals in Texas was alarmed by how many teachers spent every virtual school day lecturing and asking students to complete worksheets. One principal told his colleagues the following:

> The most common sight I see on my remote classroom visits is a teacher talking online for twenty to thirty minutes and then emailing the day's worksheets. I saw one who went on [lecturing] for thirty-five minutes. He must have stopped twenty times to tell his students to get their heads up and pay attention. For him, I think new technology means that a faster, sharper printer has replaced the purple dittos my teacher had used. After my feedback, he expressed his frustrations with the kids. I matched him with a peer who showed him how to use graphic organizers for them to take notes on his lectures. He cut his talk time in half and had them work in pairs for the other time to compare the notes they took. (G. Lard, personal communication, December 2020)

Studies of online teaching reinforce this principal's concerns about too much teacher talk and too many single-answer worksheets. For lectures, a 2016 study of *college students* noted a fifteen-minute maximum attention span (Bradbury, 2016). Brain researchers suggest even lower numbers for pre-college students (Lodge & Harrison, 2019). Other studies note that if a teacher must lecture online, as opposed to having students actively gather information via guiding questions, research rubrics, or by graphic organizers with text, it's helpful to keep online presentations in any mode short, with frequent embedded questions to check for comprehension (Chen & Wang, 2016; Giannakos, Krogstie, & Aalberg, 2016).

But a VCS allows you to engage students by different means: visuals, audio, and interactivity, synchronously and asynchronously. So that you do not get tangled in webs that distract you from your primary focus of teaching, your aim should be for students to use these tools as easily as they do social media and games. It's in your reach to gradually increase their responsibility after managing most, if not all, basic communication tools and features that you use in class (see chapter 2, page 41). There are few reasons why you cannot amplify student self-management, and there are many reasons why you should increase student responsibility by scaffolding the skills that will empower social-emotional well-being and academic achievement (Martin, Collie, & Frydenberg, 2017). Not the least of these reasons will be your increased opportunity to focus on the instructional side of virtual learning.

With the caveat that not all features appear in all VCSs, consider the following opportunities to increase student engagement through your system and maximize meaningful learning.

- **Record class sessions:** Record synchronous class meetings via your VCS capability. The recordings are helpful for students who are absent or who want to review. It doesn't hurt for students to learn how to record and save their own online interactions so they can retrieve both synchronous and asynchronous onscreen meetings.

- **Invite guest speakers:** In a lesson, teach students how to create VCS meeting invitations. After only a few months online, one fourth-grade teacher's class did most of the work, inviting students from another country to be guest speakers in a discussion of the New South Wales fires and their destruction of animal life. The teacher asserts, "It was the highlight of the year" (K. Berger, personal communication, June 2020). The U.S. Department of Education's (2009) *Teacher's Guide to International Collaboration on the Internet* offers multiple links to various opportunities.

- **Take virtual field trips to museums, historical sites, national parks, and more:** As with guest speakers, the VCS lets students become the active doers. In Austin, Texas, a high school class made all the arrangements for a virtual class expedition to Yellowstone and

Yosemite National Parks. "This year," reports the school's principal, "every club is planning its own events. Our graduation committee is planning the whole event themselves" (S. Zipkes, personal communication, December 2020).

In chapters that follow, you will have opportunities to gather ideas that can fill your online instructional toolkit. At each chapter's end, you will have an opportunity to select what will work for you. Or you can try the reproducible "Instruction Idea Gathering" (page 15) for putting all ideas in one spot.

How Do I Expand Students' Digital Skills?

When teaching online, it is important to model, teach, coach, and assess the required digital skills. From first turning on whatever digital devices, from smartphones, notebooks, laptops, or desktop PCs through which students two-way talk with you, you will have to determine what digital procedures they can perform and which they need help to learn.

In the absence of a district curriculum for digital skills, you will have to create one on your own based on your students' needs. The European Union's *Digital Competence Framework for Citizens* can help you map out the skills your students must have to complete your online lessons (Vuorikari, Punie, Carretero, & Van den Brande, 2016). The following are those that are most applicable to K–12 students (Vuorikari et al., 2016).

- Word-processing skills
- Electronic-presentation skills
- Web-navigation skills
- Email-management skills
- File-management skills
- Computer-security knowledge
- Video-conferencing skills
- How to download software from the internet (including ebooks)
- How to download computer software onto a computer system
- Computer-related storage devices (including USB drives and zip disks)
- Digital camera skills (which can take the form of knowledgably using a smartphone camera)
- Computer network knowledge applicable to your school's LMS

For each skill set listed here, assess student readiness, demonstrate the skill to students, and have students practice what they need. As soon as you model a skill, embed it into your content lessons. For example, elementary students can practice numeracy and literacy as they make bound picture books at home and read them to younger students; middle schoolers can learn to tell digital stories as they explore creating electronic storyboards; high school students can learn spreadsheet-creation skills as they prepare budgets.

The following steps sequence a learning plan that ends with students proficient in any given procedure. Adapt the plan for age-appropriate minilessons, which need not take more than fifteen minutes (for example, how to access Google Docs, how to screen share, or how to FaceTime).

1. Screen share the skill outcome in age-appropriate language or visuals (preferably both). Explain to students, "This is what you will be able to do," and share a photo or video of someone opening a document, downloading an app, or whatever skill students need to know.
2. Ask students, "Who can do the task?" They can raise their hands or use another signal.
3. Model the procedure and share a guiding rubric to identify steps for completing the procedure.
4. Share instructions with students (and, when appropriate, parents and guardians). All students get video instructions. Students who can read also get written instructions in a playbook.
5. Walk students through the steps as shown in the rubric.
6. Ask students to coach a partner using the guiding rubric.
7. As appropriate, add a practice assignment that all students watch onscreen, and coach via the guiding rubric. Identify examples of positive feedback. As appropriate, demonstrate how students can give constructive feedback, conduct a practice with students taking turns giving constructive feedback for ways you have helped them get started with online learning, return the positive feedback as appropriate, and schedule a needs-to-know workshop for those who need more help.
8. When a student shows signs of stress to this increased challenge, respond with empathy and additional opportunities to pair with a confident student or provide added one-to-one coaching in a chatroom or tutorial later in the day.
9. Encourage solo asynchronous practice and asynchronous partner practice. Encourage warm and cool feedback from partners.
10. Check weekly with a guiding rubric. Spot-check during synchronous time. Ask for a guiding rubric self-report in which students use benchmarks to identify what they did well.
11. Continue encouraging solo asynchronous practice until you observe proficiency. In this case, that means students being able to perform a task without referring to written or recorded instructions.
12. For students who struggle to master the procedures, schedule coaching that includes making a personalized learning plan with SMART outcomes and possible added coaching time.

For detailed guidance about incorporating digital-skills learning into lessons, see *Personalized Deeper Learning: Blueprints for Teaching Complex Cognitive, Social-Emotional, and Digital Skills* (Bellanca, 2021). Refer also to the reproducible "Students' Digital Skills" (page 40) to determine students' readiness for digital tools and activities.

What If the Video Conference System Crashes?

Professional TV broadcasters have to deal with glitches when an interview or video clip gets disconnected. As those professionals do, maintain your calm in the face of unexpected technical issues. You can remain calm and defuse technical issues by creating a plan B in advance; sharing it with students, parents, and guardians; making a plan C; and simply knowing that whatever can go wrong, will. With technology at the core of your classroom's operation, there is little you can do when audio and visual drop and refuse to come back. This is why contingency plans are so necessary.

Begin your contingency plan by creating two or three simple lessons for students to complete in case the unexpected happens and the system crashes. Provide playbooks to students at the beginning of the year so they have them available knowing what to do. A second option is to instruct students to prepare the assignments and save the deliverables until the class returns online. At that time, discuss the material saved or instruct students on the means to send the materials to you (by submitting it on the LMS, for example).

If there is a server crash or you have internet connectivity issues because of weather conditions or other situations, your phone will probably be the fastest way to reconnect with students.

Your shared contingency plan should include the following.

- If you lose contact and know it will continue for the rest of the day or longer, students should know you will send email instructions for an asynchronous task. For grade 2 students and older, this can include a reading or video assignment with a deliverable and, if needed, instructions for what to do such as "Check the LMS when your computer is working again to get information about missed work."

- If only some students are impacted, students should know you will email a summary of what they missed by, for instance, 6:00 p.m. that evening. That summary can include a link to the recorded class session and attachments of the materials they need that are online.

How Can I Help Students Who Have Too Little or No Internet Access?

Approximately 14 percent of U.S. families and 11 percent of Canadian families, most of whom have low incomes or live in rural areas with school-age children, lack high-speed internet (Fowler, 2020; Goldberg, 2018). Strategies for bridging the digital divide are scarce and most often grounded in poor policy and insufficient community assets—problems that extend far beyond the day-to-day instruction, assessment, and social-emotional work teachers do.

You can, however, make technological accommodations. Several of those listed here are helpful when computers have low bandwidth (and, for example, cannot stream video because it requires so much data). However, there are tricks and techniques that can allow teachers to communicate learning effectively (Hayat, 2020; Major, 2020).

- **Call and text regularly:** Especially for students without internet access, frequent contact by phone or text can make a big difference to the whole class, a group, or individuals. Your phone lets you set up Skype, FaceTime, and social media apps. By texting, direct messaging through Instagram, tweeting, and using Facebook Messenger to send reminders and notes, you can communicate with students each day. In addition to addressing their worries, you can send friendly greetings, assignments, jokes, puzzles, partner games, and feedback. You can set up small- and large-group conversations and take virtual field trips.

- **Provide digital copies:** When your system crashes, you might not be able to share documents. Sometimes, you can snail mail documents, but in this brave new technology world, that is a last resort. Consider using your phone again to send along files or connect with students, or you can set up Google Docs offline.

- **Activate offline features:** Without using the internet, students without access can download documents and tools from Google Workspace for Education. Your district's technology team can load the suite onto students' and parents' phones. With the Chrome browser, students can call up any documents stored in Google Drive. You can load all those that you need, including student playbooks, playlists, guiding rubrics, templates for your preferred graphic organizer, playbooks for parents, pacing charts and calendars, stories and text articles, and on and on. They can make project-based deeper learning end products such as storyboards, videos, podcasts, and slideshows. With phone contact, you can call students lacking internet access to complete lessons you send via email or other methods; they can turn them in using snail mail or dropboxes in the school or scattered in local libraries, stores, or social agencies.

- **Direct students to local hotspots:** There are a few different tricks here. Send students to the local library. Hotspots can be particularly effective for downloading large files that students can work on at home but may not be reliable or feasible for long periods. Google how to access hotspots for Apple and Android devices, and teach students how to use them.

- **Check in with a form:** You can call to ask students how they are doing and what support they need from you.

- **Avoid sending attachments:** When emailing documents to students by cell phone or computer, send plain text instead of rich text. Whenever possible, email lesson content two to three days in advance to give students as much time as possible to capture the email, complete the task, and return it on time.

- **Substitute audio for video:** Encourage students who lack video via internet to call in by cell phone or home phone. To ensure feelings of inclusion, let those without video know what's on the screen and call them by name at frequent intervals.

    - *Add WhatsApp (www.whatsapp.com)*—WhatsApp is an affordable messaging and calling app used worldwide. In the United States, Canada, and other countries, it comes free on smartphones. WhatsApp allows you to make video calls and offers the capacity to copy and paste texts for students to read through the app.

    - *Call on speech-to-text features*—Google Docs has a feature called Voice Typing that lets students speak and type a message. Other speech-to-text apps are available for different systems. Consider the following.

        - Apple Dictation (iOS, macOS)
        - Dragon by Nuance (Android, iOS, macOS, Windows)
        - SpeechTexter (Web on Chrome, Android)

- **Coach the strugglers:** Offer tutoring to coach struggling students. A half-hour session that unblocks the mental dam becomes a teachable time.

    - *Determine where the problem is*—Is it a digital tool problem? Is it a reading problem? Is it a meaning-of-the-assignment problem? For instance, you have given the student an assignment to analyze the literary devices in a poem. The first instruction tells him to pick a literary device. He has read the poem. He reads the instructions and then is stuck: "I can't find any literary devices." You see several and determine he has no idea what a literary device looks like even though you had shared examples during a class two days before. Ask, "Where do you think you can find the definition of a literary device?" He replies, "A dictionary?" Aha! He is beginning to solve the problem.

- *Coach, don't rescue*—Coaches ask questions and give clues so that students do the thinking and the work. You want the student to learn how to fish, not hand over a fish sandwich to devour on the spot. A struggler is someone who can't find the bait for the hook. The student in the literary devices example was blocked by a vocabulary word and didn't understand the resources available to find the answer. He traversed the digital part of his assignment with ease, searching the internet for the word's meaning, typing the answer in an email, using the spelling, grammar, and spacing tools, and as the assignment required, inserting a photo he scanned at the bottom of the text.

- *Ask the student to provide a summary*—At the end of the tutoring conference, invite struggling students to type, write, record, or tell you what they learned. By requesting a summary, you are coaching the student in how to learn, how to think, and how to solve problems. The student now has two takeaways: (1) a completed assignment with help and (2) a procedure for solving future problems with fidelity.

- **Tune in to your local PBS TV station:** For young children's educational programs, PBS has no equal. *Sesame Street* and *ABC Kids* are unparalleled as early reading, mathematics, and social skills instructors. If students have TV access, use email and phone connections to give parents the schedules and follow-up materials for these programs. If families lack TV, local libraries and businesses have been opening their doors and providing space for children to engage with Ernie, Bert, and the others.

  Encourage your district to partner with a local or state PBS station to create learning opportunities through PBS programs. For example, the Los Angeles Unified School District partnered with PBS for a full K–12 state standards-aligned educational television schedule (Los Angeles Unified School District, 2020).

- **Add private mass media to the mix:** Through Internet Essentials from Comcast (www.internetessentials.com), families in poverty can access low-cost high-speed internet. Netflix offers hundreds of hours of educational programs from its digital library. Contact parents by cell phone, snail mail, or city and church announcement with help to access these free resources.

- **Engage your community:** Whether you have one student or an entire class without internet access for more than a week, providing reliable digital access is important. With district support, you can submit lessons to a central spot on a server (such as a folder on Google Drive or Dropbox) or at a community location (Hayat, 2020).

  Rural communities with little or no internet and Wi-Fi access are pioneering the physical drop box strategy. For example, Aberdeen School District in South Dakota offered drop boxes at school entrances for students to turn in homework (Diallo, 2020). In Texas, Palestine Independent School District partnered with the local paper for students to drop assignments in unlocked newspaper vending machines as pickup stations (Diallo, 2020).

Conclusion

Acknowledging that technology is simply a tool that teachers use, and not a replacement for teachers themselves, this first chapter looked at the digital technology that commonly connects teachers to learners, and learners to each other. The tools are the means to an end. You, of course, determine the end you desire as you define your outcomes. However, no matter what those outcomes, these tools are your starting point. In this chapter, you ready yourself, your students, and their parents and guardians so that everyone is not only connected, but ready to engage in learning.

MY TAKEAWAYS

What three ideas from this chapter can best help you shift to digital instruction and prepare all students to be effective digital learners? Record your ideas here so you can make a plan later.

1. _____
   _____
   _____

2. _____
   _____
   _____

3. _____
   _____
   _____

Students' Digital Skills

Determine what digital skills students need for all the tools, activities, and other aspects of your class. Assess student readiness, demonstrate the skills, and have students practice what they need for your curriculum. After you model a skill, embed it into your content lessons.

Skill, Tool, Activity, or Goal	Students Who Are Not Proficient	What Skill They Need to Practice	How I Can Embed the Skill Into a Lesson

Shifting to Digital © 2022 Solution Tree Press • SolutionTree.com
Visit **go.SolutionTree.com/technology** to download this page.

2

Instructional Design *for* Virtual Learning

You can never use up creativity. The more you use, the more you have.
—**Maya Angelou**

Instructional design for virtual learning will have many of the same components as your traditional lesson plans. However, it requires you to think more critically and creatively and put identified students' needs at the center of more complex plans. You will have to make a concerted effort to interact with students online in much more thoughtful and empathetic ways so you can gather their thoughts and feelings about what and how they are learning.

Sometimes, the challenges of seeking student input may take you out of your comfort zone. This process may cause added concerns as you strive in your design to keep them engaged during their digital learning experiences without the visual facial and body language cues that helped in the past. This missing contact may raise your anxiety level even more, whether you are succeeding or not, in your desire to engage them in a virtual environment. During your face-to-face lessons, you could easily read body language. You may have built up a full toolkit with methods learned over several years. Remembering that "learners successfully learn when they feel a high level of teaching presence through continuous interaction with the instructor in e-learning courses" (Lee, Song, & Hong, 2019, p. 9), you will need to plan new ways to ensure your presence online so that they feel your empathy in the design you create, implement, and assess.

After this chapter, you will understand how design thinking can augment your curriculum's online lessons. Design thinking is a problem-solving process that calls on you to combine creative- and critical-thinking skills with empathy for the extra challenges your students will face during e-learning. It will help you prioritize students' needs above all considerations including time mandates, your traditional methods that you love, and what the principal wants. It relies on observing and predicting how your students might interact with their new learning environment and employing a continuous-improvement cycle of refinement for the innovative solutions you create (Tuttle, 2017). You are invited to keep in mind the words of poet and novelist Maya Angelou featured in the epigraph that starts the chapter, as you review how design thinking can connect digital tools, digital materials, and instructional strategies in lessons with deeper learning outcomes.

Research shows that using design thinking in curriculum redesign is most likely to yield positive results when teachers include the following methods to aggrandize learning in the multiple locations of digital learning—the four-walled brick-and-mortar classroom, the hybrid classroom, and remote learning spaces.

- Cooperative learning (Zingaro, 2012; Zydney, deNoyelles, & Seo, 2012)
- Project-based learning (Chen & Wang, 2016; Dede, 2014)
- Games (Sailer & Homner, 2020; Smiderle, Rigo, Marques, Coelho, & Jaques, 2020)
- Flipped classrooms (Gallagher & Cottingham, 2020; Thakare, 2018; Top Hat Staff, 2021)

As with all chapters in this book, we encourage you to spotlight the *how to*, with ideas presented to prepare you to adapt what you learn into to your e-classroom regimen. The aim is to help you enact and assess ideas that will benefit you in your digital shift not only as you consider selecting added technology tools and materials to upgrade your digital instruction but also, more importantly, how you integrate your selections in outcome-based designs for learning. First, you will have the opportunity to dig into design thinking as a driver of your planning process. Second, you will examine ways to design your own lessons with new designs that refine the best practices you have always favored.

How Do I Use Design Thinking to Adapt My Given Curriculum to Online Lessons and Projects?

When designing new lessons or adapting lessons from your past face-to-face lessons as you shift to digital designs, you will integrate new digital resources that upgrade your approach to instruction in a classroom (Hasso Plattner Institute of Design, 2018). These resources include, but are not limited to, online documents; technological tools; students' digital skills and learning needs; student engagement during asynchronous and synchronous sessions in remote, hybrid, and face-to-face classrooms; and your e-classroom management. Your empathy for the new challenges students face whenever you increase the role of technology in their lessons is shown by how you walk in your students' shoes, reconsidering how you will arrange these components in your new online lessons with their concerns foremost in mind. A case study on design thinking indicates that "design thinking, through the use of empathy, prioritizes the interrelationships among motivation, emotion, and cognition of students . . . with a deep understanding of the problems and realities of the individuals you are designing for" (Castro, n.d.).

Figure 2.1 shows the design thinking cycle. This cycle drives the creative-thinking process. You activate it each time you think about ways to integrate the many different elements, strategies, topics, and digital tools that will become deeper learning, high-engagement digital lessons (Holland, 2016). It will help if you elect to engage a peer team with you during the creative-thinking process. As you define the problem from your digital students' perspective, consider evidence-rich strategies and with digital tools. Combine your creative

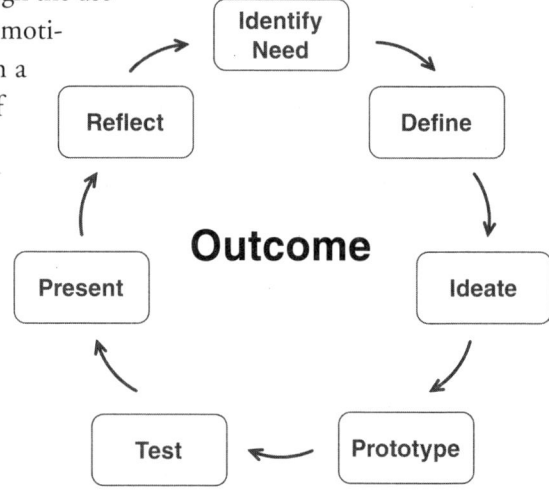

Source: Adapted from Hasso Plattner Institute of Design, 2018.
FIGURE 2.1: The design thinking cycle.

Instructional Design for Virtual Learning

and critical thinking to solve each problem. It will also help if you actively engage students early in the design process by soliciting their input from start to finish (Hasso Plattner Institute of Design at Stanford University, 2018).

This cycle is iterative; you can repeat its seven phases over and over until the plan you are refining works smoothly and produces the outcome you intend. You can elect to include students at key points or throughout the entire process. Once you have taught and assessed the prototype lesson and are satisfied with your piloted lesson design, you can begin the design cycle again, moving to the next improvement you want to build into future lessons. You may want to start with one small strategy or method change. For instance, you are not satisfied with your addition of a new method of setting up screen grids for asynchronous groups in a lesson. Your students have told you they sometimes feel left out when you are not present online to guide the asynchronous activity. Your first design thinking exercise leads you to address this concern by describing in the student playbook for these groups a more detailed set of responsibilities for the student leader's role. You observe increased participation and more thinking. The next round of feedback tells you that the concern has been ameliorated. You listened to students' feedback that said, "Thanks for calling on me."

After your success with the first small step, you can continue the design thinking cycle. The next item in your need-to-do list asks, "How do I improve student accountability in a team?" With your peer team's input, you restart the cycle and consider how you resolve the accountability issue. Your cycle continues until you feel comfortable revising a whole lesson. Of course, if you are not satisfied with a change made, you can make a quick intuitive adjustment or apply the cycle process to the targeted refinement with our "ear" attuned to students' voices.

To support your empathetic design thinking, table 2.1 details the list of steps in the design thinking process you can apply to your digital lesson creation.

TABLE 2.1: Design Cycle for Online Lesson Design

Design Step	Lesson-Design Implementation
1. Identify need.	Teacher generates many ideas to determine a shared need. For example, team members might use data to determine that they want to engage students better, increase critical thinking, or improve test scores.
2. Define problem.	Teacher defines a problem to solve, such as students putting their heads on their desks or being chronically absent.
3. Ideate solution.	The teacher generates ideas and then prioritizes a solution to try, such as a mini-lesson on muting microphones or using emojis to show raised hands, or a project on exercising voting rights.
4. Create prototype.	Teacher designs model lessons or projects to pilot alone or with team or grade level.
5. Test prototype.	Students test the prototype with a rubric targeting the innovation. Provide a rubric you have created.
6. Present findings.	Teacher presents the model to teacher teams, instructional coach, a department chair, or the principal for review and feedback.
7. Reflect and revise.	The teacher team reflects on feedback (usually verbal with a written summary) and improves the model for resubmission.

Source: Adapted from Hasso Plattner Institute of Design, 2018.

The core *creative* thinking element in the design process is *ideation*. The more creatively you or your team thinks during ideation, relying on brainstorming as the go-to strategy for generating ideas about the need you want to address, the more ideas you will have before narrowing to a trial solution.

Please note: Even the most experienced teams may stumble when it comes to engaging in a virtual ideation session. Many of the pitfalls of in-person brainstorming, such as some members sitting silently through the session while one or two of the loudest voices dominate, become even more pronounced in a virtual meeting.

The tools that your teams use for brainstorming online don't need to be fancy. An online tool like Google Docs will help. Use that tool to have participants enter ideas in a list, organize and categorize the items, perhaps with Microsoft Sticky Notes, and vote on ideas. It's essential that the meeting leader share a single screen so everyone is able to add ideas at once. Prepare the document in advance by assigning each participant a specific space to jot down thoughts, whether it's a row under a heading with their name in an Excel document, Google Sheet, or categorized sticky notes.

Although time restraints may make it tough to invite your team to participate in your design process, please consider doing so whenever possible. To make the team sessions most effective, structure your interactions as you would structure student brainstorming. Members' role responsibilities, a clear goal, review of brainstorming guidelines, and other idea-generating practices will help your team coalesce its thinking and give you the results you need. You should facilitate the brainstorm session and prep the group members. The common goal during brainstorming is for the group to generate as many uncensored ideas as possible to answer a driving question you have posed. An example of this occurs in the first season of *Ted Lasso*, when Coach Ted demonstrates how to generate a multitude of ideas during a brainstorming session without anyone making negative comments or "yes but" statements. Ted asks his team for trick play ideas. Coach Beard stands at the whiteboard and writes ideas as the *recorder*. Coach Nate plays the *cheerleader* role after the recorder adds each idea to the list without censorship. Ted, in his *facilitator* role, prompts different teammates to jump in. Slowly, then rapidly, the players give their ideas (Hunt & Delaney, 2020).

If your teammates have to meet at their online teaching workstations, you can lead the meeting, sharing the reproducible "Guiding Questions" (page 13) onscreen. Each participant assigned a role promotes full participation. You as *facilitator* call on respondents through your screen's gallery grid. You might go round-robin or wait for a member assigned as *cheerleader* to encourage volunteers. Another participant repeats all the answers, and another writes ideas on a shared whiteboard or Google Doc. You can increase the responsibilities of ideation teammates in other ways with round-robin responses, online polls, and emojis. Consider how the following roles can help everyone through the process.

- **Leader or facilitator:**
    - Finds agreements on the meeting outcome and agenda—for example, by forming the agenda from ideas provided through a Google Doc
    - Warms the group up with an "In this meeting, I hope . . ." intention or a fun warm-up activity
    - Starts the meeting on time and ensures everyone is joining in and working together throughout the agenda

- Monitors for participants who indicate they want to speak
- Makes sure everyone gets heard
- Sets an agreement for the next meeting time and deliverable tasks

- **Polling judge:**
    - Uses an instant poll or simply counts visual thumbs-up or thumbs-down to obtain real-time results when participants vote after ideation
    - Gives each participant a certain number of votes to weigh preferred choices
    - Counts and reports on the results

- **Breakout monitor:**
    - Makes sure members are on the same page regarding the task goal when the team breaks into pairs or trios (such as for a think-pair-share to discuss pros and cons) or works as a single unit
    - Ensures participants follow rules and guidelines and that breakouts start and end on time

- **Encourager or cheerleader:**
    - Prompts people to participate and encourages them with positive feedback to continue contributing
    - Intervenes if anyone is dominating by suggesting and guiding round-robin responses
    - Cheerleads!

- **Recorder:**
    - Ensures critical follow-up by typing, saving, and sharing team decisions
    - Stores all notes in a team portfolio accessible only to members

The brainstorm strategy used with your team is equally valuable whenever you want your peers to help you generate a list of diverse ideas from which you can select what works best for you. Moreover, it is a valuable tool to spur students' creative thinking. When team brainstorming as part of design thinking, consider the following two steps (Bellanca & Fogarty, 1991).

1. Share the brainstorming session's intent.
2. Review the DOVE guidelines for participation.

    D—Do give lots of ideas.

    O—Originality is essential.

    V—Variations on others' ideas are OK.

    E—Evaluate after the list is done.

Cooperative learning is the foremost method for strengthening collaboration in your peer team or with student teams. Because cooperative learning bridges P21's four Cs (Battelle for Kids, 2019)—*collaboration, communication, critical thinking,* and *creative decision making*—no other collaboration strategy is likely to spread a wider net capturing participants' attention, stimulating a variety of complex thinking skills, addressing many different issues, and including the diverse ideas of so many different points of view.

How Do I Balance the Technology, Documents, Activities, Feedback, and Assessment in Online Lessons?

When you begin designing online lessons, limit your choices to those supported by evidence. Consider the acronym RASE (*resources, activities, supports,* and *explicit evidence*). It is an evidence-based model of design thinking guidelines based on a study of eighty award-winning online instructors. It identifies four omnipresent factors from expert course designers, helping novices to experts (Martin et al., 2019). Other studies, cited in the following bullets, support the importance of each guideline.

- **Resources:** Be intentional when creating or selecting digital *resources* (including online documents) aligned with a lesson's purpose (Churchill, 2017).

- **Activities:** Make digital learning *activities* intentional and scaffold them to provide experiences and opportunities for learners to construct and use their knowledge with digital resources (Koohang, Paliszkiewicz, Klein, & Nord, 2016).

- **Supports:** Academic and nonacademic *supports* such as chat rooms and message boards are essential for online learning so that students avoid the feelings of isolation that can occur in online learning spaces (Mentzer, Black, & Spohn, 2015).

- **Explicit evidence:** *Explicit evidence* in the form of student feedback tells you how the lesson helped or hindered participation, performance, or personal growth. Your aim is to encourage two-way conversation that helps you improve your design. Ask students to share concerns, hopes, and interests via constructive and productive feedback that includes concrete suggestions for what to improve in future lessons and interactions (Bennett, Agostinho, & Lockyer, 2015; Markauskaite & Goodyear, 2014).

The reproducible "Resources, Activities, Support, and Evaluation Planning and Assessment" (page 76) offers a template to assess your online lessons before, during, and after you design them to fit your classroom's digital format. When set in a single-point rubric, the RASE factors become criteria by which teachers can give and get feedback and self-assess their instructional designs. Use the reproducible like a book of recipes. Each of the RASE sections describes a part of the whole meal. You've read all about possible appetizers, each entrée, sides, beverages, and desserts. Now it's time to make your selection. For each part of your lesson, what will you include?

What Research-Based Practices Work Best for Online Instruction?

The brief and few studies comparing universal virtual learning to in-the-classroom learning during the pandemic report inconclusive results. Although they show that virtual learning produces inferior positive results, especially among young students and less proficient students (Loeb, 2020), the sample seems much too small to draw valid and reliable conclusions. Findings about virtual learning before and during the pandemic were similar, even with drastically different environments: the data are inconclusive.

It may be years before studies can pinpoint clear, consistent data-based answers about the value of remote, hybrid, and blended learning. However, in spite of this shortcoming, there are studies that provide strong clues that technology is becoming increasingly beneficial in brick-and-mortar classrooms as well as hybrid classrooms that combine at-seat learning with remote learning. As new innovations in digital teaching and learning spread, and as teachers are able to upgrade their digital instruction skills, it is extremely likely that K–12 teachers will call on new digital practices, documents, and tools to enrich student learning wherever students learn. As you prepare to respond to this trend, a shift to digital, it's helpful to consider such data.

- **Technology increases your opportunity to engage students:** With digital tools, you increase your flexibility to increase active participation. You can do as little as ask for individual student replies on a message board. When a student doesn't answer, without embarrassing the learner, you can ask a private follow-up question. When you structure asynchronous small groups, you have only three to five students to engage in a discussion. To these situations, you can add games students love to play online as homework. With each student keeping an e-portfolio and filling it with personally created documents, you can send personalized feedback. When coaching online with a screen grid, you can move more easily from student to student (Bennett et al., 2015).

- **Technology increases student-to-student interaction and collaboration:** A digital setup lets you structure both asynchronous and synchronous small-group meetings. In synchronous time, you can shift groups from an all-class configuration in which talk is mostly by you to them with some intermittent time for small-group work. You move across the group grid, dropping into one team at a time. After you have prepared them to work as a team, you can spend more time observing each group and helping it complete a small-group task before you switch screens on your group to the next group. By structuring the interaction and defining each meeting outcome, you free yourself to increase each team's responsibility to work without your direct supervision. Once they show you they can produce the work assigned without your explicit oversight, you are ready to move them into collaborative group meetings in asynchronous time. Here they schedule their own meeting times and may invite you to visit. They don't have to sit and wait for you to tell them what to do or listen passively to you as the sole source of their information as they talk with each other to figure out rules of a game, how to build a robot, tell a puppet story, or devise wearable technology that solves a problem important to them.

- **Technology allows self-management and promotes individualized self-directed learning:** For perhaps the first time in the history of universal education, the dream of 100 percent individualized learning is becoming reality. With technology, teachers can personalize any learning experience for any student, anytime, anyplace. This new reality goes beyond sitting a student at a lone workstation, assigning a digital program, and leaving the learner alone for the program to guide them to a final test. It means teachers take a far more mindful, active role as personal guides who plan lessons and projects that allow students to select their unique paths to the final learning outcome. As they teach the most digital of natives to adapt their intuitive technology skills to navigating the curriculum, teachers leave the front of the room and work with individuals, small groups, and the whole class as their guide on the side. With a personal set of digital tools, students follow a personalized learning plan to achieve each lesson at a pace and depth that fit within their comfort zone. With a personalized plan, students, never the machine, make the choices about what pace, goals, digital tools, learning strategies, and materials will lead them to the lesson result. When help is needed, the teacher is ready to step in with needs-to-know coaching precisely for what that teacher notices or a student asks (Teo et al., 2010).

As you brainstorm during the ideation portion of the design process for practices that will enrich digital lessons and allow you to become more adept at shifting to digital teaching and learning, keep the following list of sample starter ideas in mind. When making your selections, consider these important words from researchers Youki Terada and Stephen Merrill (2020): "Logistical issues like accessing materials—and not content-specific problems like failures of comprehension—were often among the most significant obstacles to online learning." To follow their findings, put any concerns about content on the backburner, and pay closest attention to logistical issues that may interfere with the lesson.

- Know that online students are apt to feel more isolated than hybrid or in-person students. Designing digital lessons with empathy in mind allows you to plan how you can best address these concerns (Darby, 2019).

- Ensure that students are not only keyboarding but also writing by hand. Research reveals that during handwriting "more of the brain gets stimulated, which results in the formation of more complex neural networks" (Askvik, van der Weel, & van der Meer, 2020).

- Include synchronous small-group time (Gallagher & Cottingham, 2020).

- When including instructions for an assignment, do the following (Darby, 2019).

    - Provide written instructions.
    - Make sure the instructions are presented in student-friendly language.
    - Pair guiding questions or graphic organizers with instructional videos.
    - Keep videos short.
    - Provide a rubric.
    - Show multiple examples.
    - Break complicated tasks into smaller units so that students can receive formative feedback on their work as they progress, and correct their approach if needed.

- Communicate with many students simultaneously (versus meeting one to one or emailing individuals) to increase efficiency where possible. Do so on a message board, for example (Darby, 2021).

How Do I Ensure Deeper Learning Outcomes?

Deeper learning online lends itself well to outcomes-based instruction. The website Deeper Learning Hub (www.deeper-learning.org/covid19resources) offers various evidence-based resources for online learning. The Deeper Learning Hub offers free resources and courses related to six competencies: (1) content expertise, (2) collaboration, (3) self-directed learning, (4) critical thinking and problem solving, (5) effective communication, and (6) academic mindset. In addition, it offers a plethora of SEL resources to help address the empathy factor in designing lessons and ensures that teachers plan with the end in mind and students' needs first. Visit **go.SolutionTree.com /technology** for live links to the websites mentioned in this book.

You can feel confident transitioning most of what worked best in your traditional classroom lessons into the digital world. Returning to Terada and Merrill's (2020) findings, to ensure deeper learning, pay closest attention to the logistics by which you deliver instruction. Learning outcomes stay the same; you need only vary procedures or activities that match best with online learning. It's the outcome that matters, not the time or other variable logistics. For example:

- Traditional time constraints that force teachers to keep every group in lockstep don't matter. Each group can determine its own offline time and pace.
- Students who need more time to complete an offline task can take it without fearing the bell.
- For those who need less time, there are no constraints to stay seated until the dismissal bell.

When planning for deeper learning outcomes in your online classes, it is helpful to distinguish between a deeper learning lesson and a deeper learning project.

- A deeper learning *lesson* is a short (50 to 250 minutes), structured, flexible sequence of active inquiry tasks that leads to a SMART (strategic and specific, measurable, attainable, results oriented, and time bound) deeper learning outcome (Conzemius & O'Neill, 2014). For instance, you might schedule a ninety-two-minute vocabulary lesson with an outcome reading: "In the next two class periods, our team will select, find definitions, and recall ten new words from the article 'Will Coding Become a Basic Life Skill?'" (Davis, 2019). The outcome (a ten-word list) is SMART.

    - *Strategic and specific*—Selecting, finding, and recalling ten new words
    - *Measurable*—Recalling the ten words on an upcoming assessment in ten sentences
    - *Attainable*—Completing the task in a team
    - *Results oriented*—Identifying words relevant to an in-class reading
    - *Time bound*—Completing the task in ninety-two minutes (on or offline)

    Your lesson design sets up the teams with roles and responsibilities in a synchronous meeting and lets each team decide when members will work asynchronously offline to pick the words, find definitions, and help each other recall selected words through paired practice (all prior to sentence writing and the final test). The outcome ensures deeper learning because the task requires application, a complex thinking skill, when placing the words correctly in a sentence.

- A deeper learning *project* is a framework for an extended inquiry lesson requiring more than 250 minutes to complete and incorporating complex thinking to solve a problem. This time frame is necessary because the lesson will start with an outcome that requires students to engage their minds in higher-order complex thinking to produce a product. For instance, after the deeper learning lesson connected to the informational text article "Will Coding Become a Basic Life Skill?" (Davis, 2019), you take your students through a weeklong, two periods-per-day coding project in which they build gaming apps to demonstrate coding skills acquired through the year. The driving question asks: "In 900 minutes of class time, and any additional time our team chooses to spend as homework, how can we design a game app that helps our parents understand the value of coding coursework for all grade 8 students?" This longer, flexible time frame allows the complex think time for a SMART outcome that ends in a product and includes a guiding rubric.

Both learning *lessons* and their more sophisticated siblings, deeper learning *projects*, are well structured, but flexible designs prepare students to investigate a concept or solve a problem so that the outcome is SMART and deepens understanding (Conzemius & O'Neill, 2014). Within their design frameworks, always ending in a need-driven outcome, both deeper learning lessons and projects depend on your and students' choices about time, place, and activities and digital tools to produce the targeted results.

For deeper, authentic learning, the desired outcomes are those that allow students to solve problems or answer questions of importance to their understanding of the world in which they now and may eventually live. That is why it is important to base your design on empathizing with their feelings and helping them to understand what they need to know. When they feel you are listening by providing lessons from science, mathematics, history, and so on that match their cognitive and affective inquiry, you will see ears perk, eyes light up, and whole bodies engage, allowing them to focus on what they have to learn. You'll find that students' questions like "Why do we have to learn these words?" will be replaced with statements like "I get it. I see why" as they make sense of what they are learning.

Teachers aiming for relevant outcomes understand that *relevance* has three different but similar meanings.

- *Personal* relevance describes experiences that apply to students' personal aspirations, goals, interests, cultural experiences, and talents. Students may express personal relevance in statements such as, "I'm a great guitar player, and I'd like my project to include my talent" or "For our coding project, I want an app that can show my parents what I have learned. They thought the course would be a waste of time compared to taking advanced algebra."

- *Real-life* relevance describes learning experiences connected to real-world issues, situations, problems, and concerns that students feel strongly need a solution. Students may express real-life relevance in statements such as, "In our town, the river fills our basement every year, and I think a degree in civil engineering would help our town," "I am concerned that my number skills are not good enough to take algebra," or "I want to go to college so I can learn to program tools to help children with physical handicaps. I read that this is a field with a big demand."

- *Needs-to-know prior knowledge* relevance describes learning experiences that are in a means-ends relationship, as in the vocabulary lesson regarding the article "Will Coding Become a Basic Life Skill?" (Davis, 2019). For this type of relevance, one piece of content or one skill is dependent on a prior bit of knowledge. Students may express needs-to-know prior knowledge relevance in statements such as, "I am not sure of what these words mean," "I need to know the rules of the road if I am going to pass my driver's test," or "For my project, I have to learn how to measure distance and speed."

Relevance may be the most important way to ensure deeper learning. Day to day, you want your lesson and project design to include tasks and activities that align with an outcome that students have a strong desire to obtain, one that will allow them to achieve a deeper understanding of a problem in their lives but also the satisfaction for creating a viable solution.

When accomplished online, that relevance also builds the community that gives students the sense of connection necessary for overcoming the isolation that learning online—in the classroom or in remote settings—has caused so many students to feel anxious about digital learning.

What Evidence-Based Methods Promote Cognitive and Affective Online Engagement?

Collaboration and communication, two intertwined 21st century learning skills, are the heart of lessons and projects that you design. When it comes time to make your designs relevant—appealing to students' heads and hearts—the evidence-based tool most ready at hand is cooperative learning. As defined by coauthors David W. Johnson and Roger T. Johnson (2004) during their careers (1974–2020), formal cooperative learning "consists of students working together, for one class period to several weeks, to achieve shared learning goals and complete jointly specific tasks and assignments" (p. 26). Where students are located, their grade, time of day, or the tasks assigned give way to design procedures that result in the desired achievement or social skill outcomes or answers to a driving question.

A tsunami of research to support cooperative learning began with the pioneering studies by Johnson and Johnson (1974, 1989), identifying its positive effect on U.S. K–12 students, to more current research from Poland (Abramczyk & Jurkowski, 2020), studies of inclusion of students with special needs (Klang et al., 2020), and its effects in higher education (Hamadi, El-Den, Azam, & Sriratanaviriyakul, 2020) and remote or hybrid classrooms (Jacobs & Ivone, 2020). You do not have to look far for validation of this core method for classroom practice, on or offline, around the globe with all manner of students.

It's been well established that students' cognitive and affective online performance will be enriched by cooperative learning. By scheduling time to explicitly teach and assess these and other social skills, you yourself experience the first benefit: students are more mentally engaged in completing tasks and less likely to go off task with disruptive behavior. By concentrating on minilessons to improve their social-emotional skills, such as using active listening, giving warm feedback, leading teams, and resolving team conflicts, you prepare them to take increased responsibility during those asynchronous events that are out of your hearing and sight. As a result, you can expect higher productivity, more positive attitudes, and increased grit and accountability to engage students' minds and hearts and establish the foundation of the lifelong skills of communication and collaboration essential for success in the 21st century work world.

To increase student collaboration while online, cooperative learning is the go-to strategy in the effective e-learning teacher's repertoire. When you take time to teach students *how* to work together, you must leave your content for a short time-out so you can attend to what research says about the importance of procedural instruction for online lessons:

> Online learning requires high-level executive-function skills that some students may not possess. The lack of social and logistical support that is an inherent part of in-person education—where students interact with the instructor and their peers on a regular basis inside a physical classroom—means that online students must be able to manage their time well, motivate themselves, direct and regulate their own learning, and seek appropriate help when needed. But often they simply can't do all of that on their own. (Darby, 2019)

In practice, the application of this idea means addressing basic team-building procedures (like assigning roles and responsibilities and using guiding rubrics). You give students a strategy and procedures to take charge of their collaboration with self-management they can use as they work without your direct supervision. In addition, like veteran American studies teacher Arline Paul, you can adapt tactics for teaching how-to procedures by creating your own mini tools that help teams build their self-reliance (personal communication, January 17, 2020). For her classes, she devised a simple responsibility roster to track the roles and responsibilities in each class's teams. The roster keeper in each of her groups had the job of keeping the roster in the team's manila folder portfolio and updating it for her quick looks. When she shifted to remote teaching, she modified the roster, making it a folder from Google Docs. Figure 2.2 is a template of a responsibility roster.

Teacher: _____	Date: _____
Course or subject: _____	Period: _____

Team members:

Name	Role and Responsibilities	Date Due	Date Received

FIGURE 2.2: Responsibility roster template.

*Visit **go.SolutionTree.com/technology** for a free reproducible version of this figure.*

Follow the playbook's steps (see figure 2.3) when introducing the responsibility roster to the whole class.

The responsibility roster demonstrates one way to attend to the procedures that heighten online engagement. You demonstrate that when students are given structure by a skillful teacher that enables them to work together, in skillful ways, cooperative learning is the most effective approach for increasing achievement (Pitler, Hubbell, & Kuhn, 2012). Starting with digital tools that students already know and love, such as cell phones, Instagram, and TikTok, teachers take advantage of even more increased engagement.

Cooperative learning groups are an instructional grouping tool valuable both when students are physically present in the classroom and when they are working remotely to complete academic tasks in the lessons or projects you have designed. You can set up teams of students, teach the required skills, and introduce collaboration-producing elements such as team contracts, roles and responsibilities, and team-building activities that research indicates promote academic achievement as well as soft skills (Johnson & Johnson, 2017). Often surprising to novice adopters of

> 1. Introduce students to online teamwork with an explanation of how roles influence productivity, rapport, and individual accountability in professional sports teams, or other professions familiar to you or from your own experience. You can also do this with guiding questions and motivational film clips found on YouTube (consider movies like *Apollo 13*, *Invictus*, *Remember the Titans*, *The Great Escape*, and, not to be forgotten, *The Three Musketeers*).
> 2. Introduce roles and responsibilities with a screen playlist. Don't forget to discuss the responsibilities.
> 3. Identify the roster keeper as a team role. Responsibilities include making entries as agreed on by all team members and posting updates to the team portfolio. Coach students with the roster keeper role as necessary.
> 4. Check the roster updates on an age-appropriate schedule. For young or novice students (in grades K–5), you might make brief comments each day. For older and well-functioning teams (grades 6–12), one biweekly meeting will work. When checking, be sure there is observable evidence that students are doing their job in a way that helps the team reach its goal. For checking, a guiding rubric can show specific, observable behaviors.
> 5. Give the groups and individual members warm feedback as needed. Celebrate the positive and secure corrective changes as appropriate ("When I give feedback to a team member in the next session, I will make sure my words are encouraging, positive, and focus on a specific item.")
> 6. Rotate the roster keeper role with each lesson.

FIGURE 2.3: Responsibility roster playbook.

cooperative learning, the strategy also increases student autonomy (Shi & Han, 2019), as it gives students crucial practice in self-direction—a not-to-be-ignored beneficial element in successful asynchronous online learning.

It is common in discussions of the most desired learning skills to combine communication with collaboration. When it comes time for you to help students develop these skills, you will discover that both terms are overbroad. For that reason, these terms, like the others labeled as 21st century skills, need more precise naming. Instead think of them as a single set containing multiple specific, measurable skills that can lead to improvement of the broad category outcome: the collaborative skill set and the communication skill set. Now you can talk about what it is possible to do. You can name each skill in the set and define it in measurable terms. For instance, you can measure how often a student asks a higher-order-thinking question versus asking a lower-order recall question when communicating with team members. You can also measure how many complex and compound sentences that a student writes in an essay.

To identify measurable skills for collaboration or communication, it's easy to find examples via the verbs in state, national, and provincial standards. For instance, the Speaking and Listening standard SL.4.1c wants students who can "*Pose* and *respond* to specific questions to *clarify* or *follow up* on information, and *make comments* that *contribute* to the discussion and *link* to the remarks of others" (emphasis added; National Governors Association Center for Best Practices [NGA] & Council of Chief State School Officers [CCSSO], 2010a). You can construct your rubric for any specific 21st century skills by targeting what the skill sounds like or looks like. These specific skill functions benchmark *to what degree* students are able to perform them. Do students perform the function at a not yet, emergent, proficient, or an advanced level of competence? In this way, you can count or measure the amount an appropriate usage takes place and contrast it to a prior count.

The T-chart in figure 2.4 will help you determine what communication skills like *clarify* or *asks clarifying questions* look and sound like. Once you have identified these, you can set the functions in place in a guiding rubric for both instructional and assessment purposes.

Skill:

Looks Like	**Sounds Like**
An example:	My example:
A reason:	Here is what I think:
	Let me tell you why:
	My reason was:
	I did it that way because:

FIGURE 2.4: T-chart for determining what skills look and sound like.

Cooperative learning is a much-preferred instructional strategy that increases the opportunity for students to talk with each other in small numbers to achieve a single agreed-on outcome (Johnson & Johnson, 1974, 1989, 2021). The process adapted from brick-and-mortar lessons works well in any of the digital modes. In practice, cooperative learning comes in many flavors and sizes. By calling on the standards to refine the cooperative goal structures in your classroom, you can embed age-appropriate skill intervention in any on- or offline design lesson. You do so by mixing younger students, or older students unfamiliar with this approach, in pairs and threes. Group size doesn't have to be long-term groups of five or six. By keeping novice groups small, you heighten the chance each student has to spark learning. Shorter-term pairs and threes work for short, informal tête-à-têtes such as think-pair-share and paired-partner problem solving that allow young and novice students to focus on complex learning skills (Bellanca & Fogarty, 1991).

Cooperative learning groups (the means) are easily adapted to foster collaboration (the result) during online learning. Cooperative learning can look like this online.

- Breakout rooms during synchronous meetings with a student leader and other easy-to-observe roles
- Asynchronous student-led meetings completing one cooperative learning task
- Study groups that follow a list of guiding questions before the meeting and compile each member's answers during an asynchronous meeting and end with a report to the class in a synchronous session
- Instant chat messages where students alternate listening and speaking on a topic, with the session ending with agreement on a shared summary

Table 2.2 offers purposeful selections of key cooperative learning elements to maximize engagement in the online classroom. Keep this chart handy for multiple uses. Store it on your desktop in a digital folder.

TABLE 2.2: Cooperative Learning Lesson-Design Elements

Elementary Example		
Cooperative Strategy	**Digital Tools**	**Teacher Responsibility**
Paired partners Numbered roles and responsibilities Round-robin game	Notebooks Videoconference waiting room Whiteboard and video projector Breakout screen grid with a student name in each group Chat room Mic and camera with student playlists for usage Document share Document storage	Ready all devices. Welcome students. Assess digital readiness. Identify station number and letter. Lead round-robin game. Give chat room demo. Give onscreen signal demo. Review assessment rubric and student playbook with the class. Guide reflection.
Secondary Example		
Cooperative Strategy	**Digital Tools**	**Teacher Responsibility**
Trios Roles and responsibilities Team meeting Team assessment	Laptops Videoconference waiting room Breakout rooms with student playbook Microsoft Word or Google Docs Templates Online signal Mic and camera checkup	Welcome students. Assess digital readiness. Conduct Word assessment. Lead post-assessment. Guide reflection.

When building teamwork so that students will have the capability to work together productively online with a minimum of oversight from you, it is helpful to keep the following tactics in mind.

- **Start small and grow big:** Do this whatever the grade and whatever the prior experience of students with cooperative learning. When chunking your first cooperative learning tasks, try pairs first, as they allow for maximum engagement. Proceed to trios and fives to add challenge and brain power after paired teams show proficiency. For the highest level of engagement, stay small. More than five in a group can cause engagement to atrophy for one or two students (Bellanca, 2021).

- **Select equitable heterogeneous groups:** Informed by ever-continuous research, cooperative *teams* differ from homogeneous *groups*. Use the term *group* to refer to homogeneous groups that need your extra coaching to end a common content shortfall (such as ability reading groups and needs-to-know groups; Johnson & Johnson, 1974, 1989, 2021).

- **Encourage turn taking:** While some group members may elect to do less than their fair share, others may take over and do too much. Turn taking in a set sequence, or round robin, makes sure no one takes over and dominates the work. When you set up turn taking with students unfamiliar with the method, you name or point to the students whose turn comes next, or if in person, provide an object to pass each time one student finishes a statement. Each person takes a turn and listens respectively to what all others have said. During online instruction, you control turn taking by switching students on and off your video conference grid as each takes a turn in order. In breakout rooms, invite teams to create their unique symbolic objects and use them to ensure each member has a fair share or equitable chance to respond to each question in a list you have provided to the team leaders. This is another observable tactic for promoting collaboration. Make and share a T-chart with the specific looks and sounds you want to teach. Model the protocol on your whole-class grid before turning the strategy over to breakout team leaders with a student playbook for reviewing the protocol. Set the teams to work, and go room to room observing the targeted T-chart functions and giving feedback to each team.

- **Teach the jigsaw protocol to cooperatively experienced, proficient teams:** Jigsaw is the name for an advanced cooperative learning strategy that allows students or a team to gather information about a specific topic (Hattie, 2017). Each completes one part of the task and then summarizes what was learned or accomplished and teaches the content to the other group members. This works for any task that you can divide (such as multiple mathematics problems, multiple questions on a single text, and so on), so team members divide the tasks equitably.

- **Allow students to stop to think:** Before starting any communication task scheduled for synchronous team time, allow each student think time to write, think about, or rehearse what to say in response to guiding questions you have provided. For informal pairs, think-pair-share may be the most prominent and common application online. For instance, start an online session by asking all students to silently think about a coming question until you signal and write chat messages sent to a prearranged partner. After that share, use a round-robin by calling on random students to share their partners and their own ideas with all. You control who speaks with your mute button.

  Most students want to do their fair share when reporting on their solo ideas or jigsawed research to the whole class, but need a bit more time or help to prepare or build confidence to do so. In a modification of the flipped classroom, it is a helpful tactic to pose guiding questions at the end of an online session and allow overnight mulling time before students come together to share at the next session (McCarthy, 2016).

- **Schedule class time with care:** Spending time online can tire eyes when overly long. After twenty minutes of time on screen, be it with the whole class or in student teams, schedule short interludes for everyone to get their eyes off screens and relax with a drink of water, a stretch, an eye nap, a snack, or a bathroom break.

Figure 2.5 shows an example of instructions to give students in grades 3 and 5 when setting up breakout rooms. You can adapt these for older students. Schedule as many days as appropriate for students to show they can do all procedures on the list you shared.

1. Store this document in your portfolio for future reference.
2. If any members are new to this class, introduce yourselves in turn by name, and share what you like and don't like about working in a small group or online.
3. Review the guiding rubric I shared with you.
4. The person whose name is first alphabetically picks the roles for this week. For example, for student groups of two, the doer (the first person who "does" a task) and coach alternate on each round with "I do, you coach; I coach, you do." For groups of three, the roles will be the *starter*, who explains the first procedure; the *checker*, who checks that each team member can complete a procedure; and the *recorder*, who marks off completed procedures or records questions to ask the teacher. Check for agreement on your jobs.
5. Start your review of the first procedure on the list. The checker will read it aloud to the group, and the members will discuss why they think it is important. Do what you can or save questions for your teacher's visit.
6. While teams work on their small-group tasks, I will move from breakout room to breakout room to observe and give help. When I visit your online space, I will observe you before answering questions.
7. At the end, review the rubric again, and rate each other before storing the rubric in your portfolio.
8. Sign out by sharing a thanks with each other for how your teammates helped the team in this session. End on time. Return for the next class session five minutes before its start.

FIGURE 2.5: Grades 3–5 teacher playbook for breakout startup.

Here are suggested steps for introducing K–2 students in teams.

1. Start by setting up ability or other differentiated mixed pairs. Each pair will stay together for either a week or a multiday lesson longer than five days. For all-day classes, you may wish to have each student with a different partner in the morning and afternoon.
2. If health and safety require it, sit in-class students at a distance or with a cardboard divider. Each student should have a tablet or computer.
3. In preK, start modeling and practicing how to open and turn on the devices and show students how to access the camera and the microphone on the device. Show students how to send and receive messages that match their reading levels. For example, send a letter of the alphabet for each student to say in chorus with classmates, send a word for the student to read aloud, or prepare a stem statement that the student reads fluently (for example, "I am glad that I can pronounce the short *O*").
4. Review the other procedures that are appropriate for your students one by one, such as connecting earphones and making sure microphones and cameras are operating. Spread the experience over multiple sessions, allowing for practice in pairs. Students should give feedback to each other ("I like how you . . .") and reflect ("Today I learned . . .").
5. As often and as soon as possible, connect the technology lessons with students' other subjects. For example, "Let's play 'I spy' with what you learned about keyboarding today with social studies. I'll start. After my sentence, stop to think about your answer. I will call on a raised hand after I see several. I spy a way to use a small *a* in social studies." A later, more challenging stem might say, "I spy a way to use my portfolio in math."

There is no rush to get early elementary students into breakout rooms. Anne Miller, a first-grade teacher, starts students in breakout rooms when she sees signs that they are ready to read a story:

> I found it's my best signal for when to start the first two or three in a breakout room. I let them pick their first solo book. I show them how to read it online. Each reads alone until I gather them in a group, teach round-robin procedure, and pose the first question. The first sessions are a bit ragged, but once they get the hang of it, I turn the group loose to read and discuss in turn before they share with me. It's an easy entry to cooperative learning. (A. Miller, personal communication, April 2021)

For the most part, all students need to learn to work in pairs online. Following a structured sequence of mixed and matched cooperative learning tactics as Miller did, you can move students into breakout rooms one step at a time, several students at a time, until you feel comfortable and confident that they are learning together to stay on task. Keep all students online as a whole class until they show readiness to work in breakout rooms without you.

Because breakout rooms are essential for any classroom becoming filled with deeper learners, your scheduling of sufficient time to prepare an entire class to self-manage the times you cannot be with each group depends on preparing them to take on increased responsibility. By first scheduling time for students to learn how to help each other coalesce around a shared goal, the first pairs you match will learn how to function with roles such as speaker and listener for the first procedure when each starter team takes turns responding to a stem such as, "I like the main character in my story, because . . . ." Prepare instructions for your own or a grade-level team's playbook.

Share a pacing chart with students showing the schedule for the week. Consider the example in figure 2.6 (page 60). This grade 5 pacing chart for scheduling breakout rooms designates blocks of time for independent work, all-class meetings and teams, time on Skype, subject lessons leading into team project-based deeper learning, reflections, and so on. Students store each week's copy on their personal digital devices. During each morning check-in, the teacher shares and reviews the daily schedule on the online whiteboard.

When engaging students, it's best to start with what communication tools you have. For instance, in the pacing chart in figure 2.6, Chrome, FaceTime, and Skype, a chatroom, and email are the digital tools. For Skype, the teacher scheduled the solo screen or the grid for asynchronous team meetings and all-class discussions. Unless noted, she scheduled times for meetings on the grid, so she could use round-robin to get multiple responses to one question. Grid times indicate her preference for round-robins looking for multiple students responding to similar questions. Note that this teacher also scheduled time to prep the class on how to collaborate in asynchronous time as structured, cooperative learning teams. The last element of the chart to notice is her inclusion of structured team activities, such as the scavenger hunt, a people search, a Venn diagram, an exit activity, and goal setting. She employed a flipped model so students could prepare specific content study at home and bring their work to review in all-class or needs-to-know workshops.

In addition to the activities included in this sample pacing chart, there are other ways to get students working together, in addition to the traditional jigsaw and think-pair-share strategies that will work easily with digital tools like FaceTime and Skype for asynchronous distance learning experiences.

- **Holmes and Watson:** Match your students as detective partners. Ask students to identify what they could learn from Sherlock Holmes and Dr. Watson as detectives. (If students have another detective pair they prefer, substitute.) Before beginning a lesson or unit, charge student pairs to discuss a driving question about the topic. The best driving questions start with *What if? How? Why do you think?* or *What do you predict?* Pairs agree on their responses, which you sample before your talk begins. It helps to initially use a grid display. You ask the question, and then seek answers from students in a row. If you select a sequence of different questions, stop at the end of a row, and pick another row for the next questions. For instance, you might ask the first question, "What do you think Harry Potter will do next?" Invite five different responses from students who are showing on screen in the first grid row. After more reading, ask the next question, "What predictions made by the first group came true or not true?" Select the next row to respond one student at a time. When that list is shown on your digital whiteboard, ask a third row the next prediction question, and so on. For the last row, ask, "Why do you think the predictors were on target?" End with an open discussion on "What does it take to make a good prediction?" and "Why do you think detectives like Holmes and Watson need to make sound predictions?" At this point, you can return to student response in turn to structure equitable responses. Keep the element of surprise by varying rows and patterns as well as going in and out of the round-robin's response-in-turn structure. Spread five-minute round-robin interventions through the lesson.

- **Tell a story together:** This strategy requires a drawing platform or app, such as Inkist or Sketchpad. Monday, during an online session you lead, student teams brainstorm ideas for stories about objects or places they know. They vote on their choices, or you pull a choice from a hat. Then each day after, each student adds a paragraph or dialogue to the team's story, inserts an online image, and passes the story on. Let one team member add and then pass the paragraph on until you decide the story is complete with a middle, beginning, climax, and end. On the next Monday, teams take turns reading their stories. Each team in turn gets feedback for its story when the others tell them, "What I liked about your story was . . . ."

- **Collaborative comics:** Teams can make comic strips using Make Beliefs Comix, Storyboard That, or Witty Comics. There are many options available; find the tool that works best for your students. Comic strip creation works for any subject, as students can storyboard scientific, historical, mathematical, and other concepts.

- **Read-it teams:** Set up teams of two to five. Brainstorm with the class what working as teammates looks and sounds like. As members share on screen or in chat, compile a visible list of the ideas. Discuss and vote on the top five. Assign an all-class reading on the topic of your lesson. It may come from the textbook or another source. Students may even have suggestions. Give the teams a set of guiding questions, or ask students to provide them. Each group reads and answers the questions before participating in a team response that ensures everyone participates.

- **Reciprocal teaching:** Make groups of three to five students in grades 3 and up. Members take turns leading discussions in synchronous or asynchronous teams. One student guides the group with complex questions to promote complex thinking skills about the text you assign.

Monday	Tuesday	Wednesday	Thursday	Friday
8:15—Class check-in; weekly personalized learning plan (PLP) goal-setting activity; Skype grid	8:15—Class check-in online goal check; Skype grid	8:15—Class check-in partner personal share; Skype grid	8:15—Class check-in online goal check, Skype grid	8:15—Class check-in online goal self-assessment and sharing; asynchronous Skype grid
8:30—ELA; large-group Skype read-aloud: *Harry Potter*; fluency checks	8:30—World history all-class Skype; research rubric	8:30—Science, all-class Skype grid, states of matter	8:30—Mathematics and science all-class Skype with video and guiding questions; states of matter and fractions	8:30—Choice, outdoor game, all class, FaceTime
8:50—Break	8:50—Skype grid, synchronous world history informational text; independent research and checks: asynchronous Skype grid, individual breakouts	8:50—Break	8:50—Break	
9:00—Literature; independent reading and checks, Skype grid individual breakout		9:00—Matter of states independent research, notetaking, and checks, asynchronous Skype grid; individual breakouts	9:00—Asynchronous teams; guiding rubrics for literature study; avatar role selection; literature independent reading and checks, Skype grid	9:10—Break
9:20—Literature round-robin demo via Skype grid; vocabulary	9:20—World history informational text round-robin, Skype small groups	9:20—Literature round-robin; asynchronous Skype small groups	9:20—Literature avatar round-robin, Skype grid, small groups: Invent a Potter game with avatars	9:15—Literature; independent reading or team PBL; asynchronous group checks; Skype grid
				9:35—Literature round-robin review; asynchronous small groups; Skype grid
10:00—Break	10:00—Break	10:00—Break	10:00—Break	10:00—Break
10:10—Literature; all-class round-robin vocabulary	10:10—World history informational text, all-class round-robin Skype grid	10:10—Literature, all-class round-robin Skype	10:10—Literature avatar game with round-robin Skype	10:10—Literature, all-class discussion: synchronous TPS Skype
10:30—Mathematics all-class Skype scavenger hunt; add-subtract review	10:30—Math all-class Skype scavenger hunt; send off Khan Academy numeracy home study	10:30—Math all-class Skype scavenger hunt report	10:30—Share by team: "Our avatars" Skype grid	10:30—Math all-class Skype grid
			10:30—Math all-class online fraction guiding rubric; People Search team challenge, asynchronous all-class grid	
10:45—All-class scavenger hunt report TPS	10:45—All-class report, Skype grid with independent numeracy lesson games, and asynchronous class aide tutorials	10:45—All-class review, TPS and Skype grid	10:45—All-class math people search reports; TPS as Skype grid	10:45—All-class report TPS
11:00—Chat break online		11:00—Chat break	11:00—Chat break	11:00—Chat break online
11:05—Breakout check for understanding round-robin procedure in teams with independent mathematics numeracy games and class aide tutorials		11:05—Asynchronous breakout check for understanding; round-robin teams with independent math numeracy games and class aide tutorials	11:05—Breakout check for understanding, fractions FaceTime, round-robin teams with independent math numeracy games and class aide FaceTime tutorials	11:05—Breakout check for understanding, round-robin Skype grid, teams with independent math numeracy games and class aide tutorials and PBL team sessions
11:35—Lunch	11:35—Lunch	11:35—Lunch	11:35—Lunch	11:35—Lunch
12:05—Optional play break	12:05—Optional play break or asynchronous time for building team meetings	12:05—Optional play break	12:05—Optional play or asynchronous team meetings on Skype	12:05—Optional play break, independent reading, synchronous needs-to-know PBL lab, Skype

Instructional Design for Virtual Learning

12:30—Mathematics projects display on Skype and needs-to-know addition	12:30—Mathematics project offline and needs-to-know Skype grid breakouts: addition	12:30—Mathematics projects offline and needs-to-know addition	12:30—PBL overview: all-class Skype, needs-to-know addition, Skype teams	12:30—Math projects offline; synchronous needs-to-know PBL lab, addition
12:50—Mathematics projects offline and Skype needs-to-know subtraction	12:50—Mathematics project offline and needs-to-know asynchronous subtraction	12:50—Mathematics projects offline; needs-to-know subtraction Skype	12:50—Mathematics projects offline; needs-to-know subtraction, Skype teams	12:50—Mathematics projects offline and needs-to-know reading lab
1:10—Break	1:10—Break	1:10—Break	1:10—Break	1:10—Break
1:20—All-class Skype grid: roles and responsibilities in asynchronous rooms; review asynchronous breakout team grid; Skype pair practice	1:20—All-class Skype grid: asynchronous breakout team grid; pair practice observations with individual choice Google Docs; journal writing and partner sharing with daily stem: numeracy self-assessment to Google e-portfolio	1:20—All-class grid: asynchronous roles and responsibilities introduction; asynchronous breakout team grid; pair practice: states of matter TPS review; Skype	1:20—Asynchronous all-class grid: roles and responsibilities assessment; breakout Skype team grid; pair practice	1:20—All-class Skype grid: PBDL team share
1:40—Individual choice and word journal writing with daily stem	1:40—Individual choice and journal writing with daily stem	1:40—Individual choice and journal writing with daily stem: states of matter, all-class Skype	1:40—Individual choice and journal writing with daily stem	1:40—Individual choice and journal writing with weekly reflection stem
2:00—All-class volunteer journal, Skype share	2:00—All-class volunteer journal share via round-robin Skype grid	2:00—All-class volunteer journal share; all-class Skype grid	2:00—Synchronous all-class volunteer journal, shared, Skype grid	2:00—All-class volunteer journal share; weekly Skype stem grid
2:15—Break	2:15—Break	2:15—Break	2:15—Break	2:15—Break
2:20—Independent reading history; online docs via Google browsing	2:20—Independent reading, Google science docs	2:20—Independent reading online reviews: *Harry Potter*, individual FaceTime	2:20—Independent reading, Google Docs	2:20—Asynchronous Skype team, math science assessment; synchronous PBDL work teams; product share
2:40—All-class reflection; Skype	2:40—All-class reflection Skype grid	2:40—All-class reflection, Skype grid	2:40—Synchronous all-class reflection, Skype grid	2:40—All-class weekly reflection, asynchronous Skype grid
3:00—Homework assignment: Khan Academy math, division	3:00—Homework assignment; science class portal; states of matter	3:00—Homework assignment: *Harry Potter* film with guiding questions (share link)	3:00—Synchronous homework assignment: independent or asynchronous team PBDL work	3:00—Homework assignment: PBDL math science products by synchronous teams
3:10—Exit ticket, "I learned" sketch and share or show; all-class Skype grid	3:10—Exit ticket stem-write-share, all-class Skype grid	3:10—Exit ticket, Venn diagram share/ Google Doc	3:10—Exit ticket, self-assessment reflection stem: "My teamwork" all-class Skype grid share	3:15—Exit ticket, email
3:30—Exit	3:30—Exit	3:30—Exit	3:30—Exit	3:30—Exit
3:45—Parent conference by appointment, FaceTime or Skype	3:45—Office hours by appointment, FaceTime or Skype	3:45—Office hours by appointment, FaceTime or Skype	3:45—FaceTime, office hours by appointment	
4:30—End conferences	4:30—End office hours	4:30—End office hours; start parent conferences by appointment, FaceTime or Skype	4:30—End office hours	

FIGURE 2.6: Sample grade 5 pacing chart with asynchronous and synchronous breakout rooms included.

(For grades 3–5 students learning the method, you be the guide.) A second student documents the responses. Other team members answer the questions, and each gets a turn to answer. For open-ended questions, seek multiple answers to each question. For disagreements, students must back up their response with text evidence. There are four types of questions that students should learn to ask and answer with each other: (1) fact finding, (2) summarizing, (3) clarifying, and (4) predicting. A team's reciprocal interactions are meant to result in a deeper understanding of a story, poem, or informational text.

   a. *Fact finding*—What? Who? When? Where? Why? How? Start with initial questions about the story content. ("Who is Little Red Riding Hood? What was in her basket?")

   b. *Summarizing*—What is the big idea of this story?

   c. *Clarifying*—What's an example?

   d. *Predicting*—What do you think will happen next?

Once students are fluent asking and answering questions, you can assign the four types as guiding questions asked for every story they read during team or independent reading time. Start your instruction of this time-honored, evidence-strong method by embedding the method into a cooperative learning framework as a self-directed learning skill set.

What Other Digital Tools and Strategies Stimulate Collaborative Discussions?

There is a range of successful digital tools and strategies to stimulate collaborative discussions (Bates, 2019). Your challenge is how to include these in your lesson designs. Consider the following strategies.

- **Make guiding comments in discussion threads and chatrooms as well as during small-group and whole-class onscreen discussions:** Purposeful interventions guide student responses. For your interventions to have an impact, your primary responsibility is to provide the appropriate scaffolding or support with comments that help students develop their thinking around the topics ("I wonder how you connected the character [the parts] to the theme [the big idea] in your analysis?"), refer them back to study materials ("Please check out the playbook on analysis of character."), or explain issues when students seem to be confused or misinformed ("Please remember that your character analysis of Scout needs to tell you something about the Mockingbird theme"). The dynamics will vary in each interaction during a discussion when you:

    - *Set goals*—"Today's chat goal is to . . .."; "The aim for this all-class discussion is . . . ."

    - *Give positive feedback to structure participation*—"One person speaks at a time; thank you for showing the class how to do this, Keisha and Jamal."

    - *Prepare students for how to use a digital tool*—"When you want to enter the chat room, here is how . . . ."; "To mute yourself . . . ."

    - *Set up discussions by identifying roles*—"Sophie, please be our timer; Thomas, be our reader; Annal, our recorder; Elise, our . . . ."

    - *Discourage off-track comments*—"It sounds to me that this discussion is starting to bird walk."

- *Encourage the silent*—"Maria, we haven't heard from you. I'd like to hear your ideas on . . . ."
    - *Give scaffolded supports*—"That's a good point, Reggie. You have just expanded our thinking about the options, which . . ."; "Lei, thanks for clarifying that idea."
    - *Clarify*—"I'm hearing some cloudy thinking about . . ."; "Let's take a look back at what Einstein actually wrote about in the essay."

- **Choose complex tasks:** With a jigsaw strategy, you can chunk an assignment into as many equitable parts as there are team members. When dividing a task into equitable parts, it's OK for some to do more and others less as you allow for individual skill differences. For example, when there is a lot of reading required or a lab task has many steps, consider having students break into heterogeneous groups with the intention of jigsawing discussions of a week's worth of online document reading. Each team will read and summarize one article or complete one experiment and report results to the class. If a message board is cramming up with a tsunami of comments, ask teams to divide the items equitably. Each team removes redundant material from its section before sharing results with the whole class. Research shows this approach builds positive interdependence and trust among teammates (Johnson & Johnson, 1974, 1989, 2021).

- **Promote student leadership:** Daniel Zingaro's (2012) research shows that asking students to moderate an online discussion can increase participation and interaction. Student moderators who utilize the skills shown in table 2.3 (page 64) produce high-participation threads, especially when you prepare them by developing their leadership skills prior to moderating the chatroom or small-group discussion. Each time you schedule an online discussion, you can change which student leads that day's talk with a rotation that gives all a chance to lead.

- **Develop student agency:** Topics started by the teacher tend not to spark discussions as well as student-initiated topics. At the start and in the middle and end of an online session, brainstorm topics or issues to discuss. Then, you invite one student to be responsible for picking the topic and initiating the discussion with a first response. Another student or a team picked by that first responder can end the discussion with a summary or a reaction statement. For each next discussion, a new pair's voices will announce the choices. Such student involvement promotes increased cohesion and structure to the discussions (Zingaro, 2012). You can also add protocols to guiding questions and rubrics to develop student agency, and you can add protocols to our repertoire of scaffolded guiding tools, which you, and eventually students, call on as personal learning aides. Along with guiding questions and guiding rubrics, you and your students can rely on guiding protocols to add structure and keep focus during discussions.

A protocol is an organized, sequenced set of procedures for one activity or a set of activities that all participants will follow each time players enter the game. Just as every tennis match follows a sequence of accepted procedures, every discussion among your students will do so too. You want them to learn the procedures in your selected protocol. You eventually expect that all students will internalize it so they can follow the protocol even in group discussions where you are not present. The National School Reform Faculty

TABLE 2.3: Discussion Moderator Skills That Increase Student Participation

Skill	Example
Disclosing personal opinions	"Lilibet, what do you think of Diana's idea?" "I am wondering what you feel about Harriet Tubman's risks."
Using open-ended questions	"Here's the stem for today. 'Today, I learned . . . .'" "This is for everyone in the chatroom. What's your idea for how we should go forward?" "What do you believe the president should do about . . . ?"
Showing appreciation	"I appreciate how you told me that . . . ." "Thanks for sharing how you would . . . ." "Bravo. I love your reason to . . . ."
Establishing ground rules	"Let's review our playbook for how to give warm feedback in our breakout rooms." "Let's start by brainstorming norms for sharing helpful ideas to discuss hot issues in our synchronous discussions." "Here are my expectations for disagreeing with a different point of view in today's chat."
Suggesting new directions	"Wow. That's a lot of ideas. Let's move on to the next point." "Thanks, all, for sharing this list. In the time left, let's get our best thinking hats on for the last point." "If no one has another point to make, I suggest we move to consider . . . ."
Inviting participation	"I want to invite each person to make at least one comment, even if you think it's already been said but aren't sure." "I'm inviting each of you, in turn, to build on an idea you heard today, or just say 'I pass.'" "I'm asking to hear next only from those who have not yet shared."
Summarizing	"I'm inviting each of you to share what you think is the big idea in today's discussion. Write it out. I'll wait until I see each of you look up at me, and then I will call on each in turn." "I like to make a summary. Let's have someone share the big idea, and then everyone else chime in what to add to capture all that was said that's important." "Let's have each team put its heads together and summarize this discussion: a main idea, with two to three specific examples or reasons, and a concluding sentence." "In your words, what are the three ideas that capture what's most important about this topic?" "What are the key ideas you heard in this discussion that help you make sense of the topic?"

Source: Adapted from Zingaro, 2012.

(https://nsrfharmony.org/protocols) offers many protocols, as does and School Reform Initiative (www.schoolreforminitiative.org/protocols), for effective on- and offline class discussions. For online discussions, protocols are a tool for keeping teams productive, teaching discussion skills, and advancing student agency. When you share the protocols in a playbook so that each student can read the key points, you ensure that all know what's expected whether you are physically present or not. You also give a study tool that helps students practice what's expected in the process and learn a set of text-inquiry questions that deepen understanding. Elementary teachers can record and distribute the playbook so nonreaders in small groups can hear the instructions before starting the task.

How Do I Add Project-Based Deeper Learning Units to My Instructional Options?

Shifting to digitally rich project-based deeper learning units from brick-and-mortar instruction can be simple. When you trade your traditional lesson formats for the PBDL framework, start with a small digital design, aided by a design template, a pacing chart, student playbooks, and assessment tools. After the first few whole-class virtual meetings to set your design in place, your students will be eager to spend time online in individual and small-group virtual get-togethers in both synchronous and asynchronous time slots.

When students are novices to digital classroom work in the PBDL format, they'll have to abandon dependent mindsets, practices, and behaviors and discover how to stand on their own two learning feet. This expectation may be the biggest challenge your students face during the shift to digital. If your school does not have a schoolwide digital skills curriculum in place, you will have to rely on needs-to-know lab time for introducing students to the skills needed for apps and other technology they will learn within your class.

Just because PBDL let's you plan more time for students' digital tasks away from your watchful eyes doesn't mean they run free. As the year school progresses, it is important that you stay in contact with students by planning for digital workshops that address what they need to learn about working alone or with others to produce their required deliverables, such as reports and online photos of products they are making. By teaching how to follow protocols with digital playbooks, checking progress with downloaded guiding rubrics, and expecting self-managed portfolios, you will be equipped with evidence of their on-task work.

A teacher, professional developer, and PBDL consultant shared an experience with a team of Florida middle school science teachers. The teachers were concerned about abandoning their class control in the midst of a PBDL lesson.

"What if we made an assignment for our kids to spend fifty minutes of their daily learning time with no homework?" they asked (S. Zipkes, personal communication, October 2020).

To answer, he asked the teachers to brainstorm about hurricanes, a relevant Florida topic they had selected:

> "It didn't take long to list the things they didn't know about hurricanes," he said. "But they weren't sure what to do next. Ordinarily, they agreed they would show a video about hurricanes and have a discussion maybe with notes. Some offered they could have students write summaries from the discussion. To help them move to dig into PBDL

for their blended classrooms, I wanted them to take more advantage of the digital tools they had. I wanted more engagement than an interesting video on a relevant topic and a general discussion offered. I started by modeling more engaging ways to teach about the topic by calling in more technology. I formed groups of three. I asked each to list questions about hurricanes they had and post them with paper stickies on the room's green board. Groups looked at the posted items and began discussion with their peers on how to categorize the questions. Each group looked at the board and selected one set of grouped questions to research online. With the teachers, we brainstormed instructions for a research playbook. It set out research procedures to be followed by a summary writing task and a guiding rubric. Once written, I asked each team to e-share its summary with another group on a template I provided. After this jumpstart experience, I led a reflective brainstorm, which responded to their opening concern and the original driving question. Once we figured out how to fit the curriculum with their ideas, we turned to the website PBLWorks for resources available specifically for designing online PBL. That site and templates from *Personalized Deeper Learning* (Bellanca, 2021) ended with a three-and-a-half week PBDL design. It turned out well. Their need to see design thinking in action turned them into believers and doers. (R. Peters, personal communication, September 2020)

Recognizing the Benefits of Project-Based Deeper Learning

Many veteran brick-and-mortar teachers, as well as novices emerging from their first all-digital remote learning classrooms, have announced their increased shifts to PBDL and its landing as a framework for teaching with a digital mindset. From teaching *place value* in grade 1 mathematics to conducting a *nano experiment* in physics in high school, teachers have moved increasingly to blend student interests into project-based deeper learning experiences. These move digital teaching and learning beyond students mastering one isolated skill at a time, taking a test, and moving to the next lesson. There is a range of benefits that result from PBDL, not just increased achievement but also increases in a plethora of deeper learning results.

- **Outcomes:** Studies comparing learning outcomes for students taught via the project-based learning model versus traditional models of instruction show well-designed and implemented PBDL results in: (1) a deeper understanding of core academic content, (2) the ability to apply that understanding to novel problems and relevant situations, and (3) the development of a range of deeper learning competencies, including collaboration, communications, complex thinking, and self-management (Zeiser, 2016, 2019a, 2019b). The findings also indicate that students' opportunities to engage in deeper learning and the deeper learning competencies they developed were positively associated with attendance and graduation from high school. Other studies report increases in long-term retention of content, higher performance than traditional learners in high-stakes tests, and improved problem-solving and collaboration skills and students' attitudes toward learning (Strobel & van Barneveld, 2009; Walker & Leary, 2009). A 2016 MDRC and Lucas Education Research literature review found that the design principles most commonly used in PBL align well with the goals of preparing students for deeper learning, higher-level-thinking skills, and intra- and interpersonal skills (Condliffe, 2017).

- **Inquiry:** Technology can promote in-depth and collaborative investigations, which increase communication and promote active learning of complex ideas. The blending of technology in PBDL encourages students to become 21st century problem solvers. While there are many factors that contribute to the effective implementation of technology in PBDL, it is undeniable that there are positive correlations between the two.
- **Authentic learning:** When students are able to make connections between new material and the real world, it creates authentic learning environments, "Learning is stronger when it matters. Learning that matters is relevant" (Brown, Roediger, & McDaniel, 2014, p. 11).

Overcoming the Cons of Project-Based Deeper Learning

Redesigning lessons into learning projects that end with evidence showing deeper understanding of curriculum concepts and mastery of complex thinking, SEL skills, and digital skills that produce deeper learning outcomes is not a quick fix for engaging students in virtual learning experiences. It takes time. In this light, it may appear that the increased skill and time to design just one PBDL event, the most common complaint, is not worth the effort. Until the design process becomes more familiar, you may also be concerned about how much time a PBDL lesson will take students to complete as you worry that you don't have the time to cover all standards using PBDL. In addition, you wonder if you will have time in the day to prepare students to nail down the digital procedures and any other skills such as research and self-assessment. What if you ask, "Some activities I plan fall flat. How am I going to make up the time without covering less content?"

To overcome your concerns, experienced practitioners with PBDL in virtual learning urge that you think small, start with baby steps, and follow a plan. Steve Zipkes, a principal who has led school transformations grounded in digital PBDL, suggests that you design your first PBDL lesson no more than a week long with no more than five periods in synchronous time and five in asynchronous (personal communication, October 2020). Gradually, you can extend the time allotted to a short project lesson as you also increase the proportion of time students work without your immediate, physical direction. With designs that you can fine-tune and reuse, the upshot will be students' increased competency in arriving at the lesson or project outcomes and lowering of commonly felt concerns. As you work through the book, continue the deeper discussions of each element that makes PBDL lessons, filled with digital tools and documents, your preferred path to teaching.

To ensure your PBDL short lessons and longer projects are effective in the digital world, consider the following points.

- **Begin designing offline:** Offline, you can start by adopting, modifying, or transforming your face-to-face lesson plan into an online PBL. You may redesign your out-of-date plan or substitute another you create from scratch.
- **Consider best practices to heighten your chances of success (Barron & Darling-Hammond, 2008):**
    - Start with a realistic problem to solve or a project-driving question that aligns with students' skills and interests, with required curriculum standards that specify clearly defined content and skills.

- Structure group work with heterogeneous groups of two to five students with diverse skill levels and interdependent roles, a team goal, and individual accountability measured by rubrics to show student growth.

- Assess with multiple opportunities for students to receive feedback and revise their work (like benchmarks and reflective activities); multiple learning outcomes (including problem solving and collaboration); and presentations that encourage participation and end with products as results (such as exhibitions, portfolios, performances, or reports).

■ **Engage students in fieldwork:** Research indicates that collecting data and making observations increase engagement. Take teams outside school walls with a playbook to guide data-collection activities (NYC Outward Bound Schools, n.d.). Consider this virtual fieldwork by online students (NYC Outward Bound Schools, n.d.).

- Prepare students to observe and analyze with data sets.

- Teach students to do interviews over the phone, on social media, or with other technology they're comfortable with.

- For K–2 elementary students, provide links to museums, libraries, and other places where they can conduct research online or make virtual field trips with playbooks in hand.

■ **Guide the class, and then offer the technology:** From your workstation, guide the class through the design. All written, recorded, and verbal communication goes through your chosen tools. Make sure students are able to collect the data no matter where they live.

Identify what might work well or better as you assess prior to teaching, what has worked well as you assess following implementation, and what areas you can improve. Think about teaming with colleagues in a grade-level team for these reviews. Participating in a professional learning network and collaborating and reflecting on PBDL experiences in the classroom with colleagues and courses in inquiry-based teaching methods are research-recommended activities (Hung, 2008).

How Do I Design Game-Based Learning in Online Instruction?

"Games? You have to be kidding. School is for work" is a common reaction to any mention of playing online games in the classroom. If you are reacting that way, browse the term *gamification*:

> The gamification of learning is an educational approach to motivate students to learn by using video game design and game elements in learning environments. The goal is to maximize enjoyment and engagement through capturing the interest of learners and inspiring them to continue learning. (Gamification of Learning, 2021)

In the shift to digital, games have the potential to capture many students' interests and provide teachers with a valuable tool to enrich instruction. Gamification is a creative-design process, born of 21st century video game systems like Microsoft Xbox and Sony PlayStation, and Nintendo consoles like the Wii, Wii U, and Nintendo Switch. Teachers can use game elements (like narratives, immediate feedback, fun, scaffolded challenges, social connection, and so on) to modify existing lesson designs to motivate participation and foster high student agency, and sometimes, team collaboration against an "enemy" (Deterding, Dixon, Khaled, & Nacke, 2011; Landers, Auer, Collmus, & Armstrong, 2018). There is also evidence that some gaming elements increase motivation for learning. For example, implementing a transparent badge system allows peers to engage in friendly competition (Yildirim, 2017).

Knowing full well the attraction online games hold for many digital natives, determining when, where, how, and what to implement to enrich your students' online learning is important. To answer, you must respond to some other questions: What are your students' interests and talents? Is there a place for games in your synchronous designs? Asynchronous designs? Individual learning time? How can you adapt which games students may love? What game apps and websites will come into the mix?

The When, Where, and How of Gamification

A 2020 meta-analysis (Smiderle et al., 2020) captures the goals for introducing games into digital instruction: "The main goals of gamification are to enhance certain abilities, introduce objectives that give learning a purpose, engage students, optimize learning, support behavior change, and socialize." Four elements suggest the importance of gaming in digitally rich classrooms: *engagement*, *ability enhancement*, *optimized learning*, and *socialization* (Smiderle et al., 2020).

One important study discusses the impact of games in classrooms with ELs. Supported by the MacArthur Foundation at the Wisconsin Center for Educational Research, this ongoing study provides insights into the value of games on language development, problem solving, and collaboration for ELs. Meagan Rothschild, WIDA Assessment and Design Specialist, first reported in 2014 that ELs needed to ask and answer questions, explain their strategies, follow detailed instructions, and listen to colorful dialogue, all similar to the metacognitive activities that fit with other research applicable to digital instruction. She looked at how games fostered language development when supported with visuals, modeling, and interaction among players. After confirming that students' new language production was connected to these elements of the game, she is now studying next-step applications.

Consider the following playbook in figure 2.7 (page 70) for implementing gamification into your digital instructional designs.

The What of Gamification

In addition to changing traditional games into classroom games, online platforms let you create games co-joined with apps, such as GIMP or Adobe Acrobat. It is important to make sure students can operate the required digital devices before you structure the game into a scaffolded lesson design. Once students are adept with an app added to a game-based lesson, encourage them to continue playing the game in conjunction with other online lessons in different subject areas. Consider these digital resources and platforms.

- **Graphite (www.graphite.org)** is a resource platform from Common Sense Media that can help locate educator-evaluated apps, games, and websites for the classroom.
- **Kahoot! (https://kahoot.com)** is a learning platform that makes it easy to create, share, and play fun learning games. With Kahoot!, you can invite students to meet via FaceTime, Google Hangouts, or a VCS. With Kahoot!, classes can do trivia, vocabulary games,

1. Pick your first game, one that is appropriate and familiar to your students. Choose one they know, enjoy, will serve your goals, and is adaptable to be a learning digital activity. For instance, if your young students know Miss Mary Mack, you might connect the game's clapping with counting numbers. If many in a class love basketball, match it with a vocabulary study. Players score baskets for one-, two-, and three-point baskets based on a word's difficulty in spelling, pronunciation, and meaning. If you want to select a commercial electronic game such as *Angry Birds*, *Minecraft*, *iCivics*, or *Citizen Science*, be sure all students have access to the game and it fits into your lesson design.

2. Decide when, where, and how students will play. Solo or in teams? Synchronously or asynchronously? To take advantage of the cooperative-competitive studies, have students play team versus team or in a tournament so that teams in a class compete for points. Set up online team meetings as needed. For example, you could have an egg-drop team competition for a science class studying force. Let each trio schedule itself to prepare its eggs in asynchronous meeting time. Schedule all teams to drop the egg synchronously with you observe on the grid as the teams watch each other drop their eggs and earn points.

3. Set the game rules, roles, and procedures, and share them with each student digitally. In the playbook, remember to highlight vocabulary. Highlight what students are learning about collaboration, thinking and problem solving, understanding content, and so on. Do so by reflective stems and other activities as reflections at the end of each chunk. If teams can score points, describe how teams can earn each point. What are team roles for going through operations, doing procedures, monitoring game rules, keeping time, keeping score, and so on? Who tabulates points? Who resolves conflicts? Identify your role. Will you watch via a VCS? How much student self-management will you encourage?

4. Schedule the game, and share the playbook and a pacing chart on your VCS. Send asynchronous deadlines to team members with online days and times showing how you will chunk their game playing. Ten- to fifteen-minute chunks are ample once a day for young players. Small chunks let you engage players in planning a small piece, discussing strategy, and reflecting on what the game is teaching them. Make these chunks the essence of their language development. For high school students, chunk the game events and the associated formal learning elements in time amounts that fit their attention capabilities.

5. Assess the game with a focus on the outcome of the lesson. If it has teamwork, use a guiding rubric such as those illustrated in other chapters of this book. It's your choice to align the game playing to the important outcomes of your course—be it for problem solving, developing vocabulary, making predictions, asking questions, or something else. One caveat: avoid grades. Let your guiding rubric's specific benchmarks accentuate the fun, the problem solving, language development, content, and teamwork that you are spotlighting with the game. Points are OK to stimulate collaboration and positive social skills (Creighton & Szymkowiak, 2014) as long as they add up to awards, certificates, or badges for students' collaboration and determination and don't get in the way of what you want students to learn from playing the game.

6. Risk the addition. In your design, you may be adding a new product-making app such as GIMP, a free photo-editing software, or EdWordle, a free word-play app. Encourage teams to work together with the app in a collaborative-competitive format. Teams compete against each other by adding points scored on an internal team collaboration rubric. Increase the level of student motivation, and trust that the low-risk addition of game-playing formats, most notably around rote tasks, will raise the level of student engagement. As the WIDA study discovered (Rothschild, 2014), learning vocabulary is more fun and more lasting when playing with words in a game than it is when circling multiple-choice numbers on a worksheet.

7. Celebrate! Amplify the fun at asynchronous meetup times. Team members might collaborate making a team logo, song, coat of arms, or so on. They can complete open-ended tasks by which they make their team identity public. If physically together in a blended classroom, teams can gather around chart paper and map out a score sheet to share with those teams who are remote and those physically present. Or they can call on Excel or Google Sheets to keep score and share digitally with all teams.

FIGURE 2.7: Teacher playbook for game research.

collaborative competitions, and other recall quizzes. In teams, they prepare with each other; in the competition, players answer on their own devices while questions are displayed on a shared screen.

- **Classcraft (www.classcraft.com)** is a gaming platform aligned with tiered intervention practices (like PBIS, MTSS, and SEL) where students earn experience points and level up. This is a fun way to engage ELA and social studies students.
- **Breakout EDU (www.breakoutedu.com)** offers games for a variety of K–12 subjects. You can adopt lessons or create your own. For instance, biology has over fifty games to explore.
- **EdWordle (www.edwordle.net)** challenges students to increase the number of words they include in a word cloud. Alone or in pairs, while reading a story or informational text, students add words they do not know, learn them, and increase the cloud size. In a friendly competition, clouds with the largest, most diverse, and most colorful words, or with the most words that students can define, might win a fun prize. Each follow-up reading can call for breaking the record when a team competes against itself to increase a cloud's complexity or the difficulty of words picked.

The principle challenge will occur when your game adds small team collaborations. When and how will teams work together? Consider the following possible scenarios.

- All teams meet simultaneously online, with you observing or stepping in to give feedback. Because the team meetings are synchronized with your time, you rely on your grid and mute button to move out and into each space. You can still watch all the groups during collaborative tasks. When needed, you can return as many or all teams to the whole group for a Q and A session or new instructions, or you can schedule individual meetings with one or two teams or any student.
- Teams or individuals meet offline without you. They schedule their own times for team meetings to complete tasks that you assign. They choose how much time and when you meet. They need to complete the activity or task before they come back with a report in a whole-class meetup.
- Teams or individuals request time for your help. You schedule an online conference or needs-to-know, multi-student workshop.
- You identify one or more students with whom you want to meet, schedule the time, and tutor or counsel as needed.
- With some high-activity games such as hopscotch, students will have to figure out how to play, when to play, and where. You set up the teams, announce the content (for example, spelling all words from a story, naming characteristics of *Harry Potter*, or counting by tens), and tell the teams each to make up the rules to earn a score for a quiz you will give online.

For any upper-grade lesson, the full screen can serve as your go-to online tool for giving instructions, introducing a concept, explaining procedures, demonstrating practices, lecturing, or discussing a topic with the whole class. However, most efficient, whole screen, all-class presentations rank lower on the motivation and effective engagement scales when they exceed twenty minutes. They could fall to rock bottom when students have little else to do other than watch, listen, and maybe take notes.

To maintain student engagement, the most productivity will come during times when students can team to do online searches for information, discuss within a small group (guided by the teacher or by skillful self-management), play all-class games, reflect, and assess results. To ensure effectiveness of self-managed teams, it is essential to prepare members' collaborative effort before the team action starts.

For elementary students, novice ELs, and students with special needs, it is important that you hold off on planning online team tasks. Save high-energy teaming activities and games for in-classroom tasks that you can coach close-up and face-to-face. It is likely that high-energy games woven into classroom lessons will thrill these young populations, but extra care is needed to ensure that the game benefits the lesson's cognitive or social-emotional goals. For example, in a scavenger hunt for number facts or phonemic sounds, students will love the thrill of the hunt, but be sure the game helps players learn the lesson's facts and sounds.

Educators may also consider joining Playful Learning (www.playfullearning.net). Playful Learning is a growing national network of educators who are interested in conversations around game-based learning through face-to-face summits and workshops, as well as sharing ideas via the web-based portal of games and supporting materials.

How Can Flipping My Online Classroom Help?

Before the COVID-19 pandemic, teachers joined with Khan Academy (www.khanacademy.org) to create flipped lessons, where students watched video lessons at home. Students completed the assignments and arrived at the classroom ready for review and coaching by their teacher. Using universal remote instruction, teachers found increased opportunities to follow up on the home-watched videos. Among those discussed in this book are opportunities to use student playbooks and guiding questions that prompt students to anticipate *watch-fors* in a lesson, as well as chat rooms, threaded discussion boards, needs-to-know workshops, tutorials, and synchronous and asynchronous group tasks, activities, and games. Games may prove especially valuable as a flipping mechanism. The motivation of playing games increases readiness for students to do their homework and be all the more prepared to discuss what they learned in a synchronous, all-class meeting. When a teacher takes advantage of examining what research says about strategies that students can use during asynchronous learning at home and creates follow-through opportunities, the best results follow (Annenberg Institute, n.d.). When a teacher ignores research on feedback, cooperative learning, problem solving, and lesson design, flipped classroom results are mediocre at best (van Alten et al., 2019).

How Do I Engage English Learners With Online Instruction?

The Wisconsin Center for Education Research's WIDA standards (https://wida.wisc.edu/teach/standards) guide instruction that will benefit English and Spanish language learners in grades K–12. Social and instructional language, the first WIDA standard, offers instructional context to help students interact socially, build community, and establish working relationships with peers and teachers. Four other standards offer subject-specific ideas and concepts necessary for academic success in language arts, mathematics, science, and social studies. With these five standards leading the way, the Wisconsin Center for Education Research works with forty states to provide research and resources appropriate to use with a single EL in a school or an entire population of ELs.

Research highlights the benefits of games to develop English learners' language skills, collaboration, and problem-solving capabilities. Games are shown to be more effective at helping ELs with reading and writing skill development than traditional methods in an online learning community:

> Language becomes meaningful in the context of activity. And that's where true academic language development happens. It's when you create environments that elicit that kind of language. . . . Virtual gaming supports "best practices for ELLs" because it provides them with concrete experiences similar to field trips and much deeper experiences than using objects and pictures, which is a traditional and more limited ESL best practice. (Robertson, 2014)

In addition to games for ELs, researchers have pinpointed other online best practices relevant for digital instruction (Olesova, Richardson, Weasenforth, & Meloni, 2011; Robertson, 2020). These reports identify the value of providing audio and visual aids to assist English learners' language development. Consider these ideas.

- **Go visual:** When ELs can see and hear what teachers have to say multiple times, they are more likely to understand what is said. Using your smartphone or computer and Vimeo or a similar movie-making app, create short videos that students can watch at their convenience and review multiple times for practice. On videos, share greetings, prompts with sample responses, and images of examples with voice-over.

- **Go verbal:** Post playbook instructions, written examples for instructions, brainstormed lists, summaries of discussions, and other materials that ELs can read and reread on their own time. Make PowerPoints and have ELs store them in an e-portfolio folder. In addition, you can build an audiobook library of popular, age-appropriate stories. Consider the collection at the Provo City Library (www.provolibrary.com). In addition, consider FluentU (www.fluentu.com) to help students learn English from talk shows, music videos, movie trailers, commercials, and so on.

- **Make your own:** Prepare your own audio readings of stories and instructions. Make audio files to ensure that you (or a reader you select) use precise tones and dialects. You can let students make their own files when they get fluent enough to read to themselves. Listen and give feedback pointing out pronunciation errors. Set the files up in a student-accessible library and let them respond to guiding questions you record. You can also schedule needs-to-know workshops or one-to-one online tutorials (Fiock & Garcia, n.d.).

How Do I Make Up for Online Learning Losses?

Because climate change, disease variants, mass shootings, and other damaging events disproportionately affect people who are already marginalized, it helps to keep in mind how variations in instruction can counter the negative impact on learning for students who may lose more ground because their schools are not sufficiently able to provide quality teaching online in times of community stress (Engzell, Frey, & Verhagen, 2021). The most worrisome losses can occur when students cannot or do not stay connected with the technology tools (no cell phone, dropped calls, system crashes, dead device batteries, no internet access, documents lost in cyberspace, or inadequate digital skills) or other conditions including truancy or valid absences. Any of these can diminish a student's access to fruitful learning opportunities. It's important to have a backup plan to diminish these losses (see chapter 7, page 181) and enhance students' problem-solving skills and grit. These are important as short-term remedies that teachers can implement. Long-term remedies for losses caused by a community's technology shortfalls (no internet service) or family poverty (no Wi-Fi service) fall well outside your responsibilities as a teacher, but you can try to provide accommodations. Consider the following teaching approaches to diminish learning losses that can occur in online learning environments.

1. **Give students a grit goal:** When something or everything goes wrong with technology, instead of hearing "my cell phone [or laptop] died" as a reason for a missed assignment, a grit mindset says, "So what? Now what I intend to do is . . ." as students switch gears into a personal problem-solving mode. To initiate the grit mindset, adapt personalized learning plans so that personal resilience grows. Once a week, take five minutes at the start and five at the end of class to teach students how to fill in a grit plan, work on the mindset through the week, and assess results. Start with some of the little things that minimize learning time but students don't feel are theirs to control. Incorporate methods, starting with SMART goals and adding age-appropriate "I got grit" problem-solving strategies (such as a "my what works list" or self-talk to apply when something goes wrong and blocks learning).

2. **Prepare "What if?" student playbooks:** With a brainstorming or net-storming strategy, ready students for predictable tech issues with a playbook kept in the digital portfolio so they know the solution if a tech problem happens. Hold one brainstorm session to make lists of possible ways students have solved tech problems or overcome tech crash concerns.

3. **Set up a tech genius team:** Assign a team of students comfortable and confident as your in-class tech geniuses. Give each a badge or a neon jacket to put on when you or another student has a more serious tech issue.

4. **Conduct needs-to-know makeup workshops:** Needs-to-know workshops offer a "no problem" way to fill in gaps lost by tech accident downtime. Consider it a regular catch-up time for students who were ill or absent for other reasons.

5. **Try tutor time:** Tutors can work anywhere, anytime to help students stay on track and remain at grade level. Certainly, technology glitches can exacerbate learning struggles. Tutoring of all types can close gaps regardless of the cause. Arrange for older students, seniors, and other student volunteers to tutor students who lose time to technical glitches or need more time to learn an idea or develop a skill. Distance learning allows the flexibility for older students to tutor younger students from any distance for a short period of time. They can tutor a student for twenty minutes during a free time slot, and then move to their next class. They can tutor through private chats, threaded discussions, or synchronous or asynchronous meetings. Teachers could also schedule tutoring sessions during class time. Moreover, to connect tutors to students without home access to technology, teachers can set up community-located tutoring centers where tutors and students may use Wi-Fi. Libraries, coffee shops, and other public access facilities with Wi-Fi connections make strong tutor center candidates. Consider the following regarding tutoring.

    - *Predicable effects*—Tutoring is particularly effective for reading in grades K–2 and mathematics for high school students, especially when it happens during the school day. However, research shows that it is effective at all grade levels (Kraft, Schueler, Loeb, & Robinson, 2021).

- *Methods*—Receiving adequate training and support ensures tutors can successfully improve student outcomes (Allensworth & Schwartz, n.d.).
- *Extra benefits*—Tutoring can increase empathy, altruism, and self-esteem, especially in high school students and students with special needs like autism or ADHD (Greater Good in Education, 2019b; VocoVision, n.d.; Yogev & Ronen, 2014).

6. **Add learning packets:** Learning packets make it easier for students and teachers to work on the same page. Learning packets can contain the same playbooks and playlists a teacher has prepared, giving students access to the same documents, guiding rubrics, and other class aids.

Consider also using the reproducible "Resources, Activities, Support, and Evaluation Planning and Assessment" (page 76) to assess your online lessons before, during, and after you design them.

Conclusion

The design cycle encourages all educators to think creatively about how to meet students' learning needs, especially when they are exacerbated by an increasingly strong shift to digital teaching and learning. It is teachers' shoulders, however, that are bearing the heaviest weight. Traditional lesson plans published in teachers' guides fall short as they strive for more thoughtful, flexible designs to address the multifaceted needs of their 21st century learners. In addition to becoming familiar with the design cycle and its application to digital lessons, in this chapter, you explored ideas for engaging students in PBDL with gamified activities, flipped classrooms, and research-based approaches for making up learning lost by technological breakdowns.

MY TAKEAWAYS

What three ideas from this chapter can best help you shift to digital instruction and prepare all students to be effective digital learners? Record your ideas here so you can make a plan later.

1. _____

2. _____

3. _____

Resources, Activities, Support, and Evaluation Planning and Assessment

Assess your online lessons before, during, and after you design them to fit your classroom's digital format. Follow your design to implement with individuals or teams. For teams, adapt rubrics and playbooks. The first document focuses on the tools that will help you plan a lesson to teach in a digital environment; the second looks at the elements and processes for a digital PBDL.

Teacher playbook:

1. Use this template to assess each design tool before teaching with it.
2. Fill in the elements, and then invite feedback from a peer or team.
3. Implement the design, and keep notes on another copy of the template. You may want to invite a peer, supervisor, or student to observe an element and give constructive feedback on a template copy.
4. Do a final assessment. Make desired changes to think before designing the next lesson.
5. Save in a digital portfolio for making future designs.

Name:	Date:
Grade: ☐ Individuals ☐ Teams	
Subject or Unit:	
Feedback Given by:	
Resources	
Authentic and Relevant Materials <ul><li>Online content materials</li><li>Print materials</li><li>Product materials</li></ul> *Technological Resources* <ul><li>Learning management system</li><li>Video conference system</li><li>App and website access</li><li>Camera and microphone</li><li>Whiteboard</li><li>Printers</li></ul>	What worked well: To change: What worked well: To change:

page 1 of 4

Shifting to Digital © 2022 Solution Tree Press • SolutionTree.com
Visit **go.SolutionTree.com/technology** to download this page.

Activities	

Student Content Creation
- Individual or collaborative:
  - Inquiry
  - Problem solving
- Construction of knowledge and developments
	What worked well:
	To change:

Support	
Teacher Instruction and Support - Social-emotional activities - Student playbooks - Pacing chart	What worked well: To change:
Evaluation	
Outcome-Driven Skill and Content Performance Assessments - Guiding rubrics - Knowledge quizzes and tests	What worked well: To change:
Reflection on Learning in Lessons and Projects - Before - During - After	What worked well: To change:

Source: Adapted from Martin, F., Budhrani, K., Kumar, S., & Ritzhaupt, A. (2019). Award-winning faculty online teaching practices: Elements of award-winning courses. Online Learning, 23(4), 160–180. Accessed at https://files.eric.ed.gov/fulltext/EJ1211042.pdf on December 12, 2020.

Name:		Date:
Grade:		
Skill or Unit:		
Feedback Given by:		

Works Well and Why	Criterion	Needs to Improve and How to Do So
	Opens with online video	
	Includes all PBL elements with aim to engage all students	
	Advances student agency with students deciding about digital tools and other elements	
	Provides digital tools to promote student inquiry into a significant big idea	
	Develops digital skills with feedback	
	Builds collaboration among teams (if applicable) during asynchronous time	

Works Well and Why	Criterion	Needs to Improve and How to Do So
	Builds deeper learning of content with tools	
	Includes tools for special needs or language differences	
	Provides a guiding rubric to assess declared skills	
	Assesses students' skill levels for coaching needs throughout	
	Includes technological opportunities to personalize students' learning	
	Develops and then assesses cognition via digital skills	
	Highlights skills, such as product presentation, and reflections that require technology	

3

Digital Documents

Successful organizing is based on the recognition that people get organized because they, too, have a vision.
   —**Paul Wellstone**

Managing all the electronic communications, instructions, rubrics, submitted assignments, and products can quickly get cumbersome—or worse, simply out of control—if you don't have an organization plan in place. Your organization plan can include putting your files as well as students' on a file-hosting website like Google Drive or Dropbox. There is a "crucial need to organize virtual classrooms even more intentionally than physical ones. Remote teachers should use a single, dedicated hub for important documents like assignments" (Terada & Merrill, 2020). By teaching students how to manage their own electronic portfolios, you can increase their organization and digital skills and streamline access to the documents students need, increasing participation (Terada & Merrill, 2020).

This chapter explains the learning benefits of having students use portfolios to store digital products produced from their learning. It walks you through how to distribute and receive documents, how to find and manage a student portfolio system, which key documents most enrich portfolios, what to do if students lack the technology required for such portfolios, how to safeguard students' portfolio privacy, and what to know about a teacher portfolio.

How Do I Create Digital Documents to Organize Workflow?

To make it easy for you to work and communicate with older students in a digital classroom, create and save storable, form-fillable templates and pdfs that you can send to their devices for use and reuse. When you establish a baseline expectation that students will store your documents in a folder inside their portfolios, you set in place a system for enhancing classroom productivity that can far exceed the methods in pre-digital eras. In this way, you give digital natives the means to be digital learners who will become increasingly responsible for their own learning.

To start, browse for "fillable forms" so you can locate options for creating the documents that will help students make sense of the 21st century world and the massive amounts of data that flow from ever-evolving digital tools. Determine which ones will enable you to produce digital templates that will work with the expanding list of digital tools in your classroom (student playbooks and playlists, personalized guiding rubrics and learning plans, instructional strategies, templates, documents, and other work products). Pick fillable forms from Microsoft Word, Adobe Acrobat, Google Docs, or Firefly. Once you have mastered a form-filler app, you can easily create many replicable documents that will strengthen your digital organization and help students follow suit.

The following list of templates and other digital paperwork can provide the initial workflow organization in your digital learning environment.

- **Graphic organizers:** There are several steps you can take to add graphic organizers to your digital toolbox.

    a. Browse for "free graphic organizers" to find downloadable templates; save the templates you like to a folder. Or use Microsoft Word to make your own; for instance, to make a matrix, open the Insert tab, and drop down to the Tables option. Select the number of rows and columns you want, and build a matrix organizer. Fill in header titles.

    b. Look for other shapes you can use to draw custom organizers (for instance, a web). Or go to Microsoft Word's Pictures and Clip Art options on the Insert tab. Enter the key idea in the center of the organizer.

    c. Save the graphic organizer in a specific folder; fill in details each time you use it.

    d. Distribute the graphic organizer to students with a student playbook.

- **Playbooks:** *Playbook* is a term first made popular in reference to "a book containing a sports team's strategies and plays, especially in American football" (Maclean-Bristol, 2017). The word has since been adopted in medicine, business, and technology to refer to a set of instructions for completing a complex task. In the digital classroom, playbooks contain instructions for repeated tasks and serve as checklists during the tasks.

    - A *teacher playbook* is like a personal recipe book that details the steps, ingredients, and notes for special tasks done your way. You store yours in a folder as an accessible collection to remind you of the procedures you want students to follow for particular, but not regular, tasks (for example, instructions for building a specific design-it-yourself [DIY] artifact).

    - A *student playbook* contains procedures that you share and store on students' digital devices. This customized playbook details instructions for tasks you have assigned to students working alone or teams working on a digital device. When you make an assignment, you review the playbook and check for understanding. Throughout the assignment, students can retrieve the playbook document and use it as a checklist without needing to depend on you. This tool aiding with self-management becomes especially important when a student is working on a task in asynchronous time when you are offline or working with another student. If the student forgets next steps, he or she doesn't have to wait for a later conference or an email response. This guide on the side becomes the immediately accessible, go-to reminder that allows the student to continue without calling on you.

- **Playlists:** Originally used to refer to a list of recorded songs or pieces of music a disc jockey chose to broadcast on a radio show, the term *playlist* has expanded to include any list of digital files to be downloaded on a portable media player or computer. In the classroom, playlists are lists of teacher- or student-generated ideas. Once a playlist is started, students retain it in their document folders. They can add more ideas to the list, prioritize the items, or select an item for completing a task or making a PBDL product. Playlists are helpful for teacher-team members who are collaboratively developing ideas for projects and entry activities, solving technology issues, and managing digital classroom behavior, engagement strategies, and guiding rubric benchmarks, among other tasks.

- **Guiding rubrics:** Guiding rubrics are the go-to tools for assessing the outcomes, procedures, and processes in a digital classroom. You can build your guiding rubrics on what you already know about grading rubrics. The difference between these two look-alike documents is captured in a comparison of their purposes. A *grading rubric*'s primary purpose is evaluation of a performance or product in order to produce a grade. The primary purpose of a *guiding rubric* is instruction. The benchmarks in a guiding rubric teach students what is most essential to learn from a task, product, or lesson. The rubric guides your, and sometimes peers' or parents', feedback to inform students' self-assessments. You can add grades in a guiding rubric, but the guiding rubric is first and foremost a teaching aide.

  Creating your own guiding rubrics (or adapting grading rubrics that provide specific, measurable benchmarks, which inform students of what and how well they are learning) allows you to individualize assessment of any facet of online learning you select. Figure 3.1 provides a playbook for creating a guiding rubric. Copy it with your smartphone scanner, store it, and refer to it as a checklist each time you initiate a new rubric.

- **DIY artifacts:** You can organize the flow of digital lessons and PBDL unit documents that students must deliver as artifacts of their work. It's best that you set up a folder-portfolio system for all artifacts that students make (including text artifacts showing concrete evidence of their work, such as essays and stories) as well as for tests and quizzes you want

---

1. Decide on the format. How explicit you want to make the performance levels for each benchmark and how much room you want to allow for feedback will determine the format. A single-point format favors open-ended feedback. (*What did you do well?*) A multi-point format favors explicit criteria with a number rating for each item.
2. Determine who will give feedback (you, peers, or others).
3. Determine when feedback can occur (such as a student-chosen date, a specific formative date, or a final summative date) and the feedback's role (formative feedback versus final evaluation).
4. Start with a standard (subject matter from a state or national source); then transform the process (the standard's verb) and content (the standard's noun forms) into benchmarks and weighted criteria. If grading, add points for benchmark performance.
5. Make a matrix template to organize a fillable form.
6. Test the form with a colleague.
7. Scan the completed template and store it in a folder or in your digital portfolio.
8. Share it with students. Review and check for understanding. Supply a student playbook with a checklist of instructions for the self-assessment process.
9. Initiate use of the template as per its schedule.

FIGURE 3.1: A teacher playbook for guiding rubrics.

handed in. Require that artifacts be deliverable and accessible. For some artifacts that are not in text, students can take photographs or scan images of them with a smartphone or an app such as Smart Scanner.

- Students might have deliverables with sound and video content (such as podcast interviews, videos, and so on); these will require students to download special apps on their devices. Apps will also provide content from listening to stories and lectures, as well as assist students with *making-my-own* (*MMO*) audio and video products. For instance, a free podcast-making app called *Spreaker Studio* has everything students will need to create a professional-sounding podcast from a phone, tablet, or desktop. With parent permission, students can download podcast apps in a device location you determine. To download a broadcast on a specific topic they are studying, they may use Apple Podcasts, Google Podcasts, Spotify, Audible, Pandora, TuneIn, or TED Talks. To make videos for YouTube, they will need to save a video-making app such as Vimeo, iMovie, Adobe Premiere Rush, or Instagram. Be mindful when having students download apps that their devices may have limited storage capacity. Don't monopolize that space.

With any of these documents you create or adapt, a smartphone is ready to help. You can call on the phone's camera, an internal scanner, or a free downloadable scanner app (such as Fast Scanner) to copy the document and store it in iCloud or another digital storage space. When ready, send the document to student devices.

Occasionally, students may need to print documents, but mostly, the desktop printer is becoming obsolete. An up-to-date LMS should give you the capability of eliminating paper, including expensive textbooks and paper-based informational texts. The digital fillable forms you create or adopt will allow your classroom to go paperless, saving dollars and download times. And the forms will allow students to launch into online research, gathering information on any topic in your curriculum even as they refine their information-gathering skills. As students become accustomed to your library of digital forms and become comfortable and competent using these documents to self-manage their online lessons and PBDL tasks, you will spend less time going over procedures and more time coaching for deeper learning outcomes.

Standardizing these various documents for repeated use in your students' digital learning experiences will help them organize their workflow as you activate their opportunities to learn. In addition, by standardizing these documents in your repertoire of teaching tools, you make it easier on yourself to manage day-to-day flow of materials in e-folders and e-portfolios.

How Do I Organize Digital Documents?

Not following procedures and not being organized can be damaging inhibitors to student engagement, so how you prepare students to use online elements—links, documents, folders, and more—makes a difference for every virtual lesson. It is a good idea to preview your LMS through a student preview of key functions to check their accessibility. Take notes as you navigate so you can clarify for students or revise your organization (Darby, 2019). Having a colleague unfamiliar with your course review your LMS through a student-preview option is also helpful for getting navigation feedback.

Keep the following in mind when you decide where to post assignments, syllabi, and other class materials.

- **Enhance the learning environment:** Include elements of the Universal Design for Learning (UDL) framework (CAST, n.d.), which benefits all learners. A teacher's goal with UDL is to use a variety of teaching methods to remove any barriers to learning. It's about building in the flexibility that allows teachers to adjust their instruction according to every student's strengths and needs.

- **Enable text readers:** Some students use screen readers, which read text on-screen for users. You can enable text for this with your text editor's formatting tools, and provide text descriptions of anything visual, including graphs, pictures, and formulas (Darby, 2019).

- **Provide video transcripts:** On the LMS, you can offer transcripts of videos for students to watch. You can hyperlink a heading in the LMS, for example, for students to access a content page or assignment. To ensure they know to click the link for more information, add a simple line of clarification: *Click the link to access a transcript of this video* (Darby, 2019).

- **Simplify access to materials:** Avoid requiring a user to have to click more than twice get to the materials they need. Consider that if students "have to click out of a module and into another folder to watch a required video, that can be distracting—or frustrating if it's hard to find," as well as wasteful of time and mental energy (Darby, 2019).

- **Avoid the need for students to use a printer:** Students or parents and guardians can download a scanner app (such as Fossbytes at https://fossbytes.com) onto a smartphone and use it to copy and send documents.

- **Collaborate:** Consider conferring with your collaborative teacher team to decide on a consistent organization where possible, so students know what to expect and can more readily find materials from class to class. Also consider collaborating with staff who work with students with special needs to make content more accessible. For example:
    - Check with resource room teachers to learn how they use technology for students with special needs.
    - Ask social workers to identify students who have limited or no digital equipment.

How Do E-Portfolios Help My E-Classroom Organization?

An *e-portfolio* is a document storehouse accessed via a student's digital device. For instance, you may help your class set up portfolios in Google Drive. You may prefer an e-portfolio site such as b-learning (CANVAS), WordPress, or Edublog. In the e-portfolios, students will each categorize their e-documents, including rubrics, artifacts, and artifact photos, favorite tool playbooks, and other e-learning aides. So that you and the students can easily locate documents, you determine the classroom storage system with its labeled categories and subcategories (for example, Tools for Assessment: rubric templates, finished rubrics) and provide a student playbook when you teach students how to set up the categories and manage uploads and downloads.

E-portfolios help students learn the executive-function skills of self-regulation and organization. In addition to giving students the responsibilities of keeping records and maintaining order, portfolios give the teacher some time for him- or herself and for students to gain autonomy. Portfolios also provide teachers easy access to student progress and self-assessments over a period of time.

All these elements play a role in academic success, especially when it comes to online learning (Dixson, 2015; Greater Good in Education, 2019c; Jacob & Parkinson, 2015; Reeve, 2016).

For students, e-portfolios share these much-desired benefits.

- **Self-management:** Also known as *self-regulation*, this skill comes into play with portfolio use (because students must choose to put the documents in the portfolio) and portfolio organization (because they use the critical-thinking skill of categorization to decide in which subfolder to put documents). A well-organized portfolio archived for your review over time also raises the level of student accountability and responsibility; for example, it is the student's responsibility to make the digital deposit before each deadline.

- **Engagement:** Access to tools that guide them in making sense of scattered information and evaluating their own complex thinking helps students learn how to organize scattered information and tie new data to what is already stored in their brains. With an e-portfolio as the master organizing tool, more specific digital tools such as graphic organizers stimulate specific thinking patterns for organizing specific bits of information (for example, students may use cause-effect or fishbone organizers to generate connected ideas or concepts; Kailickaya & Esroy, 2019). When students make products as part of their learning, they improve problem-solving skills, including their ability to solve organization issues (Speziale, Speziale, McCook, & Letwinsky, 2016). Furthermore, evidence strongly suggests that asking students to create the tools to self-assess their work is most beneficial, in terms of both achievement and self-regulated learning, when such assessments are used formatively and supported by preparation and guiding tools (Andrade, 2019).

- **Agency:** Voice and choice are most often associated with educational agency. When students have some leeway in terms of how they organize documents and what documents they keep, this qualifies as agency. You allow students to select items that showcase their individual goals and talents. How much autonomy you give students over these choices should depend on how experienced they are with portfolio management and assessment, because they will need to understand when it is important to keep and store a document that shows growth or proficiency. The more you encourage these student-centered choices, the stronger the effect (Zeiser, Scholz, & Cirks, 2018).

- **Self-reflection:** When students reflect on the evidence of learning in a portfolio, they not only show the completed portfolio but also share reasons why they selected each item or group of items and what they learned from the process of developing the portfolio (Scott, 2006). This aligns effective portfolio practice with the cognitive processes included within the broad concept of metacognition—having students reflect on their work and think about their progress in learning (Bransford, Brown, & Cocking, 2000). Now more than ever, reports the Responsive Classroom (2019), students in distance-learning environments need time to reflect.

Where Can I Find an Effective Portfolio System for My Students?

Helen C. Barrett (2012), an advocate for portfolio adoption since 1991, offers a matrix (https://electronicportfolios.org/eportfolios/tools.html) that shows her assessment of a dozen nearly free portfolio sites that you can adapt for K–12 students. Though the information is from 2012, Barrett's recommendation for the two easiest-to-use sites still applies.

1. Kidblog at https://kidblog.org (now Fanschool at https://go.fan.school/kidblog; grades preK–6)
2. Edublogs at https://edublogs.org (grades 3–12)

The matrix helps you compare her assessments with other options she picks, such as Google Apps and Blogger. In addition, more recent LMS possibilities such as Canva and Schoology belong on the list, as do almost-no-cost DIY options available with Microsoft Word, Google Docs, and Dropbox for students who are ready for reading, writing, and adding basic digital skills to their competencies. Table 3.1 (page 88) lists options.

What Entries Most Enrich E-Portfolios?

Because working alone at a computer, especially in distance learning, can feel isolating, the e-portfolio becomes all the more important in a digital classroom. It can be a way for students to learn about and from each other, and to see how separate lessons and activities become part of a bigger picture. A portfolio is also a record showing personal accomplishment and growth. Lastly, as a place for students to store templates, instructions, and schedules, portfolios give both teachers and their students quick access to needed tools they use repeatedly. Here, we will further discuss a couple of the items that are important to include in student portfolios.

Products, or artifacts, are student-created items that give evidence of a completed performance or task. Products include written work such as essays, stories, poems, plays, and speeches. They may be text-only or may include images. Products can also be songs, websites, dioramas, posters, sculptures, and other three-dimensional printed items. If a product results from a team effort, each member includes a written portion or a photo with explanatory text and the authors' names and date in his or her portfolio.

When it comes time for students to enter an unfamiliar document or artifact into a portfolio, it will benefit students if you block out time to teach them the nitty-gritty. This will take you back to the needs-to-know assessments prior to introducing an unfamiliar tool such as iPhoto, a video-editing app, a Word template, or the process of loading an audio or video file. Conducting a needs assessment can tell you how many students need to learn the tool and how many can dig right in; it can tell you if you have some students who know the tool and can teach a workshop or provide coaching. It can also help you prepare a guiding rubric and student playbook for the tool. To assist you in preparing instruction for how to use a digital tool that is unfamiliar to you as well as the students, search for the tool's name and identify print and YouTube video tutorials that older students can use.

Instructions can explain many things: how to fill in a template, complete a task, use an app, engage in an activity, create a maker project, or conduct an experiment. Research indicates that in digital learning settings, "students place great importance on the inclusion of clear instructions for getting started in a course and consistent and logical navigation" (Ralston-Berg, Buckenmeyer, Barczyk, & Hixon, 2015). This student need for instructions accentuates the benefit of having DIY documents such as playbooks and guiding rubrics as online documents.

TABLE 3.1: Portfolio Options

Program	Grades	Information
Canva (www.canva.com/learn/design-digital-portfolio)	Grades 3 and up	If your school has purchased this platform, students can follow the online playbook design and manage their own portfolios as soon as they learn to read and keyboard. Make the setup a whole-class activity that students accomplish alone or in teams. You can turn portfolios into a yearlong project.
Dropbox DIY (https://bit.ly/3fUmnW3)	Grades K and up	Open the free version on your desktop. (You may need to buy added space.) Reserve it for student portfolios with a folder named for each student. Teach students how to share and secure documents and set up internal folders organized with an included table of contents.
Google Docs DIY (Use this tutorial to help: https://bit.ly/2WKFhrC)	Grades K and up	Starting with a Google template, students make a file folder for each document type (such as pacing schedules, essays, rubrics, and so on). Students then organize their documents into subfolders placed in a main folder. Limit access to each student's portfolio. As soon as prereaders can learn the digital skills needed to open and save a document, consider folders for sketches and first reading or mathematics products.
GradeCraft (https://gradecraft.com)	Grades K and up	This LMS helps instructors build courses and encourages students to focus on learning as they play games.
Microsoft Word DIY (https://bit.ly/3wzcdQV)	Grades 1 and up	There are two options for starting with Word. 1. Open a new document, save it, name it, and file it to be completed later. Complete a first document named "Table of Contents," and put it into a folder labeled "My Portfolio" with a student's name and date. Students will add other folders named for each specific type of document (such as playbooks, rubrics, essays, and so on). Each student stores "My Portfolio" in Archives. Instruct students to reserve Archives for their portfolios. 2. Open Templates on the Microsoft website. Instruct students on how to fill out a table of contents and then follow instructions for filling in headings. Make header titles for each type of document students will include. Again, store portfolios in Archives.
Schoology (www.schoology.com)	Grades K and up	This LMS does not have its own portfolio tool but allows users to connect to online storage from Google and Microsoft. If this is your school's platform, set up a DIY portfolio with this platform's compatible apps or a blog.

Whenever students need instruction to complete a task, it helps to share that instruction with the whole class on the LMS and with each student, parent, and guardian in a playbook so that they can keep that information in their portfolios. Because remote students can't raise a hand to call you to their desks or walk up to your desk to request clarification, sharing instructions in print docs helps minimize student dependence on you to repeat instructions. Students' ability to search for and use instructions instead of asking you to repeat them aloud in class (or to resend them) is a fair way to assess self-management and knowledge of portfolio use.

Distributing instructions with assignments helps ensure that absent students receive both. Most importantly, instructions become a readily available checklist that students can use (alone or with teams) to ensure they include all elements of a task in their work product. Figure 3.2 is an example of instructions for turning in late deliverable artifacts. These instructions are functional in the context of this discussion, as they include possibilities you may consider in your class.

Directions: Please add the date, and put these directions in your portfolio. Refer to these directions if you miss a due date.

1. Send me an email or text message that tells me what assignment you missed, its due date, and when I can expect your work. The proposed new date should be within the next three days unless you are still ill.

    ☐ Date: _____ by 4 p.m.

    ☐ Not sure. I need a conference. (If you need a conference, tell me when you will contact me during my posted conference hour to discuss what needs to be done, by what day.)

    ☐ I am sending my work now as an attachment.

2. Tell me honestly why you missed the due date for the assignment. I don't accept that your dog, your cat, or any pet ate it!

    ☐ I was ill with _____.

    ☐ I was confused about what to do.

    ☐ It was too hard or too much.

    ☐ I did not check my schedule.

    ☐ I blew it off.

    ☐ I had too much other homework on my plate.

    ☐ I had a family responsibility that I didn't plan for.

    ☐ Other: _____.

3. Sign your full name, and get a parent's full signature.

    My signature: _____ Date: _____

    My parent's signature: _____ Date: _____

4. Send the assignment.

FIGURE 3.2: Instructions for submitting missed deliverables.

How Do Students and I Manage E-Portfolios?

Portfolios in this context are digital repositories—warehouses built of ones and zeros—that retain all evidence of electronic learning documents for the year. Because "students value strong course organization" (Martin et al., 2019) and "logistical issues like accessing materials—and not content-specific problems like failures of comprehension—[are] often among the most significant obstacles to online learning" (Terada & Merrill, 2020), plan on establishing a well-organized e-portfolio management structure and method. And plan on teaching students how to create, organize, save, move, rename, and delete files, and recover deleted files.

Here are directions for how you might set up and oversee portfolio management with students. This way, you can see the big picture and then see details in context.

1. Select your platform. Consider cost. Your district may make available other, more costly tools than those described in this chapter. Adjust the following steps to your chosen platform.

2. Double-check all confidentiality and security considerations. For the United States, those include the Family Educational Rights and Privacy Act (FERPA), the Children's Online Privacy Protection Act (COPPA), and the Protection of Pupil Rights Amendment (PPRA). There are state- and school-specific considerations as well. At the semester's start, review online safety guidelines, and create and share age-appropriate instructions with students, parents, and guardians. The nonprofit organization ConnectSafely (www.connectsafely.org/eduprivacy) offers "The Educator's Guide to Student Data Privacy" (Gallagher, Magid, & Pruitt, n.d.) with considerations about laws and general app and website use. Consider the questions ConnectSafely poses to determine whether an app or website will sell or protect your students' information.

3. Choose what age-appropriate documents students may use—for example, word-processing documents (including assignments, playbooks and other instructions, and guiding rubrics), PowerPoint slide decks, JPEG photographs, pdfs, and videos. When you prepare guiding rubrics for the youngest nonreaders, use emojis they can circle. For students at that age, as well as for students with special needs or English learners, consider audio recordings to go with simple text.

4. Align student portfolios with your LMS's features. (For example, Canva has a built-in portfolio maker that may require you to eliminate a portfolio feature you want, such as guiding rubrics; you will have to customize the LMS to include this tool.) Whatever you choose, provide students accurate, thorough, written, and video-recorded instructions. Provide an overview of the organization, starting with main folders, and give steps for how to organize your system.

5. If you are grading portfolios and their contents, select a gradebook app such as PowerSchool (www.powerschool.com). If you are using a grading scale or pass-fail for deliverables, determine how you will connect grades to the portfolio, and add information with student instructions.

6. Set up the portfolio organization so students can manage it. In the directions, designate a section to deal with any settings you determine students will use as they manage their own portfolios. These settings should include instructions that let students drop in, delete, and rename files, if appropriate for their skill level.

7. Share any applicable pacing charts for the project or unit, point out the due dates, and show students the procedure for entering the data you want them to include on the pacing charts.

8. Provide a guiding rubric so students can reflect on how proficiently they are managing the contents. This feedback can come from the teacher or a student's self-assessment. Figure 3.3 and figure 3.4 (page 92) are examples of such rubrics for students' portfolio management, or their loading documents in an online folder. You need only adjust the skill and the procedural criteria for age alignment and the digital skills your students will need.

My Portfolio

Section 1

Name: _____

Class or course: _____ Quarter: _____ Due date: _____

Section 2

I am most pleased with:

I want to improve:

Section 3 Criteria	1 (Needs work)	2 (Getting there)	3 (Nailed it)	Your Reflection
Organization • Table of contents • Labeled groups • Labeled entries with dates • Sequenced entries				
Consistency				
Completeness of entries				
My Feedback				

FIGURE 3.3: Guiding rubric for assessing students' portfolio management.   continued →

Student Playbook

1. Fill in the information, section 1.
2. Skip section 2: the open-ended questions. Come back to it at the end of section 3.
3. In section 3, rate each criterion, and add your feelings or thoughts about a criterion in the reflection box to the right.
4. Go back to the "did well" and "need to improve" questions in section 2. Add your ideas and feelings here.
5. Submit the document to me. I will review it and send you my feedback.
6. Decide on how you will use your ideas and my feedback to improve your portfolio.

Visit **go.SolutionTree.com/technology** for a free reproducible version of this figure.

Name: Jorge Lopez		Date: January 16
Teacher: Ms. Lorbochar		Class: ELA 5
Feedback from: Myself		Skill: Add a document into my Google Drive portfolio.
What I Did Well	**Criteria**	**How I Can Improve**
	Identify my document with name, date, and driving question.	
	Start a blank document and select an appropriate template.	
	Load my document on the template.	
	Attach and label tables, clip art, and images.	
	Attach the appropriate rubric.	
	Save the document to my portfolio, in the right folder.	
	Set it up to share with the teacher only.	

FIGURE 3.4: Student self-assessment for portfolio management.

Visit **go.SolutionTree.com/technology** for a free reproducible version of this figure.

9. Determine roles and responsibilities for yourself, students, parents and guardians, and other staff for each lesson or project stored. Instructions for each project should include information about these roles and responsibilities.
10. Consider what functions you will open to students (for example, student permissions). Check student readiness to use these functions, and identify expectations for proper use.
11. Walk students through their first lesson. Determine what they must include in the portfolio. Table 3.2 suggests ideas. Visit **go.SolutionTree.com/technology** for a longer list of artifact ideas.
12. Spot-check entries for organization and completion. If they are not proficient or acceptable, let students know that they need to reorganize, and tell them what the consequences will be if they do not. For example, you might return a file to a student for editing and request he or she join a needs-to-know workshop to reexamine how to complete a file. If this is a solo student problem, plan a time to coach the student one to one.
13. Share warm corrective feedback if needed for entries (for example, "This is really well organized, but this rubric is in the folder for our previous project. Please make sure that this rubric gets to the right folder by the end of today"). You can use different methods, such as sending a direct message or sending a quick emoji and letting students know what the emoji message refers to. This feedback is important to students' continued learning about organization and self-management (Martin et al., 2019).
14. Conduct quarterly formative and end-of-year summative assessments for the organization of the portfolio collection as per the rubric. To balance the numbers, have a rotation schedule so you have one-eighth of your students for reviews each week.

The following sections offer more information about checking for proficiency and organizing portfolio folder structures according to grade level.

TABLE 3.2: Common Portfolio Contents

Expectations	Templates	Artifacts
Class norms	Examples of completed templates include:	Audio recordings
Cooperative-learning norms		Charts and graphs
Actions you will take for missed deliverables, including a schedule for make-up work, grade penalties, or private conferences	• Parent communication letters	Completed rubrics with feedback
	• Personalized lesson plans	Graphic organizers
	• Guiding rubrics	Journals
Contact-loss contingency plan	• Surveys	Lab reports
Instructions (for technology, assignments, assignment turnover, and portfolios)		Lesson and project deliverables
Student profiles (About Me–type assignments)		Photographs
		Reflections
Procedure charts		Slides
Pacing charts		Tests and quizzes
Syllabi		Videos

Check for Proficiency

Once students are reading and writing, conduct a needs assessment with a quick survey (using, for example, SurveyMonkey or Google Forms). Enter criteria and invite students to rate their proficiency, assuring them that not knowing how to do something simply means it is time for you to teach them. Explain the reason for checking what they can do, and share on your screen a needs assessment document. Most online poll sites provide instructions or prompt you on what steps are needed for completion.

You can list multiple criteria, such as the following. If you do not think of every skill students will need, ask them if they feel proficient in the skill as it comes up.

- I can make an outline.
- I can make subfolders for each lesson.
- I can upload artifacts and rubrics into a lesson folder.
- I can upload video, slides, and charts.
- I can share my folders.

Students can, for example, rate something *0* for "No, I can't do this," *1* for "I'm OK at this," and *2* for "Yes, I can do this easily." Check poll responses by asking students to go online and access the poll tool; then ask the class to try the first task in the poll. If students haven't successfully done the task, they need coaching on it, and you may need to ask the students to reassess their skills.

- If proficiency is split so that roughly half the class is ready to go, but half is still struggling, invite those who can do the task to pair and chat online with someone who doesn't know how. If the number of students who need to pair up is large enough, take time at the start or end of the next day (elementary grades) or class period (upper grades) to schedule a ten-minute needs-to-know workshop. If not, let the pairs pick their own times as soon as possible. The student who knows can demonstrate setting up a folder organization like the one you first shared on a half screen and then help the still-learning partner adjust his or her own to match the model. If you lead a needs-to-know workshop on your master screen, you can re-demonstrate for all. End by asking each attendee to complete his or her reorganized model before the next day. Review the submissions and schedule onscreen group coaching for those who still need help.
- If just a few students do not yet know how to do the task, schedule a coaching session outside class time.

Organize Portfolios According to Student Grade Level

In elementary classes, a student-managed e-portfolio highlights the subjects in the grade's curriculum. The table of contents lists the folders and subfolders students fill as the year progresses. Middle and high school teachers who teach a specific subject may choose folders with item categories such as plans, artifacts, feedback, rubrics, and reflections in a consistent sequence. The simplest format lets students organize contents by lesson. Figure 3.5 shows an example of an elementary portfolio organization, and figure 3.6 (page 96) shows an example of a secondary portfolio organization. Your role is to guide students in making their portfolio, staying organized, and assessing their portfolio organization with the guiding rubric (figure 3.3, page 91) as the year progresses.

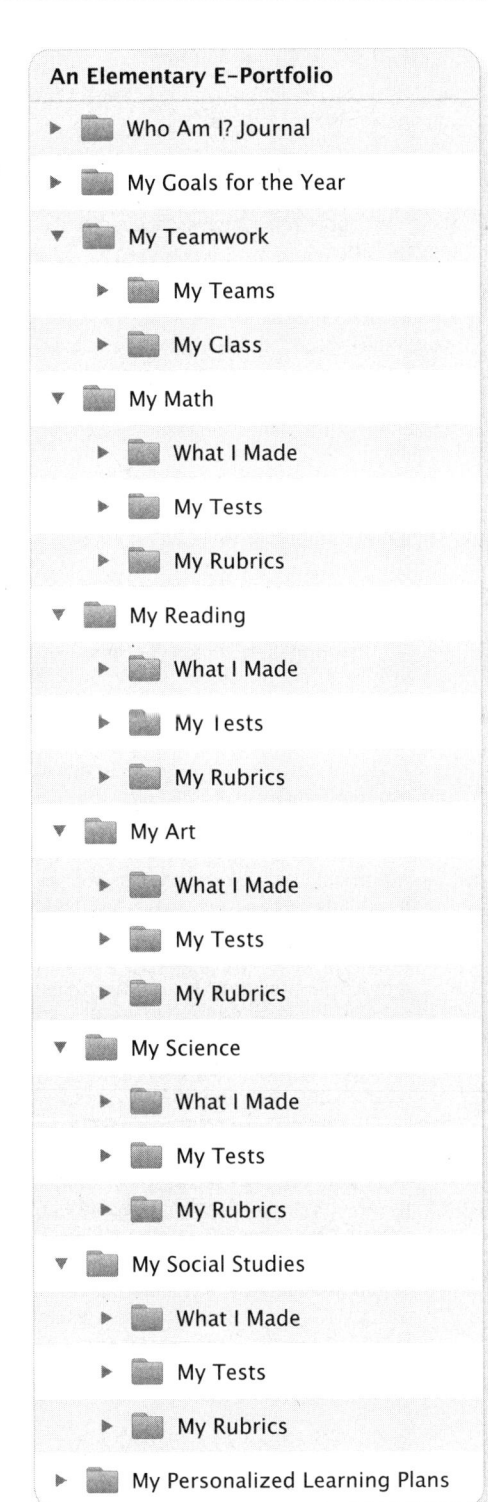

Student Playbook

1. Make a labeled folder for each of the items in the table of contents.

2. Label two subfolders (My Teams, My Class) for the My Teamwork folder.

3. Label three subfolders (What I Made, My Tests, My Rubrics) for each subject folder.

4. When you have an item to enter in a folder, add the date first and then load it into the folder when I ask you.

5. Fill in each folder.

   a. In your Who Am I? Journal, you will enter items about yourself. I will give you stems to complete, such as, "Today, I learned . . ."; "My favorite book is . . ."; "I like friends who . . ."; and "This week, I am pleased that . . ." or items that you want to put in anytime. This is your private book. You and I decide who can read it. Please keep your code private.

   b. In My Goals for the Year, you will have a chance to think about and write down your goals. You can change them anytime you want.

   c. In My Teamwork, you will keep your guiding rubrics for working with a partner, small groups, and the whole class. Date and file these in order. As the year goes along, you can learn how to become a better teammate and friend in many ways.

   d. In each subject folder, you will keep three folders. Please enter the contents for each one. When you finish a required task, such as a poem you wrote or a slideshow you made, I will teach you how to put a copy or photo of it in the folder. That will be a fun project each time. I will also show you how to put tests and rubrics in their folders.

   e. In My Personalized Learning Plans, you will keep those plans and their rubrics. Here, you will work on your own goals that you told me about in the My Goals for the Year folder. You will be in charge of picking out what or how you can learn better every week.

FIGURE 3.5: Example elementary portfolio organization.

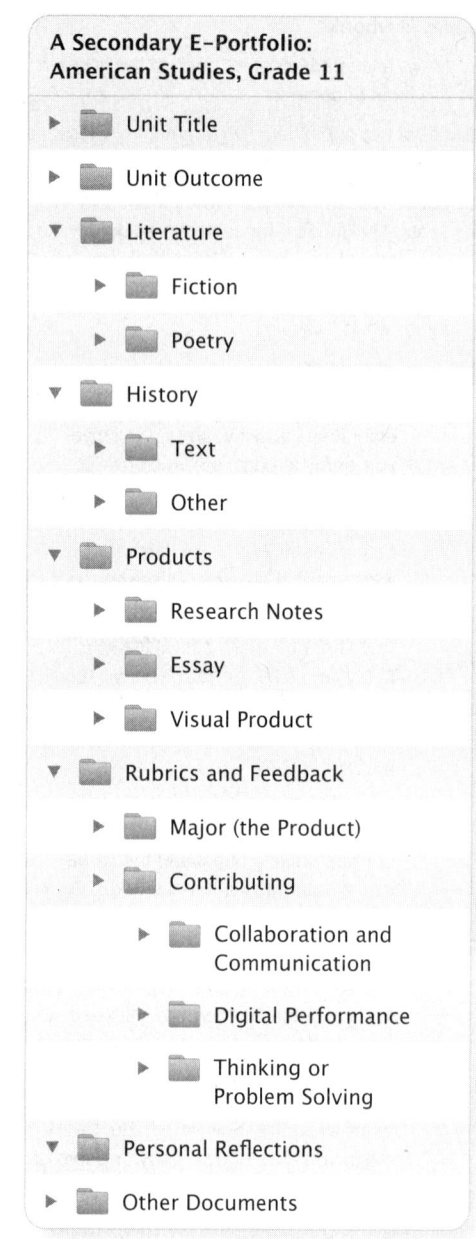

A Secondary E-Portfolio: American Studies, Grade 11

- ▶ 📁 Unit Title
- ▶ 📁 Unit Outcome
- ▼ 📁 Literature
  - ▶ 📁 Fiction
  - ▶ 📁 Poetry
- ▼ 📁 History
  - ▶ 📁 Text
  - ▶ 📁 Other
- ▼ 📁 Products
  - ▶ 📁 Research Notes
  - ▶ 📁 Essay
  - ▶ 📁 Visual Product
- ▼ 📁 Rubrics and Feedback
  - ▶ 📁 Major (the Product)
  - ▶ 📁 Contributing
    - ▶ 📁 Collaboration and Communication
    - ▶ 📁 Digital Performance
    - ▶ 📁 Thinking or Problem Solving
- ▼ 📁 Personal Reflections
- ▶ 📁 Other Documents

Student Playbook: American Studies

1. Identify the unit folder (for example, Puritan Era) you open in Microsoft Word.
2. Make a labeled Word folder for each item in the table of contents (for example, Literature).
3. Make and label each subfolder required (for example, Poetry).
4. When you have an item to enter into a folder, add the date first, title it, and then load it into the appropriate folder (for example, *The Scarlet Letter*).
5. Make and label the next level of folder with specifics as identified.
6. Fill in each folder.

   - In Personal Reflections, you will enter assigned reflections as well as any you want to add. If you do not want me to read the latter, please say so on the document. I will give you stems to complete, such as, "My writing goal in this unit is . . ." or "My teamwork has improved because of . . ." This is your private portfolio. You and I decide who can read it. Please keep your code private even from teammates.

   - In Rubrics and Feedback, you will keep your guiding rubrics for final products. They will address the outcome products that show what you are learning about (for example, Puritan life and society). You will have other rubrics, such as a collaboration rubric for working with two partners and the whole class when online, as well as a digital performance rubric for the digital element in your project (for example, a shareware video with storyboard) and for a thinking skill (for example, drawing conclusions). Date and file these in order. As the year goes along, you can learn how to become a better teammate and friend. You will also keep the master rubric for the unit. It will ask you to measure a reading comprehension goal as well as characteristics of your final product. You will do a self-assessment at the start of the unit and weekly until the final assessment. You will receive feedback from your teammates and me to consider. Please date and sequence each rubric entry.

   - When you finish a required reading task, such as a chapter in the unit novel, add new ideas to the unit concept map after your team has completed all tasks for that chapter.

   - For the final product, include (in order) your notes, design plan, team and idea rubrics, and phone photographs of the product. I will conduct a workshop for all who need to know how to upload the photos on a brochure in a Word template.

FIGURE 3.6: Example secondary portfolio organization.

In addition to serving as an instructional strategy that develops students' analytical thinking through categorization, the portfolio is meant to provide an opportunity to reflect (see chapter 4, page 103) and to share practical, observable data about students' progress and productivity with parents.

- For primary students, you will find it helpful to allot several twenty-minute online mini-lessons to walk them through the task of preparing their table of contents. If they are not yet readers and writers, you may schedule time each day to talk one-to-one with them as you fill in information for their e-portfolios. Follow this preparation task with round-robin, one-to-one conferences to help them make entries. As some become ready to read and do the entry tasks themselves, group them for coaching. As a coach, take the opportunity to include coaching of their phonemic awareness, numeracy, and vocabulary development. For extra coaching, write mini-playbooks so individuals can go to a central space and practice.
- For readers, start with a whole-class whiteboard session. Make the introduction a hands-on demonstration so that students each are labeling their own folders and perhaps making a first rubric assessment to learn what's most important in this process. In the first eight weeks, schedule minutes to coach students as they each make their individual folder entries. Start round-robin checking in week 4 with the portfolio guiding rubric. By quarter 2, assign folder entry as independent, self-directed homework with a quarterly rubric review. Schedule needs-to-improve workshops as you identify problem areas.

What If Students Lack the Technology Needed for Electronic Portfolios?

You can incorporate portfolios into your class even if students lack internet access, sufficient bandwidth, or digital devices. Consider a good old-fashioned folder divided into sections and filled with required materials. Just as you could choose this option in a physical classroom, you can adapt it for distance learners.

- For 100 percent remote learners with no internet access and no Wi-Fi, you will have to rely on mail services to collect semester or quarterly portfolio packets (or arrange for drop-off and pickup by way of volunteers, or your own transportation). For elementary students, you can send the sectioned folder and a set of instructions, a guiding rubric for the parent or guardian to read, and pre-stamped, pre-addressed envelopes for the portfolio's return. Ensure the district provides plenty of postage for a full portfolio.
- For hybrid classes, schedule a time to set up the folders early in the semester. Within the first two weeks, complete the setup and check on the first items students have placed in the folders. During the quarter or semester, students deliver scheduled documents to your face-to-face class and place them in the folders. Set up the sequence so they deposit documents, write reflections, and get peer feedback while in the classroom. You may require all documents to stay in the folders or allow students to take documents home and save them for an end-of-year review.

Figure 3.7 (page 98) shows a pacing chart for scheduling a real-time portfolio activity. Duplicate the following months until the final month of school.

Pacing Chart

On portfolio entry days, students send updated portfolio entries with assignments that result in an artifact submission after two weeks.

After students make entries on their own time, the teacher spot-checks them by a rubric and sends a request to students who will benefit from coaching about their portfolios.

Month One	Monday	Tuesday	Wednesday	Thursday	Friday
Week One			Needs assessment given Teacher introduces portfolios	Lesson one: Whole class Portfolio structure starts	
Week Two	Lesson two: Whole class Students create folders and subfolders together	Students complete setup on their own	Students make entries on their own time	Lesson three: Whole class Artifacts	Teacher randomly contacts students to check for compliance through next week
Week Three	Teacher coaches students for portfolios	Lesson four Students review portfolios with partners	Teacher coaches students for portfolios	Teacher directs first entries into folders (for example, first reflections)	Teacher does random quality spot-checks of entries made
Week Four	Students make entries on their own time	Students make entries on their own time	Students make entries on their own time	Portfolio entry: Students make entries on their own time	
Notes	Teacher spot-checks and invites students to coaching	Monthly team portfolio review	Teacher spot-checks and invites students to coaching	Whole-class, week four Five-minute reminder to update entries	

Months Two to Seven	Monday	Tuesday	Wednesday	Thursday	Friday
Week One	Students make entries on their own time	Students make entries on their own time Teacher reviews portfolios by last names A–F	Students make entries on their own time	Students make entries on their own time	Teacher randomly contacts students to check for compliance through next week
Week Two	Students make entries on their own time	Students make entries on their own time Teacher reviews portfolios by last names G–L	Students make entries on their own time	Students make entries on their own time	Teacher randomly contacts students to check for compliance through next week

Week Three	Students make entries on their own time	Students make entries on their own time Teacher reviews portfolios by last names M–R	Teacher provides coaching for portfolio issues	Students make entries on their own time	Teacher does random quality spot-checks
Week Four	Students make entries on their own time	Students make entries on their own time Teacher reviews portfolios by last names S–Z	Students make entries on their own time	Portfolio entry: Students make entries on their own time	Teacher randomly contacts students to check for compliance through next week
Notes	Teacher spot-checks and invites students to coaching	Monthly team portfolio review Teacher reviews portfolios by last name	Teacher spot-checks and invites students to coaching	Whole class, week four Five-minute reminder	
Final Month	**Monday**	**Tuesday**	**Wednesday**	**Thursday**	**Friday**
Week One	Students make entries on their own time Teacher coaches students for portfolios	Students make entries on their own time	Students make entries on their own time Whole-class final presentations	Students make entries on their own time	Teacher prepares students for final portfolio presentations
Week Two	Students make entries on their own time Students submit final portfolios	Students make entries on their own time	Students make entries on their own time	Students make entries on their own time	Teacher randomly contacts students to check for compliance through next week
Week Three	Students make entries on their own time Students submit final portfolios	Students make entries on their own time Students prepare product presentations	Teacher coaches students for portfolios Students finalize portfolios	Students prepare portfolios for the final whole class	Teacher reviews requirements for final rubric submission with the whole class Guiding rubric
	Students give presentations	Students give product presentations	Students make entries on their own time Students prepare product presentations	Students make entries on their own time Students give product presentations	Teacher randomly contacts students to check for compliance through next week
			Students and teacher have product assessment conferences and student reflections	Overflow day	Assessment conferences continue (five minutes each)

FIGURE 3.7: Pacing chart for scheduling a portfolio activity.

How Do I Safeguard Students' Portfolio Privacy?

The first step in privacy protection is setting guidelines for keeping the information students store in portfolios secure. The following guidelines extend to all work that students complete online.

- **Keep passwords private:** This is a challenge for many students, but forgetting or ignoring this guideline is not an option. No one but the teacher may enter a student's portfolio without the student's permission. Hold a frank discussion about bullies who steal private images and share them on social media *and* the real-life consequences of sharing private information on social media. Articles such as "Yes, College Admissions Officers Do Look at Applicants' Social Media, Survey Finds" by Alyson Klein (2020) make good discussion starters.

- **Be wise about social media:** The social media beloved by students can motivate communication. As you weave social media opportunities into remote lessons, help students examine each medium's pros and cons, including damage from social media, and decide which is wise for learning and which is not so wise (or educational).

- **Add permissions passwords:** When students submit homework assignments or deliverables in a lesson or give and get feedback, those contents are for your and the students' eyes only. Let students know in the strongest terms that violating online permissions protocols is a violation of the trust that binds all class members together. Show students how to restrict anyone other than you, their peer team members, or their parents or guardians from viewing, printing, editing, or copying content. Students cannot change these restrictions unless you give them a permissions password.

- **Sound spammer alarms:** It's important to teach and reinforce that any email, text, or external document received may not be benign. Spammers love to entice the unwary into sharing information they shouldn't. While you can set up protection against spam that encrypts your and your students' digital communications, spammers will eventually find a way to sell the latest fad appealing to your students' age group. Encourage students never to open an email or social media contact from a person, a phone number, or an email address they are unsure about or do not know. Tell them to delete the unknown and forget about it. They should never, never share personal information when they don't know the person asking for it. They should never even ask the person a question.

- **Keep parents and guardians in the loop:** Parents' and students' privacy rights are mandated by law. Your school or district must make these rights known to parents. You can help by proactively addressing parents' concerns for students' data safety and security, perhaps with an email to class parents or a discussion in online parent-night conferences.

A second step of protection is installing spyware protection on your LMS to watch over all connected devices. Although there is no guarantee that hackers won't break through these barriers, they are a strong line of defense. The ultimate defense will be determined by how well students follow the guidelines after you teach and reinforce each guideline's value.

What Should I Know About My Teacher Portfolio?

Your teaching portfolio is where you store information about your professional practice. It can include a variety of information: lesson plans, assignments, personal reflections, and written and recorded instructions, for instance. Like student portfolios, a teacher portfolio will have subfolders for these different targets. Depending on their purpose, teaching portfolios could include different collections of materials, consisting of background information (résumés), teaching artifacts (classroom video recordings, lesson plans, and student feedback), and professional information (recommendations and formal evaluations). Prepare an assessment portfolio for evaluations by your supervisor. Creating a developmental showcase—which shows evidence of your gradual, innovative additions of research-based practices and new digital skills in an online portfolio—would benefit your application for a promotion or a job in another district.

Conclusion

By including instructions, templates, and expectation and performance documents in their e-portfolios, you give students access to the guidance and resources they need whether working synchronously or asynchronously. Additionally, the portfolios foster student self-management, metacognitive self-reflection, and assessment, collaboration, and organization skills. When you use these digital tools, you gradually transfer record-keeping responsibility (including for student assessment) to students, thus reducing the load on your shoulders to track their performance and growth throughout the year. Starting with documents you make, such as guiding rubrics and playbooks, students can learn how to traverse your digital system. From planning to implementing to assessing, this chapter has provided you with templates, model schedules, and other documents that will help students see the relationships that small pieces of lessons have to learning outcomes, tying together the many events of the year's study. In short, their portfolios show them their year's travel across the landscape of your curriculum.

MY TAKEAWAYS

What three ideas from this chapter can best help you shift to digital instruction and prepare all students to be effective digital learners? Record your ideas here so you can make a plan later.

1. _____
   _____
   _____

2. _____
   _____
   _____

3. _____
   _____
   _____

Mindful Engagement *in* Digital Classrooms

Technology is just a tool. In terms of getting the kids working together and motivating them, the teacher is most important.
  —**Bill Gates**

Capturing and maintaining students' interest in learning can be tough, and distance learning makes it even tougher. Students face many more distractions at home than in a controlled classroom, such as family members talking, dishes clattering, or doorbells ringing. A vast number of magnets—everything from caring for younger siblings to playing video games or napping—pulls students away from teachers' tenuous control, too often leaving them unmotivated to show up for class or stay on task when present. In the worst scenarios of remote learning, students at home are truant. Other students come onscreen, watch and listen to their teacher for a few moments, and then drop their heads on folded arms or twiddle with anything their hands can touch, including the mute button. Some get up and amble offscreen. The list of low-interest, no-engagement signals is endless.

Attracting and keeping twenty to thirty students mentally locked into digital instruction is a top challenge remote teachers face. While being physically present in a hybrid or blended classroom may increase the chances that teachers will engage their students during an online task, simply sitting students in front of a screen and having them listen or fill in a worksheet are a quick step toward wandering and lost minds. By themselves, even the fanciest VCSs, laptops, and other digital devices seem to have little effect in sustaining the attention and engagement needed to produce reliable academic results (Zhu, Kaplan, Dershimer, & Bergom, 2011). Teachers in hybrid and blended classrooms have found other distractions when digital tools enter the instructional mix. Students sometimes sneak unapproved digital devices to send Instagram messages or scroll through TikTok on the sly as they sit in digital carrels.

The Glossary of Education Reform (2016) defines *student engagement* as "the degree of attention, curiosity, interest, optimism, and passion that students show when they are learning or being taught, which extends to the level of motivation they have to learn and progress in their education." This definition suggests that student disengagement, in contrast, shows up as boredom or lack of interest, passion, or inspiration. The concept of student engagement is predicated on the constructivist belief that learning improves and achievement increases when students are asking and answering questions, collaborating and communicating, and solving problems and making decisions about what (the content) and how (the methods) they are learning. A pre-pandemic study shows there is "a moderately strong and positive correlation between overall student engagement and academic achievement" (Lei, Cui, & Zhou, 2018).

Literature on student engagement during remote and hybrid learning shows students' minds scarcely stay attuned to the online learning events teachers design. On the other hand, a search for literature on engagement via instructional strategies turns up a cornucopia of studies that show what teachers can do to increase student engagement.

To encourage teachers to strive for passionate, mindful student engagement, best-practice researchers have highlighted the effects of teaching strategies such as the following (Hattie, 2016; Marzano, Pickering, & Pollock, 2001).

- Cooperative learning
- Advance, graphic, or visual organizers
- Higher-order or complex thinking, such as:
    - Comparing and contrasting
    - Testing hypotheses
    - Summarizing
    - Setting objectives
- Feedback

Teachers can adapt these instructional practices to their now more-digital classrooms (Hattie, 2016; Marzano et al., 2001). As you have already noted in the prior chapters, and as you will see in the remaining chapters, there are a variety of ways to integrate each strategy into digital lessons, with different digital tools and materials expanding when or where a lesson may occur. When well used, these strategies have high potential to engage students' minds and hearts. What teachers have in hand to increase brains-on, hearts-on learning is the opportunity to construct lessons suitable to multiple forms of highly engaging digital instruction for those who sit in brick-and-mortar classrooms and those who sit in cyberspaces. By combining prior knowledge of evidence-based practice with digital tools and materials like those discussed in chapters 1–3, K–12 teachers can construct new ways of teaching that will impact learning outcomes in the same way as in pre-pandemic classrooms. Just as teachers in one-room schoolhouses were forced to adapt to new ways of teaching with the multigrade schoolhouses in the late 19th century, 21st century teachers have to consider how they will change their instruction with the switch to digital classrooms.

What does *mindful engagement* mean in a digital classroom? Biologist Jon Kabat-Zinn (2003), the person who is credited with articulating a common *mindfulness* definition, says it "is awareness that emerges through paying attention on purpose, in the present moment, and non-judgmentally" (p. 143). Education researchers Jeongju Lee, Hae-Deok Song, and Ah Jeong Hong (2019) define students engaged online as follows:

> Successful and engaged online learners learn actively, have the psychological motivation to learn, use prior knowledge well, manage their learning schedule, and utilize online technology effectively. Moreover, they have great communication skills and are proficient in both cooperative learning and they are self-directed. (p. 4)

Prior to assessing engagement, designing engaging lessons is in order. In addition to just designing online instruction for achievement, if you want to increase your students' online engagement, you will need to add attention grabbers, peer interactions, and communication strategies. For example, when students come onscreen, you have to grab their attention. For their entry, you can be a historical figure and ask them to guess who and why. In the middle of a lesson, you can show a video with guiding questions to focus students' attention as they watch and lead the discussion after, or you can send out a poll asking students to vote on which historical figures from a certain era contributed most. Beyond these easy-to-do engagement strategies, what research-backed strategies increase engagement during distance learning? This chapter offers ideas.

In addition to the strategies you pick to grab and keep students' minds and hearts involved, research shows that activities that promote the following social-emotional outcomes lead to higher engagement from students who are learning online.

- Autonomy
- Goal setting
- Community
- Reflection

The subsequent sections cite that research and reveal strategies for including these elements to deepen mindful engagement in your classroom.

How Do I Increase Student Engagement by Building Autonomy?

Autonomy refers to people's need to know that they have choices so they can govern or manage their own behavior, emotions, and cognition as they see fit. Children increase their autonomy as they move to adolescence and childhood to the degree that significant others, including teachers, parents, and older siblings, relinquish their natural feelings of control. For adults to relinquish the power and control they hold over children is a delicate balancing act. Remote classrooms, and to a lesser degree hybrid and blended classrooms, put added strain on teacher-student control relationships. However, remote classrooms, and to a diminishing extent other 21st century classrooms caught in the shift to digital, provide a significant opportunity for teachers to help students expand the degree of autonomy that leads to increased and productive engagement. Expanding their autonomy gives students a voice in making choices about how and what they learn. When this occurs, teachers are rewarded when they hear student agents able to declare, "I can do this myself!"

Online learning in any delivery mode depends on students being able to self-manage or self-direct their learning. Autonomy is crucial to students practicing that self-management (Gallagher, 2020; Shi & Han, 2019). Many digital tools, such as VCSs; strategies such as cooperative learning; and materials such as student playbooks (already mentioned in this book) boost autonomy. Cooperative learning during asynchronous and synchronous times and online problem-solving discussions, for instance, is a "you can't do without" instructional strategy that helps students internalize the belief, "I am the master of my fate" (Shi & Han, 2019). Student voice and choice become ever more important online when you cut the ropes holding what and how students learn from your control and gradually push students to increase their level of responsibility to set goals on the road to self-direct their learning.

Increasing autonomy does not necessitate throwing students into the learning lake to sink or swim on their own. All students have the potential to benefit from an immersion during which you teach them how to swim. To this point, a study of at-risk students has determined that increasing teacher support is especially crucial for at-risk students learning online, as these struggling students look for less risk and more certitude: "These strategies need to facilitate opportunities for self-pacing and autonomy in the learning experience while ensuring that appropriate guidance and monitoring are in place" (Lewis, Whiteside, & Dikkers, 2014, p. 6).

It stands to reason that all students, whether they are at risk or not, benefit from added support when they receive increased autonomy, which is especially risky and especially beneficial in a digital world. As the digital guide on the side, you are the one who designs how you will modify your brick-and-mortar teaching style. You can increase the challenge for all students to center their expanded digital learning potential.

In the first three chapters, your review of digital tools, digital materials, and a digital design process uncovered some big-ticket items in the digital store.

- VCS tools (for example, gallery grids, breakout rooms, chat rooms, and remote learning stations)
- Portfolios
- Communication tools for digital lessons and PBDL units (for example, email and social media)
- DIY materials (for example, guiding rubrics, playbooks, and playlists)
- Evidence-based instructional strategies (for example, cooperative learning and games)

It's your decision to avoid doing for students what you can teach them to do or what they can already do for themselves. Making this decision suggests that you are coming close to Einstein's declaration, "I never teach my pupils; I only attempt to provide the conditions in which they can learn" (Goodreads, n.d.a). His thought reaffirms that it's OK to mediate growth of your students' autonomy by teaching them how to learn in new ways so they can make authentic choices about how, what, when, and where they can learn in the wider world of digital learning.

The preceding listed digital tools, materials, and resources set the stage for your leadership in expanding student autonomy. When you empower students by developing the digital, social, emotional, and cognitive skill sets related to each item, you are readying students to take charge of their own digital learning and speak with their own voices. To ensure this happens, you prepare them to make decisions that will lead to positive outcomes. Your primary leadership tools are those enabling words and actions that advance your goal to produce self-directed learners who stand on their own two feet. Consider in the following guiding rubrics (figure 4.1 and figure 4.2, page 108) what the mediation of autonomy looks and sounds like in digital classrooms. First, use the appropriate grade-level rubric to self-assess the degree to which you are already promoting student autonomy in your digital learning environment. After, rescore the rubric of your choice to assess changes you make over time.

How Do I Engage Students in Goal Setting?

Goal setting is a practical and effective way to connect with students who are disconnected from you by physical space. It becomes all the more important when students are at a distance from their teachers, as happens to a greater degree in remote classrooms and a lesser degree in blended classrooms. Even when students are online in a brick-and-mortar computer station, the separation is wider when they communicate through cyberspace.

Name: _____ Grade: _____

Instructions: Mark to what degree you give students a choice. Score yourself: 0 = not at all, 1 = less than once a month, 2 = at least four times a month, 3 = twice a week, 4 = daily.

The Looks and Sounds of Autonomy: Elementary Teacher Self-Assessment

1. VCS
    a. _____ I prompt students to answer higher-order questions on the grid.
    b. _____ I ask open-ended guiding questions on the grid, giving each student a chance to answer.
2. Portfolios
    a. _____ I use a rubric with students asking them to self-rate a product they made.
    b. _____ I let students decide what documents go into each section.
    c. _____ I let students choose and assess a personal improvement goal.
3. Collaborative teams
    a. _____ I teach students how to be responsible in a team role.
    b. _____ I help students self-assess their team contributions with a guiding rubric.
    c. _____ I prompt students to reflect on their peer relationships in the classroom.
4. Digital lessons
    a. _____ I model, coach, and help students self-assess new digital skills in a lesson.
    b. _____ I ask students for ideas so I can help them improve their digital skills.
    c. _____ I let students tell me what they need to know about digital tools we are using.
    d. _____ I schedule free time for students to do games and activities on their devices.
5. DIY materials (for example, guiding rubrics, playbooks, and playlists)
    a. _____ I provide guiding rubrics and other templates for teams to construct their own.
    b. _____ I provide input and coaching for student needs-to-know workshops and tutorials.
    c. _____ I provide coaching and resources for product making.
6. Evidence-based instructional strategies
    a. _____ I prepare and encourage students on how to give positive feedback to their peers and me.
    b. _____ I set up opportunities with prompts for students to give and get positive feedback during asynchronous and synchronous activities.
    c. _____ I ask students to assess collaboration and problem solving in all activities.
    d. _____ I look for ways and put into practice ways to encourage autonomy and self-direction.

Review your responses, and then complete these open-ended prompts.

What I am doing best is _____.

What I am going to improve is _____.

I am going to do so by _____.

My timeline is _____.

FIGURE 4.1: The looks and sounds of autonomy—Early elementary-grade guiding rubric.

*Visit **go.SolutionTree.com/technology** for a free reproducible version of this figure.*

Name: _____ Grade: _____

Content Areas: _____ Date Completed: _____

Instructions: Mark to what degree you give students a choice. Score yourself: 0 = not at all, 1 = less than once a month, 2 = at least four times a month, 3 = twice a week, 4 = daily.

The Looks and Sounds of Autonomy: Upper-Grade Teacher Self-Assessment

1. VCS
   a. _____ I prompt students to answer higher-order questions on the grid during synchronous instruction.
   b. _____ I prepare students to work in cooperative groups to define their own roles, self-assess, and set their own schedules in asynchronous time.
   c. _____ I prepare and ask students to lead discussions or other all-class tasks, such as group reports, presentations, and games on the grid.

2. Portfolios
   a. _____ I let students self-rate a product and share that with peers and myself for feedback.
   b. _____ I let students decide or place what documents go into each section.
   c. _____ I let students choose and assess a personal improvement goal.
   d. _____ I give students feedback on their portfolio rubric.

3. Collaborative teams
   a. _____ I ask students to define responsibilities and select team roles.
   b. _____ I let students self-assess their team interactions with a guiding rubric.
   c. _____ I prompt students to reflect on their peer relationships in the classroom and team.
   d. _____ I schedule but let student teams plan their own community-building activities.

4. Digital lessons and projects
   a. _____ I ask students to peer coach and help other students learn and assess new digital skills needed for a lesson or project.
   b. _____ I encourage students to add new media skills to their repertoires as they select products for PBDL.
   c. _____ I engage students in design of lessons and PBDL.
   d. _____ I equitably engage students in taking classroom leadership roles.
   e. _____ I let students tell me what they need to know about what and how we are learning in a unit.
   f. _____ I invite students' feedback on how to increase their autonomy.
   g. _____ I encourage free time for students to do games, activities, and offscreen team-building collaborations on their devices.

5. DIY materials (for example, guiding rubrics, playbooks, and playlists)
   a. _____ I include student feedback guiding rubrics in subject areas.
   b. _____ I provide student playbooks for new activities related to lessons and projects.
   c. _____ I assist students in locating new materials, local resources, and digital tools for lessons and PBDL.

6. Evidence-based instructional strategies
   a. _____ I teach students how to give positive feedback to their peers and me.
   b. _____ I set up opportunities with prompts for students to give and get positive feedback during chat rooms, discussion boards, and grid think-pair-shares.
   c. _____ I ask students to solve problems related to stories we are reading.

Review your responses, and then complete these open-ended prompts.

What I am doing best is _____.

What I am going to improve is _____.

I am going to do so by _____.

My timeline is _____.

FIGURE 4.2: The looks and sounds of autonomy—Upper-grade guiding rubric.

*Visit **go.SolutionTree.com/technology** for a free reproducible version of this figure.*

After teaching students how to set goals during digital learning, some useful options for you to make goal setting a routine include the following.

- Have students self-set goals that challenge them to lead, talk more, or increase their team role contributions; read more; or complete other out-of-your-sight digital tasks with a goal that they report to you in a weekly email. This added contact, enriched with your feedback about the students' accomplishments, is the starter bond.

- Maintain students' personal interest in an important topic by asking them to share a report with you in sessions. You can schedule these sessions daily in small online groups or less often in an entire-class chat room or discussion board.

- Ask students to set lesson goals and capture the results in rubrics for their e-portfolios; keep them connected on a scheduled basis. On a schedule you provide (see chapter 3, page 81), arrange for team and individual feedback on goals via a small-group chat or an asynchronous team-lead session.

- Ask asynchronous teams to set and assess goals each time they meet; this allows you to reinforce the value of goal setting and help teams self-manage the meeting time.

- Teach students how to adapt goals so they become SMART outcomes. When upper-grade teams are collaborating in making a PBDL product, you can expect them to follow the SMART model so they can assess the product more precisely and present it to the class via the VCS.

In short, studies show that "across a variety of grade levels, subject areas, and studies, effective goal-setting practices help students focus on specific outcomes, encourage them to seek academic challenges, and make clear the connection between immediate tasks and future accomplishments" (Nordengren, 2019). Identifying learning goals helps students take more responsibility for their education (Wright, 2015).

ALARMS is an acronym for waking up students or calling students' attention to goals that make your expectations explicit and measurable. With ALARMS, there are no fuzzy targets. Instead, you clarify your expectations with lessons whose goals are as follows.

- A = I will be *actively* engaged in getting to this goal.
- L = I can *link* this goal to the lesson's goal.
- A = I believe this is *achievable*.
- R = This goal is *relevant* to me.
- M = I can *measure* the ways you will know I reached the goal.
- S = I know *specifically* what I have to do.

Goal setting that leads to specific and measurable achievement results is best learned *from doing*, not from hearing lectures about its history, famous goal setters, benefits, or methods. ALARMS reminds you, as a teacher, that active engagement needs to be built into the ALARMS lesson criteria. You make each criterion as observable and countable as you can. This not only lets students see how to produce a measurable outcome, but also tells students exactly what you expect them to know or do and what the resulting product will look like.

Your role is to demonstrate how to set up the first goal and to coach students in following suit. Make the first goal experience simple and straightforward. As the semester progresses, enhance goal setting with your online coaching of accomplished goals and selection of age-appropriate activities to maintain interest and refine the skill.

Keeping a goal journal is another option, as it helps students learn to manage time and can help them practice their handwriting, which triggers different brain activity than typing does (Askvik et al., 2020). Once a week, ask students to spend ten minutes reflecting on their academic or social-emotional goals. You might ask students to try sketchnoting—"creating a vocabulary of symbols and arrows that you can use to represent ideas" (Gobir, 2021).

Research shows that sketchnoting can help build relationships (by having teachers and students create sketchnotes collaboratively) and increase autonomy (by letting students choose whether to use sketchnoting or take notes traditionally, and choose how to record information; Gobir, 2021). Artist and author Wendi Pillars (as cited in Gobir, 2021) suggests taking ten of the most important words or concepts in a lesson and creating a "little visual library." Pillars adds that students can have "one icon or one little sketch" instead of "a bullet point . . . at the top of [their] notes" for the week.

How Do I Build Community to Enrich Online Learning Time?

Students love to belong in a community. Early on, young children find buddies. Some go on to cliques and gangs. Some tag walls with their group name. Some join sports teams and wear the team paraphernalia. Most text each other and live in social media.

Not all such communities are healthy, but you can capitalize on this need to belong, which increases each year young people are in school, as you address the need for inclusion. At the height of the COVID-19 pandemic, when remote learning separated friends, a chief rallying cry among students was "I love talking to my friends. I hate not seeing them every day" (S. Kahler, personal communication, 2021). The stronger your students feel about separation from friends, the greater the opportunity you have to bring them together. Their desire to communicate face to face with friends is your lever to transform them into a community of learners with a common goal and shared interests.

Community is defined as "a feeling of fellowship with others, as a result of sharing common attitudes, interests, and goals" (Lexico, n.d.). Each time you encourage small teams to work together to strive for a collaborative goal or to build a project based on common interests, you build that community. When you mix and remix online student teams throughout the school year so that they feel fellowship with their teammates, you build the whole-class community. You, as a leader, can deepen the bonds in that community so the shared goal accelerates and deepens learning for all community members.

The more remote the learning, the more you can call on tools to span the interpersonal gaps it creates. It's up to you to nurture student-student relationships that bridge those gaps. You can do this by making your classroom environment interaction rich in the following ways (Borup, West, Graham, & Davies, 2014).

- In an elementary school classroom, start each day with a five-minute all-class opportunity for any student to express cares, comforts, or concerns (the three Cs). Lead the way until students have the level of comfort necessary to share one of the three Cs. Say things like, "I am concerned that our internet connection died and some of you didn't get to finish sharing your answers," and "I want all of you to know that Raoul became an Eagle Scout last night."

- In a middle or secondary school classroom, lead a five-minute three Cs session once a week. Say things like, "I noticed that some are having a hard time speaking up in the chat room. I'd like to hear some ideas for how to help."
- Send private notes via text message celebrating students' special accomplishments. Say things like, "Last night, I saw you dance a solo at the Ruth Page Center for the Arts. That's a bravo."
- Structure free online time for students to hang out in a VCS room or chat online after lunch.
- Mix and match pairs and roles in small teams. Be sure everyone knows what to do, and then let them select an informal game to play online or an informal team activity to do, such as making a team logo or flag to show and tell the class how it represents certain talents of the team members.
- Set a standard each week for the amount of collaborative time students will spend in synchronous and asynchronous work. Increase the time each week until you observe students deeply engaged in the tasks you assign. If you are a middle school teacher, set your weekly goal for 70 percent; in K–3, look toward a 50 percent goal.
- Set a second standard to engage in pure community-building activities, including team-building games during recess, for thirty minutes per day in elementary school. Average thirty minutes per month in middle and secondary school.
- Teach grades 4 students and older to sketchnote during VCS all-class or small-group meetings that have a lot of talk time (with lectures by you or presentations by peers). Sketchnoting allows listeners to sketch and draw what they are hearing and to escape looking endlessly at the VCS screen (Gobir, 2021). At the end of a session, invite pairs and threes to give "I like" feedback in a round-robin, focusing on relationship building and mentioning the need to have students write and draw by hand.
- Go to https://museumhack.com/virtual-team-building-for-remote-teams, where you'll find several activities that build relationships. Instructions are provided; your responsibility is to select an age-appropriate game or make a game age-appropriate.

A sense of community is important to any learning space but is of particular importance to engagement for students learning virtually. Boras and colleagues (2010) note that opportunities to heighten communication among students, and between student and teacher, may be prevalent in emerging online classroom communities. In addition, an online learning–specific study finds that an "emotional sense of belonging can be a major factor in the prevention of dropouts and help students to engage in classes" (Lee et al., 2019, p. 9).

Cooperative learning, even though it is not the only way to build online communities, spans the space between academics and social-emotional learning (SEL) as the best time-tested, evidence-based method for igniting fires of student engagement (Gillies, 2016; Kupczynski, Mundy, Goswami, & Meling, 2012). From an SEL perspective, cooperative learning is a go-to strategy that builds "more caring, supportive, and committed relationships, and greater psychological health, social competence, and self-esteem" (Johnson & Johnson, 1989, as cited in Eredics, n.d.). By adding cooperative learning as a routine structure in a digital classroom, teachers enable students to become more adept at learning with others and working as a team to produce a shared product. At scheduled intervals, teachers heighten engagement by holding students individually accountable for their contributions to a team's final work products by both surprise assessments and preannounced assessments of graded teamwork. Be aware that graded quizzes don't motivate all.

For most preadolescent and adolescent students, peer relationships may be the primary—if not sole—reason for attending school. However, it is important to remember that constructive social-emotional learning is essential for earlier learners as they start on the path to a healthy adult life (Kupczynski et al., 2012).

The following list includes ideas that not only develop students' digital skills for learning but also help build your community of learners.

- **Start with yourself:** In a brief video, introduce yourself. Doing this lays the groundwork for how your students meet each other, initiating the interdependence, trust, and mutual respect at the heart of a collaborative community of learners. Tell students, for example, where you have lived, what you like to do in your free time, and what family and pets you have. You could tell them why you became a teacher or share a funny story about yourself. Make it simple and record the video with your phone.

- **Share your schedule:** Contact families and students prior to school and then, in the first few days, talk with students and send home a document and video stating the best ways and times to reach you, plus your office hours. Invite them to contact you. Research shows that "both the tone of a short syllabus and the presence of statements normalizing reaching out for help can influence student intentions to contact instructors for help" (Gurung & Galardi, 2021). Figure 4.3 is an adaptable template for the teacher availability document you send home.

- **Make an initial phone call:** If you're an elementary school teacher, or another teacher who has just a single class or two, call each student. Refer to them all by name. Be personal and personable. Make your voice smile. Say who you are and why you are calling, and then go immediately into checking on their well-being and readiness to start school. Ask only clarifying questions with a strong focus on any empathy needed as you check the students', parents', or guardians' tone.

- **Make follow-up calls:** As often as possible, but no less than once a quarter or whenever you sense a student needs a lift or has been absent from online sessions, call and talk with students. Listen hard for feelings of isolation and anxiety. Follow up with parents as needed, especially about the student's tone. Keep academic solutions for yourself. Your aim is to keep students engaged and feeling positive about school. If you are having difficulty with phone contact, go to an app, text, or email to start contact.

- **Keep parents and guardians in the loop:** Especially when trying to draw a hesitant student into online attendance or participation, let parents know your concern, and encourage them to have their child respond to you. When all else fails in your outreach, talk with your principal or school social worker to devise a plan of action. Chapter 9 (page 205) has more about communicating with parents and guardians.

- **Continue building community:** Select and schedule other activities that allow you to build peer relationships in your new community, and invite students to make suggestions.

Teacher: Mr. Boisson	
Date: September 25	
Contact information: 555-317-8821 oboisson@thisschool.edu	
My office hours are Monday through Friday from 8 a.m. to 9 a.m. Please get in touch! I am here to help, answer questions, and connect you with resources. Don't be shy. • I am available during my regular office hours except those marked with an *X*. • The best days for online conferences with you or your parents are marked with a *C*. • The best days for coaching are marked with a *W* and show start and end times. Please text requests with two possible days and times that work for you. If I don't respond in twenty-four hours, repeat your request. Indicating a reason for requesting coaching in the space for notes in your text helps me prepare, but including a reason is optional and confidential. Keep this in your portfolio.	

	Monday	Tuesday	Wednesday	Thursday	Friday
October 1–5		X	X	C	
October 8–12				C	
October 15–19	X	W 8–10	X		X
October 22–26					
October 29–November 2					
Notes					

FIGURE 4.3: Teacher availability.

Open every day with one or more icebreakers so students can follow the axiom, "There are no strangers here, only friends who have not met." Practice these procedures to make it easy for students to share items or photos.

- Introduce yourself with items you are comfortable sharing: pictures of yourself growing up, trips you have taken, items from your workspace, and the like.
- End each day with a share time so that one or more students can show their own items— favorite music, items from their workspaces, or pictures of their shoes, for example—and say how they are.
- Play two truths and a lie about student interests. You start. Round-robin through the group to share, and have others vote on the lie.
- Start any small-group coaching by inviting the group to brainstorm questions such as, "I always wanted to ask about . . ." or "I'd really like to learn about _____ this year." Start an interest chart on a spreadsheet by student name. Build the chart as the year goes on. Use it as a guide to plan lessons around the most common topics or for students to reference for PBL ideas.

- Conduct a survey using a free polling app, such as Crowdsignal (https://crowdsignal.com) or SurveyMonkey (www.surveymonkey.com). Gather responses on interests, hobbies, talents, and feelings about the coming year.
- **Move from smaller groups to the whole class:** When your groups are becoming small communities, start gathering them all together in whole-class meetings. Make a list of ideas gathered from your community-building sessions, and share them.
  - Help each group make a word cloud (try www.edwordle.net) and share it with the whole class. Teach the groups to self-manage procedures for screen sharing.
  - Take a poll (as discussed previously), and then help each group develop a graph of its own results. Make an all-class graph that combines the results. Show graphs side by side on the whole screen, and let students ask clarifying questions so they can respond to commonalities and differences as you expand both complex thinking and SEL skills together while also building relationships.
  - With the results of the poll, create a class newsletter. Get a free template from Google Docs or another site. Invite students to contribute parent-approved photographs that don't show students' faces (or ask students to edit the faces out before sending the photos), nominate a student of the week, and write a short article about that person. Add notes about upcoming units, include an activity schedule for the week, and offer a brain-break idea. Make sure to include your contact information and office hours. Post the newsletter on your LMS, and email it or send it to students, parents, and guardians via an app such as Remind (www.remind.com). A parent volunteer may be able to help.

Remember when choosing activities like those described in the following two sections, which offer elementary- and secondary-level peer-learning activities, that you are doing the following.

- Fostering a sense of community
- Activating students' collaboration
- Setting up your role as a guide on the side as students engage with each other in achieving a common outcome
- Helping students learn digital skills
- Explicitly teaching the first social skills students will develop throughout the year
- Engaging students in problem solving
- Raising the level of engagement one more step by asking students to assess both their peers and themselves in their collaborative efforts

Elementary School Peer-Learning Activity

The following is a peer-learning activity that is appropriate for elementary students.

1. Students are in the VCS waiting room. They also have all the materials listed in these instructions ready at each station.
2. When students enter, invite them to wait for you to unmute them and welcome them by name. If very young students are physically present, have them sit on a rug, spaced out.

After all are settled, hand out tags with numbers and letters that indicate which students are in pairs (for example, 1A and 1B, 2A and 2B, and so on), and send the pairs to find digital learning stations with their respective numbers, sit down, and not touch the digital tool.

3. After online attendance, introduce yourself by name and say your favorite dessert. Invite students to introduce themselves by first name, number-letter combination, and favorite dessert. Use a guided round-robin, opening one mic at a time and then shutting it off.

4. When done, thank all students for sharing. Welcome the class, and share your pleasure about their presence.

5. Match numbered partners or screen pairs with their numbers and names visible on your master screen.

6. Show pairs how they can privately chat to each other with the chat feature on their devices. (In-meeting chat allows each student to send a private chat message to a partner within an online meeting.)

7. Invite all to enter their number on chat and then, after you demonstrate how, share it with their number partner on chat. When both receive the message, they raise a hand and hold it up until all have signaled. Help those who may have difficulty. Celebrate with a silent windy hurrah (putting two hands over your head and shaking to make wind).

8. Invite all to use the large index card and three markers at their station to draw and color their favorite dessert, add their screen number or letter, and, when their partner is ready, take turns sharing their first name, dessert, and ID number and letter. (*A* goes first.) When both have shared, they should turn back to the teacher's station and sit quietly. (Note: Sitting at a distance may raise the decibel level. Get used to it during sharing activities. This first activity will help you decide the maximum decibel level needed for partner share-alouds. If your primary students can read and write, adopt the dessert-share element so they can print info in the chat room.)

9. When all are ready, go back online. Use a number or letter wrap so each student can in turn share his or her first name, number-letter combination, favorite dessert, and reason why. Before starting, invite the class to follow these onscreen guidelines. Demonstrate each one.

    - Make sure your camera shows you and your partner from the top of your head to your shirt or dress top. If not, give a thumbs-down signal until you see the change is OK.
    - Keep your mic off when it's not your turn. When the teacher calls your number and letter, open the mic and turn it off when finished.
    - Listen carefully to each person. After each person shares, the teacher will surprise someone by asking him or her to name the last person's favorite dessert or reason.

10. Stop when you see eyes fading, or after five minutes. Return later that day or the next so you can continue until all have shared. After the last one, call for the windy hurrah.

11. After all have shared, invite students to give a thumbs-up or thumbs-down signal after each of the following statements. Make a note for each *yes* count.

    - I know how to open the chat room.
    - I want more practice with the chat room.

- I remember my number and letter for partner work.
- I know how to silently signal my partner yes or no.
- I know how to speak quietly when asked.
- I know how to listen carefully to each speaker.
- I know a way to help my teacher, my partner, and other students work together.
- I learned something new about my partner today.
- I know a way to silently celebrate a good job.

Thank the class and ask for a windy hurrah.

12. Later that day or the next, regroup and invite the students to focus on ways to help the teacher, the partners, and the class work together. Remind the class how to signal onscreen, and then seek several responses for helping you, partners, and others as you play the numbers or letters chat game. You can separate the question into three (teacher, partners, and class). End with a silent windy hurrah.

13. Start your community of learners by establishing daily online procedures, practicing digital procedures for chatting or talking via the synchronous grid, and engaging in a getting-to-know-new-friends activity.

Secondary School Peer-Learning Activity

This activity assumes only that students can open their digital devices, get to your VCS waiting room, and produce a Word document or Google Doc to share online. You can pair any students who can't produce a document with other students who can.

1. After welcoming everyone and introducing yourself, introduce the first task. Jumping right in will signal that in your class, it is important to act and interact.

2. Ask everyone to open a Word document and open a business-letter template. Explain that they will be "attending a business meeting" during which they will introduce themselves.

3. Review document text instructions, and test their ability with phrases. Introduce some general business-letter terminology (such as *salutation*), and give examples.

4. Have students indicate with a physical thumbs-up when they are done doing this work. Invite anyone who wants or needs extra coaching to attend your office hours or another time you have set aside for that.

5. On return, set students in groups of three. Spot-check by asking for examples of each completed element from at least two members. Give feedback and respond to any requests for assistance.

6. Show students how to communicate with one another in a trio, with a screen split to show the person and his or her copy of the business letter. Check for their ability to do so.

7. Set up groups to collaborate with the following roles.

    - The *timekeeper* shares when each member's five minutes of sharing in the group meeting and the team's agreed-on time for assessment are up.

- The *manager* designates the order of introductions and leads discussion so each has a fair chance to comment or ask a question.
- The *reporter* will guide assessment and report to the whole class the group's results in a five-minute summary.

8. Have students type answers to the following questions in their documents.
   - What was your header, and why did you choose it?
   - What was your quote, and why did you choose it?
   - What was the most important point you made, and why do you say so?
   - What did you learn about your team members?
   - How well did team members each carry out their role?
   - How informative to the group (on a scale of 1–5) was each report?

9. Set a due date for putting next week's deliverables (the finished letter and team assessment) in the teacher's inbox. Teams will schedule their own asynchronous time and share letters.

10. When back online via the VCS waiting room, check attendance, and be ready to divide the whole screen for each member's inclusion with name and group number visible.

11. Call for group assessments from reporters; they should last five minutes. Invite all to listen for similarities in assessments. (Depending on the number of groups, complete reports in this session, and debrief with an all-class reflection.)

12. Debrief with whole-class responses to the following. Distribute responses among all.
    - What similarities did you hear among reports?
    - How were roles helpful? Give examples.
    - What did you learn about your peers in the interviews?
    - How can you or I improve technology to get everyone involved?

13. Establish your personalized two-way communication via email. Because you may have one hundred or more students total, you cannot email each one on a regular basis. However, you can communicate with each via email at least once per month or as needed when anyone is late to class, late with an assignment, or otherwise shows signs of struggle or disinterest.

How Do I Stimulate Mindful Online Reflections?

As brain researchers have posited over and over, mindful reflection is a very important brain-based activity that enriches lifelong mental health from early childhood forward, in both one's private life and one's professional life (McTighe & Willis, 2019; Meyer, 2004). Reflective thinking increases students' autonomy as they examine how they are advancing their self-direction. It benefits their goal-setting efficacy as they learn to set personal goals, act on them, and then reflect on efforts to achieve those goals. In a community, students can reflect on what they are giving to and receiving from the development of relationships (Miller, 2018). In addition, mindful self-reflection advances how well they use the tools for learning as they assess the development of the digital, social-emotional, and complex cognitive skills needed to become competent and confident about how they learn in any environment.

Mindfulness is a key ingredient in the reflection recipe. Mindful reflections are those that prepare students to become more aware of their learning environment, thoughts, and emotions, and to apply their new insights to mindful actions about what choices they are making and how they are making them as they learn. For this generation of digital learners, mindful reflection becomes a two-purpose key. First, it helps counter the negative impact of technology on student decision making. Second, it enhances the decision making that students of this generation will require to become successful learners and citizens.

1. **Countering the negative:** In the digital learning world, social media enabled by smartphones and other related technologies has eroded how digital natives, addicted to these popular communication tools, make decisions. As their smartphones appear to grow out of their ears, the social media that drives their technology-controlled interactions makes it difficult for them to decide what is true and what is false, what is fact and what is fake, what is rumor and gossip versus what is verifiable. This difficulty is especially hurtful when poor decisions negatively impact students' still-developing interpersonal relationships.

2. **Energizing the positive:** In digitally active classrooms, social media enabled by smartphones and other related technologies enables teachers to counter the negative effects of these e-tools. After teaching their digital natives how to use social media and the other e-tools available for use as learning tools, they can call on mindful reflections that benefit students' goal setting, agency, and interpersonal relationships. Mindful reflection increases students' awareness and decision-making abilities. It also moves students to action as they interact with their peers, learn to concentrate on desirable learning outcomes, think about how to use and assess their digital tools and what information they learn, and try to more effectively control digital media in all aspects of their lives.

The content of mindful reflection prompts requires your thoughtful consideration. It's important that you act on the information about mindfulness. For the most mindful responses, you will want to provide prompts that ask students to take action on what they learn about content and the e-tools they are using to get to deeper understanding. Add synonyms of *transfer*, *use*, and *apply* to these prompts. Go to https://thesaurus.com for lists of synonyms to adopt in prompts and questions.

Reflection is a metacognitive process that involves thinking about thinking. When teachers of any grade or subject want to increase students' metacognition so that they become more aware and understanding of their own thought processes, attitudes, and feelings, they can prepare instructions, ask guiding questions or provide guiding rubrics, and allow students to choose what and how much they want to say. They can increase student autonomy by encouraging students to schedule their own times for reflection and choose the topic of their self-reflections. These self-managed reflections can occur anytime and anyplace, before, during, or after lessons and projects. They may target a goal, a lesson outcome, a completed task, a collaboration, or an instant self-hurrah.

In any case, self-managed reflections can start with prompts such as, "Today, I learned . . ."; "In today's workshop, I wondered . . ."; "With this idea, I want to . . ."; or "What I learned today will help me to . . . ." Or they can start with guiding questions such as, "Why do you think . . . ?" "How did you feel when . . . ?" "How will you apply . . . ?" or "How will _____ help you?" Students might also receive graphic organizers, such as webs with a thinking prompt like, "What do you predict will happen in the next chapter?" "What are some ways you can use this lesson?" or "What were the three ideas in this article that most surprised you?" or access fishbone organizers that ask, "What do you want to show as the causes of (event)?" After posting the question as a chat or discussion room thread, a sketch to share on the VCS gallery grid, or a verbal round-robin sharing on the gallery grid, you designate a time for students to think and prepare a response. When it looks as if all have finished thinking because at least ten seconds of wait time have passed or students have signaled "ready" by turning their organizers facedown, you initiate the next strategy (for example, round-robin, think-pair-share, or an exit comment).

Whichever approach a teacher takes and however much time a teacher devotes to student reflection, this powerful mechanism confirms the words of American philosopher, psychologist, and educational reformer John Dewey (1933): "We do not learn from experience . . . we learn from reflecting on experience" (p. 78). Learning to reflect on experience is most effective when it is intentional—when either the student or the teacher purposely asks about a learning experience with prompts and guiding questions. If you remember that reflections can occur in any basic communication media—written, spoken, or drawn—you can vary the activity. You might ask for a write- or sketch-pair-share instead of a think-pair-share, or ask students to sketch or write a response to a guiding question, post a journal response in a portfolio, or write an exit ticket on a sticky note. Whatever the medium, allowing students sufficient time to reflect slowly and carefully is the goal.

You can prevent students asking, "How do I do this?" when you ask for reflections by modeling what you expect. You do not expect them to mimic your thinking. You do want them to reflect on the topic in the method you provide. When you check for understanding of the method, ask for demonstrations, selected at random. Once you see or hear responses, coach extension by asking appropriate and noninvasive clarifying questions ("It would help your responses if you shared an example") or encouraging more extensive responses ("I'd like to hear more about that" or "When thinking about how you might do better, I'd suggest you brainstorm a list. Maybe set a goal for five more ideas?").

When some students struggle to respond, they will say, "I pass," or be silent in a round-robin, in a chat, or on a gallery grid. Others will not hand in a sticky note. You can give these students a private online conference in which you coach them one-to-one to write or speak on the next day's prompts. You can also pair them with a peer helper or have them attend a needs-to-know workshop in which you lead a brainstorm of ideas to the next day's prompts. Be sure to give sufficient wait time for the reticent reflector to reflect, or say, "As an option, anyone in the class can tweet or message their response, but I do want one from all." Whenever your prompts stimulate self-efficacy, the feeling of *I can*, self-management, and the taking of action steps determined by the students, you deepen the effects of learning the content, skills, and outcomes of online learning and lead students to self-prompt the mindful reflections you model and coach.

Effective K–12 teachers who value complex cognition and metacognition are not shy about providing regularly scheduled reflection prompts that challenge students to react to their academic performance. Mindful reflections on content are a first step. Teachers can use the preceding prompts and guiding questions as well as the following grade-level strategies to encourage those reflections.

- Primary-grade teachers commonly ask kindergarten or first-grade students questions during directed reading-thinking activities. In these activities, a teacher reads a story or informational text passage to the class or a small group. The teacher will follow the factual questions with prediction questions such as, "What do you think will happen next?" and then, "Why do you think so?", which is a fundamental metacognitive query.

- Middle-grade mathematics teachers may ask students to think about how they went about solving a geometry problem: "With your mind's eye, walk me through the steps you took to solve this problem. Then tell me why you think you took correct steps." In this instance, the open-ended *why* leads to a reflective response.

- High school music teachers may ask students to explain how they interpreted a musical score: "I appreciate your interpretation. Now walk me through your reasons for how you interpreted the first bar." Asking for reasons is a variation on a "Why do you think so?" request for students to think about their reasoning choices.

Teachers can up the ante to next-level metacognitive questions by calling for responses that include feelings.

Taking time for reflection when students are online may be fairly easy to implement. Teachers who introduce a mindful reflection strategy will coach students to take their time to think. Taking time to think is becoming a much-in-demand workplace skill, but it is not an activity that students generally feel comfortable implementing on their own. However, teacher-initiated reflection can become a daily expectation when students are waiting for the roll to be called or other preclass business to be finished. By posting "Today's reflection" on your digital whiteboard with a prompt related to the previous night's homework or the previous day's breakout room meetings, you can ask students to submit a response in the chat room or perhaps save it for the day's opening activity. You can follow a similar tactic with exit-ticket prompts when every student has three minutes of free time before class ends. These prompts could include, "A question I have about today's lesson is . . ."; "Today, I am glad we discussed . . ."; "An idea I want to follow in my next research task is . . ."; or "I see I can improve my _____ by . . . ." When students become comfortable thinking in response to your prompts, you can begin encouraging them to pick their own prompts at times when they are able to stop and think about their thoughts and feelings.

Mindful reflections will take more time when students write, type, or sketchnote their thoughts and feelings (Gobir, 2021). But these are methods that allow you to provide more extensive feedback than if students are only sharing aloud. You can encourage deeper, more extensive, and more detailed reflection with open-ended reflections in journal entries or on a guiding rubric after a project-based learning task or lab. For instance, you may schedule ten minutes of reflection time every Friday with a stem such as, "This week, I improved my note taking by . . ." or "What I want to do better with my note taking is . . . ." Or if students have spent the week working in a remote asynchronous group, they can conclude by reflecting on what they each learned about content and collaboration and post the statement via your email.

Prompts are key to effective responses. The following list captures a range of possible prompts.

- **Basic stems:** Like twigs on a tree, stems start new growth. Sentence stems begin with *I* or *we* and add a verb that prompts students to write, speak, or draw a response to share with you or the class. Try stems such as, "In this lesson, I learned . . ." (or replace *learned* with *discovered, am pleased, am proud,* or *wondered*) and "What if I . . . ?" to start. Increase the mindfulness until students are mostly thinking about how they will transfer what they have learned into action steps with such prompts as, "Tomorrow, I plan to follow your feedback by . . ."; "In my next project, I plan to improve my team participation by . . ."; or "As a member of this class community, I want to set a new goal that will . . ."

- **Guiding questions:** Ask an open-ended question to prompt student answers. After a short wait allowing each student to frame a response, students take turns answering questions such as, "In this lesson, what did you learn?" "What was difficult to learn?" "What was easy to learn?" and "Why was learning this important?" As students become more adept with their responses, provide two or three guiding questions in sequence that turn their reflections into mindful responses: "What was the most important lesson you learned about your thinking skill today? Why do you think you are saying that? How are you going to apply that lesson?"

- **Plus-minus-interesting:** This three-in-one mindful question tactic, invented by Edward de Bono (1985), asks for students, alone or in a team, to brainstorm their end-of-lesson reflections, indicating pluses, minuses, and interesting questions to ask. For example, a group of students might collaboratively determine, "What were the pluses or benefits of using the graphic organizer in this lesson? What were the minuses? What interesting questions do we have about applying the ideas we collected?"

- **Poll-group-repoll:** Launch a poll with your preferred polling app, and ask students open-ended, mindful questions that will generate divergent responses. Figure 4.4 provides an example. After polling the class, post the results. Guide a discussion of the results, and then ask each student to set a goal indicating what action he or she will take. Relaunch the same poll so students can see if their responses have changed. Anchor another reflective class discussion on any changes to students' answers.

- **Who's on First?:** Ask students to each vote on how they much they agree with an idea on a scale of 0 to 5 (0 = not at all, 5 = very much). For example, ask them, "How much would you like to improve your reading comprehension?" or "How much do you want to expand your digital skills for making group products?" Then break students into groups

---

1. Which of these ideas will be most important for improving your team's collaboration?
    a. ☐ New roles
    b. ☐ Defined responsibilities
    c. ☐ A clear goal statement
    d. ☐ Agreed-to behaviors
2. Which of the following best describes your contributions?
    a. ☐ I talk too much.
    b. ☐ I let other members talk too much.
    c. ☐ I don't talk enough.
    d. ☐ My comments miss the point.

FIGURE 4.4: Poll question examples.

of up to four to discuss the issue and give each other ideas before each student makes a personalized learning plan (PLP) with an action goal stimulated by the discussion. At the end of the PLP time, students will complete a self-assessment of the self-targeted skill.

- **Transfer prompts:** Transfer prompts are those that move students to action. They are at the core of mindful reflections designed to promote action. You can move students into mindful deeper learning by focusing your prompts backward or forward, near or far.

    - *Backward-transfer prompts* ask students to recall past learning experiences. For example, when students have used a graphic organizer to enrich their learning, you might use prompts such as, "I would change how I used the fishbone in my last science lab by . . ." or "After reviewing my concept map on our discussions of the Jazz Age, I wish I had . . ."

    - *Forward-transfer prompts* ask students to speculate about future applications of an idea, skill, or tool. A sample forward-transfer prompt would be, "Next week, I will improve my participation in my asynchronous group by . . ." or "To prepare for my participation during tomorrow's threaded discussion, I want to . . ."

    - *Near-transfer prompts* help students make small cognitive leaps, such as making connections backward and forward in your course. A sample near-transfer prompt is, "From today's discussion about the Trail of Tears, I learned that I need to read with attention to detail. Tomorrow, when I am reading the next chapter, I will ask myself five starter questions for gathering detailed information."

    - *Far-transfer prompts* challenge students to take giant steps as they transfer skills or knowledge learned in one course to other courses, applications outside the classroom, and future and lifelong learning possibilities. A sample far-transfer prompt would be, "This graphic organizer could help me in my after-school job by . . ."

The following sections address quick reflection, deeper reflection on cognition, and reflection on teamwork in more depth.

Quick Reflection Example

Schedule time for five-minute forays into metacognition, like those listed in the preceding section. If the five minutes you planned for disappear at the end of a lesson, invite students to reflect after the lesson as an asynchronous assignment. Figure 4.5 is an example to replicate.

Figure 4.5 features quick reflection prompts for middle school students. This example sets students up for a daily reflection activity they can complete in the VCS waiting room before admission to class. The same model might be used to create an asynchronous activity or an exit activity for the end of each class.

Deeper Reflection Example

In addition to providing quick reflection prompts, teachers can infuse more extensive reflection into the school day by using question stems and prompts that guide cognitive reflection and focus it on content or initiate metacognitive reflection about the complex thinking students have been utilizing. Students will need more stop-and-think time to consider what happened or why, how a lesson or concept impacted them, or how they might respond or adapt their responses in the future. As students show competence and reliability in completing sentence-long and then

> As we discussed, I am sharing directions for guiding your reflection on your mathematical thinking. This month, I want you to focus on how precisely you are thinking as you complete math assignments. "Attending to precision" is a mark of a mathematically proficient student. Each day, I expect you to complete a one-paragraph writing. I have included a playlist of prompts to help you get started. Make your choice. You may repeat any prompt as often as you like. Store your reflection in section 3 of your portfolio. As you know, I will be asking members of the class to share their thoughts with no comment from others. Who gets asked to share is by surprise, but anyone can respond, "I pass today."

> **Directions:**
> 1. Select your prompt.
> 2. Tell how you did so with up to three examples from today's lesson.
> 3. Date and put the file in your portfolio.
> 4. Share a copy with me by the end of class each day.

> When attending to precision, check the following criteria for self-assessing your response. Prepare to explain your thinking about how well you did on last night's homework and why each is important for your mathematical reasoning.
>
> - _____ I use clear, explicit definitions in my reasoning.
> - _____ I use clear definitions in my discussions.
> - _____ I state the meaning of the symbols I choose, including using the equals sign consistently and appropriately.
> - _____ I am careful about specifying units of measurement and labeling axes to clarify the correspondence with quantities in a problem.
> - _____ I calculate accurately and efficiently and express numerical answers with a degree of precision appropriate for the problem context.

FIGURE 4.5: Quick reflection prompts about problem solving in mathematics.

whole-paragraph reflections, consider making a reflective assignment that uses a specific model, such as a concept map on which students can post one-word descriptors or a graphic organizer students can use to analyze and interpret causes and effects related to an outcome.

Most standards statements start with an action verb such as *analyze*, *compare*, or *differentiate*. The verb signals how the student is meant to think about a concept (as in, "Compare the two microorganisms"). Because learning standards apply in remote classrooms, standards-aligned reflections are appropriate anywhere, anytime, and for any subject.

The key word for daily reflections is the verb *thinking*. To build students' habit of thinking about thinking, a daily prod helps. At the end of each class, students can finish a two- or three-sentence stem in a group chat or daily log: "Today, I learned . . ."; "When I predicted . . ."; "I was pleased that . . ."; or "When finding data to support the claim, what I did best was . . . ." You can have students file the completed stem in a subfolder titled *My Thinking*, or save it to share in the next day's online session at the start of class. You can choose how complex stems are based on how much synchronous class time is available. If time is short, you can elect to assign the metacognitive task for completion during students' self-managed asynchronous time.

Figure 4.6 (page 124) shows an example of an end-of-year reflection on how seventh-grade students increased their engagement during a teacher's history instruction.

| Name: Winston Hill | Date: June 1 | Teacher: Mr. Jones | Period: 5 |

Dear Mr. Jones,

In your class, you asked us to be responsible for what we learned.

In September, you told us about different ways to pay attention during your online lectures. You said if we did these, we would be prepared for all the high school and college lectures we would get in our online classes. I am now going to answer the three questions you wanted me to think about. I hope this is what you wanted.

First, I did a good job of having my notebook ready when I entered the waiting room every day. I missed only one time. I also had my laptop charger ready to go on most days. I now also keep a battery charger with me. I also added a column on the right of the study sheet I made in Google Docs. When I wrote notes, I followed the outline you gave each week in your portal. I got better with that too. I used my text color highlighter on the toolbar when I was getting ready for a test. It helped me underline the stuff you said was important.

Second, I need to get better at using bolding and big and small letters to separate important ideas. I put down many facts. For your tests, this made it hard to study. I wasn't very good at keeping everyone's opinions straight during discussions. I still can't always tell when a fact is different from an opinion.

Third, I need some more help paying attention during discussions. When other kids got into arguments during our team meetings and you weren't online with us, I could never figure out how to keep them straight.

Sincerely,
Winston

FIGURE 4.6: Deeper student reflection in a digital academic area.

Reflection on Teamwork in a Community Example

Give small groups the opportunity to provide you with thoughtful feedback on how you and they are building collaboration in your learning community. There are several ways to do this. First, you can prompt their reflections on the value of your community and their contributions to its construction. Second, you can prompt feedback to you about your contributions. Third, you can prompt a dialogue about shared responsibility for a community's construction among all its members; this dialogue can include recommendations and discussion of how you and the class members can take action to improve feelings of inclusion and shared responsibility.

Academic standards can serve as a framework for inciting mindful reflections that target how students think, feel, and plan to take action related to what they are learning. These standards give you an easy means to target content and process with metacognitive and social-emotional prompts. When promoting reflection on community building, you face a tougher challenge. A helpful way to promote this reflection is to follow the example of teachers in Sydney, Australia, where PBDL is the predominant form of instruction. Jo Dulin, a middle-grade science and mathematics instructor, describes how she focused on community building with her students during the COVID-19 pandemic:

> I wanted to make sure that my kids felt a sense of belonging. My experience in the states before the pandemic taught me how a strong community lent itself to their involvement in science labs and mathematics discussions. When my kids were shut out of the classroom,

as short a time as it was here, it was even harder to figure out where to begin. I decided to brainstorm with my class the whole idea of a community. On my home computer screen, I shared a government slide that introduced the importance of community in the Indigenous culture. I assigned groups of three to research online about this culture, and we had an all-class discussion that extended two class periods. It was a topic that excited them. From that I asked them to brainstorm ideas of what makes a culture. That was tough going. I had to do lots of cueing and clueing so they could make the transfer. It took a little more time than I had planned. In the end, we had a list. I built the best ideas from the list into a guiding rubric like the ones I had learned from my Advanced Reasoning in Education Global PBL Academy in Arlington Heights [in Illinois]. I set the rubric up so the teams in the PBDL on marsupials I was designing could reflect on how they were building community. I don't remember all the criteria. I do remember, however, that I asked them to think about what they were doing and what I was doing to build our class community. I think their feedback to me was more important than mine to them. I got lots of ideas from our chat room. (J. Dulin, personal communication, 2021)

Later that year, Dulin connected her class with a class in Chicago. They talked for free on Skype for twice the time planned. Their topic was "advice to give each other about how community helps us learn" (J. Dulin, personal communication, 2021). Responses to the experience from the Australian side of the conversation included:

- "I learned how important community can be to a family. We became a family too."

- "I discovered that Skype made it easier for me to talk. I had to get to know everybody."

- "Mrs. Dulin said, 'There are no strangers in our class. Only friends we have never met'. We can become friends on the way to Australia and talk to each other a lot."

- "I was really scared about talking to a whole bunch of students on the computer. I learned it's easy. I think I can do it more." (J. Dulin, personal communication, 2021)

Responses from the American class included:

- "I just learned today that the ocean didn't matter. I can learn new ideas from people across the ocean."

- "I think we are a community. Even though we speak different English, it doesn't matter if we listen to ideas."

- "I want us to call again. I had to stay up late for this one, and it was fun. I learned a lot about community. I think I have to speak up more." (J. Dulin, personal communication, 2021)

Following this discussion, Dulin spent more time in the week building community. She asked her students what they had learned about community. At first, she had to give some time to keeping everyone focused on the community question. Almost all students were overexcited about talking to their peers in another country. They found it tough to get past their interest in the friends they had not met in person and the country that was so far away. With more guiding questions and time to think, her students told her what else they wanted to do with the other class and with the topic itself. She invited their feedback. By the end of her 250-minute mini-inquiry, Dulin was able to take their feedback and construct a guiding rubric for community building.

In the case of formal two-way feedback (Hattie, 2017) between students and a teacher, you can see how reflection can build positive student-teacher relationships that include feelings of belonging, trust, and respect as you look for opportunities to expand the digital conversation throughout the school year. Dulin says she repeats this sequence "starting each quarter" (J. Dulin, personal communication, 2021).

You can also build online communities by other means. Cooperative learning, suggested as a practical tool to enhance mindful reflections, fits this bill. It increases achievement and bonds virtual teams during synchronous and asynchronous times. Individual students form cooperative teams; multiple teams enrich communication and collaboration throughout their whole class, a much larger team.

The forms in figure 4.7 and figure 4.8 help students reflect on teamwork. When you encourage learners to think about their contribution to the success of increased communication and collaborative work—applied first to their teams and then to their entire classroom, with your feedback and peer feedback in the same form—you can increase the speed and power of your community's effects on student learning. This double impact fuels the building of a classroom community. Figure 4.7 facilitates open-ended responses in order to promote mindful reflections; it helps show how mindful student reflections can lead to student feedback and to student action.

Directions: Please answer one or all of the questions with specific examples. If you are providing feedback to me, I would welcome that you do so before _____.
What we like about our teamwork is:
We appreciate that you help our team by:
We would like more help from you with our team to:

FIGURE 4.7: Open-ended reflection on teamwork.

*Visit **go.SolutionTree.com/technology** for a free reproducible version of this figure.*

You can substitute a guiding rubric as shown in figure 4.8, which identifies desired outcomes.

Student:	Date:
Class:	Period:

☐ Solo

☐ Team Members:

Names are optional.

Directions: You are giving your teacher feedback. Each student will rate each item that fits your team's experience. Add specific comments explaining your rating. Submit by email or the LMS in the Assignments tab by Friday, April 4. I will keep all communication private. Thanks in advance.

Rate how I (your teacher) have helped your team develop one or more items. If desired, give an example of how I have done so.

0 = Not helpful at all
1 = A little helpful
2 = Helpful often
3 = Always helpful or helpful in a big way

Rating	Outcome	Comment
	The teacher helps our team members know our responsibilities.	
	The teacher helps our team members develop trust with one another and with the teacher.	
	The teacher helps ensure that our team members do their fair share of tasks.	
	The teacher helps me feel included in this group.	
	The teacher helps our team members bond with each other.	
	The teacher helps create an environment in which team members respect each other's ideas.	
	The teacher helps our team members learn the material.	
	Other:	

FIGURE 4.8: Guiding rubric with team agreement.

*Visit **go.SolutionTree.com/technology** for a free reproducible version of this figure.*

Let students discuss and agree on responses. Encourage but do not require individual student-author identification. Especially before students feel they can trust you with their responses, you need to let them feel safe in anonymity. A two-way guiding rubric from students not only helps them reflect on what's important but also stimulates them to offer thoughtful feedback on how you are helping their collaborative learning improve. When you add the component of two-way student-teacher feedback, it increases students' agency and positive relationships with you and their peers, which are extra important to students engaged in remote learning. You can adapt the example on a tool such as SurveyMonkey (www.surveymonkey.com), Kahoot! (https://kahoot.com), or another survey app for student phone use.

How Do I Create Community in Hybrid Classes in Split Locations?

Hybrid lessons, with their mix of some students in a walled classroom and some in remote learning stations, create unique problems that prevent community building, result in student disengagement, and spark teacher confusion. The most significant issue occurs when students in one location or the other feel they are not part of a lesson. Most often, this occurs with remote students who are not in the teacher's physical presence. In order to maintain inclusion and equity, it is very important for teachers to have proactive contact with students wherever they may be.

Balancing instruction so that all students are equitably included was difficult enough with all students sitting in one location, before universal distance learning. Hybrid learning ups the ante. Many strategies that helped you respond to a single classroom location can stay in your hybrid classroom's instructional toolkit (for example, round-robin responses, wait time, cooperative groups assessed for individual responsibility, and so on). However, you can also add the following strategies to your equitable inclusion repertoire so that students are and feel equitably included.

- Schedule whole-class end-of-day meetings (elementary) or start-of-week and end-of-week meetings (middle and secondary). Put all students on the gallery grid, and conduct an activity that encourages all to participate. Use goal-setting think-shares at the start and stem-shares at the end with round-robins on the grid.

- At the end of a lesson, preferably one in which a product shows the result, allow time for a show-and-tell. Match partners or partner groups on the gallery grid so they can present to each other. Be sure to give feedback to all groups.

- When remote students are working in groups online, have students in your physical space do the same. Visit them each in turn, observe them, and give feedback.

- Devise other times for matched individuals, pairs, or larger groups (no more than five members) to play a game or complete an activity together as a single group. Structure the activity so that students can respond in turn and leave no one out.

- Plan small-group interactions, such as giving feedback, talking in a chat room, or sharing results of a completed activity. Set up a leader role in the groups. The leader will call on each person to take a turn or invite students who are hanging back or seem overwhelmed to make a comment.

- Hold whole-class morning and end-of-day meetings. According to education columnist Jin-Soo Huh (2021), "Starting and ending the day as a whole class helps students create bonds by hearing from remote and in-person peers." Second-grade teacher Merced Fletcher turns her computer around so in-class students can see online students and vice versa (Huh, 2021).

You can take advantage of your screen grid by using it to assign student leaders who invite participation, rotate roles in small groups, and structure response turns in round-robins. You can also schedule needs-to-know SEL workshops with invitations to students who are uncomfortable engaging in front of the whole class or on the digital screen. For those students, you will do well to check for feelings about their place in class. So that you include all students in each learning location on an equitable basis, set up a four- to six-student committee to meet with you online and discuss how well your intent to equitably include all is working. Ask the committee members to help make equitable inclusion a classroom project with a specific outcome and an assessment.

The following sections describe three of the key ways to create an equitable and inclusive community in hybrid classes.

Have Class Discussions Online

Put all students on an equal footing by conducting all discussions online, with both groups responding online. Make it a priority to be adept at the technical mechanics of keeping both in-person and remote learner groups onscreen and in the conversation. This applies with both chat room and face-to-face time. Consider doing the following.

- To help recall who is who in a chat room, ask remote students to chat in all capital letters, in contrast with in-person students. In this way, you can immediately see which group is chatting and check names to invite nonparticipating students in with a friendly "Hi, Tomas. We haven't heard from you. Would you like to share your thoughts?" even if the answer is *no*.

- Assign an *includer* role to a student, whose job is to watch who from the group is chatting and who is silent. Rotate this role and provide instructions detailing the best tactics for engaging a silent group member.

- Group two to five remote students for think-pair-share (or write- or draw-pair-share) contributions. If shy students are asked to share in a smaller group first and receive affirmations from partners, they can build confidence. When it comes to sharing with everyone on the big screen, the most confident students can do that. This will give shy students a chance to see they could also do that, and they can later do so with encouragement from peers in the smaller group.

- Adapt the strategy "That's a Good Idea" with grades 4+ groups. Designate which group, in-class or remote, starts a class discussion. (You need the same number of groups in each space.) Each group meets in its space and predetermines the order in which the group members will respond to members of a predesignated partner group. For example, the first responder in the remote group makes the first comment. Then the first responder in the in-class group responds, "That's a good idea because . . ." A recorder in each group writes down each idea and each response on a T-chart (in two lists). The responders alternate, with a validation each time—"That's a good idea because . . ."—until the circle is complete and there is a list of good ideas with a *because* reason for each.

To start this high-energy, strong-bonding activity, practice with only one two-group partnership (one group in a hybrid classroom, and one group in a walled classroom). When you coach the first group, say the name of each responder whose turn comes up. Working out the kinks can be hard until you see the activity done, but co-solving the problems can be fun.

- If you notice discord while observing small groups during a hybrid class, make a note and later check on how the students in a group resolved any disagreement. If the issue continues, intervene with a private chat with the group leaders on your shared screens. Start by saying, "I noticed . . . ."

Make Sure All Students Engage in Chat Discussions

At the start of each semester, share chat room interaction guidelines with the entire class. For instance, discuss the DOVE mnemonic and feature the DOVE guidelines on the whiteboard, shared to all digital devices.

- Do give warm feedback.
- Original and different ideas are encouraged.
- Variety of views is important.
- Evaluate only when evaluation is asked.

A minilesson with response examples will clarify acceptable practices when chatting. For example, it is acceptable to say, "I appreciate how you expanded on my idea when you said, 'It's also a good idea to . . . .'" Such a response encourages participants to build on each other's ideas and expand the conversation. If students post unacceptable responses such as, "Where in outer space did you come up with that idea?", correct these conversation killers with warm but firm feedback that points back to the *D* in DOVE—for example, "I want to encourage us all to follow *D* and give warm feedback." Warm feedback sounds like, "I am not sure what you mean by that idea. I would like an example of the idea."

Check In With Students About How Involved They Feel

Assess how students feel about their engagement. In a quick way, these check-ins can help express honest empathy (for example, "I am sorry to hear that you felt left out in yesterday's chat. I experienced that same feeling last week when . . ."). Once a week or at least once a month, you can send a poll or survey to all students about their feelings of inclusion. Use this feedback to adjust instruction so that all are included. For instance, if several students indicate they don't think you are equal in whom you call on, ask them to say what would help. If you know which students feel this way, have a private chat with them and ask for advice about how to make things better.

Beyond these simpler strategies, teachers who include single problem-solving lessons in short-term (one-week) inquiries and problem-based learning in long-term (six-week) investigations can ensure all students feel included by doing the following.

- Schedule different days for dropping into small-group meetings. Although all groups of three to five students meet at the same time, you should post and follow a round-robin schedule for dropping in. Posting a schedule shows that your time with them is fairly distributed.
- Post your office hours for groups to contact you for coaching or private conferences.

What if a student complains, "You're not teaching us?" Don't be surprised. It is most likely to come from those students who do well taking notes and recalling information for a good grade (Center for Inspired Education, 2018). These students have learned how to do those things so well that they are often at a loss to think about or solve a problem for themselves, a challenge that increases when learning goes digital (Walma, 2020). When you are not around to ask, they may feel at a loss.

You can prepare yourself to mitigate worries about problem-based learning with a calm explanation of what research says about the need for increased self-direction. Also, you can openly acknowledge that self-directed learning is an important part of achievement. Start with the Hechinger Report (Diallo, 2020), and browse for answers to the question of how to engage students with self-direction in remote classrooms. You will then be well on your way as an engaged investigator of all you need to know to prepare your thirty-second elevator pitch. In short, the Hechinger Report (Diallo, 2020) discusses how students of distance learning are less engaged. Without engagement, there is far less achievement. When you start with cooperative-learning and problem-solving skills (plus the other strategies described in this book), you can turn passive, compliant learners into learners who can figure out what to do when the going gets tough and there is no one to hold their hand. The goal: students finding their own way.

Conclusion

By building in autonomy and community, teaching goal setting, and training students to reflect on their learning, you multiply engagement, whether your class is fully online or hybrid. By giving students some agency, teaching them how to set goals and then monitor goals for themselves, helping them use cooperative social skills to create a cohesive community, and coaching students to apply their cognition and metacognition to reflections, you provide digital natives with the skills for engaging as deeper learners.

MY TAKEAWAYS

What three ideas from this chapter can best help you shift to digital instruction and prepare all students to be effective digital learners? Record your ideas here so you can make a plan later.

1. _____

2. _____

3. _____

5

Positive Interaction *and* Social-Emotional Learning

It is not about technology; it's about sharing knowledge and information, communicating efficiently, building learning communities and creating a culture of professionalism in schools.
—**Marion Ginopolis**

In this chapter, you will explore how to engage students in constructive interactions with you, with other students, and with the digital tools they use. Here, you will explore ways to enrich social-emotional learning and prosocial skills that enable students to manage their own interactions—academic and social—and do so at a distance.

Social-emotional learning (*SEL*) is the process of developing a wide range of skills, from coping with feelings to making decisions, that are vital for school, work, and life success. The Collaborative for Academic, Social, and Emotional Learning (CASEL, 2020), a leader in the field of SEL, identifies five core competencies that make up SEL.

1. **Self-awareness:** Knowing your own emotions, strengths, and challenges and how they impact your actions; having a growth mindset about your skills

2. **Self-management:** Self-regulating and using executive-functioning skills, like planning and organization, impulse control, and goal setting

3. **Social awareness:** Understanding other perspectives, showing empathy, respecting diversity, and understanding social norms

4. **Relationship skills:** Building and maintaining relationships, communicating clearly, cooperating, and resolving conflict

5. **Responsible decision making:** Making positive choices about how to behave and interact with others; thinking about how your actions affect yourself and others

These skills are labeled *prosocial* because they are positive, helpful, and intended to promote social responsibility, social acceptance, and friendship (Committee for Children, 2021).

You will also explore how you can respond to distracting and dysfunctional behaviors when students are online, what you can do if students continue unacceptable behaviors, and how some restorative practices can help maintain your learning community in the face of obstacles.

How Do I Develop Students' Social-Emotional Skills?

Before the *how*, it is important to review the *why*. In the 2010s and 2020s, educators have paid more attention to social-emotional learning. Often in reaction to reports of increased bullying, states such as Illinois have added K–12 SEL standards (Illinois State Board of Education, n.d.). The Illinois standards, set well before the COVID-19 pandemic led to widespread remote learning, encourage teachers to (1) "develop self-awareness and self-management skills for school and life success," (2) enable students to "use social-awareness and interpersonal skills to establish and maintain positive relationships," and (3) "demonstrate decision-making skills and responsible behaviors in personal, school, and community contexts" (Illinois State Board of Education, 2020). Because online learning increases the need for students to regulate and manage their online presence, teachers obviously need to provide skills and motivate attitudes that enhance how students work online.

Literature examining the role of SEL skills during online communication argues that successful online learning depends on interpersonal skills more than traditional learning does. Online learning and education technology expert Ben Kehrwald (2008) states that teachers need to put considerable effort into developing interpersonal interaction skills, which he calls the key feature of contemporary online learning. In a 2017 study, Helen G. M. Vossen, Maria Koutamanis, and Joseph B. Walther draw the conclusion that self-esteem, a principle result of peer interaction, plays a more important role in virtual classrooms than in face-to-face classrooms.

Examining the following resources, which address SEL, will provide you with age-appropriate strategies to embed in your classroom lessons, either for highlighting a specific SEL skill or inserting SEL into a content lesson.

- *Evidence-Based Practices for Assessing Students' Social and Emotional Well-Being* (Hough, Witte, Wang, & Calhoun, 2021)
- *SEL Lessons for Online Learning (Middle School)* (Greater Good in Education, 2019c)
- *Encouraging Prosocial Actions in Students* (Greater Good in Education, 2019a)
- *PBL + SEL + Trauma-Informed Teaching for the Times We're In* (Adams, 2020)

Research suggests that the following are key strategies that will boost student SEL.

- **Cooperative learning:** The University of California, Berkeley's Greater Good in Education (2019b) site promotes prosocial behaviors with a spotlight on building interpersonal relationships and empathy. It states, "Reviews of the research on cooperative learning show that it has a range of positive effects for students: heightened academic effort and achievement, improved interpersonal relationships, and increased psychological well-being" (Greater Good in Education, 2019b). The site further notes, "Especially when students work together in structured groups—with guidance on how to communicate and collaborate with each other—they not only perform better, but are more helpful towards each other and build stronger group identities" (Greater Good in Education, 2019b).
- **Mental health check-ins via technology:** Sarah Matusek (2021) reports on a mental health check-in innovation that one educator developed during the COVID-19 pandemic:

    In St. Louis, a seventh-grade language arts teacher adapted her own classroom check-ins. Before the pandemic, Adia Turner asked her Long International Middle School students to place sticky notes with their name on a "mental health wall" within categories that spelled out different feelings. Sometimes the exercise prompted her to follow up with individual concerns. With the shift to digital learning, she collects that data through private weekly Microsoft Forms—using memes to illustrate moods—and has expanded her questions to include what they're grateful for. One student expressed thanks for the "clothes on my back and food in my house."

A 2018 meta-analysis of long-term impact studies shows that students in SEL programs score ten points higher in academic achievement than those not in such programs (Mahoney, Durlak, & Weissberg, 2018). In addition, SEL programs reduce the number and seriousness of off-task disruptions. The programs produce students with more positive attitudes about themselves, others, and school, and students with an increased ability to manage stress and depression and improve their skills, attitudes, and prosocial behavior over the long term (Mahoney et al., 2018).

Self is the adjective that delineates the starter SEL competencies: self-awareness and self-management. The other most common SEL competencies—social awareness, relationship skills, and decision making—each start with the more complex skills students need to manage their online interactions. In the digital world, teachers who integrate the development of these skills into the school day give students the tools needed to function cognitively and emotionally (Kehrwald, 2008), most importantly in a digital world but wherever students may walk and talk.

Researchers have created a questionnaire, called the *Online Self-Regulated Learning Questionnaire*, whose results can help you plan which students might need a bit more guidance based on their responses (Barnard-Brak, Paton, & Lan, 2010a). Post this questionnaire online, and adapt it as a needs assessment that students can volunteer to complete and email to you. Address the most significant needs in your lesson designs—for instance, "environment structuring, goal setting, time management, help seeking, task strategies, and self-evaluation" (Barnard-Brak, Paton, & Lan, 2010b). You may also want to help students develop SEL skills and attitudes by asking them to self-assess their readiness for making a PLP with a focus on an SEL skill.

Review the questionnaire template in figure 5.1 (page 136) to determine which statements will best help your students improve their self-awareness, self-manage their interactions in person and online, and make decisions (thereby meeting the Illinois State Board of Education [2020] standards). This questionnaire template will allow your students to self-assess what they are doing well and not so well, which they can improve as they learn online. Note that the subscales highlight the most important elements addressed in the item column. For younger students, scale down the scale, and pick one or two statements from each area. On your VCS gallery grid, read the statement, and ask the students to vote with five fingers (0 = not yet, 5 = every day in every way). Note the two or three lowest-scoring items, and ask the class to brainstorm ideas to improve those items. Let each student pick an item from the brainstorm. At the end of a week, ask the students to share on the grid what they did well to improve their item. For older students, start the year with an online start-of-class, all-class assessment. Share the questionnaire document (or one subscale), and ask students to self-score. Once a week, take a subscale, and invite all to come prepared to talk online about what items they do well (and how) and what items they need to improve (and how). Encourage them to steal good ideas from others!

A schedule is a basic tool that provides the consistent and predictable structure researchers note is helpful for students to develop self-regulation. Including social-emotional activities

Item	Subscale
1. I set standards for my assignments in online courses.	Goal Setting
2. I set short-term (daily or weekly) goals as well as long-term (monthly or for the semester) goals.	
3. I keep a high standard for my learning in my online courses.	
4. I set goals to help me manage studying time for my online courses.	
5. I don't compromise the quality of my work because it is online.	
6. I choose the location where I study to avoid too much distraction.	Environment Structuring
7. I find a comfortable place to study.	
8. I know where I can study most efficiently for online courses.	
9. I choose a time with few distractions for studying for my online courses.	
10. I try to take more thorough notes for my online courses because notes are even more important for learning online than in a traditional classroom environment.	Task Strategizing
11. I read aloud instructional materials posted online to fight against distractions.	
12. I prepare my questions before joining in the chat room and discussion.	
13. I work extra problems in my online courses in addition to the assigned ones to master the course content.	
14. I allocate extra studying time for my online courses because I know it is time-demanding.	Managing Time
15. I try to schedule the same time every day or every week to study for my online courses, and I observe the schedule.	
16. Although we don't have to attend daily classes, I still try to distribute my studying time evenly across days.	
17. I find someone who is knowledgeable in course content so that I can consult with him or her when I need help.	Help Seeking
18. I share my problems with my classmates online so we know what we are struggling with and how to solve our problems.	
19. If needed, I try to meet my classmates face-to-face.	
20. I am persistent in getting help from the instructor through email.	
21. I summarize my learning in online courses to examine my understanding of what I have learned.	Self-Evaluating
22. I ask myself a lot of questions about the course material when studying for an online course.	
23. I communicate with my classmates to find out how I am doing in my online classes.	
24. I communicate with my classmates to find out what I am learning that is different from what they are learning.	

Source: Barnard-Brak, Paton, & Lan, 2010a.

FIGURE 5.1: Online self-regulated learning questionnaire.

and connecting them to your SEL goals can be helpful and certainly can reassure parents and guardians that you are attending to SEL goals as well as to academics in your schedule. For example, Vernoy Johnson, a high school mathematics teacher, makes it a top priority during parent-teacher conference nights to share the importance he places on peer interactions when his students are learning to solve problems (personal communication, February 2021). Bev Miller, who teaches ELA in a seventh-grade team, sets up teams of five students on the first day of school each year (personal communication, February 2021). She designates the social skills important for collaboration as a team meeting target during the first period at the start of each week. She locates team-building games through a digital search. After a game, she has students reply to the sentence stem, "What I learned about communication is . . ." or a similar stem for five minutes. For additional structure ideas, consider the partial example of a third-grade teacher's online SEL activity schedule in figure 5.2 (page 138), noting the daily detail. Each day in this schedule repeats the same times not only for the content but also for the SEL competencies the teacher has selected.

Elementary school students and secondary school students have different SEL needs.

Elementary School

According to developmental psychologist Nancy Hill and social entrepreneur Latoya Gayle (2020), elementary-age students require "a consistent and predictable daily schedule." As they explain:

> Having a set time each day for focusing on specific academic subjects, physical activities, and leisure time has been shown to reduce anxiety. For example, younger children find comfort in knowing that they will see their teacher at the same time each day and know that it is followed by playtime, quiet reading, and writing. (Hill & Gayle, 2020, p. 5)

Hill and Gayle (2020) recommend posting a daily schedule so that students know what to expect and follow, which gives young learners "a sense of security and calm" (p. 5). When online, share a pacing chart, which is a mirrored scheduler of the activities planned for the week. Ask students to include the chart in the Other Documents section of their e-portfolio so they, you, or their parents can refer to it.

Middle and High School

Posted schedules in the upper grades offer the same SEL benefits as in the early grades. But upper-grade, self-contained content classes present a slightly different challenge for including SEL in the schedule. Knowing that course content takes precedence in most middle school and high school classes, researchers studying the impact of digital learning on preteens and teens emphasize these students' increased vulnerability when traditional, in-person time with friends is cut. Furthermore, teens identify online groups and forums as important parts of their social lives and as spaces where they can meet new people and receive support to cope with tough times (Anderson & Jiang, 2018). If no teen is an island, class schedules identifying times for online groups and forums can provide some predictability about when and how teens can meet up with friends during online school.

Time	Academic Area	SEL Activity	Skill Focus
8:30	—	**Check-In** Have students each check into the waiting room, turn on their camera, ready their workstation, and share a reflection with a partner based on the prompt, "My thought for today is . . ."	Self-Management Social Relationships Self-Awareness
8:45	—	**Comfort and Concern Circle** Ask the class about any concerns felt today. Review empathic listening.	Self-Awareness Social Relationships
9:00	Reading	**Guided All-Class DRTA** With the book *Juneteenth Junkie*, ask questions such as, "What does it feel like to celebrate this new holiday with family and friends? How does the main character feel about Juneteenth? How do you know? What else do you know about this day? Why is the main character called a *junkie*?"	Self-Awareness Social Awareness
9:30	Reading: Vocabulary and decoding	**Cooperative Trios With Roles** Make a list of new vocabulary words. Visit breakout rooms to observe how students perform their roles and, if all students are included, how they help each other decode each word.	Self-Management Social Relationships Decision Making
9:50	Break	Free-reading, snack, and bathroom break	Self-Management
10:00	Science lab: Force and motion	**Race-Day Pairs** Have students in pairs take turns with a rubber-band race car going down three different ramps and record the times and distances on a chart. Have pairs finish self-assessment rubrics, clean up their workspaces, and put the rubrics in their portfolios.	Social Relationships Decision Making Self-Awareness
11:00	Class assessment; breakout rooms	**Stems in Turn** Have students take turns on screen responding to the stems, "During science, I helped my partner when . . ." and "I am pleased that I was able to . . ." This helps students practice listening to others.	Social Awareness Social Relationships Self-Awareness
11:20	Mathematics: Multiples of 100	**Team Show-and-Tell: Our Game Board** Have each team show and explain its number-100 game board during class with a title and explanation of who wins and how they win. The game must ask players to use multiplied combinations that get to 100. Each team plays a demo round and answers questions after. Another team, selected by the teacher, tells what it liked about the first team's game. Invite teams to prepare a list of what social-emotional and digital skills they needed to make and show the game. Continue on the following day as needed.	Self-Management Social Relationships Decision Making

FIGURE 5.2: Third-grade pacing chart for SEL activities.

How Do I Engage Students in Prosocial Behavior?

Managing a class means something different when students are in a completely separate physical space than the teacher. Laying out some of the difficulties for teachers of virtual classes, *Washington Post* reporters Joe Heim and Valerie Strauss (2020) state that online learning management can mean:

> having to monitor issues from attendance and appearance to whether the dozens of children or teenagers on the screen in front of them are engaged, sitting still, keeping their cameras on, answering questions, not eating or drinking, not petting their dogs and not bickering with siblings.

Like when teaching in real time with students seated in your physical classroom, identifying the prosocial behavior outcomes necessary for learning in a group is a crucial and reliable starting point. Evidence has long stipulated that if your students achieve your measurable outcome, they give you the needed evidence to move on (Sessums, 2020). It's no different in the virtual classroom. There, your outcomes ask that students conquer your curriculum and leave at year's end as more competent thinkers and problem solvers, solid citizens in a digital society, and friends who deeply understand the content you have taught.

Your class requires the integration of a digital skill set, which includes the teaching of netiquette, online safety, and manipulation of learning apps, in addition to social-emotional skills such as self-awareness, self-management, social awareness, relationship management, and responsible decision making (CASEL, 2020). Your students require this not for a test but for immediate application to learning tasks.

Three simple norms are your touchstones for guiding all student-student and student-teacher prosocial interactions during online or hybrid instruction.

1. Focus on reaching the goals of every lesson as well as you are able.
2. Respect all persons in your online classroom.
3. Respect the equipment and materials you are using to learn.

Setting expectations, getting to know your students, communicating clearly and inclusively, and dealing with infractions are all ways to foster prosocial behaviors in students, whether they are learning online or not.

Set Expectations

It follows you can jump-start your hybrid or fully online instruction by developing outcomes that create a community of mutual trust and respect, which engage learners who interact in positive, supportive ways. Hattie's (2009) *Visible Learning* meta-analysis, plus a number of studies about the effects of feedback from online college and adult learning classes (Coulthard, 2003; Sadaf, Martin, & Ahlgrim-Delzell, 2019), suggests that effective feedback retains its viability as a tool for managing prosocial norms in virtual classrooms. When you add high expectations to the mix by providing feedback on social skills, you increase the likelihood that students will pay attention to what you are asking when it comes to their role in trusting and respecting you and each other (Johnston, Whitley, & Shank, 2019).

The following considerations help you set expectations for students to apply SEL skills in digital environments.

- **Outcomes:** You lay the foundation for positive interactions essential in a digital learning community when you identify your class or course outcomes. If your outcomes include SEL aims such as collaboration and self-management, you have jump-started construction of your virtual learning community by stressing the importance of students' treating each other with respect.

- **Norms:** The social norms of mutual trust and respect direct how all students are expected to behave in your collaborative learning community. These norms guide students on self-managing how they interact both online and offline with the whole class, with small groups, and with you, and how they work on solo tasks. Figure 5.3 features a list of three expected prosocial norms that can guide students as they work online with each other. Post the figure online for all to keep in their e-portfolios. The figure also features a student playbook passage that tells students how the class will use the norms.

When you look at what you can say and do as the manager of norm-supporting interactions, it helps to review the threefold classification from the National School Reform Faculty (n.d.) at Brown University, as shown in figure 5.4. When giving any type of feedback, examples are practical; your goal is to reinforce how the student is making a positive change. Feedback is more likely to induce change when the student acts on a desired goal and when your tone (warm or cool) matches your words. Your *I* statement is essential, as well as your enunciation of change you observe.

Norms

1. Respect each other in word and deed.
2. Help each other in word and deed.
3. Respect the equipment and materials.

Student Playbook

Post this list in your e-portfolio. In the first month of school, I will lead a netstorm (if that's a new word for you, it means a chat room brainstorm) online. We will add specific behaviors you think will meet these norms.

After the lists are made, you can add other ideas.

I will ask you next quarter to include ideas from these lists as skills for you or the class to develop. We'll talk about the ideas and set up a rubric so you can self-assess how well you are meeting the expectation.

In the third quarter, I will ask you to give feedback to each other during asynchronous team meetings. You can add the feedback to your personal improvement plan.

I believe it's very important for you to act on what you learn, including what you learn about talking with your classmates and giving and taking feedback that will help you become a better teammate.

Thanks for your cooperation.

FIGURE 5.3: Working-together norms with a student playbook.

Behavior	Warm Feedback An all-positive recognition of constructive behavior	Cool Feedback A tone of disapproval of a specific, unhelpful behavior	Hard Feedback Feedback that identifies the behavior and provides a next-step expectation
Distracting	I appreciated your effort when I saw that you _____ today.	—	—
Dysfunctional	—	I am displeased when you go against our _____ norm. I am wondering why . . . How will you . . . ?	—
Repeat Disruption	—	—	I am pleased you understand why I am unhappy that you chose to . . . For your return to class, I expect . . .

Source: Adapted from National School Reform Faculty, n.d.

FIGURE 5.4: Feedback for promoting positive online interactions.

- **Positive expectations:** To meet your expectations for a collaborative learning community where mutual respect, reciprocal help, and complementary support thrive, share positive expectations that will guide students to act in a framework of shared values. The following are examples of positive expectations.
    - "I am pleased to see how you have waited to enter our screen by reviewing last night's homework."
    - "I thought it was a good idea when you respected Ruiz's answer."
- **Procedures:** Set procedures for maintaining norms in an online learning community. In figure 5.5 (page 142) the left column shows example expectations for interactions among people, and the right column shows expectations for interactions with and while using technology. As mentioned, make sure to check that all students know your classroom and required technology procedures. Write complete instructions for each procedure (and consider also recording a video of the instructions). Discuss how misuse can distract or become a disturbance. Post all the procedures on the LMS and class portfolio repository, and send copies to each student (to put in his or her portfolio) and to parents in your initial communication.

Figure 5.6 (page 142) is a sample expectations document you could share with grades 3–5 students. You can easily modify it to meet students in any grade where they are, though if you teach K–2, make sure not to have more than three behaviors per category, read the items to students, and identify one behavior a month. For those earliest grades, discuss specifics with the class, and then follow each discussion with a drawing activity about the behaviors. Start by announcing a draw-pair-share, and tell the students which expectations they can use as the subject of a sketch.

With People	With Equipment
<ul><li>Respect privacy.</li><li>Give constructive feedback.</li><li>Take your turn.</li><li>Stay on topic.</li><li>Use the agreed-on method for showing you have a response or question.</li><li>Share as asked.</li><li>Listen to and look at who is speaking.</li><li>Perform team roles and responsibilities.</li><li>Help and respect others.</li><li>Keep your team agreements.</li><li>Follow game rules.</li><li>Keep appointments for coaching and with groups.</li><li>Ask for help.</li></ul>	<ul><li>Enter the waiting room on time.</li><li>Dress according to the code.</li><li>Have all materials ready.</li><li>Mute and unmute when asked.</li><li>Save and share responses and documents.</li><li>Keep food and drink separate from tools.</li><li>Clean devices.</li><li>Date, label, and identify yourself on documents.</li><li>Block and report spam, phishing, and password sharing.</li><li>Cite sources.</li><li>Pay teacher-requested fees.</li><li>Turn off your phone.</li><li>Turn on your microphone, earphones, and camera.</li><li>Exit when released from class.</li><li>Follow app procedures.</li><li>Do not access unacceptable websites.</li></ul>

FIGURE 5.5: Expectations for interactions with people and technology.

Readiness

- I have materials ready for conferences and class.
- I am on time for conferences and class.
- I complete assignments on time.
- I bring my charged technology to class and to meetings.
- I only go to approved websites.
- I review all my posts before submitting them.

Respect

- I take my turn during discussions.
- I speak only for myself.
- I give helpful feedback.
- I honor the rights, beliefs, customs, and privacy of others.
- I listen to others.
- If I wouldn't say it to my parents or teachers face to face, I don't type it.
- I post only thoughtful responses.

- I address my peers by first name.
- I clarify my point of view when asked.
- I take care of my technology.

Rules

- I attend every class and breakout session.
- I am on time to all class meetings, breakout sessions, and conferences.
- I keep my PIN confidential.
- I never use or share another person's PIN.
- I never bully another person.
- I do not steal another's work.
- I always cite my sources.
- I do not eat or drink when I am using my technology.
- I reserve any technology loaned from school only for schoolwork.

Responsibility

- I help out at home.
- I follow class procedures.
- I follow DOVE guidelines for team meetings.
- I complete my homework.
- I identify myself in all online communications.
- I only post positive emojis.
- I stay on task even when the teacher is not present.
- I keep a schedule of classes and conferences.
- I take notes.
- I give feedback to my teacher and peers when asked.
- I manage my online and offline time responsibly.
- I report inappropriate or suspicious online behavior to my teacher.
- I keep my portfolio organized.

Resilience

- I try to do my best work.
- I ask for help.
- I check my work.
- I assess my work as honestly as I can.
- When a technology problem occurs, I problem solve.

Source: Adapted from Center on Positive Behavioral Interventions and Supports, 2020.

FIGURE 5.6: SEL chart for prosocial behaviors.

For example, tell them, "What does it look like in your team when you respect your partner? Remember this is your picture. It can be different from everyone else's. Just turn the page over when you are finished." After seeing most have turned their sketches over, ask students to each hold up their sketch to their digital device's camera in turn and say how the image shows they respect their teammates. Be sure with all ages that you ask them to take a turn, hold the image to the camera, speak loudly and clearly for all to hear, and listen without comment or facial expression to each other. If you feel the class is ready, ask all the students to give a visible but silent windy hurrah (two hands waving in the air) after each presented image.

After reviewing this chart in the first week of school or inviting teams to brainstorm what each interaction can look and sound like, have each student store a copy in his or her portfolio. On a set schedule, or when you notice student interactions out of alignment, guide an online group or all-class discussion to encourage those prosocial behaviors to return. The chart can also serve as a reference during a one-to-one online conference with a student whose behavior is violating a class norm.

Get to Know Your Students

Often forgotten is the opportunity to build SEL skills that bond the classroom community. Five minutes a day of bonding will keep the disciplinarian away as well. To establish and then build on the bonds that make it easier for students to speak up, give feedback, and work productively in teams, pick at least five minutes each week to get to know your students.

In primary classes, start getting to know your students with SEL-focused stems in a round-robin on your gallery grid. To keep it short, let five students a day respond at the very start of class. Let each say something about a personal talent or skill, or a favorite time of day or memory. In middle grades, switch to Friday five-minute chat posts, where students share feedback to the class or to a team: "Thanks for . . ."; "I liked it this week when . . ."; or "It helped me this week in the group when . . ." Ask secondary students to post online sticky notes to a teammate; again, pick the stem.

To learn more about how to help all in a class get to know you and each other, go to these webpages.

- *Getting to Know the Whole Student in Distance Learning* (Furman, 2021)
- *Prospect's Descriptive Processes: The Child, the Art of Teaching, and the Classroom and School* (Strieb, 2011)
- *The Descriptive Review of a Child* (School Reform Initiative, n.d.)

Communicate

Communicate your expectations with students as well as with parents and guardians about what you want to happen in students' digital class time. To do this, you can build on the traditional methods from your brick-and-mortar classroom. In addition to the traditional forms and messages—classroom norms, syllabi, and your support hours and contact information—consider adding the following communication strategies as appropriate for all to know and act on.

- **Keep copies:** Students can store a copy of norms and other guidelines in their portfolios, and you can keep a copy posted on a waiting room screen. You can refer any student or parent to these guidelines and share them electronically as you need to during a private conference.

- **Post (and screen share) classroom rules:** Refer to norms posted for onscreen behavior and procedures announced in student playbooks. Include opportunities to discuss norms and procedures, model them whenever you reteach, and allow time for practice as needed.
- **Prepare transitions:** For example, before a change from an all-class screen to breakout rooms, announce what is happening and (if necessary) do a quick procedure check. Share a student playbook and sample individuals to explain key instructions.
    - "Before you break into separate rooms, I want to review this guiding rubric that focuses on the DOVE guidelines. Rolando, I want you to start. How do you and your teammates follow the *D*?"
    - "Sally, I think your turn is next. Can you share how your team brainstorms so that all ideas are original?"

  When students are reentering the classroom, signal time remaining at five and two minutes with a visual timer. If students are doing a team or solo task, signal the end countdown. Show timekeepers in asynchronous teams how to use a timer.
- **Rely on routines:** Schedules and pacing charts provide students with a way to know what happens at a given time each day. Taking time to learn routines at the beginning of the school year (such as the entrance to the waiting room, round-robin rules, and signals to express the need to ask a question) will lower distractions and disruptions. The time you invest at the start of the year to prepare students to manage procedures and comply with norms will pay off in increased instructional time and a more respectful community—just like in a physical classroom.
- **Review the schedule:** If you are going to change the master schedule or a weekly pacing chart, let students know in advance—don't just say so. Share the change with both students and parents in an email or other message, and post a notice on your class landing page (such as the LMS). To check for understanding, put all students onscreen and then ask for a show of thumbs-up or some other visible action. A thumbs-up means, "I can name the change." Follow with a random callout of two or three thumbs-up students to repeat the change, and then ask those who had their thumb sideways ("Not sure") or down ("Nope!") to repeat what they heard. Check to see that all have read the message and made a note in their own schedules.
- **Celebrate procedure and norm compliance:** When you see the majority of students onscreen following a procedure, give a hurrah with a celebratory emoji, such as a giant happy face with heart eyes or an avatar you create. Accompany the hurrah with words describing what you are observing: "Wow, am I glad to see so many of you signaling your readiness to enter!" Call for a celebration when a large majority of students is behaving as expected and you don't want to call out the few who are not. But don't forget to unexpectedly cheer when all are complying.
- **Foster autonomy:** Having a voice and being able to make autonomous choices are healthy for young people and increase motivation through voice and choice. The path to agency can start with the smallest choices that convey the message, "You are responsible." Examples for that student agency include choosing to either respond in a round-robin or say, "I pass"; stepping out of a learning space for a stress break; picking team roles; and

adding ideas in a brainstorm. Voice and choice do not apply for procedures. Behavior is a choice, and choosing not to comply comes with a consequence. Read more about autonomy in chapter 4 (page 103).

- **Accentuate the positive:** By setting norms and procedures as goals to reach and acceptable ways to act, you highlight what to do and what not to do. This lets you teach positive ways of interacting, just as you teach positive ways to write a paper or complete a lab assignment. With warm, cool, and hard feedback, students can learn from their experience through supportive statements such as, "I appreciate how this group is taking time to assess team responsibilities," or "I like that you said you quoted Ben Franklin. In future podcasts, please attach a complete citation with the date and source." You can read more about goal setting in chapter 4.

- **Explain reasons:** Assumptions such as, "You should know better," are not helpful. To avoid assumptions when addressing the norms and behaviors you expect, explain the reasons for them through statements such as, "Remember that arriving early to the waiting room lets you get ready for class so we can all start together," or "I'm talking about doing your fair share because our learning community depends on it. If one piece is missing, then it keeps everyone from meeting his or her goals, and your teammates can lose trust in you."

Deal With Infractions With Restorative Justice

Restorative justice is a classroom management approach that asks that a student take responsibility for an offense against a classroom norm and make it right to you and affected classmates, and it asks that the community help the offender restore lost trust by adhering to classroom norms. Restorative practices are corrective, not punitive, respectful actions taken by you and the community of learners to help rebuild any broken bonds caused by the offender. Mutual trust and respect are the values that underscore the practices.

In classrooms committed to student-centered SEL, respectful of all outcomes, there is no room for punitive discipline (Smith, Fisher, & Frey, 2015). A teacher's response to a digital distraction or major disruption is required to be about reparation and learning, since "restorative justice is aimed at repairing the harm a student has caused and teaching him or her to learn from the experience" (Heim & Strauss, 2020). Instead of, "You can't participate in asynchronous small-group activities anymore," the response is, "We must discuss what steps you will take to get back online and how you can make this right." When restorative principles guide your reaction to a disruption in class norms, you can expect them to bring longer-lasting, positive results (Fronius et al., 2019).

In a restorative context, short-term practices such as muting microphones, shutting off video screens, or sending a student to a waiting room as punishment are not acceptable. Any may be a temporary step that teachers committed to restorative practices take to end the disruption for the moment. The dismissal should allow the offender the preannounced *if–then* choice to return if he or she is ready to stop the behavior. However, to ensure that mutual trust and respect are the core operational values of their online classroom and that the next steps will bring the students back into the classroom community, repeat offenses and shutdowns will require that an online teacher-student conference take place as soon as possible. In the conference, the teacher's aim is to help the student repair the damage caused to teaching and learning as well as to the trust bonds. Remember the following when applying this approach.

- When a student breaks the trust and respect bonds created with the class, the action you take must be consistent with justice values aiming to re-establish the injured trust relationships (International Institute for Restorative Practices, 2006) as soon as possible. One-to-one private conferences are best.
- Equitably apply these practices for each offender no matter what the student's race, ethnicity, sexual orientation, religion, socioeconomic status, physical condition, or mental condition.

To be clear, your reliance on restorative principles and practices and your exclusion of punishment do not make you soft or naive. It is to everyone's benefit when you take immediate, identical action with any student's damage to your online class's positive norms so you can return the student to full class citizenship as soon as possible.

To make the restorative process as simple as possible, it helps when you ground your responses in a well-defined, achievable, prosocial outcome that results from a personalized mutual trust and respect agreement. In the short run, such an agreement is meant to replace the distraction or disruption, be it small (fiddling with entry buttons) or gigantic (cyberbullying), with a constructive interaction. You want the student to follow classroom norms in the long run. More importantly, your restorative response aims to help the student with new ways to overcome his or her difficulties and follow prosocial norms in the classroom, not just for the next week but the rest of the school year.

How Do I Address Distractive or Dysfunctional Behaviors?

Even if you are fastidious in fortifying a climate of trust and respect with daily doses of social-emotional skills attention, preparing yourself for what can go wrong is sensible. And when a student's actions or words take your attention away from a teaching task, interrupt peers' learning, or make it tough to teach that student, asking yourself, "How do I address these interactions?" is smart. Knowing the difference between distractive and dysfunctional behaviors, knowing how to handle small distractions in proportion, and knowing how to handle continued disruptions differently will help you answer this question. The following sections cover these topics.

Know the Difference

It is helpful to define each term—*distractive* and *dysfunctional*—in the context of digital instruction. Student interactions that distract from a norm are those that take you or other students' attention away from a lesson's goals. A student turning off her screen or laying her head down on her computer as you review an activity's instructions may distract you. Another student who doesn't do his job as breakout team timekeeper may distract teammates. When a student checks a text during a lesson or steps out of a breakout activity, this is a distraction. Students who flash faces onscreen, toggle chat keys, or play a solo video game during an online question-and-answer session may take attention away from a lesson's goals.

Dysfunctional online student interactions are ones that interfere with peers' completing an online learning task or your reaching an online lesson's goals. Examples of such interactions include repeatedly muting or engaging in other distracting behaviors; physical or verbal abuse; off-color language, jokes, or stories; shouting and arguing with other students; or damaging equipment.

In the first dysfunctional group are repeated distractions such as habitual tardiness to all classes or breakout sessions; side conversations; interruptions; late or incomplete homework; ignored small-group responsibilities, including assignments; inappropriate dress; swearing, disrespectful comments, or inappropriate jokes; and disrespect in word or action toward you, other professionals, or visitors to the class. Other distractions such as having bad netiquette or not returning emails can move from an occasional distraction to an ongoing dysfunctional event.

In the second dysfunctional group are egregious major infractions. Any single occurrence of the following requires a restorative action as immediately as possible. First, you hold a one-to-one conference with the student and inform the parents in writing with a copy to the principal. Second, schedule an online or in-person restorative conference, inviting anyone offended by the action (for example, you, the team, or a parent).

- **Using prohibited websites:** Obviously, any school-issued laptop will likely block certain websites, but some students may sneak a view.

- **Cyberbullying:** When one or more students send a message that threatens, intimidates, makes fun of, or tells lies or suggestive stories about another student, that is cyberbullying. According to the Transforming School Discipline Collaborative (2020):

    Any communication that is threatening in nature within the online class discussion board, chat function in synchronous (Zoom, etc.) instruction, or online harassment of classmates on social media should be considered an immediate concern. These comments include anything that is harassing, profane, obscene, suggestive, solicitous, indecent, sexually explicit, pornographic, threatening, abusive, defamatory, libelous, derogatory, discriminatory, or hate speech. (p. 27)

    Most cyberbullies leave a traceable trail, which makes this offense one of the most dysfunctional in a virtual classroom where you are working hard to build trust and respect among a community of learners. Worse, cyberbullying can have a lifelong negative impact on a victim's mental health (Hurley, 2018; Lockhart, 2021). When cyberbullying, sexting, or other similar opprobrious misbehavior occurs, you should notify the principal first and plan the restorative action.

- **Breaking confidentiality:** When a student shares any correspondence meant only for that person, that is breaking confidentiality. This includes private feedback or any written document. It also includes sharing one's own or another student's password or PIN. Success in having students give and get feedback is built on a sense of trust in the community. Breaking confidentiality cracks open the safe and shatters the victim's ability to trust you and peers, and can have a long-lasting effect on relationships.

- **Plagiarizing:** Citations are required for all text taken from a website or other source, for indirect or direct quotations. Please reiterate this to all students, giving examples of plagiarism and making clear that it is theft. When these instances occur, your restorative approach should include a series of tutorials so that you can teach the proper way to apply and cite resources and discuss one-to-one plagiarism's harm. Some teacher practitioners of restorative justice have asked students to write to authors, explain what they did, and invite a response from the authors.

- **Sexting:** This behavior includes sharing any lewd images or inappropriate or suggestive messages. Holding restorative conferences between the victims and the perpetrators can be a valuable practice. Remember, however, a victim of sexting may feel too ashamed to participate.
- **Being truant:** Any unapproved absence from scheduled online classes, including those occurring asynchronously, qualifies as truancy. However, truancy should not be considered a punishable offense. When the student cuts him- or herself out of a team task, you and the team can confer with the offender, highlighting the truancy's negative effects on any collaborative task's completion and the extra burden on other members. When the student is truant from one class period or more, school referral to a social agency or the school social worker is an appropriate restorative action.

In the context of restorative problem solving, it is important to remember that students of color and poverty have been victimized by inequitable treatment and inequitable reliance on punishment for online offenses (Riddle & Sinclair, 2019). Not only has school discipline in the form of punishment fallen disproportionately on Black and Brown students, but it stands in the way of offering them equitable opportunities to work collaboratively in online learning communities. Superintendent L. Oliver Robinson points out, "[Racial] disproportionality in things like suspension is real," and it has been exacerbated during the massive switch to remote learning (as cited in Matusek, 2021). Robinson says, "Until that is completely addressed, the impact of the disproportionality can be significantly minimized or mitigated" (as cited in Matusek, 2021). In this light, restorative practices become all the more important.

When discussing these major infractions with students, be specific and thorough in your explanation, sharing examples where appropriate, explain the infractions' serious nature and impact on others, and mention the student who distracted or disrupted the learning process. Use your judgment about how you should introduce each and what is age appropriate. Should you include a formal lesson or hold a discussion after an event, for instance? The following sections discuss how to go about handling small distractions and continued disruptions.

Handle Small Distractions in Proportion

For lesser offenses that continue, or about which students want to argue, you must make a judgment call. Does the student receive an email in which you express your unhappiness more bluntly? An invitation to a one-to-one conference? A parent conference? It is up to you and your school to determine the step you will take based on a behavior's severity, its continued impact on your teaching, and its impact on other students and on the mutual trust and respect needed to make the class go well for all.

Some digital distractions create unique problems and may require you to evaluate the student's intention. For instance, what if a student makes fun of a peer's religious clothing during a chat? This could be a naive and insensitive act, an empty-headed and callous remark, or a major cyberbullying offense. Here, use your professional judgment, but maintain your consistency. When unsure, set up a private FaceTime or Google Hangouts conference with the student, report your observations, and allow his or her response. Don't jump the gun, but prepare that you may have to go beyond with a restorative conference.

You may wish to require nonpunitive, restorative conferences for a preset number of class or small-group tardies, an unexplained absence, missed assignments, or other, more serious concerns in which the student shortchanges his or her education. For the most part, these behaviors fall into the category of distracting because they interfere with your time to prepare, teach, or assess lessons.

To make a swift judgment guided by principles of restorative justice, you will want to react promptly to what you are seeing or hearing with cease-and-desist cool or hard feedback. For instance, when you see a student sneak a peek at a smartphone, you may say, "Reginald, I see you have your phone out again when you are supposed to be completing your concept map. I expect you to put it away now and get to the map. If you choose to stay with the phone, you will be asking me to send you to time-out." If necessary, you will follow up your feedback by sending the student to your digital waiting room. As soon after class as possible (perhaps relying on a precomposed email), bring the student back online with only you, or if you have shut off the student's camera and mic for a more serious incident, contact the student via email to set up a one-to-one conference. At that conference, identify the elements in figure 5.7, and advise the student that he or she will have to attend a restorative conference with three students you select to discuss and come up with a plan for avoiding the infraction in the future. Why are students involved here? In Reginald's case, it's because his infraction caused you to stop your teaching and focus on his phone work. He will have to agree to a plan that will prevent him from work stoppage in the future. If the student doesn't show, inform the student's parents or guardians and your principal.

What to State	Example of How to State It
The problem	
Your feelings	
Either a stronger invitation to stop or a simple problem-solving process so you and the student can identify the norm that the student is having difficulty following	
The reason for the norm	
How the student, perhaps with your or another student's help, can solve the problem	

Source: Adapted from Greene, 2014.

FIGURE 5.7: Problem-solving template for a restorative conference.

*Visit **go.SolutionTree.com/technology** for a free reproducible version of this figure.*

Positive Interaction and Social-Emotional Learning

A simple contract may follow, laying out a small, chunked plan that will enable the student's immediate return online. The problem-solving discussion and all-win agreement open the waiting room door. The student-teacher agreements for restorative steps answer the questions, "What am I going to do differently?" and "What help do I need from you and my classmates?" Figure 5.8 features a sample restorative contract for primary students. Figure 5.9 features a sample restorative contract for secondary students.

My name: Billy

What I did: I called Marie a bad name. She cried.

How I feel now: 😱

What I will do: Say I am sorry. Not use that word at all.

Recorded by: Elliot 4/4/21

FIGURE 5.8: Sample restorative contract—Primary.

Student name: Ellen Micheale

Date: 4/15/2021

Teacher: Mrs. Binder

Class: Grade 11

Restorative justice team members: Susie Lockhart, Janson Trompley, Michael Lupin

The issue: I blew off our team meeting yesterday. Went to Cubs game.

The response: I kept the group from finishing our product assessment. It still is not done. I have to do my piece. I agree to prepare my piece and send it by email to Mrs. Binder and each team member. My deadline is tomorrow. I will be at our next meeting on Tuesday so we can discuss the whole team assessment and finish the product. If I do that again, I will have to do future projects this year by myself.

Signatures

Student: _Ellen_

Restorative justice team members: _Susie_ , _Janson_ , _Mike_

Teacher: _J. Binder_

FIGURE 5.9: Sample restorative contract—Secondary.

Handle Continued Disruptions Differently

What happens if a student repeats a disruptive behavior or stops following a commitment to improve, such as being on time or attending group meetings? Then it's time for tough love! Institute a restorative procedure that involves parents. If the student breaks other norms, start with a notice about the first breakdown, and then go to a one-to-one restorative conference. A second breakdown can initiate a report to a peer justice team (if you have one set up with classmates who were disrupted) with parents and guardians.

For the repeated behavior, consider using psychology professor and author Ross W. Greene's (2014) collaborative and proactive solutions model. Greene's model "dramatically reduced both discipline problems and punishments for the most challenging children and adolescents" (Lewis, 2016). The model asks you to take the steps in figure 5.9 (page 151) when conferencing about repeated norm violations. These are the same steps you would take with a major violation.

Adopting Greene's (2014) recommended practices begins with your list of digital classroom disruptions that you find irksome. This personal list may contain annoyances similar to those in your physical classroom (whining, text messaging, or swearing, for example). Others may be more serious issues because they are threats to another person's physical or emotional safety or the student's own safety, or repetitions that indicate a more serious issue.

In this context, it is important to urge the student to take control by owning his or her behavior even as you show empathy and avoid a power struggle over norms. Your aim is to heal broken trust and foster respect in relationships, return the student to the online classroom, and continue with all the remote learning opportunities you are providing.

How Do I Address Failure to Adhere to Prior Agreements or a Major Dysfunctional Behavior?

Any major norm-smashing interaction or event requires immediate attention. Once you have clear evidence that a student has violated a norm with a major dysfunctional behavior or failed to adhere to prior agreements to change a pattern of disruptive interactions, you up the ante. Immediately contact the student online with cool feedback, and inform the student of your decision to notify his or her parent or guardian. Stay firm but encouraging, and do not engage in debate. Your statement may sound like one of these.

- "I am going to inform _____. I will explain what has happened and invite your side when we meet."
- "I am not open for debate now. Your mother and I will listen to your side when we meet."

Failure to Adhere to Prior Agreements

Email the parent or guardian with a requested date. Copy your principal on the email, and then call the parent or guardian until you make contact. Explain why the student has lost online learning privileges, and provide next-step instructions, including the time and date for a mandatory online conference as soon as possible that week. Provide the student with assignments to complete solo and dates to email each to you. Remember that "banning a student from Google Meet for multiple classes is similar to suspending a student from school for a couple of days" (Transforming School Discipline Collaborative, 2020, p. 22). That's never your prerogative. However, by getting the principal's approval and providing the student with assignments to complete, you see that the time-out is a time for you, the disruptor, and the class to continue through the lesson. If the parent cannot meet the online date, arrange a different time as soon as possible, and consider letting the disruptive student attend class events in mute mode. Meet with the student alone to agree on conditions for class participation until the parent can meet.

Be sure your language in any correspondence emphasizes your restorative intent, is specific about the behavior, and expresses a desire to resolve the issue within two days. Figure 5.10 is an example email.

> November 12
>
> Today, your child, _____, distracted her classmates and me by making extensive off-topic comments (including swearing in the whole-class chat during instruction). She and I had discussed the same off-topic behavior on October 29. We agreed that she would avoid this behavior. However, she did not. I do not wish to punish her for this behavior. I want to find a way for her to be present in our class full-time without going against the behavior norms (such as by swearing or engaging in other verbal abuses online).
>
> I would like to have a thirty-minute conference tomorrow, November 13, at 7:15 a.m. via FaceTime on our smartphones. She should join us. If you don't have this app, she does. You may wish to borrow her phone and use the speaker mode. If you cannot meet at this time, please email two or three convenient times in the next two days. Thank you.

FIGURE 5.10: Restorative email to a parent or guardian.

Anytime you have to send a restorative email to a parent or guardian regarding repeated or disruptive behaviors similar to the one in figure 5.10, do the following.

- Inform the parent or guardian why you are calling, summarize what happened, and reiterate the information you provided. Keep in mind that this call may arouse parent defensiveness or anger. Be ready to stay out of conflict, keep cool, and avoid arguing.
- Schedule a phone or in-person conference with the student and parent or guardian no later than two class days after the repeated disruptive event or major infraction.
- Maintain a firm, respectful tone.
- Confirm the time and date with emails to the student *and* parent or guardian.
- If the student's follow-up to the first conference's agreement does not produce the agreed-on results, follow these same procedures for the next conference. Consider inviting the school social worker, counselor, or principal.
- Keep copies of any agreements and communications in the student's personal record, or if part of district policy, send a copy to the principal.

Major Dysfunctional Behavior

Research indicates that restorative justice programs have helped reduce exclusionary discipline and narrow the glaring racial disparities in how discipline is meted out in schools. The evidence is a bit more mixed or inconclusive on two other fronts: (1) school climate and (2) student development (Gregory & Evans, 2020). However, studies also suggest that the approach's success depends on how well it is organized and how well the plans are implemented. When the approach is used to respond to major dysfunctional behavior, it works most effectively when practice closely adheres to restorative justice principles (for example, give no punishment and restore trust).

For a major offense, students need to know that you mean what you tell them during the first class meeting of a semester: violation of class norms with any of the major offenses will result in instant loss of the chance to learn in your online community, an immediate restorative conference, and involvement of a parent or guardian. Reiterate that the principal has approved your practice. As your classroom rules—posted on a classroom portal or mailed home in a packet—make clear, any major infraction will require a same-day (as-soon-as-possible) conference with you and the principal or the principal's representative whenever feasible.

When you share your principal-approved practice with parents and students, it will help that *equitable* restorative justice is your approach to classroom management, as opposed to punishment. In that communication, it will help if you explain why you prefer restorative justice and how you make it work in your digital environment. Send this home in a start-of-year packet, post it on a portal, or discuss it during the first fall parent night. Consider telling parents and guardians about the following.

- Define the term *restorative justice* and your reasons for this approach.

- Explain how you will set up a small team of students who were offended by the disruptive or continued behavior. Describe how you will determine the justice team members if the offenses disrupted all class members, usually by lottery from among volunteers.

- Describe how you will schedule between three and five time slots in the first two weeks of a semester to prepare everyone as a possible restorative justice team member. Do this in the context of setting expectations for a positive, trusting environment of mutual respect with an emphasis on positive interactions. You can engage older students by making your introduction an inquiry lesson with the expected outcome that all of them will be able to define the concept of restorative justice, how it will work, what value it has, and what their responsibility will be as members of a trusting and respectful community.

- State how you will form a justice team from among individuals who may be harmed by someone's major dysfunctional behavior.

Prepare a reproducible template that a restorative justice team can use to record its decisions. Figure 5.11 also includes instructions from a student playbook that describe how a teacher will set up a restorative discussion. The team recorder will give you all written documents to secure.

How Do I Deal With Student Stress, Anxiety, and Depression?

It is important to recognize if a student is having stress or is very anxious or depressed. According to a study conducted by Reem M. Ghandour and colleagues (2019), 3.2 percent of three- to seventeen-year-olds in the United States (approximately 1.9 million) have diagnosed depression. A study conducted by Rebecca H. Bitsko and colleagues (2018) asserts that anxiety and depression have increased over time in U.S. students. The number of six- to seventeen-year-olds in the United States diagnosed with either anxiety or depression increased from 5.4 percent in 2003 to 8 percent in 2007, and to 8.4 percent in 2011–2012 (Bitsko et al., 2018). The number of six- to seventeen-year-olds in the United States "ever having been diagnosed with anxiety" increased from 5.5 percent in 2007 to 6.4 percent in 2011–2012 (Bitsko et al., 2018). The number of six- to seventeen-year-olds in the United States "ever having been diagnosed with depression" did not change between 2007 (4.7 percent) and 2011–2012 (4.9 percent; Bitsko et al., 2018). You might consider it a "silent epidemic" (Anderson & Cardoza, 2016). According to Meg Anderson and Kavitha Cardoza (2016):

> Up to one in five kids living in the U.S. shows signs or symptoms of a mental health disorder in a given year. So in a school classroom of 25 students, five of them may be struggling with the same issues many adults deal with: depression, anxiety, substance abuse. And yet most children—nearly 80 percent—who need mental health services won't get them.

Our class:

Our names:

Date:

The problem:

The details:

The student's side:

What we considered:

Our recommendation:

Signature:

Student Playbook

1. Set your restorative justice team members' roles and responsibilities.
   - After the teacher re-explains the team's immediate goal, the team's responsibility, and the hearing procedure, the leader facilitates interactions among the team members and the mediated student (the term we will use to describe the student whose return to class the restorative justice team is seeking to resolve) by making sure all who wish to speak can do so in a respectful way. The leader also introduces witnesses and the student's advocate and appoints the recorder and timekeeper.
   - The team recorder fills in the template and gives the completed copy to the teacher.
   - The team's student advocate helps the mediated student explain his or her perspective on the event and calls on any student witnesses.
   - The team timekeeper keeps the session in the agreed-on timelines.
2. Explain your role in this restorative hearing.
3. Preview the case.
   - Answer, "What was the student's offending behavior?" and "What do you expect from the team?"
   - Construct your student playbook. In it, define team roles and responsibilities, hearing procedures you have identified, and the hearing schedule. (Generally, each teacher identifies desired procedures.)
   - Review the template with the team.
   - Stress the need for confidentiality of all deliberations.
   - Offer help as needed, especially about the tone with which students ask questions, ways to listen actively, and methods to clarify summations.
   - Answer questions.
   - Review with an emphasis on your expectations, and encourage students' best efforts.
   - Conduct a practice hearing as needed.
4. Complete your in-session role as agreed on with the team. (The teacher is always present in some role.)
5. After the restorative hearing, schedule a thirty-minute debriefing session with the restorative justice team, asking guiding questions such as the following.
   - What difficulties did you encounter?
   - How well did you resolve these difficulties?
   - What else did you do well?
   - What help do you need to improve the next case?
6. Celebrate the team's effort with positive feedback. Either file a commendation in each team member's personal folder or email each team member's parent or guardian with something such as, "I'm pleased to share that [student's name] participated in a peer mediation today. I especially want you to know . . ."
7. Celebrate the mediated student's participation, demeanor, and decisions. Encourage the student to follow through with the agreement's terms, and let the student know what will happen if he or she follows through on the agreement or chooses not to do so. You will follow up with positive feedback affirming the student's effort and successful compliance or identify a breakdown that requires, as per the agreement, a follow-up meeting.

FIGURE 5.11: Restorative discussion template.

*Visit **go.SolutionTree.com/technology** for a free reproducible version of this figure.*

Mayo Clinic researchers note that excessive time with technology and social media can fuel feelings of anxiety and depression (Balzer, 2019). Long hours of online learning, plus the seven hours per day that adolescents commonly give to social media outside of class, can result in less sleep and trigger feelings of being out of control (Rogers Behavioral Health, 2019). Although some students may act out when they are anxious, others may disappear into a shell. Those students won't signal their feelings by disruptions; they will stop participating, come late or skip sessions, or go completely offline. When you see any of these behaviors, it's important to pay attention.

When it comes to psychological evaluations, teachers are left out in the cold until a 504 plan or individualized education plan (IEP) is created. Although you, as a teacher, are not expected to resolve the serious emotional and psychological issues causing stress, anxiety, and depression, you should be aware of them and to whom you need to speak about your concerns. Currently, there are no mandates on reporting concerns about a student's mental health. It is just an unwritten rule that the teacher should know who to go to. Stuck between a rock and a hard place, teachers do not have much they can or should do besides reporting such issues to a school psychologist, social worker, or school counselor. Unfortunately, action on a concern is no guarantee that help will arrive. Such an alert requires jumping through many hoops. Sometimes, there are so many hoops that a student doesn't get the needed help and tragedy unfolds. Once you have reported to the school official who can make a request, the more important questions are, "What can I, as a teacher, do to help students who are showing signs of stress, anxiety, or depression?" and "When students are online, what signals might I look for?"

Although sometimes a single major incident can trigger a blowup, it is likely that any major mental breakdown will be preceded by a pattern of repeated dysfunctional interactions, such as events of verbal abuse and bullying, physical abuse, sexual confusion, antisocial behavior, neglect, or aggressive behavior, any of which produces feelings of worthlessness or hopelessness. The more regularly and repeatedly these events occur, and the feelings that follow appear, the more important it is for teachers to talk with a counselor, social worker, or other helping professional. A single mild instance of anxiety is not likely a significant signal. However, combinations, repetitions, and serious mental breakdowns (intense mental distress) tell you it is time to talk with a counselor, social worker, or school psychologist. Unless you were trained and certified to serve as a social worker, counselor, or psychologist, you cannot be expected to provide needed services to students who display signs of stress, anxiety, or depression. When you do notice signs suggesting a student might be depressed, panicked, or overanxious, don't feel compelled to take on the role of rescuer. What you can best do instead follows.

- Be vigilant during online sessions, paying particular attention to students with special needs for danger signs.

- Take what you see and hear seriously, and say that to the student. (An overview of signs to watch for follows.)

- Express your concerns to any health service professional or counselor in the school (that person must inform the parent), as well as the principal. If a school lacks mental health resources, the principal can make a home connection and, as needed, refer the student to local services or local physician. Refer to the following overview for signs that a student may need help.

Signs of stress involve noticeable behaviors that are mild forms or precursors of anxiety and depression. These signs may include the following.

- Biting fingernails
- Whining
- Weeping
- Presenting with dark-ringed eyes
- Reacting listlessly

Signs of depression include the following.

- Participating noticeably less often
- Losing interest in formerly favored class activities
- Losing one's appetite
- Having constant headaches
- Yawning frequently and putting one's head on one's desk
- Complaining of tiredness or lack of sleep
- Making statements about being sad, hopeless, guilty, or powerless
- Having sudden arguments with friends, family, or teachers that end in abrupt withdrawal
- Expressing boredom
- Showing an increasing pattern of late or missed attendance to breakout and chat rooms, deterioration of work quality, or missing assignments
- Not responding to communication from the teacher

Signs of anxiety include the following.

- Breathing rapidly
- Sweating
- Having trembles, muscle twitches, or finger or leg shakes
- Reporting feelings of danger, panic, or dread
- Having trouble focusing on anything other than what's worrisome
- Being overly concerned about online work, deadlines, the amount and difficulty of work, the members of one's team, or feedback from team members
- Displaying disproportionate fears that teachers, parents, and friends will be angry

When you notice a student is struggling with depression or anxiety, it's important that you discuss this with the student in a very gentle and caring way. Empathy (putting yourself in the student's shoes) is critical. Display empathy by discussing and showing that you care and can make a difference to that student. If there is a more serious case, you should report it to the school counselor.

Teachers, administrators, and other school staff must also be knowledgeable about depression and anxiety because these disorders can seriously impair academic and interpersonal behavior at school (Hammen & Rudolph, 2003). Those staff can use the following list of strategies to help a student with depression or anxiety.

- Give frequent feedback on academic, social, and behavioral performance.
- Teach the student how to set goals and self-monitor.
- Teach the student personal problem-solving skills.
- Make a PLP for grit with the emphasis on learning needed to feel in charge of one's life.
- Coach the student in ways to organize, plan, and execute tasks demanded daily or weekly in school.
- Develop modifications and accommodations to respond to the student's fluctuations in mood, ability to concentrate, or side effects of medication. Assign one individual to serve as a primary contact and coordinate interventions.
- Give the student opportunities to engage in social interactions.
- Frequently monitor whether the student has suicidal thoughts.
- Develop a school-home communication system to share information on the student's academic, social, and emotional behavior and any developments concerning medication or side effects.

Conclusion

Social-emotional learning is intended to promote skillful prosocial behaviors and help students maintain healthy interpersonal relationships, including those they have with you and their peers during online learning. Helping students develop their prosocial skills by increasing their self-awareness, self-regulation, interpersonal relationships, and sense of justice even as they work to learn your course content is a challenge that all teachers must address. In this chapter, you reviewed an SEL needs assessment template (figure 5.1, page 136) that you might use as a tool to introduce SEL behaviors that help students become the managers of their own behavior. Teacher considerations for helping students develop and manage these behaviors included the following.

- When you set up schedules and pacing charts that provide a time structure, and you share positive behavior norms and a system for encouraging positive self-control, you make it easier to hold to values of mutual trust and respect as the standards that guide your digital classroom's interactions.
- When you teach the skills that promote awareness of how students interact in a classroom so they are contributing citizens of a mini society, you also put in place the conditions for correcting any damage to that society and for supporting it as a community of learners.
- When restorative justice, in principle and practice, becomes your favored best practice, you increase the chance that all class members will contribute to maintenance of the preeminent values of trust and respect you favor. Punishment for violating these core principles and distracting or disturbing your teaching or other students' learning is considered an unacceptable violation of mutual trust and respect.

- When a student in an online community of learners distracts or disrupts you or other students, you must restore trust by asking the offender to be responsible for restoring the broken bonds. Punishment that excludes a student from learning is damaging. Instead, have a problem-solving session, led by the offended peers in the online community, conducted in your presence. The teacher and peers reach an agreement, spelling out the specific path the student must walk in order to restore trust and his or her rights as a community member.
- When a student reacts to the isolation imposed by technology by becoming very anxious, distressed, or depressed, you are encouraged to refer the student to school personnel who are certified to respond to and assist him or her.

MY TAKEAWAYS

What three ideas from this chapter can best help you shift to digital instruction and prepare all students to be effective digital learners? Record your ideas here so you can make a plan later.

1. _____

2. _____

3. _____

6

Feedback

A major role for teachers in the learning process is to provide the kind of feedback to students that encourages their learning and provides signposts and directions along the way, bringing them closer to independence.
 —*Lorna Earl*

A story to start: Ralph opened his chat room.

"Ralph," he read, "I was pleased to receive your revised personal learning plan. I like how specific you made your goal. Adding the timeline with assessment dates and the specific count of poems you intend to analyze sharpened the focus. I have one added suggestion to improve the plan. Would you be willing to expand the assessment criteria in the rubric with a criterion that specifies the elements you will include in the analysis, such as the poet's use of metaphor?"

Ralph clicked his response. "Not sure what you mean. What other elements should I be looking at?"

Feedback is the information that a teacher gives to a student before, during, or after an activity, performance, or lesson; it is the written or spoken communication between a student and a teacher that contributes to a final assessment or evaluation about the degree to which the student has achieved a goal or outcome. Teacher feedback helps a student set goals, assists the student's progress to those goals, and goes into making an assessment. That feedback process can result in a grade, the shortest and least helpful feedback, or it can result in a written or spoken description of the completed performance or product's value with suggested recommendations for improvement.

Effective feedback will answer three major questions, asked by a teacher or by a student: (1) "Where am I going?" or "What are my learning goals?"; (2) "How am I going to get there?" or "What progress am I making toward the goals?"; and (3) "What do I need to do next?" or "What activities will help me make better progress?" According to John Hattie's (2009, 2012) review of over 800 research studies relating to student achievement, the most effective feedback for increasing achievement helps the learner look forward and backward in a reciprocal conversation; this has double the impact that regular teaching strategies have on student achievement. Hattie's revelations opened a floodgate of studies, such as the Sutton Trust and Education Endowment Foundation (Higgins et al., 2013) report that enunciates clear criteria for assessing feedback quality and reinforces how feedback enriches self-management, peer cooperation, positive teacher-student relationships, and self-direction.

Online-specific research confirms that "synchronous class time is most effective when it is built around small-group peer interactions and direct teacher-to-student feedback" (Gallagher & Cottingham, 2020). Participants in a study about award-winning online teaching practices declare the "importance of providing timely, actionable, and substantive feedback, through formative assessment strategies of quizzes, discussion posts, online meetings or synchronous sessions, short papers, projects," and other metrics (Martin et al., 2019, p. 201). With a sharper focus on feedback research in online learning, this chapter will answer what effective feedback looks like online, what online feedback best practices are, how students can give you feedback, how students can give two-way feedback, and how you can engage students in peer-to-peer feedback.

What Does Effective Feedback Look Like in a Virtual Classroom?

It should be made clear that providing and receiving feedback require much skill and time in every classroom. The model advanced through Hattie does not invoke a mere stimulus-and-response routine; this model requires teachers to have the following.

- High proficiency to set up a high-trust classroom climate between student and teacher
- The ability to deal with the complexities of multiple judgments
- Deep enough understanding of subject matter to provide feedback about tasks or relationships between ideas
- Willingness to encourage self-regulation
- Exquisite timing to provide constructive feedback the student will value

To be able to devote time and thought to feedback that is interactive and reciprocal, teachers must automate other instructional tasks. This way, they can provide the richest learning opportunities for a full class of students. If, indeed, feedback is doubly powerful, as Hattie (2009, 2012) suggests, you will need to block more interactions and gather the resources to be responsive to everyone's feedback needs (Hattie & Jaeger, 1998).

Because students ultimately learn by constructing their own learning, it is crucial that teachers understand and appreciate how formal and informal feedback contributes to the equation so that assessment becomes a powerful instructional tool as well as an assessment tool. The more you can immerse the giving and getting of feedback in an instructional process whereby students learn from the feedback, the more they are going to master the material and complete their goals for a lesson or project and for the entire course of study. When students experience setting challenging goals and self-assessing with your targeted, specific feedback as they work through lessons and projects, you promote their feelings of self-efficacy to tackle ever more challenging tasks that will lead to deeper learning outcomes.

Many of the most effective informal and formal feedback tools at your disposal in a brick-and-mortar classroom are available for online adaptation.

- Informal feedback methods give you and students quick and immediate information. Among the informal methods you will recognize are color-dotted note cards and hand signals to check for understanding, side and summary notes on essays, exit slips, sticky notes to attach to peer work, drop-by-the-desk tête-à-têtes, and one-on-one conferences. None of these need to be abandoned online. In addition, when online, you can add other informal feedback tools such as digital sticky notes, screen mutes, plus–minus emails, tweets, and other social media features.

- To a far greater degree than for informal tools, you can expand the opportunities for formal feedback when in digital classrooms. With formal online assessments, you and students have much more time and many more digital tools to transform your feedback into effective teaching and learning. First, note that the mechanics of two-way feedback in a digital classroom differ only in the use of electronic media. In addition to the standard written paper or face-to-face conference—which is almost impossible to schedule with, say, twenty-nine other students needing simultaneous attention—students and teachers can type online feedback on a chat board, in an email, via social media, or via the comment features in Microsoft Word and Google Docs. They wait for the other to respond in a private chat as soon as he or she can, or respond immediately in the context of a chat discussion. They can synchronously or asynchronously show images or text, send comments back and forth, talk on solo screens, take multigrid gallery walks, or take advantage of apps such as Kahoot!, Quizlet, Peergrade, Padlet, Kaizena, and CampusKnot.

Confidentiality is always a big issue with feedback. The most effective feedback involves personal goals. Students tend to respond more to feedback when they trust that what you and they are saying in a personal feedback dialogue is sure to remain private. Sometimes, however, the feedback you want to share involves the whole class. For that, you maintain privacy by providing a summary and examples from unnamed sources, such as saying, "I found that more than 60 percent of this class's answers lacked proper footnotes. For instance, a number of you did not footnote the source of the article on climate change."

Online, you have many flexible tools that let you engage in private, personal feedback conversations. You can communicate via private chat, email, or text message to a single individual or share private documents via Google Docs. When you aim feedback at one student, everything you and the student say is best said after an explicit statement of confidentiality. It is a personal communication and is no other student's business unless the receiver invites others to read or hear it. In all methods, start with feedback that builds your students' trust in the feedback process. Influential researchers Wayne K. Hoy and Megan Tschannen-Moran (1999) claim that benevolence and reliability are two routes to trust. Giving students feedback that is warm (benevolent) reaffirms "confidence that one's well-being . . . will be protected," while reliable (consistently given) feedback builds trust (Hoy & Tschannen-Moran, 1999, p. 187, as cited in von Frank, 2010).

The most common form of feedback in schools is one-way feedback on a grade report. The teacher gives a grade and may or may not use a red pen to record a nice, but not very helpful, comment such as, "I like this" on the side of an essay. In those cases, the teacher misses the chance to initiate a feedback conversation with a pointed but open-ended question such as, "What support do you have for this claim?" to which the student can give a thoughtful response.

The least common form of feedback in the classroom—two-way communication—invites reciprocal responses. Business guru Peter F. Drucker (1954) was among the first to identify two-way communication as a means to ensure that evaluation reviews lead to improved job performance. In schools, an early form of two-way communication appeared as two-way writing evaluations conducted in ELA classrooms. One version of the two-way conference started with the teacher writing feedback comments on a student's story or essay before they met to review the teacher's suggestions and consider how the student intended to change the work. The teacher could discuss ideas with the student, listen to the student's ideas, and let the student choose a different way to write the story. Two-way feedback gains power and effectiveness by including such conditions as a focus on goals and flexibility to adjust (Hattie, 2009, 2012).

Many variations of this practice evolved over the years until researcher Hattie (2017) concluded that feedback has double the impact on student results than any other teaching strategy. He also notes that feedback is best experienced as a two-way communication process (Hattie, 2017). The student and the teacher enter a dialogue that best starts during a course's or grade level's first online session and ends on the last day of class. In this context, feedback to and from students and adults involved with learning in the classroom (especially the teacher) continues throughout the school year, adding to the mutual trust and respect that enhance deeper learning.

Remember that when giving feedback, trust comes first. The giving and getting of feedback both benefit when teachers consider each of the following types of feedback.

- **Warm feedback** is best used in the beginning when trust is low. Make specific, positive statements with an invitation to respond (for example, "I am pleased to see how you are listening to your partner's ideas and telling her the specifics you like").

- **Cool feedback** works best when trust is starting to show, and students welcome increasingly reciprocal conversations. With permission from a student, ask probing or clarifying open-ended questions, or make open-ended statements ("Since you gave me the OK, I'm going to push you to think harder about how you are interacting with your team. I mentioned your specific feedback yesterday. My question now is, "How do you feel you can use feedback to get your team members to follow through on your ideas?").

- **Hard feedback** is helpful when trust is strong between teacher and students, and when students make it clear that reciprocal conversation is welcome. With permission, offer recommendations to help the student improve a task or reach a goal, and check for action acceptance or modification ("I appreciated the list of ideas that you came up with. I think it was a big plus for you to ask your team members to help take action steps based on feedback. Bravo! Now, I'd like you to get the best ideas into a PLP with a clear action goal. Do you want to try that?").

Table 6.1 has examples of what a teacher might say or write so that students accept and act on a lesson's intended outcomes.

TABLE 6.1: Feedback and Trust

Warm Feedback (Starter, Low Trust)	Cool Feedback (Familiar, Some Trust)	Hard Feedback (Strong Trust)
• "I see excellent use of . . . ." • "On page 2, I see a good example of . . . ." • "Attention to detail is evident in the following areas . . . ." • "I like the way that you have . . . ." • "I think it is a good idea how you _____ because . . . ." • "I am pleased to see how you . . . ." • "What do you think about what I said?" • "How do you feel about what I have written?" • "Would you like to pick a meeting time so I can help with your next steps?"	• "I wonder if this fits your goal?" • "It looks like you wanted this to _____, but I'm not sure it does." • "What if . . . ?" • "Can you give me _____ examples of . . . ?" • "It is hard to tell what the goal was." • "I don't see what element is . . . ." • "It looks like you're missing . . . ." • "How do you think you can realign this task to your goal?" • "How can you make _____ more specific?" • "How can you improve . . . ?" • "I'd like you to send me an email with the times you can meet online."	• "Does this do what you wanted?" • "Does my suggestion help you meet your goal?" • "Will my recommendation consistently provide similar results?" • "How do you think my feedback will help you reach this goal?" • "What changes will you make to get this _____ straight?" • "What do you want to do so you reach your goal?" • "What do you think should happen next?" • "Where do you want to go from here?"

Source: Adapted from School Reform Initiative, 2020.

That is what distance-learning feedback *sounds* like. It *looks* like technology making it easier to give students feedback. You are probably already using the basic technology necessary for providing one-way feedback and for engaging students in two-way feedback. You need only prepare students for two-way feedback by adding to online tools with which they can move from being passive receivers of one-way feedback to joining you as givers and getters of the various types of feedback. The tools in table 6.2 are helpful for expanding two-way feedback.

TABLE 6.2: Two-Way Feedback Tools

Tool	Situation
LMS tools	Your LMS might allow you to make annotations on student work submitted through the program, which keeps you from having to download the assignment. Built-in rubrics with automatic point tallying will also save time. Your LMS might also let you program in feedback for assessments that are automatically graded. For example, an incorrect answer might generate a response asking the student to review a certain part of the week's recorded lecture. Your LMS might also allow audio feedback on submitted assignments.
Portfolios with lesson folders or a single feedback folder with skill subfolders	After students have received feedback, remind them to save and store any feedback documents in their portfolio in the correct locations.
Guiding rubric templates	When students are learning SEL, academic, or digital skills, provide them with a guiding rubric for each specific skill. Make a template (such as a Microsoft Word template) so you don't have to recreate the wheel each time.
Synchronous tools (FaceTime, Google Hangouts, or another video-conferencing app; recordings from Kaizena [www.kaizena.com], SoundCloud [https://soundcloud.com], or Vocaroo [https://vocaroo.com])	When you or students' peers want to share one-to-one feedback with students, it's best to pick tools that allow users to hear each other's tone of voice and even see each other's facial expressions, both of which play a part in feedback reception.
Asynchronous individual tools (LMS, private video-conferencing grid, chat messages, Google Docs, Microsoft Teams, ClassDojo)	When you are sharing one-to-one feedback with students, use a digital tool that allows you to do so with a schedule that is out of sync with other instructional events.
Asynchronous group tools (message board, LMS, ClassDojo, Google Docs, Microsoft Teams, Flipgrid, CampusKnot)	When you or students' peers are sharing one-to-many feedback, use a digital tool that allows for asynchronous group use.

Not all available tools are listed because they change so often. But this table and "75 Digital Tools and Apps Teachers Can Use to Support Formative Assessment in the Classroom," an article by former manager of innovation and learning at Northwest Evaluation Association, Kathy Dyer (2021), can be good resources to start with. As you end a feedback conversation, invite students to store any outcomes in an e-portfolio. Engaging students in a dialogue about feedback itself will also help them learn about the feedback process. Make that dialogue both a private and a class chat; again, students should store what they learn in their portfolios. The stored discoveries will make helpful guides on the side to which they can refer as they perform future tasks, practice skills, and try to improve their proficiency by giving feedback to and getting feedback from you and their peers.

What Are Online Feedback Best Practices?

John Hattie and Helen Timperley (2007) have collected in a meta-analysis multiple studies' findings about what makes feedback effective.

- Effective feedback should occur as soon after the event as possible.
- Effective feedback should be continuous.
- Effective feedback should be clear.
- Effective feedback must be goal directed and specific.
- Effective feedback must focus on a goal-oriented task or skill, not on a person.
- Effective feedback must provide opportunity for elaboration in manageable (chunked) units.
- Effective feedback has the most impact in a climate of respect and trust.
- Effective feedback has the most impact when it comes from a reciprocal agreement.

Not only must teacher-to-student feedback conversations meet these effectiveness criteria, but student-to-student feedback must as well. That means teachers need to explicitly instruct students about this process, thereby empowering them to take charge of their own learning. You can provide that instruction by offering a guiding rubric described in this chapter's Use Guiding Rubrics section. Additionally, because you are almost certainly employing both asynchronous and synchronous time in your class, consider this: feedback provided in asynchronous time may be the most powerful (Ene & Upton, 2018). To put this into practice, store your guiding rubric and playbook instructing students on how to engage in two-way feedback in their e-portfolios. Show them how to use the guiding rubric and give each other feedback in an early lesson or project. Throughout the year, have them call on the rubric to give feedback to and get feedback from their peers with whom they may work online throughout each quarter. Schedule time each quarter for asynchronous reviews of the rubric.

The following sections cover the best practices of creating rapport, using audio feedback, and using guiding rubrics during online feedback.

Create Rapport

A meta-analysis by digital education researcher Jeffrey Martin (2019) supports the necessity of rapport among students in online classes. This rapport expands on Hattie and Timperley's (2007) trust and respect criterion. Martin (2019) describes the positive effects of prompting student autobiographies; life-story books that answer personal questions that students select; "getting to know you" video-conference sessions via Google Hangouts, Zoom, or Skype; and family photo albums as tools and strategies to build trust and respect among students.

In addition, Martin (2019) urges inclusion of feedback in virtual classrooms. At the core of the online feedback process, Martin (2019) suggests, is the teacher's ability to engage students through actions like the following. This list includes in parentheses some examples of things teachers can say while creating rapport through these actions.

- Sharing academic and nonacademic interests and life histories
- Making course expectations and accomplishments clear (which occurs when you begin communicating them at the beginning of the school year or semester)
- Using interactive digital tools like tutorials, chat rooms, and message boards to go with a VCS, which have gallery grid controls (such as Zoom and Skype)
- Dialoguing about student interests and goals ("I see you have listed three possible goals for this project. Can we chat tomorrow at 2:20 about these?")
- Asking questions that allow for two-way feedback about the quality of student productivity ("What do you think is your best work in this portfolio?" "How can you make this goal statement more specific and measurable?" "How can you make this discussion of Maya Angelou's poems more relevant to your life?")
- Designing assessments that highlight feedback ("Each Friday, please complete the rubric by gathering and summarizing your partner's feedback." "After you finish the wall mural with your team, invite plus and minus comments from passersby with an attached comments box." "In this PLP, I would like to see you refine your goal statement and make the criteria you will use to show how well you have done more specific.")
- Collaborating with students in synchronous and asynchronous activities ("By Friday, I want each team to submit its plan. Here is the schedule this week for your asynchronous team meetings. On Tuesday, I will visit each team to observe how you collaborate and watch you make your project goal.")
- Engaging students in team-to-team feedback, which helps members of student teams bond as they aim for a common class goal ("This end-of-year project requires each team to contribute a piece. It's a jigsaw. In your teams during asynchronous time, you will research one of the women scientists listed and uncover the impact on her particular field. You will show each of the completed steps listed to another team. The schedule of matches is posted on the front bulletin board. Using the guiding rubric, each team will share its goal and its work, and ask for feedback. In the class periods allotted, each team will give and get feedback.")

Use Audio Feedback

Audio feedback, as mentioned earlier, is something teachers should consider. One study focused on English learners shows that recorded audio feedback, best accompanied by written feedback, has positive effects for online students (Olesova et al., 2011). Those benefits include "increased student engagement and greater understanding of the instructor's intent because of the availability of tone and intonation. Students perceive audio feedback as personal and enjoyable, and it helps increase their interest and feel the instructor's care" (Olesova et al., 2011, p. 40).

Use Guiding Rubrics

During distance learning, guiding rubrics are important for enhanced two-way feedback (Wisniewski, Zierer, & Hattie, 2020). The ideal format is a two-way guiding rubric that is shareable online (Lee et al., 2019). A rubric is a very good assessment tool and an excellent scaffolding mechanism. Through a lesson, the rubric serves as a guiding checklist as well as a way to structure the assignment (Panadero & Jonsson, 2013). The criteria clarify expectations in a variety of ways that help students organize their study.

With a guiding rubric in hand (or stored in an online folder), students know where to focus; they can find relevant details and reduce time spent on details that are not pertinent to the important concepts. Guiding rubrics also increase students' presence online (the result of emotional and mental engagement) by helping them understand what they need to do for an assignment. With a guiding rubric, students can participate more actively in two-way feedback with each other and their teacher in more positive working relationships. The rubric becomes a social contract blending rules, expectations, and assignment details, which are co-reviewed throughout the task and foster a community of learners (Roblyer & Wiencke, 2003).

Although guiding rubrics may look at first glance like grading rubrics, the two differ in spelling, purpose, and result. A *grading* rubric is an *assessment* tool that allows a teacher to award a grade based on benchmarks or quality indicators for each lesson or topic covered in a unit. It provides the minimum feedback in the form of a number or letter. To arrive at a grade from a rubric, the teacher lists benchmarks or criteria for the overall goal performance. Each benchmark indicates one criterion for judging the performance. For each criterion observed, the teacher assigns points. Points are scaled and totaled as a grade. Effective teachers will review a grading rubric at the start of a lesson or project so students are all equally informed of what it takes to earn grades. During the lessons, a teacher gives formative quizzes on the content, all graded to show students how well they are learning parts of the content, such as vocabulary words, dates, names, chapter questions, or sample problems. Teachers may compose course rubrics indicating how formative assessments (such as quizzes, essays, vocabulary tests, and discussions) add up to the final grade.

A *guiding* rubric is first and foremost an explicit *teaching* tool for the content and skills expected to result from alignment to a standard. As such, it always focuses on outcomes rather than on coverage of material. It is intended to teach concepts and skills by designating the most important elements of a standard as the guide through a lesson. Students engaged in active learning continuously refer to the rubric's benchmarks or criteria for quality to guide their activity and assess its complex cognitive outcome. As a result, students internalize the benchmarks so that they more deeply understand the key concepts and skills and transfer them to other lessons.

Guiding rubrics prepare students to self-assess what and how they learn, allowing teachers to shift the responsibility and increase student autonomy. Effective use of guiding rubrics asks that you give students these rubrics in age-appropriate formats at the start of a task or lesson so they know the expectations and how to improve their study. Figure 6.1 shows an elementary example of a guiding rubric, and figure 6.2 shows a secondary example. Students are responsible for storing the documents on their devices and sharing them as directed by the teacher so they can obtain feedback.

Name:	
I saw or heard that	
_____ You added many ideas.	
_____ Your ideas were different.	
_____ Your ideas added to others' ideas.	
_____ You helped make the final idea special.	
Project title:	**Date:**

FIGURE 6.1: Elementary example of a guiding rubric.

Team members: Jana, Pham, Luisa			
Date: 10/1			
Unit title: Investigating Cultures			
Skills: Teamwork, research, understanding other cultures			
Criterion	**Done Well**	**Improvement Needed**	**Agreed-On Means to Improve**
We used seven or more research questions.	We worked on these in class and together outside of class.		
We used reliable resources.	We used some resources from that country's government.		
Each team member fulfilled the given role.		We had trouble keeping time.	We'll use a timer next time.
We picked a driving question that interested us about the culture.	We did this together in class, but we worked on making ours a little different when we met asynchronously.		
Each team member followed classroom online norms and behaviors.	Yes		
Each team member added ideas during online brainstorming.	Yes, Pham especially had a lot of ideas.		
We selected multiple sources of information.	We had to choose at least five, and we did.		
Each team member checked information for accuracy and documented our online sources.	We did our Works Cited page.		
We helped each other when having difficulty understanding sources.	Jana had some questions about one source, so we talked about it in our group meeting.		
We found enough information to avoid biased answers.		We had trouble finding websites that gave us information about negatives.	We will ask our teacher.
We have enough data to draw valid conclusions to answer the driving question.		We think one more source that talked about the country's challenges would have helped us do this better.	We will each find another source.
We are pleased with our understanding of our issue or culture.	Yes!		

FIGURE 6.2: Secondary example of a guiding rubric.

Guiding rubrics benefit online students because they provide these students with an easily accessed document they can store on their digital devices, share online with peers and the teacher for feedback, and use to assess their progress in understanding key concepts and big ideas. With the proper encouragement and guidance on how to self-assess, every student can schedule his or her own time offline to capture feedback from peers, teachers, or mentors. As with the teaching of any new procedure, it's most beneficial to introduce the self-assessment process early in the school year. Set aside three to five hours to teach it. Start with a guiding lesson in which students can have fun arriving at a goal (for example, tying a shoe, building a tower of cards, or dropping an egg without breaking it). Set up the activity as a timed game. When all is done, give students three open-ended questions to answer: (1) "What did I do well to reach my goal?" (2) "What can I improve?" and (3) "What help do I need?" In a think-pair-share, encourage students to self-assess their process and outcome with these questions. For the all-class share, record responses on your digital whiteboard. Finish by discussing self-assessment with the same three questions. At the end of each of the first month's lessons, repeat the process with fun variations, but always end with a discussion of "How can I improve my self-evaluation?" In the following month, you may wish to add a guiding rubric on self-evaluation.

By including guiding rubrics as tools to focus assessment on academic content and skill goals with corrective feedback (cool or hard), teachers can allot time to asynchronously give and get feedback (Elola & Oskoz, 2016, 2017). During their asynchronous one-to-one time with the teacher, students don't have to worry about bells signaling that time's up. With sufficient time to incorporate feedback and to reflect, students are free to look back at what and how they have learned, consider multiple perspectives, and make plans to improve.

How Can Students Give Me Feedback?

One-way feedback from students to you can be informal or formal. For informal feedback, start with simple visual signals. A VCS often has built-in options for this; for example, you may have students raise an e-hand so you can gather immediate feedback about whether the whole class understands a concept. On Zoom, tell students how you want them to use this feature (for example, they can use the feature to ask questions or to vote). Students click on the icon labeled Participants at the bottom center of their computer or phone screen and then click on the button labeled Raise Hand. You respond verbally, or if you have a survey app ready, you can gather the questions or data and plan when you will respond.

You can rely on other conventional signals by asking students to visibly show a thumbs-up ("I got it"), a thumb to the side ("My understanding is cloudy; not sure"), or a thumbs-down ("I'm lost; help needed") or display green, yellow, and red index cards onscreen. The number of middle signals (thumb to the side, yellow) quickly tells you whether you are going to stop, reteach, and clarify for all or if you should schedule a time for a needs-to-know workshop. And red signs tell you that these options are all the more important. When the numbers at red are small, schedule time immediately after the whole-class session to meet with those whose feedback indicated a need for help. There is no general rule for how you respond to the feedback other than to use it to adjust your day's schedule.

For formal strategies intended to gather feedback, choose age-appropriate options, and determine how often and when you want student feedback. Here are options you can add to your toolkit.

- **Knows–Needs to Know–Learned (KNtKL) graphic organizer:** Students in grades 3–12 can share what they know about a topic you are about to teach or a skill you need to introduce. Distribute a Knows–Needs to Know–Learned graphic organizer to teams of three, and have them complete the What We Know and What We Need to Know columns in breakout rooms or together, asynchronously, prior to class. Describe the topic or skill so students have some ideas for the What We Need to Know column, and compile the feedback. Make a guiding rubric with the list of what they need to learn. After the lesson is done, go back and have the teams fill in the third column, What We Learned. The KNtKL graphic organizer, a variation of Donna Ogle's (1986) classic K-W-L (Knows–Wants to Know–Learned) format, is shown in figure 6.3.

- **Sticky notes:** During class, with their cameras on, students can send words via digital sticky notes to complete a prompt such as one of the following.
    - "The three most important things I know about _____ are . . . ."
    - "Today, my goal is . . . ."
    - "I hope that . . . ."
    - "I'm worried that . . . ."
    - "I don't understand why . . . ."
    - "Last night's homework was tough because . . . ."

  When class is ending, students can respond to after-class statements such as the following.
    - "I discovered that . . . ."
    - "My question is . . . ."
    - "I didn't understand . . . ."

  No sticky notes? Substitute an email, text, chat, or message on the message board.

- **Three-write-share:** To build positive relations, complete online sticky-note feedback with this activity. You can use small sticky notes on the Microsoft Word app to create online sticky notes. Set up student groups of three in breakout rooms so each group can show its work on the VCS (for example, Skype or Zoom) grid screen. Provide a prompt such as, "The best feature of this [collage, concept map, wall art, and so on] is . . ." to which the groups can provide positive feedback. Positive feedback shows the giver respects the receiver's work, effort, ideas, and so on and builds a feeling of trust. You can also make a prompt with an *I* statement, where a positive verb follows *I*, left open for students to fill in the blank ending. Your choice of prompt goes a long way to ensure that feedback is timely.

Topic:		
What We Know (K)	**What We Need to Know (NtK)**	**What We Learned (L)**

Source: Adapted from Ogle, 1986.

FIGURE 6.3: KNtKL graphic organizer.

Be sure to encourage sincere, honest, and specific feedback with each statement. Encourage each student in turn to make a unique statement or say, "I pass."

Name a recorder, and let each group agree on its response to share with you. Students need only internalize the positive feelings generated by sincere and honest recognitions directed from a positive prompt you provide.

- **Chat back:** Invite pairs or trios of students to open a chat thread where they respond in turn, giving each other specific feedback. Start with sentence stems. Engage with one stem or one rubric criterion at a time. You can rely on this technique for only peer-to-peer feedback, or you can include your comments in the discussion. For instance, after Manuel explains an idea, Susan goes next with her feedback and a question: "Manuel, I like the idea that we can ask for permission to paint murals in the Seventh Avenue substation. Whom do we ask?" You can jump in with a warm response such as, "Sue, I think that's a good idea. Manuel, I would also suggest that you _____ when you follow through with Sue's idea to . . . ."

How Can Students Give Effective Two-Way Peer Feedback?

Two-way peer feedback can produce advantages that improve student outcomes: students are more engaged, stimulated, better able to reach goals, and better equipped to transfer what they have learned (Boud & Molloy, 2013; Carless et al., 2006). When written, peer feedback leads to increased collaboration—crucial to virtual learning—and achievement.

With trust as the starting point, you can enrich two-way feedback with instruction on how to give feedback, keeping the best practices noted by Hattie and Timperley (2019) in mind. The following sections give two-way feedback options for the beginning of a lesson and during and following it.

Beginning a Lesson

Use a KNtKL variation of K-W-L to help readers in grades 3–12 organize information before, during, and after a unit or lesson in any subject. The KNtKL graphic organizer (figure 6.3, page 171) can engage students in a new topic, activate prior knowledge, share unit objectives, and allow teachers to monitor students' learning. Teachers can change the organizer's indicators to make it helpful for when students are giving and getting feedback (Hattie, 2012). The first column of the KNtKL organizer can list the criteria for the task (such as *reading aloud with fluency*). In the middle column, students type what they need to improve. In the last column, they assess their effort to improve with each indicator.

During a Lesson

Jill Fletcher (2019), a curriculum coordinator for the state of Hawaii, asks students to write down key themes, questions, and ideas about a topic or lesson on a single page (much like a study guide) and include artwork or imagery if they would like. Students can take this opportunity to write by hand or type, draw with different materials, or utilize graphics in different programs; middle and high school students can blend in video or other media. Students can create their graphic organizer in a tool like Canva or Google Slides, or photograph the paper version of their graphic organizer and submit it as an image file.

According to Fletcher (2020), the teacher's job in this case is to set up two rubrics and review both with students before they start the activity. The first rubric guides students' thinking about their process (in this case, the creative-writing process); the second rubric assesses the final outcome. To the very end, the teacher favors warm feedback. In formative contacts, the teacher bases feedback on the rubric criteria (for example, "I think you will improve the poem if you start off with a metaphor," or "Thanks for emailing the final copy of your poem. Bravo for including a metaphor in the first stanza as we discussed! I also liked how you expanded the metaphor through the poem. Now share with your team members to see what they say"). After students hear the teacher's feedback, they work with their partners for five or ten minutes to give warm feedback on each other's product. ("When you are done, email me the rubric with your partner's feedback and any changes. Don't make the changes, but tell me if you think they would help or not and why.")

Proposing a less time-consuming method, Tom Hines, a seventh-grade social studies teacher in Media, Pennsylvania, reports that he finds out what's up with WhatsApp (www.whatsapp.com; personal communication, September 23, 2019). He videoconferences with students to review the guiding rubric. Then, he breaks students on the gallery grid into groups of five to discuss the rubric (using Instagram Stories' polling feature) and see if there are questions. Via chat, students send questions they can't answer within their teams. He responds on the chat so all can see his responses (T. Hines, personal communication, September 23, 2019).

Bev Fisher, a retired chemistry teacher in Chicago, asked her students to maintain an online lab journal (personal communication, October 2020). At the start of a unit, she invited lab partners to review the journal rubric. It laid out the lab technique criteria with sketches and summary descriptions of what students would learn. Fisher allotted time for students to make daily journal entries, but they did summaries as homework and shared them with her on a schedule. After she spot-checked the summary emails, she added feedback (B. Fisher, personal communication, October 2020).

The first semester was all warm feedback as Fisher built trust with students. She left it up to each student to follow through on her feedback. One by one, they began to respond to her warm invitations and encouragement (B. Fisher, personal communication, October 2020). In the second semester, Fisher added cool feedback with suggestions for improvement. Every eight weeks, she required students to use her feedback and their self-assessment to tell her how they improved their lab techniques. (Such feedback might be, "I'm pleased to see how you are asking your teammates to check your technique. To improve your technique, I want you to follow through on at least one suggestion you get after the next lab and implement it. When you do your own rubric, tell me how you followed through. Thanks.")

Following a Lesson

To follow up after a lesson, you can have students respond to a sentence stem on a message board using electronic sticky notes, or you can have them share their responses in a chat. For example, you could show students, "Please post on this class's message board your completion of this stem: *The most important thing I learned and used from peer feedback in this lesson's labs was . . . .*" No names are needed. When students are ready, they can access the stem responses on their own (the teacher can take a screenshot of the responses if the class has used a chat) and give more detailed responses in a shared rubric.

If you want to organize and facilitate added two-way feedback at the end of a lesson, try Flipgrid (https://flipgrid.com). With this tool, you can create a screen to facilitate discussion of the day's topic (for example, the driving question on the topic of flotation could be, Why does a boat float?).

Students post video responses to the driving question, which appear in your gallery grid. At the end of a screen-share lesson, you review the guiding rubric you gave to students at the lesson's start so they can assess the final outcome and reflect on what they learned. You then respond with feedback to their entries. The tool allows a process reversal, with each student requesting specific feedback for one or more criteria by posting the question in his or her own box in the grid. In this way, students can ask why they were scored the way they were according to the rubric.

How Do I Engage Students in Peer-to-Peer Feedback?

Teachers for grade 3 and higher who adopt feedback as a primary instructional strategy are most likely to reap the benefits of peer-to-peer feedback when they integrate the evidence-based strategies given in this chapter throughout every school day both synchronously and asynchronously. In whatever grade a teacher introduces feedback, it helps to continue developing students' feedback skills with at least one guiding rubric each month. For example, you can end a yearlong unit with digital skill outcomes as reasons for developing feedback skills. If you are teaching primary students, a yearlong keyboarding goal might be appropriate. Over the year, a rubric will guide assessments showing how well the students can perform writing tasks with the alphabet and number keys (the first eight weeks), manipulate the F keys (the second quarter), and so on. In pairs with a guiding rubric aimed at the basic digital skills, students observe partners entering data for a grade-level-appropriate writing task and review the final product. When students show they are becoming confident and competent giving and getting feedback under your watchful eye during synchronous lessons with the target skill (for example, manipulating F keys), you can move them into asynchronous team lessons to enrich their meetings and increase productivity. At this point, peer feedback has to stand on its own, with students able to manage constructive communication. Gradually, you can release secondary students to give and get feedback with smartphones or to exchange feedback via FaceTime, chat, and so on.

Figures 6.4 and 6.5 show examples of writing and digital skills standards and directions for grade 3 students to practice peer-to-peer feedback.

Name: Darian	**Date:** April 4
Standard: "With guidance and support from adults, use technology to produce and publish writing (using keyboarding skills) as well as to interact and collaborate with others" (W.3.6).	
Resource we will use: *Nikki and Deja* by Karen English (2007)	
Directions: Practice your keyboarding skills, including using the Tool menu. Also use the spell checker and review your work. Type one answer to this prompt: "In today's chapter, Nikki and Deja showed they were friends when . . ." Use the spell checker to correct misspellings. If you had none, please say so on your form.	
When you are finished: Share your example on Google Drive with your partner. That partner will review your work and answer the prompts in the guiding rubric. Your partner will put the finished guiding rubric on Google Drive in that same folder.	

Source for standard: National Governors Association Center for Best Practices (NGA) & Council of Chief State School Officers (CCSSO), 2010a.

FIGURE 6.4: First peer-feedback task for grade 3.

Directions

1. Record your name, the date, and your teammate's name. That teammate will write your feedback.
2. Agree on your team role and what you will do in that job.
3. Make sure you have your rubric.
4. Look at the criteria, and type an *X* in the Yes column or the Not Yet column, depending on whether your partner met that criterion. Keep the rubric close so you can look at it while you work with your teammate.
5. Put your responses to the prompts on Google Drive, and let your partner know the guiding rubric is ready.
6. Your partner will put the finished guiding rubric on Google Drive in that same folder and let you know when it's ready.
7. Read the feedback and send a thank-you to your partner.

Name:	Date:

Teammate name:

I think you expected:

I like this because:

What you did well is:

Yes	Criteria	Not Yet
	Your feedback meets the standard, and all the words are spelled correctly.	
	You helped teammates use the spell checker.	
	You helped teammates use the Tool menu.	
	You gave teammates specific ideas to help with keyboarding.	
	You did your assigned team job.	

FIGURE 6.5: Second peer-feedback task for grade 3.

*Visit **go.SolutionTree.com/technology** for a free reproducible version of this figure.*

With age-appropriate content, secondary teachers can replicate the example by sending the rubric document to each student with portfolio instructions and a review of how students and teachers can talk with each other and share documents. Figure 6.6 (page 176) is your teacher playbook. It will guide your presentation of the rubric to your students.

In figure 6.4, a given standard does not need to call for feedback, but feedback is the chosen strategy to initiate collaboration. Note the selection of a single-point rubric as the preferred format so that students can respond with warm prompts: "What I think you did well is . . ." and "I like this because . . . ." Model and check every student's ability to perform the specialized keyboarding tasks prior to teamwork.

1. Share and review the student instructions, making the expectations (the standard) and resources clear.
2. Share the guiding rubric. (The example in figure 6.4, page 174, uses the guiding rubric in figure 6.5, page 175.)
3. Explain the vocabulary, including *cool feedback*, *warm feedback*, *hard feedback*, *criteria*, *prompts*, and other key words you select from this lesson.
4. When the activity is complete, have an all-class discussion. Ask for thumbs-up or thumbs-down to the following questions.
   - Did you receive specific answers in the Yes column?
   - Did you receive specific answers in the Not Yet column?
   - Who liked having specific and positive feedback?
5. Give warm feedback to the responses from the form in figure 6.5. Direct the feedback to the whole class prior to partner feedback.

FIGURE 6.6: Two-way feedback guiding rubric—Teacher playbook.

In addition to formal feedback, informal strategies such as the following can promote productive student feedback skills.

- **Warm word hugs:** In the first week of K–3 classes, start daily online circles with warm verbal hugs. Provide a prompt such as, "I like it when you . . ." and then move around the class so each student can offer a verbal hug—such as "I'm happy that you . . ." or "I think it is a good idea when you say . . ."—preferably to one other student. To make sure that hugs are as equitably distributed as possible, model first by explaining what you are doing and why. Tell the class that each morning, you will go around the circle and give a verbal hug to five students. By the end of the week, each student will get a hug. Explain that on some days, someone might need a special hug—because that person had a rough day, for example, or shared that he or she lost a pet. Otherwise, warm hugs are the norm: "Yesterday, I was glad that Rico . . ." or "I was pleased when Shannon . . . ." Gradually, ask for volunteers to help you, but keep an eye on equitable distribution.

- **EdWordle poster:** Make a *Warm feedback is . . .* word cloud using EdWordle (www.edwordle.net) to share with the class onscreen. Hang a large copy behind you so students will see it each time you are online with them. In the week that you hang it, spend a few minutes each day discussing one or two of the criteria for friendly and helpful feedback and modeling what the criteria sound like.

- **Product and performance rubrics:** While students are working on—and after they have completed—a writing assignment, an art project, a science demonstration, a dance performance, or the like, match students in mixed-ability pairs. Each student will share with the other a completed task using words or images with the guiding rubric you gave the class (for example, students might share a sketch of a favorite character from a story they just read). Model how to use the rubric with warm feedback. After checking for understanding, ask pairs to write rubric-based warm feedback to each other.

- **Say-it-with-love go-round:** With the class, ask each student to share a personal talent while everyone listens. Pull a name from a hat (or use an app like Pickster for Apple at https://apple.co/3aXFFqv or Random Name Picker for Android at https://bit.ly/33tdZWt to do the same thing electronically). The chosen person says, "I love it when you are able to [talent]," or "It's great to have [talent] because . . . ." Do five a day until the go-round is complete.

- **Friendlies for all:** Show students how to send sticky notes to each other. Each day, ask a volunteer to select a peer who hasn't yet been focused on to pick the "you're it" student. All the rest of the class will send a warm feedback statement in this form: "[Student name], I like it when you . . ." or "What is special about [student name] is . . . ."

- **Three statements:** After pairs or trios have worked together on a shared task, review guidelines for warm feedback, model an example, and then invite each group's members to give each other responses to these three statements.

    a. "What I liked about working on this task with you was . . . ."

    b. "I think we would do better if . . . ."

    c. "You could help me do better by . . . ."

- **We agree:** This is a version of three statements. After pairs have worked together on a shared task, ask them to make a single list agreeing on the pluses and minuses and ways to improve how they worked together. You can ask them to follow a guiding rubric for teamwork.

How Do I Keep Track of the Correspondence Generated by Two-Way Feedback?

To keep track of correspondence generated by two-way feedback, first keep it small and simple.

If you are a primary teacher, select just one yearlong outcome, such as the keyboarding example discussed earlier in this chapter. Use the formative reviews scheduled throughout the year to introduce two-way feedback. For instance, in the first quarter, concentrate on one set of skill outcomes: keyboarding the letters and numbers. Start the guiding rubric with criteria identifying each piece of that skill in a simple medium, such as a one-sentence tweet or an *I learned* stem. Gradually add other keyboarding skills, shown on emails or a Facebook post. For students who struggle at any point while learning to keyboard, schedule needs-to-know labs so they can receive added guidance. With the rubric, you alone give feedback to the students so you can model how to use the rubric. Gradually increase student challenge: give students a more challenging writing task, require an increased show of proficiency with the keyboarding skill, and invite students to tell you what they are doing well, what they find tough to do, and what they need help with. The last question is an invitation for students to join in the assessment by opening the door for you to give feedback. From this point forward, encourage the students to say and do more as self-assessors with the guiding rubric as a road map. More and more, you can say, "I see that you have only one example. May I suggest some others?" By providing warm encouragement to help with an open-ended invite, you are more likely to draw even the shyest students into the feedback dialogue.

If you are a middle or secondary school teacher, you can do more during small start-up conversations with teams of students. After you have given a lesson assignment to the whole class, you divide the students into teams, still in asynchronous time. While four-fifths of your teams work on the task, you visit one team online via the gallery grid, interrupting the task, and introduce the guiding rubric. It could be a digital skills rubric for applying keyboarding skills to an app such as Kahoot! or CampusKnot. Start by modeling the guiding rubric. You show how to give warm feedback with this rubric. Check for understanding before you leave this first team and go to each other team in turn via your gallery grid. In a second visit, show each team how to use the chat feature so that every team member will make a warm statement about the team's helpfulness with the task. Specify which indicators on the rubric they can use to assist them in this round-robin feedback. When this is done, ask the team to brainstorm responses to you: "What did you do that helped the team learn how to give feedback? What was not helpful? What could you have done differently?" You will likely have to encourage the team members that it's OK to give you feedback via anonymous answers to those three questions. If the level of trust required for all three is too high, start with the first question, and model warm feedback they might consider (for example, "Your instructions were very specific" or "I liked your examples"). In weeks after that, follow up with suggestions to improve (for example, "You used big words I don't understand, like *onomatopoeia*, and didn't show me examples. I would do better with an easier word and an example"). Give this specific feedback via an *I* message.

Engaging students in two-way conversations online can be difficult. What you do to encourage participation makes a significant difference. Hattie (2009, 2012) notes that a focus on outcomes leads to an emphasis on evidence-based best practices of two-way feedback. These tough-love devices can raise the quality and quantity of students' voices in chat rooms and gallery grid discussions. Through round-robin responses to sentence stems, technical hand signals, surveys, guiding questions, and guiding rubrics for assessing participation, you can gently overcome student hesitance to participate in the crucial conversations you initiate and continue throughout the school year.

Conclusion

Feedback is a powerful instructional strategy. Hattie's (2009, 2012) research says that it's the most powerful method at your disposal for increasing student achievement. As this chapter's opening quotation indicates, feedback is about encouraging learning and providing students with signposts and directions along the way to bring them nearer to independence. Feedback is best shared in ways that encourage students to become independent, self-managed learners. Immediate, specific, constructive, ongoing, goal-oriented feedback raises achievement, improves relationships, strengthens trust, and enhances student learning and engagement. Feedback can be a thread tying together the tapestry of students' learning online. To obtain the best results, first, make sure students feel trust, and second, make sure they learn how to become partners in the feedback process. The partnership that results from your high expectations and close attention to the development of feedback skills benefits individual learners and helps build the community of trust that enables feedback to take hold. Because the community of learners in an online environment, be it physically separated by carrels and dividers in a walled classroom or by remote locations across a district, is so scattered, those receiving effective feedback—from teacher to student, from student to teacher, and from one student to another—must trust the words are meant with benevolence. That will help everyone reach their goals no matter what intervening spaces might block deeper learning.

MY TAKEAWAYS

What three ideas from this chapter can best help you shift to digital instruction and prepare all students to be effective digital learners? Record your ideas here so you can make a plan later.

1. _____

2. _____

3. _____

7

Assessment *in a* Digital Environment

In education, the term assessment *refers to the wide variety of methods or tools that educators use to evaluate, measure, and document the academic readiness, learning progress, skill acquisition, or educational needs of students.*
—**The Glossary of Education Reform**

A story to start: "These are terrible grades," Lane's father growled. "And how can anyone be so stupid as to get a B– in religion?"

Lane stared at her shoes.

"So what does it mean? How do you explain these?"

Lane mumbled. "Don't know."

"Don't know? What did Mrs. Schmidt say?"

"Nothin'. It's the grade that counts."

In this chapter, you will read how you can drive assessment by engaging students with a plethora of digital tools and strategies to make a shift to deeper learning outcomes. You will examine how to assess virtual learning that embraces shifts from traditional grading and standards-based grading to standards-based assessment, in which you embed two-way feedback to drive how you most productively evaluate, document, and coach students' digital learning performances with the standards in mind. If you have already moved to standards-based grading, you will see how to adopt simple digital tools to initiate the transformation of your assessment practices so you go beyond letter grades to assess standards-aligned performances with two-way feedback.

The chapter begins with a self-assessment tool that you can adapt to review your current performance on the road to deeper learning outcomes, gather feedback from dialogue with your professional peers, and shift any vestiges of traditional brick-and-mortar grading practices to adoption and refinement of assessments that help you chart student improvement in your digital environment. Aided by technology, forward-looking teachers have the necessary means to reengineer their assessment tools so that these tools—including guiding rubrics and feedback—instruct as well as measure. You will explore online, lesson-embedded assessment practices (many of which will already be familiar to you from your brick-and-mortar experience) and engage students in them. Afterward, you will have the knowledge to adapt and adopt what you read in this chapter so you can expand options for two-way feedback in digital assessments. These options will enrich your coaching of student performance as a guide on the side in digitally rich brick-and-mortar classrooms and especially in remote classrooms. In the end, the chapter will help you extend the notion of two-way feedback with a playbook that allows you to make your own guiding rubrics for a highly engaging digital classroom. It asks you to invite your students to give you feedback on the quality of your digital instruction so that you have the information you need to improve how you teach while you shift to a more digital learning world.

How Can Technology Enhance the Assessment Process?

In order to answer this question, it is important that everyone understand assessment is broader and deeper than putting grades on formative quizzes, worksheets, and final exams. It's arguable that documenting achievement of recalled information through traditional letter grades as the principal source of assessment is ineffective (Klein, 2020) and a waste of time. More likely, the quest for grades stymies academic motivation and inhibits meaningful learning (Kirschenbaum, Simon, & Napier, 2020) when addressing 21st century students' deeper learning needs. A single letter or number on a quiz, test, or essay does little to teach a student. An *A* may reinforce a good feeling. It may make a student feel proud. Or it can result in the opposite. A *D* or *F* may discourage a student. There is no evidence to back up claims that grades motivate students to work harder and achieve more. What traditional grades do well is provide specific numbers for teachers to record in their system, for high achievers to boast about on college applications, and for report cards to keep interested parents up to date.

Grading and *assessing* are not synonyms, although they are commonly mixed up in common parlance. Traditional grading provides a single number for reporting a percentage of knowledge gained in a specific period of time. Assessment is a process that helps teachers inform students and parents or guardians about how the students are improving (or not) in key skills.

Since their advent in 1785 at Yale University (Grading in education, n.d.), report cards have dribbled down to elementary schools. Their original emphasis was to announce to college students that their professor had determined their work was sufficient to pass a course. By the end of the 20th century, elementary schools digressed from spotlighting basic academic achievement. Many added effort, attendance, friendliness, homework completion, and citizenship to the mix. Some relied on grades to reward compliance (Tyre, 2010). In the worst scenarios, some teachers have used grades to punish boredom and noncompliance, especially with students of color who live in poverty and Black and Brown boys identified as disobedient (Palmer, 2021).

Following the advent of universal standards at the turn of the 21st century, some schools adopted standards-based grading, ostensibly to return content evaluation to center stage. Rather than traditionally grade students on a competitive curve, teachers who use standards-based grading measure student performance against standards adopted by their states. Teachers are required to align the knowledge and skills they test with these standards. Students are commonly graded as exceeding, meeting, or falling below the standard, again with a number or letter grade as the end result. Grades have remained; the process, for good or bad, is standardized.

On the positive side, standardized students are not pitted against each other. Each supposedly has an equal opportunity to meet (show competence) or exceed (show proficiency) a standard when performing a skill (the verb in a standard statement), including applying that skill and others to deeper understanding of the standard's stated content (the stated direct object). For instance, these standards each follow the typical verb-to-direct-object pattern: "Represent and solve problems involving multiplication and division" (Common Core mathematics standard 3.OA.A; NGA & CCSSO, 2010b) and "Use mathematical representations to support the claim that atoms, and therefore mass, are conserved during a chemical reaction" (Next Generation Science Standard HS-PS1-7; NGSS Lead States, 2013).

The negative side turns up whenever schools set the standard at a level that is substantially higher than previous achievement levels they expected. In addition, many schools give little help to students so they can connect the standard with the tasks they are assigned, the graded tests they get handed back, and the outcomes they are expected to reach. As a result, a relatively high percentage of students fail at least some part of the standards in the first year, including an especially high percentage of non-college-bound students in schools attended by poor Black and Brown populations (Feldman, 2018). In addition, the emphasis is still on a "grade" that a student earns. No danger signs are erected when the quality of instruction falls short or hidden biases present themselves. Unless teachers make the more skillful effort to teach with the grading rubrics that they are supplied with and turn each rubric into an instructional strategy rather than a summative, single-digit report, they lose the opportunity to stimulate interest in stated learning outcomes and the content and skills that drive understanding to deeper outcomes.

To move beyond assigning grades, including standards-aligned grades, means you must do more with standards assessment. If you want to ensure all students have an equitable chance to become competent or, better yet, proficient, it's important to stir their interest, enable their talents, and give intrinsic reasons for learning what your curriculum says. To teach in this way necessitates more than saying, "No more grades." It requires you to continue instructing as if grades were the most important outcome from a lesson, project, or course. With the digital shift, you have a unique opportunity, much of it provided by the many digital tools available for you to assess rather than grade. You can start with a commitment to a different way of assessing students' achievement and skill development in the context of what they need to know and do as 21st century deeper learners. The different way starts with a new mindset about the nature of learning, in which assessment that helps students explicitly learn more and more deeply from the coursework you and they are assessing together becomes the starting gate. In this context, assessment is never a red grade at the top of a quiz, test, or essay they produce to show what they recall from what you taught in a lesson or entire course. It is never a summative mark on a report card. In digitally rich classrooms that take standards seriously, you call on standards-based assessment, a process that empowers students to achieve at the highest level by listening to your feedback and determining what they will do differently in the immediate future.

To help you assess your own competence as a standards-aligned assessor committed to deeper learning outcomes for all students, you can examine your own aims and performance as you consider how to increase the impact of your assessments and move beyond grades. You could also chunk the indicators into groups, taking only a few at a time as you ask your peers in a collaborative team to observe how you implement a chunk and give you suggestions to improve.

In the playlist that follows (figure 7.1, page 184), you will find criteria for a dual assessment of factors that influence your assessment practice. Follow the playbook after the playlist so you can rate yourself and think of reasons for each rating. Note how this model begins with simple numbers to rate criteria but moves from numbered feedback to a request for an action plan. This is but one approach that incorporates feedback, so assessment becomes a helpful learning tool. In addition to using it for a solo self-assessment, you can transform the items into driving questions for a yearlong discussion of assessment's role in engaging students for deeper learning outcomes. As you will note after the playlist and playbook, you can share your selections as a template and then enter into an ongoing online chat about them with your peers.

Teacher Playlist

Consider the following criteria for assessment practices.

1. _____ You want students to develop intrinsic motivation and own their learning as shown by less concern about points and grades and fewer questions such as, "Will this be on the test?" or "Will this be graded?"

2. _____ You present lesson goals and project outcomes in student-friendly, conversational language with specific results identified (for example, "I'd like you to explain why you chose these three strategies to solve your measurement problem," or "Please review the five criteria that identify how your video tells a story").

3. _____ You provide the scaffolds and schedules for synchronous and asynchronous works so that each student can achieve a standards-aligned lesson outcome.

4. _____ On quizzes and tests of knowledge as well as all other products returned to students, you provide specific warm, cool, or hard feedback.

5. _____ Your lessons require products at the application level for the lesson's standard (for example, "A story video will show me that you can use the tools to tell a story with a beginning, middle, and end").

6. _____ For results that are embedded in a product (for example, an essay, slide share, video, or lab report), you provide guiding rubrics that allow for feedback from you and peers.

7. _____ For results that are embedded in a product (for example, an essay, slide share, video, or lab report), you provide guiding rubrics that allow for self-assessment.

8. _____ You prepare students to self-assess and reflect on their own learning by modeling and coaching each.

9. _____ You encourage students to select their own activities for meeting a mutually agreeable lesson or deeper-learning project outcome.

10. _____ You provide students with the skill development to learn from you and their peers.

11. _____ You provide assistance and support for students to set and meet personal goals in ways that are conducive and adaptable to face-to-face, hybrid, and digital learning spaces.

12. _____ For each lesson or PBDL outcome, your rubrics allow for digital feedback that shows how students can take specific steps based on your feedback to improve their performance (for example, move from basic performance to competence and proficiency).

13. _____ To improve student performance, you introduce digital tools (for example, sticky notes, chat threads, emails, social media, and so on) to provide personalized, constructive feedback, which enables each student to improve and accelerate the accomplishment of mutually agreed-on outcomes.

14. _____ You show that you value equity by assessing your own self-assessment practices to see that any students of color who live in poverty receive equitable opportunities for two-way feedback and necessary support to achieve their personal goals and end-of-year grade-level outcomes.

15. _____ To help parents or to meet distinct requirements that grades are required, you transform your rubrics and test scores into grades backed by digital files.

Teacher Playbook

Review this playbook for instructions on completing the preceding self-assessment.

1. To assess yourself with the indicators, provide two scores in the blank space beside each indicator. The first score indicates the value you attribute to an indicator. The second indicates where you currently stand with actually embedding the value in your digital classroom practices. Each score is based on a scale of 0 to 5.

Value
0 = I don't value this.
1 = It's a nice idea, but not very important to me.
2 = It's a good idea, and I need to learn more how-to.
3 = It's an important value for driving my students' learning.
4 = I strongly value this and want to do it better.
5 = I highly value this idea and want to introduce it to colleagues.

Performance
0 = I don't do this.
1 = I like the idea, and I will study it more.
2 = It's a good idea, and I need to try out a strategy to see how the idea works for me.
3 = It's an important value for driving my students' learning, and I will include it in a personalized learning plan for next semester.
4 = I strongly value this, and I will work with my supervisor or PLC to plan, implement, and assess a lesson or project.
5 = I am doing this on a regular, intentional basis with a high degree of satisfaction in lessons and projects and want to refine it by planning, doing, and assessing lessons that will result in measurable deeper learning outcomes for my class.

2. Tabulate your scores, and look for how a value matches or does not match your current performance. This will provide a snapshot of what you can do to bring more productive assessment to your digital classroom.

3. Rank the top five items you most want to improve. Go to your notes at the end of prior chapters, and recall items that will help you make a personal improvement plan based on these responses. Take one step at a time, and work with your grade-level team or your PLC to implement and then reassess each item. At a minimum, you can make a plan and implement it. And you can assess how you close the gap between what you value and your increasing level of skill as a teacher who calls on assessment to move beyond grading and to advance students' deeper learning.

FIGURE 7.1: Teacher playlist and playbook for assessing student performance.

How Do I Assess Student Learning in a Digitally Rich Learning Environment?

There seems to be little consensus on how to assess virtual student learning. This does not need to be so. Here's why.

- **Assessment still drives instruction:** Digital assessment is not a three-headed monster. Digital assessment tools promise to make standards-based assessment less work and more informative.

- **Most standards-aligned curricula have not changed:** It is still possible to assess student performance aligned with a preK–12 curriculum. Even if a teacher's curriculum is not aligned with a federal, state, or provincial set of standards, he or she need only search online for standards that will help in planning standards-aligned lessons and projects for online instruction.

- **Remote learning expands opportunities for teachers to adopt paperless assessment practices:** This reduces the rote work of assessment in situations when district policy requires you to grade. For example, after you have engaged students with a guiding lesson rubric, you can move it through a digital rubric maker. This "speeds up the grading process by allowing you to click on the appropriate criterion and automatically tally the points and calculate the grade" (Fiock & Garcia, n.d.). Chat rooms, VCS grids, Google Docs, and Microsoft Word documents stored in folders provide opportunities to give and get feedback and story documents to show a complete body of work in an organized fashion.

- **Digital assessment tools make it easier to communicate with parents about student progress:** More frequent and clearer reports are a direct path to assuaging parent concerns. For instance, sharing assessment documents with the parents of struggling students provides them with more clarity and with opportunities to engage more deeply in giving the students positive help.

These reasons make it sensible and practical for teachers to not only eliminate the range of concerns about online assessment but also organize online lessons that provide valuable opportunities to assess for deeper learning outcomes. Those changes reinforce the value of assessing standards-aligned skills and content, as well as encourage students to transform from digital natives to digital learners.

As you uncovered in chapter 6 (page 161), teachers have multiple opportunities to introduce better two-way feedback into a process that highlights assessment as a teaching strategy (Fiock & Garcia, n.d.). The following list is a start-up playlist of additional ideas. All the methods for providing feedback given in table 6.2 (page 165) are available for assessment as well.

- **Socrative** (www.socrative.com) helps with digital assessments in two ways. First, you can use it to set up your own content quizzes and analyze immediate results. Because its analysis feature keeps your focus on patterns and outcomes, you can give corrective feedback centered on fine-tuning instructions to obtain lesson results and move away from individual grades. Second, you can use the same feature to set up a guiding rubric. Instead of stating a criterion, you can ask a question such as, "How well are you able to [enter a standard statement or sub-statement]?" as the criterion. You can use the reciprocal responses as fodder for added discussion, replanning the lesson to fill in gaps, or save them for added responses at other places in the lesson or project.

- **Nearpod** (https://nearpod.com) is an app that connects to Google Play. With it, students can choose virtual reality, science and mathematics simulations, and other content via open-ended questions, polls, quizzes, collaborative boards, and more. With its emphasis on student agency, teachers can only access a student's page with his or her OK. This site's high bar on student agency can work against teacher-guided assessment. Try sharing a document or a file of a guiding rubric on your whiteboard. Students copy the document so you can teach them how to complete rubrics and share them with you, along with the other work they finish on this app.

You can also access Darby (2021) to further expand your possibility playlist. No matter which assessment tool you select, that tool is only valuable if it shows to what degree a student has achieved a standard skill-aligned outcome.

Can I Abandon Assessment in Certain Situations?

Even if your system crashes and all virtual connections are lost in cyberspace—whether for one class period or several days—do not eliminate assessment. In the worst possible scenarios that obliterate a well-planned lesson, you will have ready-to-go emergency lessons or activities in your back pocket, just as you would have for a substitute teacher. Every moment is a teachable moment. If student stress is high and interferes with your intended lesson, you can drop that lesson and switch to one for calming students' nerves. If calm nerves are the outcome at the end of a short game, soothing read-aloud, meditation, humorous video, or some other SEL activity, you can fit your assessment questions to the activity. Prepare a multiday reading assignment—guided by five or six questions and a rubric—that students will save in their portfolios for their return online in case they will be offline for a longer period of time.

How Can I Address Cheating in Distance Learning?

Research doesn't support claims of rampant cheating in online learning. In fact, at the college level, the few statistics available indicate that online cheating is slightly less prevalent than in-class cheating, with the majority happening via plagiarism and substitute testers. There are no substantive studies that address K–12 cheating in remote learning. That is not to say it is not happening. Here is what you can do to help prevent it.

- Set norms and procedures that dissuade cheating, and teach the rules for citing all direct and paraphrased quotes.
- Write critical-thinking, open-ended questions that students cannot answer by doing an online search.
- When in doubt, dialogue with students in a needs-to-know lab. Identify examples of students not identifying authors, and coach students on the needed changes. If examples still appear, engage in one-to-one coaching and restorative practice.
- Monitor students while they test by watching the whole class via the VCS.

How Do I Assess Online Cooperative Learning?

Cooperative learning is a go-to tool for initiating collaboration in a digital classroom. Remember that assessment drives instruction; assessment of how students work together can also raise their level of concern and drive quality work with you and your peers. If you are assessing students' cooperation in their teams, you can increase productivity by heightening their skills through constructive feedback. You sharpen the focus on what skills students can develop when you add a guiding rubric for teamwork or collaboration. When all is said and done, cooperative learning gives you the most well-researched and battle-tested instructional strategy (Harris, Brown, & Harnett, 2014).

Cooperative learning formats make it easy for students to learn how to give constructive feedback in any of the digital learning scenarios. First, as you would in a brick-and-mortar classroom, prepare your rubric. Second, decide on what digital tools (for example, the VCS grid, email, and Microsoft Word documents) you will need to share the rubric with all in the class, prepare them to use your selections well, and check for readiness. When you prepare students to give constructive feedback using a two- or three-way reciprocal process and digital tools that allow for feedback, you double down on their achievement motivation (cooperative learning's impact on achievement multiplied by feedback's impact on achievement means even higher achievement).

Be forewarned, however, that peer assessment doubled by cooperative learning requires careful preparation. Avoid getting in the weeds with students making light of self-assessment. It requires a maximum of mutual trust, modeling, open and honest discussion, and the highest expectations for honesty; that combination can bring unparalleled engagement as you present and guide the ultimate opportunity for student empowerment. It's imperative to take your time teaching the skills of cooperation and feedback and strengthening the skills with your coaching feedback, preferably with guiding rubrics.

The elementary-level example in figure 7.2 is accompanied by instructions for engaging young students to assess their teamwork. This is a first guiding rubric for a classroom as young as preK. As students show increasing ability to manage the technology, you call on the rubric as a multidimensional teaching aid. You teach and refine the skills with feedback that takes students back to the rubric's criteria. Eventually, as with any lesson, your aim with lessons on feedback given and received in teams is for students to internalize the skills and self-manage their team assessments when working together to improve productivity.

Name:	Date:
I shared ideas with my partner.	👍 👎
I listened to my partner.	👍 👎
I took turns with my partner.	👍 👎

FIGURE 7.2: Elementary-level example of a cooperative learning assessment template.

*Visit **go.SolutionTree.com/technology** for a free reproducible version of this figure.*

Squeeze in the prep for peer assessment instruction during online times where collaboration is natural (for example, chat rooms, partner problem solving, and asynchronous interviews). Grow how students perform roles, follow guidelines, make decisions, and so on by first modeling a practice and then coaching their adoption of the practice until it becomes a competent skill they can do on their own. During each successive use, add new skills and new instructions. Those scaffolded instructions result in students advancing their cooperative learning applied to assessment, digital skills, and content-area skills. Ask students to keep the instructions in their digital portfolios for review at the start of each lesson.

Adjust the following instructions to your classroom configuration. These instructions assume a hybrid or remote classroom with one-to-one capability. Assess your K–3 class to determine prior experience with cooperative learning and guiding rubrics.

1. Share the rubric and your face on a split screen.
2. If you have prepared students on how to add an emoji or another symbol for every rubric criterion, invite each of them to store the document.
3. Explain to students that they are learning how to tell you what they do well when they work with a partner.
4. Match distant partners in breakout rooms on the VCS grid. Match face-to-face partners sitting at a single computer station.
5. Walk students through the rubric. Tell them you want them to work together by sharing ideas, listening to each other, and taking turns as they discuss the indicators on the rubric.
6. Complete a fun wraparound activity with students each taking turns saying their name and their favorite ice cream flavor (or favorite hobby, book, or band). The next person has to repeat the names and ice cream flavors from all prior responses. Promote encouragement as the list gets tougher and longer. Afterward, show the collaboration rubric again. Tell students you will read the rubric. After each item, students will give a visible thumbs-up or thumbs-down to their camera. Demonstrate how they can do this, and check their camera placement to show their full-face images. Coach them on adjustments as needed.
7. Thank students for responding, and prompt those who don't respond to show their thumbs-up or thumbs-down.
8. Give all-class warm feedback after each indicator is discussed.
9. Repeat the same procedure in a chat thread in which students work together, giving each other feedback about teamwork. Read questions so each student can signal thumbs-up or thumbs-down about his or her partner's work. Do a round of *I*-first feedback, such as, "I thought that my team listened to each other." On the next activity, add a round of *I* feedback with an indicator (for example, "I appreciated how everybody listened to me when it was my turn"). For future practice, show students how to embed emojis as signals in the chat thread with a cool comment. (See chapter 6, page 161.)
10. If you observe any students having difficulty managing the technology, schedule an asynchronous workshop or a one-on-one conference.
11. Once three-fourths of the students can manage the technology for whole-group responses, teach them how to email their responses so they can give each other more detailed feedback. If young students are just starting to learn email, teach them how to spell their names and copy a date on an email before they enter the message or add emojis.

12. Add new cooperative criteria such as the following throughout the semester.
    - "I appreciated how I or my team followed the teacher's instructions."
    - "I was pleased how I or my team completed my task."
    - "I found it helpful when my team or an individual explained ideas."
13. As needed, hold one or more all-class discussions of what is hard to do and what is easy to do with this rubric. Be sure to illustrate cool feedback with a desired corrective action. (For example, hard equals, "I found it hard today to comment on our teamwork since there were too many off-task distractions. I would appreciate it if we all took responsibility to stay on task." Easy equals, "I found it easy to stay focused when Tom, our team recorder, took time to share his notes every five or so minutes.") Use this information as feedback for any coaching students need about their self-assessment.
14. In the second semester, continue to chunk criteria additions and the ways students interact in breakout sessions. By the third quarter, most should be able to complete an independent self-assessment and store it in a folder. At the end of the year, structure a summative self-assessment with this guiding rubric shared to your LMS and stored in a folder.

Once young students are competent readers and writers, you increase partner dialogue even as you decrease your own reading and writing. By the end of kindergarten with students who started with preK, expect that your coaching will have resulted in three-fourths of your students being sufficiently proficient with the digital, self-assessment, and peer communication skills and understanding cooperative benchmarks so they can self-assess their teamwork with a guiding rubric and without a student playbook. For the other students, schedule added coaching until 98 percent of them can assess themselves online free of their given instructions. Continue needs-to-know workshops or conferences to coach the remaining 2 percent.

For any secondary grade, start the school year with a team rubric as your needs assessment to check what students already know and what they need to know about working in a team. What do the results tell you about what your students need to know regarding the digital technology, collaborative criteria, or self-assessment used in your class? As needed, schedule instruction for either the whole class or small groups. You can also create an online student playbook for those who need an aid to help them learn the skills. Figure 7.3 shows a cooperative learning template for an upper-grade guiding rubric; teacher instructions follow the figure. Each student stores both the template and completed assessments in his or her online portfolio according to your written instructions.

Adjust this rubric to fit dissemination for digital assessments. This version and these instructions assume students are at remote learning sites and already have portfolios prepared. Change the language as needed to adapt this rubric for hybrid and blended scenarios.

1. In the first week of class, share this template with instructions for storage in portfolios. Coach any students who do not know how to digitally store, fill in, or share the template with you or peers.
2. Present the rubric to the whole class. After each student fills in the top section, walk through the rating system and encourage students to provide their interpretation of it before you give your clarification.

Student name:
Project or lesson:
Course: Period:
Date:

1 = Your teamwork isn't yet where you think it needs to be.
2 = Your teamwork is getting there, and you have some ideas for how to further improve it.
3 = You are doing just fine.
4 = You can give evidence that your teamwork skills are superpowered.

How Well I (or We) Did Something	Score and Reason
Perform the assigned role (see the playbook).	
Follow guidelines for teamwork.	
Agree on an outcome and stay focused on it.	
Ask clarifying questions.	
Encourage others to work through a disagreement for a win-win solution.	
Give warm and honest feedback.	

FIGURE 7.3: Secondary-level example of a cooperative learning guiding rubric.

*Visit **go.SolutionTree.com/technology** for a free reproducible version of this figure.*

3. Explain the *I* versus *we* in the criteria—that sometimes, students will assess themselves (*I*), and sometimes, they will assess their whole group (*we*). Note that you specify this in accordance with how you want them to assess themselves or each other. You only have to make minor wording changes for each of the variations you want. For instance, if you are asking for students to self-assess, it's *I*. If you want peer feedback, it's *we*.

4. Show the DOVE guidelines on a split screen.
   - Do give warm feedback.
   - Original and different ideas are encouraged.
   - Variety of views is important.
   - Evaluate only when evaluation is asked.

   Ask students to offer clarification of each statement. Seek multiple ideas for each guideline before discussing and summarizing each one's value in promoting ongoing teamwork.

5. Clarify warm feedback with examples and nonexamples.

6. Invite students to discuss benefits of self-assessment in school and life and their concerns about self-assessment. (Some example concerns might be, "Will I be graded on collaboration? If so, how often?" and "How do I know the feedback is honest?") Paraphrase and clarify the benefits and concerns. Add others to each list that you think are important. Be ready to respond to the most predictable concerns. Determine with your students which solution will bring short-range results (such as honest self-assessments, increased trust, and increased teamwork) and which will provide long-range results (such as intrinsic motivation and lifelong learning skills).

7. Determine what instruction students need, such as on pronouns, the DOVE mnemonic, or digital mechanics (filling out and sharing the template, for example).

8. Explain how assessments are scheduled.

9. Conduct a closing reflection. For example, you could ask students to complete this sentence stem: "One thing I learned during this session is . . ." If time is short, invite each student to write an online sticky-note response and submit it to you by text or email.

After an introductory lesson focused on this rubric, schedule a procedure review prior to any activity or lesson that engages students via cooperative learning. As they show increased proficiency in managing the digital skills and confidence with self-assessment, expect students to assume increased responsibility for rating themselves. As students become more skilled team players, see that they schedule time for inter- and intrateam feedback and self-assessments in their team plans.

How Do I Assess Project-Based Deeper Learning in a Digital Environment?

The following instructions will guide your assessments of PBDL lessons and artifacts in your digital classroom. This example focuses on the end product created to show what students have learned from the project. Adapt it for other products (graphic organizers, survey charts, and so on) that contributed to their understanding or to their use of digital tools (apps, spreadsheets, asynchronous teamwork, personalized learning plans, and so on) in the project for which you want a formal assessment.

1. Review the PBDL's end-product criteria in a guiding rubric. Be sure all students in the class have a copy of this rubric stored on their digital devices.

2. Review the sample rubric first, and note how digital tools are integrated and digital skills are invited.

3. Take notes on what digital tools your students will need to know how to use to accomplish each element of their projects. What procedures will they have to follow? How will they learn the procedures? It will help their digital acumen if you include a guiding rubric for the digital skills or tools, especially for those new to them as learning tools.

4. Use the guiding rubric to assess each sample lesson.

5. Let the rubric inform students of your performance expectations.

6. Plan your lesson with design thinking in mind and rubric in hand.

7. During your pilot implementation, if you are a secondary teacher with more than one class subject to this design, decide on the number of classes in which you will pilot the plan.

8. Schedule formative assessments to include student feedback. Either use a polling app or allot time for feedback with the whole class. Take notes, ask clarifying questions, and ask for options.

9. Invite a colleague to observe your class. Explain what part of your plan this colleague will observe—students in action? Your facilitation? After the observation, ask your colleague for cool and hard feedback. Take notes, ask clarifying questions, ask for options, and express thanks. If synchronous online feedback times don't work, invite answers via email or some other method.

How Do I Assess Engagement?

According to Marcia D. Dixson (2015), associate vice chancellor for teaching and learning at Purdue University Fort Wayne, "Student engagement is critical to student learning, especially in the online environment, where students can often feel isolated and disconnected. Therefore, teachers and researchers need to be able to [assess] student engagement." Dixson's (2015) study validates the online student engagement scale. Visit **go.SolutionTree.com/technology** for a link to Lee and colleagues' (2019) article *Exploring Factors, and Indicators for Measuring Students' Sustainable Engagement in e-Learning* that features the analysis results and a table of assessment indicators.

Additionally, follow these teacher steps to create guiding rubrics that will ask students for their feedback to you about their engagement as deeper learners in a digital classroom. Note how the factors (psychological motivation, peer collaboration, and so on) each have several items ready to become indicators in your rubric.

1. Select the format. Do you want a single-point or multiple-point rubric?

2. Select which and how many factors you intend to include. For each factor, select the items.

3. Adapt the language as necessary for your purposes. For instance, the first factor includes a generic assessment of online classes. If you want to use this rubric for feedback throughout your upper-grade classroom, modify the generic statement "online classes" to read "your remote classroom" or "your blended classroom." Do the same for each item you select from this factor. The other factors will need less modification to fit a ninth- to twelfth-grade digital classroom. You may wish to do more editing for fourth- to eighth-grade students or reduce the number of items.

4. Determine the purpose and schedule to use this rubric as an anticipation guide at the start of a course or school year.

    a. If you only want to measure changes in student attitude as a result of your online instruction, you can end the semester or year with a second survey.

    b. If you want feedback on any of the factors so you can make changes in your instruction, add dates for formative feedback at the end of each quarter for this purpose. It will help if you ask for specific examples to illustrate a given rating, plus a response to "What can I do to improve?"

    c. If you want to accentuate a single factor that's in your personalized learning plan, such as learning management or community support, reduce the rubric to that factor's items.

5. Analyze the data, and construct a goal within a personalized learning plan so that you can take advantage of this assessment feedback to improve your teaching in digital environments.

Conclusion

Lorna Earl once said, "A major role for teachers in the learning process is to provide the kind of feedback to students that encourages their learning and provides signposts and directions along the way, bringing them closer to independence"—as chapter 6 prefaced this chapter. In this chapter, you uncovered the key role that feedback plays in enabling teachers to bring their digital students "to independence." You were able to review how well-tailored assessments go beyond letter and number grades on report cards. Guiding rubrics structure two-way feedback that makes it more possible to engage students in what and how they are learning with tools that also inform how you can improve your instruction so it documents academic readiness, enhances learning progress, and meets your students' educational needs. In short, in this chapter, you learned how-to practices so that your assessments, fueled by two-way feedback, not only report students' performance but also become a major driver of engagement and achievement.

MY TAKEAWAYS

What three ideas from this chapter can best help you shift to digital instruction and prepare all students to be effective digital learners? Record your ideas here so you can make a plan later.

1. _____
   _____
   _____

2. _____
   _____
   _____

3. _____
   _____
   _____

8

Students *With* Special Needs

Children are not a distraction from more important work. They are the most important work.
—John Trainer

Teaching students is a tough job. Teaching students with challenges is harder. Teaching students with challenges in a virtual learning space makes for the hardest situation. That doesn't mean it can't be done and done effectively, though. In this chapter, you will investigate emerging information about various modes of learning and different methodologies that specialists and teachers of students with special needs in traditional classrooms can use to guide their charges in an online learning environment. After examining the challenges faced by students who have special needs in virtual spaces, you will delve into how-to information about providing online lessons and interventions. This includes lists of cognitive learning and social-emotional strategies adapted as aids to online learning, ways to assist parents, and what the Americans with Disabilities Act (1990) requires for equitable instruction of children with special needs.

This chapter was written from the perspective of students who have already been diagnosed and given an IEP or 504 plan. It was written this way because the diagnoses of students with disabilities are an exceptionally long process and contain many parts; it could be a book of its own. This book is intended to help teachers work in the current situation with students who already have IEPs to help elevate the virtual learning experience. So, the real question is: How can educators help their students who have already been diagnosed to learn in a virtual setting? That question is best answered first so that the teacher can then adapt what's needed to the IEP.

What Challenges Occur While Teaching Students With Special Needs?

In addition to missing the proximity, body language, and eye contact so important between a teacher and learners with special needs, there are added complexities when figuring out how to provide instruction and communicate with parents and students about mandated specialized services and supports, testing, and accommodations:

> One huge hurdle, teachers say, is determining if both the learning and services students are accustomed to receiving in school—things like gross motor remediation and behavioral therapy—can even be offered in a home-based setting or through digital resources. (Fleming, 2020a)

These challenges of teaching special education online are discussed in the following sections.

- Ensuring individualized education plan fidelity
- Identifying gifts, interests, and talents
- Teaching social-emotional skills

Ensuring Individualized Education Plan Fidelity

The wide spectrum of disorders, and the fact that each student with special needs has different issues, makes the job even harder. It is often difficult for practitioners to translate common accommodations identified for a traditional environment to a virtual setting. Unless your state mandates otherwise, review each student's IEP or 504 plan to note what has been identified as the most important goals, objectives, and services for the student (Arundel, 2020). This will assist in lesson planning, differentiation, and earmarking growth indicators to benchmark for the year. Each plan needs to be explicit about online tools and strategies the student can use.

When one student has two or more challenges (such as a learning disability plus an anxiety disorder, or autism spectrum disorder and epilepsy), teachers have the added challenge of addressing what is called *comorbidity*. Teachers must identity and address these with interventions that not only address the comorbidity but also ensure that the interventions work online. Online learning can increase the issue of comorbidity with students. For instance, a physically challenged student may show signs of anxiety or depression ignited by inability to manipulate a keyboard. A student with bipolar disorder may experience mood swings and show anger bursts and disrespect in online statements or the chat room. A student with dyslexia may find new difficulties reading text in a chat room so the teacher sees the volume of work declining or no written work at all. This all means that general education classroom teachers not only have to sharpen their observation skills for an IEP student's primary special need but also be on the lookout for possible signals of a second issue such as anxiety, depression, mood swings, temperamental behavior, sabotages of the communication tool, and so on. Signals can run the gamut from drops in online attendance, missed appointments, silence in chat rooms, incomplete or deteriorating work, angry or disruptive outbursts, grief, or a dark tone to comments. Please note that a student in any grade can show these signs that are easily mistaken for bad behavior. Students with special needs display signals that must be considered in context with the students' primary disability diagnosis so that teachers can address them with the most appropriate online intervention. For instance, for the physically challenged student who is angry and frustrated because he cannot manipulate the keyboard, focusing on the anger is insufficient. A teacher will have to communicate the issue to the special needs coordinator to make an adjustment to the IEP, which helps the student use a dictation device that bypasses the keyboard. With that out of the way, the special needs coordinator can assist the teacher in helping the student manage his anger or make a special referral to a school social worker.

When addressing whether an intervention will work online, a classroom teacher should confer with the special educator in charge of the student's IEP. The special educator is likely to be much more informed about the options available not only to assist the student with the dual accommodations but also assist the teacher in carrying out the extra intervention.

Failing to list all intervention methods in the context of online learning then leads to extra difficulty. For instance, a student with a reading disability and anxiety disorder combination may not show anxiety in a classroom or resource room with a physically present adult; the absence of that support when online brings the anxiety to the surface. It follows that to avoid any negative consequences, teachers must check that the full array of interventions necessary in a virtual environment is listed.

It is very important to review each student's IEP or 504 plan prior to preparing any online learning activities. Double-check that the selected interventions include appropriate online interventions. When it comes to planning online learning for students with multiple disabilities, IEPs are still needed, but with extra care that information for each disability or disorder is listed in the IEP. Overlooking comorbidity issues can have damaging consequences, the least of which may be increases in off-task online behavior. One consequence is an increase in the severity of an emotional disability; this can become apparent during online classes and in some cases lead to trauma and illicit drug use (National Institute on Drug Abuse, 2018). Even when the comorbid issues are identified, omissions can occur when only one disorder's accommodations and interventions are listed. Kathryn Fishman-Weaver, director of academic affairs and engagement for Mizzou Academy, suggests "that teachers evaluate which IEP goals are achievable in the new environment, and then work with families to break learning targets into manageable benchmarks" (as cited in Fleming, 2020a).

For instance, students with dyslexia are often predisposed to making errors with sequenced details. When reading a book, these students may skip words in a sentence or add words that aren't there. Their teachers know the strategies that have worked in brick-and-mortar classrooms. For this challenge, a teacher who has utilized tape recorders, chunked tasks, taught text highlighting, provided copies of guiding questions and rubrics for small chunks of a lesson, paired empathetic peer tutors, posted visual aids, and so on needs to adapt these to online instruction.

One way to ensure IEP fidelity is making sure to hold and attend IEP meetings. Teacher education assistant professor Kathleen Bautista (as cited in Nelson, 2020), says "it's wise to schedule them at the beginning of the year with your administrator, parents or guardians, and support providers to ensure everyone is on the same page" for all *online needs* for each student reviewed. Increase the meeting structure with goals, roles, responsibilities, guidelines, and end times. Record the meeting and store it with names of all students reviewed in each meeting. Record and store your meetings with a copy in each student's file. As mentioned elsewhere, it is important to record classes for student access. To that end, after a meeting, schedule online time to review the lesson, coach, or tutor as called for in the IEP or as you see fit.

Identifying Gifts, Interests, and Talents

When students with special needs have mild disabilities, sometimes their talents and interests are overlooked. For instance, students with autism are sometimes considered to have severe mental disabilities. Temple Grandin, one of the first individuals identified on the autism spectrum to document the insights she gained from her personal experience, currently is a university professor teaching animal science. The talents of Helen Keller, Elon Musk, Howie Mandel, and Vincent van Gogh were often ignored under the cover of misdiagnoses. Research shows that most learners with special needs tend to be highly aware of the environment, more curious than average, and highly intuitive and insightful; think mainly in pictures instead of words; think and perceive multidimensionally (using all the senses); and have vivid imaginations (Silverman, Iseman, & Jeweler, 2009).

When teachers look closely for talents and interests in students with special needs, they are likely to discover the best approaches for engaging these students online. You can find a variety of career interest surveys online, including picture-only career interest interviews such as those on Truity (www.truity.com/test/photo-career-quiz). After identifying a student's possible interests, interview the student to uncover examples or reasons for the selected interests and then build learning activities to match. For example, with a student who expresses interest in building objects, you could teach mathematics measurement by building three-dimensional geometric figures. As an alternative, set up peer partner interviews between students of similar interests. Gather these data and plan lessons, such as the geometric example, so that you address these interests.

Teaching Social-Emotional Skills to Students With Special Needs

A study of parents reported by NPR (Kamenetz, 2020) reported the disastrous impact of distance learning on students with special needs during the pandemic:

- Four in 10 say they were not receiving any support at all.
- Just 1 in 5 report that they were receiving all the services their children are entitled to.
- 35% report that their children were doing little to no remote learning, compared with 17% of their general education peers.
- And, 40% of parents of special needs children were concerned about their children's mental health, compared with 23% of parents of other children.

Perhaps the most practical way to support students' mental health is for teachers to put more emphasis on units and lessons that support the social-emotional well-being of all students in a classroom. With cooperative learning and other activities and strategies rich in SEL coupled with content, teachers can begin to address these needs. For instance, when the curriculum calls for primary students to meet a standard, such as RL.2.3 (NGA & CCSSO, 2010a), the teacher selects a relevant story with SEL discussion material (like *A Terrible Thing Happened* by Holmes & Pillo, 2000). A high school physics teacher could include research projects on Stephen Hawking, who suffered from amyotrophic lateral sclerosis (ALS), to discuss the anxiety he faced working with technology. Further, consider the following.

- Plan for small-group meetups in synchronous time. This can be a stress-free time for students to become adept with how to use a video conference system, play online games you adapt to the split screen, and complete self-awareness activities such as a round-robin sharing in response to stems ("Today, I am glad . . ."; "Today I feel excited by . . .").

- Set up heterogeneous home groups to rotate membership monthly, with group roles that rotate weekly. These longer-lasting groups (as opposed to other groups that may function for a one-day task or a week's lesson) build a sense of belonging, safety, and security, as well as students' empathy and SEL skills. Place one student with special needs with one or two general education students. When using only partners, try to select general education students who are empathetic. You may want to schedule a needs-to-know workshop to ready general education partners in ways they can be inclusive.

- Set up guidelines for equitable involvement of every home group member.

- Encourage visible learning for all in a group or class. When presenting, make learning visible by including visuals, such as showing student playbooks for hands-on activities for all to see. Use a split screen as a visible teaching aid that group members can refer to as needed. For instance, if a student with special needs is the encourager and forgets what she does in this role, the playbook will allow her partner to help her review.

- Make sure to teach to the whole class, since that "is vital in creating a social presence and routine for your students" (Nelson, 2020). Scheduling care and comfort minutes for students to share their concerns or worries, talk informally with friends, play a game that does not have a specific curriculum skill as the outcome, learn ideas or skills with each other, and enjoy each other's company as an online community become more important during online learning (Nelson, 2020). You guide the opportunity for all to respond, taking extra care to draw out the concerns that may hinder students with special needs from participating in the day's lesson.

What Transferable Skills Benefit Students With Special Needs When Online?

The following tools are especially valuable for engaging the minds of students with special needs, so they not only learn a course's content but also learn the transferrable skills and strategies that empower their future learning. Every teacher should keep a secure digital file of key documents for each student. When a team is making new plans and IEPs for a student with special needs, teachers on the team can share these documents for review to all who have password access. The students' IEP team should decide who does the following tasks.

- **Needs assessment:** How well can this student perform a specific cognitive or SEL task relevant to the IEP? Start with gathering information about what the student knows or can do in respect to the task outcome. Give the student a complex cognitive task to complete, such as finding key words in a text or making two groups of objects alike. See what you observe, and record what you observed and your conclusions. Record these and add them to the student's IEP folder. Determine how you will include results in an IEP. You can do this assessment in a private online conference.

- **Personalized plan:** When your assessment determines that a special needs student should develop a skill in your curriculum, either make that function a priority in an annual IEP with appropriate interventions or make a string of short-term personalized learning plans. The following are examples.

    - *Precision*—In all mathematics assessments, set a criterion for precise answers. Ask the student, "How close are these measurements?"

    - *Accuracy*—In all English language arts assessments, set a doable criterion that identifies how well the student can write or speak an accurate response, such as spellings of key words from a story, punctuation in a sentence, or evidence to back up what a character does or says in a story. Ask the student to do the test task at least twice: "Show me each punctuation mark in this sentence."

    - *Impulse control*—The student's goal is stopping to think before acting. Create a guiding rubric to go with this goal and ask the student, "How many seconds did you stop and think today before you . . .?" (for example, "answered this question").

- **Guiding rubric:** Any teacher on a student's IEP team can create a guiding rubric for use with the student. For a targeted SEL cognitive function such as impulse control, a classroom, resource room, or special needs teacher can create a guiding rubric for the student to keep in his or her portfolio. Often, it is to everyone's advantage when the team agrees on the function to target. One teacher will conduct the conference with input gathered by other members. Have a common format for the rubric that allows self-assessment as well as teacher feedback. Rubrics should be accompanied by a five-minute conference with each student to review each week's progress. Figure 8.1 (page 202) is a sample student playbook teachers can adapt by changing the example entries. Older students can share the completed rubric each Friday by emailing it to the teacher.

> 1. Your goal is to be a better "What if . . . ?" thinker. Your daily objectives are in the list. You can decide whether to give yourself a score or not on your daily objectives in the list. I'd prefer to have your comments rather than just a number. For instance, tell me why an objective is important for you.
> 2. Please have your weekly rubric in my email box by Friday at 4:00 p.m. No one else will see what you say.
> 3. End the email by telling me in general how you are getting better at this skill.
> 4. By the following Monday, I will send my feedback. Please store everything in your portfolio.

FIGURE 8.1: Student instructions for guiding rubric.

How Do I Differentiate Instruction for Special Needs Students?

In the United States, federal law, under the Free and Appropriate Public Education for Students With Disabilities regulation of section 504 of the Rehabilitation Act of 1973, states that students with learning disabilities should be educated alongside their non-disabled peers "to the maximum extent possible." Sixty-six percent of "students who have learning disabilities [should] spend 80 percent or more of their school day in general education classrooms" (National Center for Learning Disabilities, 2020).

When it comes to learning online, the federal placement requirement does not change, nor does the need for effective differentiated instruction. When students with special needs are online with peers, it is important that instruction that includes students with special needs be offered in small chunks with more time spent in small groups, alone or with peers, and in one-to-one meetings with teachers. Differentiated activities designed to increase engagement, along with fun games to increase SEL, can go a long way in creating a comfortable virtual space for students with special needs (James, 2020).

To differentiate instruction that meets a variety of student needs in a mainstream classroom, incorporate best practice strategies that you can easily adapt to inclusive online learning.

For example, consider using student response systems. By asking students to vote visibly using colored flash cards or hand signals, you make time for collaboration that allows you to gauge student understanding and differentiate instruction. In addition, you can create online quizzes that automatically assign differentiated follow-up activities or assignments based on the student's comprehension of the material (Bellanca, 2021). For example, ask students to be makers as they create an alphabet book or a Wordle, collage about a historic event, or graph to show results of a hands-on science experiment. As you introduce the making of a product at the end of a PBDL lesson, you may want to check for understanding of the instructions provided in the student playbook. You ask for students to show a red dotted index card ("I have no idea"), yellow, ("I have a question"), or green dotted card ("Good to go"). These tell you what, when, and how you may respond. For instance, if a student with special needs signals red or yellow, you can send the rest of the class on to the next step off the grid and support the student who needs extra assistance.

Also review the benefits of using paired partners and tutors (page 74). The program Best Buddies (www.bestbuddies.org) is a worldwide organization that pairs partners who assist persons of all ages with intellectual developmental disabilities in forming meaningful friendships with their peers, securing successful jobs, living independently, improving public speaking and self-advocacy and communication skills, and feeling valued by society.

Finally, try using HyperDocs (https://hyperdocs.co), digital lesson plans to help students do independent work asynchronously. When you personalize a HyperDoc and link it to an IEP, students with special needs can move through an assignment or whole lesson at their own pace. You can teach to small groups or individual students with specific goals and sequenced activities and differentiate due dates for deliverables (Harris, 2018).

How Do I Ensure Compliance With the Americans With Disabilities Act?

The Americans With Disabilities Act of 1990 is a U.S. law that attempts to ensure everyone has accessibility to resources, including online instruction. All public schools in the United States must comply with the ADA (1990). In addition, the course syllabus should include an accessibility statement for students that outlines ADA procedures.

- **Hyperlinks:** Make sure all your hyperlinks, or links, are in text. When you search, you can look for link leads as shown in these examples.
    - TITLE DOC can be found here: http://TITLE.com.
    - To view TITLE, click here.
    - To view TITLE, visit http://TITLE.com.
- **Text design:** When designing, typing, or writing material, make sure the font is readable. Steer clear of serif fonts like Times New Roman and Palatino. Acceptable sans serif fonts are Arial and Helvetica. Use the same font in all your documents and online text. That minimizes variation and helps students stay focused. Also consider font color and contrast. Use a dark font on a light background. Avoid using bright backgrounds. It is good to use the less-is-more approach.
- **Images and graphics:** Only use visuals if they are relevant to the content and easily visible (high resolution). Do not use animations (such as gifs) or blinking images. Make images and graphics ADA compliant by adding a tag for alt text. Most LMSs have an alt tag option.
- **Audio and video:** Keep audio or video clips between three and ten minutes. You may have to create several videos this length to cover a single topic or set of instructions. Also, use MP3 (audio) or MP4 (video) file formats to ensure compatibility.
- **Documents:** All text in digital documents should be searchable, allowing learners to search for words or phrases. If a PDF document is not searchable, an accompanying plain text version should be available. When linking documents within a course, the label of the link should have the file extension type at the end (.doc or .docx for a Word document, .ppt for PowerPoint, or .xlsx or .xltx for Excel).
- **Tables and charts:** Any table or chart needs to have identified headers and labels as well as summaries.

Conclusion

This chapter investigated various modes of learning and different methodologies that specialists and teachers of students with special needs in general education classrooms can use to guide their charges in an online learning environment.

As noted, the diagnoses of students with disabilities are an exceptionally long process and contain many parts; it could be a book of its own. We intended to help teachers work in the current situation with students who already have IEPs to help elevate the virtual learning experience. Make sure that you review, assess, and follow each student's IEP goals and benchmarks, strategies, and interventions so that you accurately understand the online learning needs of students with disabilities.

MY TAKEAWAYS

What three ideas from this chapter can best help you shift to digital instruction and prepare all students to be effective digital learners? Record your ideas here so you can make a plan later.

1. _____

2. _____

3. _____

9

Communication *With* Parents and Guardians

Productive collaborations between family and school, therefore, will demand that parents and teachers recognize the critical importance of each other's participation in the life of the child.
— **Sara Lawrence-Lightfoot**

Partner is the term that encompasses but does not adequately describe a parent's role in a student's online learning—especially for those in elementary school, even more so for those who are not yet reading and writing, and perhaps most for those who have students with certain special needs.

In this chapter, you will learn what best-practice research demonstrates parent-teacher partnerships should include. The chapter continues with a compliance-aligned model charting four ways—each with a selection of specific how-to strategies—of making the most effective parent-teacher partnerships for advancing students' online academic achievement.

Education scholar Sandra Wilder's (2014) meta-analysis of parent and guardian engagement clarifies what practices are especially important when classrooms go virtual. Most important, her study notes, are the positive relationships and shared expectations among parents, students, and the teacher. Most discouraging, she notes, is the delegation of parents to be homework helpers (Wilder, 2014). This plays out in Grace Chen's study (2020) that "a parent's interest and encouragement in a student's education affect the student's attitude toward school, classroom conduct, self-esteem, absenteeism, and motivation." In short, in crucial digital parent-teacher relationships, parental expectations for high academic achievement of their children must take precedence over practices that expect parents to become homework assistants.

Casual communications, including when someone, especially a parent, explicitly says that "School is important; I expect you to try your best" during daily conversation, not only enhance academic performance but also have a positive influence on student attitude and behavior relative to in-school, online, and at-home responses (Loughlin-Presnal & Bierman, 2017).

In some schools, teachers encourage families to review report cards, help their children manage (or simply limit) TV and online time, oversee homework schedules, talk about post–high school plans and college applications, and above all do their best. In the digital world of learning, parents can help their children manage screen time, take brain breaks, become familiar with the VCS and other digital tools for communicating with teachers, stay in touch with the teacher, and encourage their children during online time. Asking parents to tutor mathematics or help write essays is not on the list of helpful practices.

During the COVID-19 pandemic, common involvement requests were that parents and guardians oversee their young children's homework, check completed tasks, tutor basic skills in reading and mathematics, read aloud, and guide science experiments. Adding to parents' at-home load and anxiety by asking them to teach specialized material such as Common Core State Standards mathematics or Next Generation Science Standards is likely to fail—even with parents who were mathematics and science majors (Willingham, 2020). What sense does it make for a teacher to hand over instructional tasks to parents who may not understand the content, are not trained to teach, or simply don't have the time?

Teachers can partner with parents and guardians with evidence-based ways to promote high expectations. The RASE model (Churchill, King, Webster, & Fox, 2013), which poses the following four teacher-asked questions, is a starting place for two-way communication between teacher and family.

1. **R:** "What *resources* can a parent use to suggest strategies used by academically successful learners?"
2. **A:** "What *activities* will help a parent communicate high expectations?"
3. **S:** "What *support* can a teacher provide for parents wanting to show high expectations?"
4. **E:** "When parents want to show high expectations, what is their role in *evaluation* of a student's school performance?"

With these four teacher-asked questions, parents who have digital access can better prepare for an online conference. In addition, online conferences, especially if offered on a more flexible schedule than the one-time-a-year 7 p.m. to 9 p.m. conference, allow parents with many children, single parents, and parents with work schedules conflicting with conference night schedules to find a time when they can attend an online conference. When parents or teachers feel a special conference is available, they can initiate an online contact and set up an online conference at the most convenient time. Further, online parent conferences are more accessible to (some) parents: "Virtual communication has offered an efficient replacement for in-school conferences, which were often derailed by parent work schedules and child care" (Matusek, 2021).

The following sections address the resources, activities, support, and evaluation (or assessments) that teachers can communicate about and provide to families.

What Resources Help Parents and Guardians Communicate High Expectations for Digital Learning?

A packet sent to families to start the year and a monthly contract outlining expectations are resources that can help you communicate with parents and guardians as an introductory connection. Just be prepared to send snail mail packets if some parents lack internet connection or a digital device. You can fill the packet with ideas to help parents share with their children the all-important high expectations they have for efforts and growth, which are so important for academic performance and their faith in their children's ability to learn (Wilder, 2014). You can supplement this packet with monthly email invitations for parents to read other ideas on your classroom website, or tweet encouraging statements to parents with ways to help their children learn online.

A Packet to Start the Year

After introducing yourself to parents and guardians, send families a packet with some information that can help them throughout the year. Put as much of the packet language in the parents' or guardians' preferred language. (Talk to your school's parent liaison, support staff, or language teachers for translation help if necessary). After sending hard copies and electronic copies of the packets (one of each version for one family is fine, since not everyone will have an electronic option), let everyone know they are on the way. The following represent a sample list of items for an introductory packet.

- The daily schedule
- Ways to contact you
- A map for setting up a child's learning place so it is most conducive to the student's at-home study
- A reading list with books available from the local library or online, marking those that are free to download
- A survey asking about family concerns and hopes with an easy-to-answer set of questions
- Ways parents can help with online learning (such as giving encouragement, setting a schedule, or contacting the teacher)
- Ways families can show their high expectations for their children's academic efforts

For the survey, use a simple online polling app like Poll Everywhere (www.polleverywhere.com/mobile) or SurveyMonkey. Offering the survey multiple ways is important because you'll get more responses when people can use the method they prefer (Jacobson, 2018). Ask what concerns families have about the school year, including content, technology, and accommodations. No later than the first week of the year (or semester, depending on the duration and whether you get new students throughout the year), send an email that has the following. Make sure to include a link to a video recording of you talking about these items and giving the same information that is in the documents.

- An introduction
- Your contact information
- Your goals for the year
- Your wish for parents' involvement (such as attending quarterly or semester online conferences with you and their children, using encouraging words to the children, or staying in touch when a worry arises about digital learning)
- What days and times work best for them for attending conferences, with a note about what the conferences are for and how important they are
- Offers of support (such as finding a peer tutor for online asynchronous help)
- A promise that you will not ask parents and guardians to tutor academic content

Figure 9.1 (page 208) is a sample welcome letter. It can help improve parent engagement if, every eight weeks, you send a follow-up invitation asking for parents' involvement in one specific way, such as "early this week, set up your child's personal, quiet-as-possible digital learning place" or "early this week, set up a daily schedule for your student to do digital homework assignments." Make the emails as personal as possible, using the recipients' last names and their children's first names.

> Dear Ms. Jordan,
>
> My name is Margaret Kim. I am Luke's teacher this year. I want to introduce myself and let you know how you can get in touch with me.
>
> I've been teaching for five years and am originally from Los Angeles. I have a cat named Kwan.
>
> Please share with me any concerns you may have about this school year. You can ask any question and voice any concern that you or your child have. I will keep these things confidential.
>
> If you need to contact me about something, I am available at mkim@ourschool.edu by email or the school learning platform at http://ourclassportal.edu.
>
> I hope that your child will enjoy learning in my class. I look forward to it!
>
> Sincerely,
> Margaret Kim

FIGURE 9.1: Sample introduction letter.

After you receive the survey results about concerns and hopes, schedule a meeting to discuss them. During the meeting, reintroduce yourself and address the expressed concerns. Also talk about the role of the parent and the power of high expectations. Focus on how families can best help their children with words and actions that convey high expectations, including the following.

- Minimizing TV, phone, and social media time
- Encouraging talent and interest exploration
- Talking about dreams and goals, including future educational and trade school plans
- Scheduling and sticking to homework time
- Ensuring the proper amount of sleep
- Explaining the importance of participating in class
- Modeling and talking about showing grit (and more grit) as you stick with tough tasks

Encourage contact if parents and guardians get more than average resistance from their child on any of the academic expectations, including going online for class. A particular resistance may be a sign that a student needs more instruction or is struggling with something that requires an additional resource, such as a school counselor or even a vision or hearing assessment. For parents of sixth-grade students and up, offer information about college and articles with online study tips to share with their children, and stress the value of talking with children about post–high school education opportunities.

Also include a survey to identify the state of internet access and availability of digital devices. Here are sample survey questions to modify, distribute, and gather data for your instructional planning and accommodations. For each, give students the option to choose *Do not know*.

- Does your home have internet?
- If you have internet access, is it high speed?
- If you have internet access, is it cellular, Wi-Fi, or ethernet?

- Do you have a computer that your child can use all day? Is it a Chromebook, Apple, or Windows-based computer?
- Does your child have all-day access to a smartphone (like an iPhone or Android-based phone) or tablet?
- Does the device that your child will use for school have Microsoft Word?
- Does the device that your child will use for school have a video conference system (also referred to as a VCS) like Zoom or Skype on it?
- Does the device that your child will use for school have a microphone and camera?

Some parents won't know the answers to these questions. Giving them instructions for how to check their internet speed and computing platform, and for the existence of programs and a microphone and camera, is a good idea, depending on your school.

A Monthly Contact

Monthly contact is a happy medium between keeping in touch with families and inundating them with communications, which may lead to their disengaging as digital home helpers (Jacobson, 2018). Share your weekly class calendars and pacing guides with two items: (1) class time and (2) daily deliverables. Invite parents to review the schedule and check with their children whether they are up to date on the required work. No tutoring requests! If parents or guardians want to, they can ask their child to copy the deliverable via email, text, or social media.

Ask the parents and guardians of K–2 students to share their email addresses and smartphone numbers, if they have them, so you can share information with them as well as with students. After grade 3, consider creating and assigning the student role of communications manager, and explain that this person is responsible for sending the schedule and other important change information to parents. Rotate the role between two students per month, and confirm that families are receiving the communications by random spot checks or during calls you want to make for other issues, such as a student crying online or an overactive mute finger.

Inform parents about the availability of online lesson recordings and offer a link to your welcome video, sharing that class sessions will be there as well. Ensure, of course, that only invitees are able to access the videos. (For example, make sure they are set to private on YouTube). If a student has a conflict with an online scheduled lesson or activity, adults can direct the student to listen to the recorded lesson. Offer parents recorded and written instructions for accessing a recording or video for a scheduled lesson or activity, and offer an online meeting for those who need further instructions.

For K–2 and any other prereading students, ask parents and guardians to check their child's technical proficiency. For instance, the adult should ascertain whether students can open a laptop and open files. As the teacher, you will prepare students to work the basic devices (smartphone, Chromebook, and so on) and the free downloadable apps and sites they will use. Send students instructions and ask them to practice with the device. If parents are concerned about their own lack of digital skills with any device, arrange for instruction for them or a convenient one-to-one digital call.

What Activities Help Parents and Guardians Communicate High Expectations?

The following activities can help create a partnership between you and families so that students get the message from both about high expectations of them.

- **Poll parents and guardians:** Ask for parents' feelings about what students are studying, how they think their children are doing, and other details. An online survey will calculate the data automatically. Figure 9.2 is a sample survey. Most poll apps and websites will automatically tally the results for you. You might want to invite a group of parent or guardian volunteers or classroom assistants to compose, edit, and then analyze the results, as long as names are left out of sight and confidentiality is ensured.

Dear families,
Here is this month's survey. Your feedback will tell me how my class is helping your child. I would like to know your answers to the following questions. Your expectations for these tasks will help your child succeed in school now and in the future. Please share the importance of these tasks with your child. If you want to add comments, please type into the textbox at the bottom of the questions. Thank you for helping.
Sincerely,
Señor Alvarez

Choose a number to indicate your level of agreement. 1 = Not at all 2 = A little bit 3 = Mostly 4 = Completely	
1. You know when homework is due.	
2. What the class is learning will help your child in the future.	
3. Your child is doing his or her homework without you.	
4. Your child knows how to sign in to online classes alone.	
5. This is what I like about class so far:	
6. This is what I don't like or think is not working about class so far:	
Comments:	

FIGURE 9.2: Parent online survey example.

*Visit **go.SolutionTree.com/technology** for a free reproducible version of this figure.*

- **Hold private digital conferences with parent, guardian, and child at least once per semester (and ideally, once per quarter):** By personalizing invitations, you increase chances for a positive response (Heerwegh, 2005). Propose talking points and ask parents and their children to RSVP with any questions they would like to discuss during the meeting. Refer back to your start-of-year packet, which ideally surveys parents and guardians for good days and times for them to attend digital conferences and highlights a conference's purpose and value. Figure 9.3 is a sample performance-review conference invitation. Of course, you may hold other types of conferences, such as for chronic misbehavior. This template is an adjustable model to fit other reasons for conferences. However, knowing it's a performance review that every teacher does keeps the academic focus.

Dear Mr. and Mrs. Jacobs and Mariana,

Please join me in an online conference next Friday, January 12, at 2:00 p.m. We will discuss what Mariana did well this last quarter and what she needs to improve next quarter. Please respond to this communication with email, text, or a message on the LMS that this time and day are acceptable. If this doesn't work for you, please let me know an alternative day and time. Thank you.

FIGURE 9.3: Sample performance-review conference invitation.

- **Be prepared with specific recommendations for academic or social-emotional growth:** During the conference, stress the positive with warm feedback and, where applicable, explain how the student's performance will put him or her in a good position to graduate from high school and apply for higher education or trade school, even if you are teaching elementary students. As soon as possible, it's helpful for every student to hear this specific high expectation. That expectation declared loud and often plants the importance for higher learning, in whatever form the student may elect, for living and learning in the high-tech, high-information digital work world.

- **Share weekly summaries saying what students have been and will be learning:** Include specific examples. Once students move beyond K–6, secondary teachers can collaborate to send a weekly message communicating about different content areas. Add guiding questions to structure the summary (for example, in social studies: What topic are we studying this week? Who are the most important figures? Why is the time important? How will students learn about this topic in our digital classroom?).

- **Have students create a monthly blog or podcast to capture learning about a topic:** Share the link to the website or audio file with parents and guardians. Students can put a hook for their parents and guardians in the blog or podcast. For example, for an elementary class: "Dear Mom or Dad, Thanks for sharing your story with me. In my podcast, I hope you can find my secret reference to Rex, our family dog. Please listen and tell me what it was!"

  For upper-grade classes: "Dear Mom or Dad, I would appreciate your answer to the three questions our team asked in our math blog. If you would send me your email answer, I would love you forever and ever."

How Can I Support Parents and Guardians as They Show High Expectations?

A letter communicating ideas for ways to show high expectations is one way you can support families.

- **Respond to concerns:** The most effective response to your invitation for concerns is to answer individuals with a one-to-one meeting. Seek solutions prior to the meeting where necessary so you can share ideas and resources. During the meeting, listen, give warm feedback, and seek agreement on how to resolve any issues. Follow up in any way agreed to during the meeting. If you uncover the same concerns from many families (such as how to access the LMS), set up a parent meeting through a VCS. Record the meeting for those families who cannot attend at the scheduled time. Invite concerns, listen, and clarify, and then agree on helpful solutions. When a solution is outside your range of authority, seek future involvement of the principal or other individual with appropriate authority and expertise.

- **Help families set up their children's workstations:** Encourage parents to find as private a space as possible for their child's workspace. Share the checklist from figure 1.5 (page 29).

- **Let parents know about new digital tools and the role they can play in advanced education and future jobs:** Share usage instructions on your LMS and in an email or text to parents. Let them know what you have already done with the tools in class. Figure 9.4 provides suggestions that you can adapt to help families participate in a relevant learning activity. You might want to assign middle school students the responsibility of guiding their parent's or guardian's involvement; share these instructions with students.

Dear families,

We will begin using _____ in our studies this coming week. As your child opens _____, you can help by going over the following points with him or her.

- **Be clear about goals and expectations:** Ask your child, "What do you want or expect to learn with this app or website? How do you think it will help?" Share the goal and help your child understand how the app will benefit class.

- **Set parameters:** For example, ask, "What are your teacher's guidelines for being safe while using the app or website?"

- **Review the class norms for privacy:** Ask, "How are you keeping your passwords and login safe?"

- **Warn your child about in-app purchases:** Explain, "Do not click on any options asking you to upgrade or to buy something."

- **Encourage learning directed by your child (self-directed learning):** Ask, "What is your personalized learning plan for becoming really good with this app or site? How will your plan help you learn with this app?"

- **Check how ready your child is to use the technology:** Ask, "Show me how to open and manage this app or site."

Please contact me with any questions or concerns.

FIGURE 9.4: Parent instructions for new apps and websites.

*Visit **go.SolutionTree.com/technology** for a free reproducible version of this figure.*

- **Provide instructions and ideas for encouraging good time-management and work habits during asynchronous learning time:** Highlight the importance and benefits for students controlling their academic future. Figure 9.5 (page 214) provides a sample parent and student letter. You can adapt it for students' ages. For instance, brain-break time for elementary students—to rest, have a snack or bathroom break, or do a fun activity—should stop after ten minutes. Middle and high school students can add doing solo academic work, reading a book, or talking in a private chat with a friend. These students should participate in and receive instruction up to twenty or thirty minutes and then have a five-minute break. Read student reactions during instruction. Obviously, passive listening will merit quicker breaks than breaks during intense engagement. For a chart of average attention spans by age, refer to the article "Normal Attention Span Expectations by Age" (https://bit.ly/3nCA0vp; Brain Balance Achievement Centers, 2021). For longer breaks, look at SEL and team-building activities and games, or encourage students to stretch, get a drink of water, or take a bathroom break. Make student-specific instructions to include with this message.

- **If you need to schedule a conference to address a behavior incident, do so immediately:** Don't wait until the quarterly performance conference. Keep this conference separate from the performance review, but do not shy away from the need for the student to change the behavior. In the online conference, clarify the purpose of the meeting to the parent and emphasize the need for a realistic solution. End with an agreement among you, parents, and the student, and follow up with a summary of the agreement and a thank you.

What Is the Parent's or Guardian's Role in Student Assessment?

First, early in the school year, invite them to participate in student assessments. Cheerlead the importance of their constructive feedback in the process. Create and share weekly presentations or request a recording of their child's sharing of an "I learned this week" or similar open-stem completions. Rehearse how to finish a stem even if the first responses are one sentence brief. Schedule the presentations with part of your class each week. Gradually, once students can read, add a guiding rubric with indicators students can use to make stem responses. Each student can invite parents or guardians and share a rubric with them. The students can also invite parents to give warm feedback by completing a response stem such as "I am pleased that . . ." or "I am proud that . . . ." Teachers can delay starting this practice until the end of the first quarter and after students have worked with the teacher to make self-assessment stems. In messages sent home via the classroom website, a teacher should prepare parents so they understand what a rubric is, why it is important, and how they should use the response stem to start their answer. Using stems enables (and controls) warm feedback. Later in the year, the option exists to provide parents with a digital lesson on warm feedback and its value for students.

- **Send a weekly warm feedback prompt:** Offer something such as *I liked . . .* or *I am proud . . .* to share with their child's self-assessment of a skill they observe, such as time management, grit, digital literacy, or problem solving. Heighten the assessment effectiveness by coupling a student's target skill. This will give families the opportunity for short but effective conversations with each other. (See table 6.1, page 164.)

Parent and Guardian Letter

Dear families,

You can help your children handle learning time when they are not in class. Research shows that good work habits make a big difference in classroom success! Please take five minutes or so to ask your children how things are going in class (or, even better, "How is _____ going?" with the blank filled in with a specific topic, assignment, or book you know your children are working on. As you talk and listen, it is important to do the following.

- Clearly say that you believe your children are able to learn hard things.
- Suggest ways your children can manage time (like doing homework before playing or practicing how to estimate how much time it takes to do something).
- Explain how these skills will benefit your children in the future.

I have included the following other helpful ideas here. These ideas are also on our class portal (http://ourclassportal.edu).

- Be in class on time.
- Put the class schedule somewhere you can see it, so you know when things happen.
- Keep your workspace organized. Put everything back in the same place.
- Start your day with enough time to do what you need to do before class.
- Use the instructions that the teacher gives you.
- When possible, move away from distractions like TVs that are on or people who are talking as you are in class or doing work.
- For projects that take more than one evening, plan a daily schedule for finishing them on time.
- Work on one task at a time, for fifteen or thirty minutes (without phone distractions). Take breaks in between, getting up, taking a bathroom or water break, doing some stretches, or listening to a song.
- Store documents and projects in the right folders in your online portfolio.
- Ask for help from team members, teachers, or parents.

Thank you!

Mr. Tsai

Student Letter

Hi everyone! Scientists have studied how to remember more information and save brain energy.

1. Have a goal.
2. Take regular breaks while you work, with a time limit for breaks and work.
3. Use a timer to keep your break schedule.

Let me know if you have any questions or ideas to share. See you in class.

Mr. Tsai

Source: Adapted from Grade Power, 2018.

FIGURE 9.5: Parent and guardian tips for encouraging asynchronous work habits.

- **Invite parents and guardians to have coffee with you online:** Use either a VCS or chatroom. Acquaint them with the key digital tools you use at the first meeting and then gather feedback each subsequent quarter.

How Do I Help Families With Primary-Grade Digital Learners?

Early elementary students' undeveloped self-management, literacy, and digital literacy skills leave these young learners more dependent on explicit, time-consuming, step-by-step adult guidance. Colin Seale, author of *Thinking Like a Lawyer: A Framework for Teaching Critical Thinking to All Students*, reminds us that "Parents are the experts on their children . . . Teachers, on the other hand, are the experts on instruction" (Seale, 2020). Although more and more children arrive at school with some digital skills, it will help families if you immediately assess all students so you know what they still need to learn. That can include simple skills such as turning on and logging into a laptop, using a mouse, and sending and receiving documents.

The European Union has created the Digital Competence Framework for Citizens (Vuorikari et al., 2016), a digital curriculum—available at https://bit.ly/39ostss—and many classrooms throughout the U.S. are also teaching digital literacy and citizenship (Deye, 2017). Follow suit. Plan your first month of instruction to include teaching these skills to all early learners and any older students who need them. Support parents and guardians by providing basic VCS links and login instructions and a list of technology tips in your start-of-year packet. Also post them on the LMS and create and share a video or just audio of these basic instructions to share as well, in case that works better for them. If families are struggling with a particular technical issue, also provide written and recorded instructions. It's an even better idea to offer a class for parents who need to learn the same skills, including keeping online communications safe and secure.

After sending the technology survey that goes to families in their start-of-year packet, collate the data so you can see where problems might arise. Your analysis should ready you to pick the spots were students and parents have the greatest need to know. With that information, you can design one or more sessions for parent signup. The checklist in figure 1.5 (page 29) can help parents and guardians prepare their children for technology use. Add items that you feel will benefit; remove those that don't apply. Parents and guardians of students in preK through grade 4 should review the document. Students in grades 5 and up can review what's working and what's not and report directly to you.

What Should I Be Aware of Regarding Parental Consent, Law, and Student Privacy?

Some parents are concerned about who can see information on their children and want to know that hackers cannot change a student's grade or enter false information into the online student records. Others are concerned about school records showing up on Google or other information-gathering sites. Teachers can best respond to parents concerned about student safety by sharing instructions for privacy settings. Explain that they should set privacy on their computers and phones, and explain what federal mandates apply to school districts.

U.S. Federal Laws

Districts and charter management organizations are required to follow standards for protecting student data confidentiality. This applies to educational websites, too: "teachers and schools must have proven parental consent before students provide any personal information to third parties" (EDpuzzle, n.d.). The following laws are especially important.

- **The Family Educational Rights and Privacy Act** (FERPA; 20 U.S.C. § 1232g; 34 CFR Part 99) is a federal law requiring privacy of certain student education information in both print and digital formats. FERPA generally prohibits schools from disclosing personally identifiable information from a student's education records to a third party without written consent from the parent (or the student, if the person is eighteen or older). At the same time, however, FERPA allows exceptions. For example, schools may share personally identifiable information, without consent, with designated school officials who have a legitimate educational interest. Parents and guardians should know that "third parties may be considered school officials if they are performing a service for which the school would otherwise use employees" (EDpuzzle, n.d.). In short, contracted service providers are considered by the courts to be school officials who are allowed to act as school officials.

- **The Children's Online Privacy Protection Act (COPPA)** of 1998 (15 U.S.C. 6501–6505) is a federal law that protects children under age thirteen who use commercial websites, online games, and apps. The law requires schools to make sure that websites students use are safe and secure. To ensure students' safety under the law, teachers should preview each site, game, and app they ask students to work on has legal language describing due diligence about student data.

District or Charter Management Organization (CMO) Compliance Rules

Know your district or CMO compliance rules. Ask your school IT specialist or principal to show you how the school is following legally mandated practice. The Data Quality Campaign and the Consortium for School Networking (2014) offer a list of principles for using and safeguarding students' personal information. Many respected education organizations, including the ISTE, National Center for Learning Disabilities, and American School Counselor Association support the principles. Teacher teams should ask their school or district's IT specialists how it follows these principles and push for specific examples that respond to parents' and guardians' specific concerns. Be sure that you are doing the same.

Some of the principles follow. Visit http://studentdataprinciples.org/the-principles to see all the principles.

- Student data should be used as a tool for informing, engaging, and empowering students, families, teachers, and school system leaders.

- Students, families, and educators should have timely access to information collected about the student.

- Educators and their contracted service providers should only have access to the minimum student data required to support student success. Everyone who has access to students' personal information should be trained and know how to effectively and ethically use, protect, and secure it.

- Any educational institution with the authority to collect and maintain student personal information should provide a designated place or contact where students and families can go to learn of their rights and have their questions about student data collection, use, and security answered (Data Quality Campaign and the Consortium for School Networking, 2016).

Your Compliance Practices

Before storing the recommended compliance principles, review your own practices. Store documents after ensuring you are in compliance with the local, national, and school guidelines and laws. If a parent or guardian raises a concern, respond with the same medium that the parent or guardian used to communicate with you. For instance, if a parent emails you to ask about how you keep your rubrics, feedback, or grades confidential, respond by email with examples. If someone contacts you by phone, return the call. It is likely that talking with you will allay their fears. Figure 9.6 shows a sample email response to a concern about online document safety. Discuss your response with your principal or district IT manager before sending the message. The school may have a specific response to share instead. If you should have multiple parent concerns about online security and data, plan a conference. Include your principal or designated IT person in the planning and conference.

Dear Mrs. Kelly,

I appreciate that you contacted me about your concern. As I understand it, you are concerned about how I keep Bernard's computer data secure. I do that by following our district policy and federal law.

All data on my computer and the school's servers are protected by security software and other safety measures. If my response does not address your worry, let's talk more. If you would like, I can invite our principal, Dr. Ericka Brown, or information technology director, Scott Ng, to confer with you. We can do so online with Zoom or in person at a time convenient for everyone. Thank you.

Sincerely,
Mr. Cooper

FIGURE 9.6: Sample document protection for written responses.

The following ideas, for parents and guardians, mirror what you convey to students on a consistent basis—especially about not revealing who you are online and not sharing passwords (EDpuzzle, n.d.).

- **Safely keep and share data:** Never include a screenshot or other document containing private student data via email or other non-secure medium. If sharing feedback on your child's rubrics, I will show you how to blur the information so that your student is not matchable with his or her data.

- **Never share your child's personal data by email, chat, or other unsafe means:** Google Drive and Dropbox are password protected so that you can safely share assessment information or other documents that way.

- **Require that your child rely on online security devices, including PINs and passwords on all devices used for schoolwork:** Insist on accountability for maintaining PINs and passwords private. Make sure your child knows that your family does not ever share PINs or passwords.

- **Require your child to make all devices password protected:** You can also enable encryption on laptops. Consider downloading a device-finding app (such as Find My at www.apple.com/icloud/find-my) to devices. If he or she loses a registered device, set up a quick way to alert you or the teacher.

- **Insist that your child follow the teacher's deadlines for shutting down portfolios and assessment folders:** Unless there is a reason that your child and I have agreed on for carrying a folder into a next academic year, I will let your child take home folders. You may want to keep this copy in your secure files for future reference. If you wish, I will delete the folder.

- **Ask me about essential information in my class records:** I will remove any information you don't need when your child is no longer in my class. This is a safeguard for maintaining your child's right to privacy.

Conclusion

With everyone's increased readiness to communicate via ever more digital tools, so too are expanded opportunities to engage parents in productive communication about how best to partner in productive virtual learning for every student. The RASE model is a best practice and shapes support and activities that can engage parents and guardians in their children's academic development. Remembering that less is often more, and your systematic plan to take one step at a time with well-selected strategies can engage families in concert with you in each student's distance learning. Showing parents how to maintain high expectations in a digital learning environment with specific ideas for parents to help students manage the technology are key features. E-communication through your classroom website, starting in the first days of school and continuing through each semester, is highlighted with sample letters and playbooks you can adapt.

MY TAKEAWAYS

What three ideas from this chapter can best help you shift to digital instruction and prepare all students to be effective digital learners? Record your ideas here so you can make a plan later.

1. _____

_____

_____

2. _____

_____

_____

3. _____

_____

_____

REFERENCES AND RESOURCES

Abramczyk, A., & Jurkowski, S. (2020). Cooperative learning as an evidence-based teaching strategy: What teachers know, believe, and how they use it. *Journal of Education for Teaching, 46*(3), 296–308.

Adams, L. (2020, April 22). *PBL + SEL + trauma-informed teaching for the times we're in* [Blog post]. Accessed at https://pblworks.org/blog/pbl-sel-trauma-informed-teaching-times-were on September 27, 2021.

Adler, A. (1998). *Understanding human nature*. Center City, MN: Hazelden.

Aguilar, N. (2020, April 16). Remove a participant in a Zoom video call & ban them from joining again. *Gadget Hacks*. Accessed at https://smartphones.gadgethacks.com/how-to/remove-participant-zoom-video-call-ban-them-from-joining-again-0286813 on September 20, 2021.

Alexander, K., Entwisle, D., & Olson, L. (2014). *The long shadow: Family background, disadvantaged urban youth, and the transition to adulthood*. New York: Russell Sage Foundation.

Aljraiwi, S. (2019). Effectiveness of gamification of web-based learning in improving academic achievement and creative thinking among primary school students. *International Journal of Education and Practice, 7*(3), 242–257.

Allensworth, E., & Schwartz, N. (2020). *School practices to address student learning loss* (Brief No. 1). Chicago: UChicago Consortium on School Research. Accessed at https://consortium.uchicago.edu/publications/school-practices-to-address-student-learning-loss on October 3, 2021.

Alliance for Excellent Education. (2014). *West Virginia digital learning: Report to the governor, legislature, and West Virginia Board of Education*. Washington, DC: Author.

American Academy of Pediatrics (AAP) Council on Communications and Media. (2016). *Media use in school-aged children and adolescents* [Policy statement]. Accessed at https://pediatrics.aappublications.org/content/pediatrics/138/5/e20162592.full.pdf on April 23, 2021.

Americans With Disabilities Act of 1990, 42 U.S.C. § 12101, et seq. (1990).

Amos, J. (2014, December 16). *Core of the matter: Equity and deeper learning (#CoreMatters)* [Blog post]. Accessed at https://all4ed.org/core-of-the-matter-equity-and-deeper-learning-corematters on September 20, 2021.

Anderson, M., & Cardoza, K. (2016, August 31). Mental health in schools: A hidden crisis affecting millions of students. *NPREd*. Accessed at https://npr.org/sections/ed/2016/08/31/464727159/mental-health-in-schools-a-hidden-crisis-affecting-millions-of-students on September 27, 2021.

Anderson, M., & Jiang, J. (2018). *Teens, social media and technology 2018*. Washington, DC: Pew Research Center. Accessed at http://publicservicesalliance.org/wp-content/uploads/2018/06/Teens-Social-Media-Technology-2018-PEW.pdf on October 3, 2021.

Andrade, H. L. (2019). A critical review of research on student self-assessment. *Frontiers in Education*. Accessed at www.frontiersin.org/articles/10.3389/feduc.2019.00087/full on October 3, 2021.

Annenberg Institute. (n.d.). *The Research Partnership for Professional Learning*. Accessed at www.annenberginstitute.org/rppl on October 2, 2021.

Arundel, K. (2020, October 6). *IEPs altered to reflect distance learning service changes, but at cost to schools*. Accessed at www.k12dive.com/news/iep-changes-to-special-ed-services/586104 on October 3, 2021.

Askvik, E. O., van der Weel, F. R., & van der Meer, A. L. H. (2020). *The importance of cursive handwriting over typewriting for learning in the classroom: A high-density EEG study of 12-year-old children and young adults*. Accessed at www.frontiersin.org/articles/10.3389/fpsyg.2020.01810/full on April 20, 2021.

Ausubel, D. P. (1968). *Educational psychology: A cognitive view*. New York: Holt, Rinehart & Winston.

Autor, D. H., Levy, F., & Murnane, R. J. (2003). The skill content of recent technological change: An empirical exploration. *The Quarterly Journal of Economics, 118*(4), 1279–1333. Accessed at https://economics.mit.edu/files/11574 on April 23, 2021.

AZ Quotes. (n.d.a). *Elliot Masie quotes*. Accessed at https://azquotes.com/quote/1498943 on February 26, 2021.

AZ Quotes. (n.d.b). *Michelangelo quotes*. Accessed at https://azquotes.com/author/10049-Michelangelo on January 30, 2021.

AZ Quotes. (n.d.c). *Sara Lawrence-Lightfoot quotes*. Accessed at https://azquotes.com/author/39522-Sara_Lawrence_Lightfoot on February 25, 2021.

Bailenson, J. N. (2021). *Nonverbal overload: A theoretical argument for the causes of Zoom fatigue*. Accessed at https://tmb.apaopen.org/pub/nonverbal-overload/release/1 on April 17, 2021.

Balzer, D. (2019, April 1). *Mayo Clinic minute: Is a rise in teen depression linked to technology, social media?* Accessed at https://newsnetwork.mayoclinic.org/discussion/mayo-clinic-minute-is-a-rise-in-teen-depression-linked-to-technology-social-media on October 3, 2021.

Banderas News. (2008, April). *"The grid" could soon make the internet obsolete*. Accessed at www.banderasnews.com/0804/nt-thegrid.htm on January 20, 2021.

Barak, M. (2012). From "doing" to "doing with learning": Reflection on an effort to promote self-regulated learning in technological projects in high school. *European Journal of Engineering Education, 37*(1), 105–116.

Barnard-Brak, L., Paton, V. O., & Lan, W. Y. (2010a). *Profiles in self-regulated learning in the online learning environment*. Accessed at www.erudit.org/en/journals/irrodl/2010-v11-n1-irrodl05150/1067795ar.pdf on April 15, 2021.

Barnard-Brak, L., Paton, V. O., & Lan, W. Y. (2010b). *Profiles in self-regulated learning in the online learning environment* [Abstract]. Accessed at www.erudit.org/en/journals/irrodl/1900-v1-n1-irrodl05150/1067795ar/abstract on April 15, 2021.

Barrett, H. C. (2012). *Selecting a "free" online tool for ePortfolio development*. Accessed at https://electronicportfolios.org/eportfolios/tools.html on September 20, 2021.

Barron, B., & Darling-Hammond, L. (2008). *Teaching for meaningful learning: A review of research on inquiry-based and cooperative learning*. Accessed at https://eric.ed.gov/?id=ED539399 on October 2, 2021.

Barzilai, S., & Blau, I. (2014). Scaffolding game-based learning: Impact on learning achievements, perceived learning, and game experiences. *Computers and Education, 70*(C), 65–79.

Bates, A. W. (2019). *Teaching in a digital age: Guidelines for designing teaching and learning* (2nd ed.). Vancouver, British Columbia, Canada: Tony Bates Associates. Accessed at https://pressbooks.bccampus.ca/teachinginadigitalagev2 on October 2, 2021.

Battelle for Kids. (2019). *Frameworks and resources*. Accessed at www.battelleforkids.org/networks/p21/frameworks-resources on December 14, 2020.

Bell, S. (2010). Project-based learning for the 21st century: Skills for the future. *Clearing House: A Journal of Educational Strategies, Issues and Ideas, 83*(2), 39–43.

Bellanca, J. A. (Ed.). (2015). *Deeper learning: Beyond 21st century skills*. Bloomington, IN: Solution Tree Press.

Bellanca, J. A. (2021). *Personalized deeper learning: Blueprints for teaching complex cognitive, social-emotional, and digital skills*. Bloomington, IN: Solution Tree Press.

Bellanca, J. A., & Brandt, R. (Eds.). (2010). *21st century skills: Rethinking how students learn*. Bloomington, IN: Solution Tree Press.

Bellanca, J. A., & Fogarty, R. (1991). *Blueprints for thinking in the cooperative classroom* (2nd ed.). Palatine, IL: Skylight.

Bellanca, J. A., Fogarty, R. J., & Pete, B. M. (2020). *How to teach thinking skills: Seven key student proficiencies for college and career readiness* (2nd ed.). Bloomington, IN: Solution Tree Press.

Bellanca, M. J., Koney, A., & Bellanca, J. A. (2015). *Science alive! Creating next generation science projects*. Northbrook, IL: International Renewal Press.

Bennett, S., Agostinho, S., & Lockyer, L. (2015). Technology tools to support learning design: Implications derived from an investigation of university teachers' design practices. *Computers and Education, 81*, 211–220. Accessed at https://ro.uow.edu.au/sspapers/1245 on September 29, 2021.

Bentley, K. (2020, June 8). 9 million students lack home internet for remote learning. *Government Technology*. Accessed at www.govtech.com/network/9-Million-Students-Lack-Home-Internet-for-Remote-Learning.html on September 15, 2020.

Bergman, P., Lasky-Fink, J., & Rogers, T. (2018, July). *Simplification and defaults affect adoption and impact of technology, but decision markers do not realize this* (Harvard Kennedy School Faculty Research Working Paper Series RWP17-021). Accessed at www.hks.harvard.edu/publications/simplification-and-defaults-affect-adoption-and-impact-technology-decision-makers-do on December 13, 2020.

Berkeley Center for Teaching and Learning. (n.d.). *E-portfolio*. Accessed at https://teaching.berkeley.edu/resources/assessment-and-evaluation/design-assessment/e-portfolio on October 3, 2021.

Bitsko, R. H., Holbrook, J. R., Ghandour, R. M., Blumberg, S. J., Visser, S. N., Perou, R., et al. (2018). Epidemiology and impact of health care provider–diagnosed anxiety and depression among US children. *Journal of Developmental and Behavioral Pediatrics, 39*(5), 395–403. Accessed at www.ncbi.nlm.nih.gov/pmc/articles/PMC6003874 on October 3, 2021.

Bitter, C., & Loney, E. (2015, August). *Deeper learning: Improving student outcomes for college, career, and civic life*. Washington, DC: American Institutes for Research. Accessed at https://air.org/sites/default/files/downloads/report/Deeper-Learning-EPC-Brief-August-2015.pdf on February 4, 2021.

Blumenfeld, P., Fishman, B. J., Krajcik, J., Marx, R. W., & Soloway, E. (2000). Creating usable innovations in systemic reform: Scaling up technology-embedded project-based science in urban schools. *Educational Psychologist, 35*(3), 149–164.

Bond, M., Buntins, K., Bedenlier, S., Zawacki-Richter, O., & Kerres, M. (2020). Mapping research in student engagement and educational technology in higher education: A systematic evidence map. *International Journal of Educational Technology in High Education, 17*(2), 1–30. Accessed at https://educationaltechnologyjournal.springeropen.com/articles/10.1186/s41239-019-0176-8 on February 18, 2021.

Bond, S. (2020). A must for millions, Zoom has a dark side—and an FBI warning [Audio broadcast transcript]. *Morning Edition*. Accessed at www.npr.org/2020/04/03/826129520/a-must-for-millions-zoom-has-a-dark-side-and-an-fbi-warning on December 14, 2020.

Borup, J., West, R. E., Graham, C. R., & Davies, R. S. (2014). The adolescent community of engagement framework: A lens for research on K–12 online learning. *Journal of Technology and Teacher Education, 22*(1), 107–129.

Boubouka, M., & Papanikolaou, K. A. (2013). Alternative assessment methods in technology enhanced project based learning. *International Journal of Learning Technology, 8*(3), 263–296.

Boud, D., & Molloy, E. (2012). Rethinking models of feedback for learning: The challenge of design. *Assessment and Evaluation in Higher Education, 38*(6), 698–712. Accessed at www.researchgate.net//241683246_Rethinking_models_of_feedback_for_learning_The_challenge_of_design/citation/download on October 3, 2021.

Bradbury, N. A. (2016). Attention span during lectures: 8 seconds, 10 minutes, or more? *Advances in Physiology Education, 40*(4), 509–513. Accessed at https://doi.org/10.1152/advan.00109.2016 on October 1, 2021.

Brain Balance Achievement Centers. (n.d.). *Learning on the move: Awesome activities for kinesthetic learners*. Accessed at www.brainbalancecenters.com/blog/learning-move-awesome-activities-kinesthetic-learners on June 12, 2021.

Brain Balance Achievement Centers. (2021). *Normal attention span expectations by age*. Accessed at www.brainbalancecenters.com/blog/normal-attention-span-expectations-by-age on December 1, 2021.

BrainyQuote. (n.d.). *Tony Robbins quotes*. Accessed at https://brainyquote.com/quotes/tony_robbins_134116 on February 26, 2021.

Bransford, J. D., Brown, A. L., & Cocking, R. R. (Eds.). (2000). *How people learn: Brain, mind, experience, and school.* Washington, DC: National Academy Press.

Brengard, A. (2015). *Build tech success with students' help.* Accessed at www.naesp.org/resource/build-tech-success-with-students-help on April 17, 2021.

Bridgeland, J. M., DiIulio, J. J., Jr., & Morison, K. B. (2006, March). *The silent epidemic: Perspectives of high school dropouts.* Washington, DC: Civic Enterprises. Accessed at https://docs.gatesfoundation.org/documents/thesilentepidemic3-06final.pdf on April 23, 2021.

Brody, L., & Honan, K. (2020, September 3). Help us get better at remote instruction, NYC public school teachers ask. *The Wall Street Journal.* Accessed at https://wsj.com/articles/new-york-city-teachers-want-more-lessons-on-remote-instruction-11599147400 on February 4, 2021.

Brown, J. S., Collins, A., & Duguid, P. (1989). Situated cognition and the culture of learning. *Educational Researcher, 18*(1), 32–41.

Brown, P. C., Roediger, H. L., & McDaniel, M. A. (2014). *Make it stick: The science of successful learning.* Cambridge, MA: Belknap Press.

Bryant, J., Child, F., Dorn, E., & Hall, S. (2020). *New global data reveal education technology's impact on learning.* Accessed at www.mckinsey.com/industries/public-and-social-sector/our-insights/new-global-data-reveal-education-technologys-impact-on-learning on September 28, 2021.

Budhai, S. S. (2020). Fourteen simple strategies to reduce cheating on online examinations. *Faculty Focus.* Accessed at https://facultyfocus.com/articles/educational-assessment/fourteen-simple-strategies-to-reduce-cheating-on-online-examinations on February 3, 2021.

Bui, S. (2020, November 19). *Top educational technology trends in 2020–2021.* Accessed at https://elearningindustry.com/top-educational-technology-trends-2020-2021 on September 28, 2021.

Burns, R. (1786). *Poems, chiefly in the Scottish dialect.* Kilmarnock, Scotland: Wilson.

Butler, P. (2006, October). *A review of the literature on portfolios and electronic portfolios.* Accessed at https://uncw.edu/cas/assessment/docs/resources/eportfolioprojectresearchreport.pdf on September 25, 2020.

Butler, T. (n.d.). *On the clear evidence of the risks to children from non-ionizing radio frequency radiation: The case of digital technologies in the home, classroom and society.* Accessed at https://radiationresearch.org/wp-content/uploads/2019/04/On-the-Clear-Evidence-of-the-Risks-to-Children-from-Smartphone-and-WiFi-Radio-Frequency-Radiation-Final-20201.pdf on September 25, 2010.

Cambridge, D. (2008). Layering networked and symphonic selves with electronic portfolios: A critical role for eportfolios in employability through integrative learning. *Campus-Wide Information Systems, 25*(4), 244–262.

Canadian Radio-Television and Telecommunications Commission (CRTC). (2020). *Communications monitoring report 2019.* Accessed at https://crtc.gc.ca/eng/publications/reports/policymonitoring/2019/cmr1.htm#a1 on September 15, 2021.

Carless, D., Joughin, G., & Mok, M. M. C. (2006). Learning-oriented assessment: Principles and practice. *Assessment and Evaluation in Higher Education, 31*(4), 395–398. Accessed at www.researchgate.net/publication/295568484_Learning-oriented_assessment_Principles_and_practice/citation/download on October 3, 2021.

Carroll, M., Goldman, S., Britos, L., Koh, J., Royalty, A., & Hornstein, M. (2010). *Destination, imagination and the fires within: Design thinking in a middle school classroom.* Accessed at https://stanford.edu/dept/SUSE/taking-design/proposals/Destination_Imagination_the_Fire_Within.pdf on February 2, 2021.

CAST. (n.d.). *About Universal Design for Learning.* Accessed at www.cast.org/impact/universal-design-for-learning-udl on September 23, 2021.

Castelo, M. (2020, July 30). How schools are bringing CTE programs online. *EdTech.* Accessed at https://edtechmagazine.com/k12/article/2020/07/how-schools-are-bringing-cte-programs-online on December 13, 2020.

Castro, L. (n.d.). *Introduction to Design Thinking methodology.* Accessed at https://lucianocastro.com/introduction-to-design-thinking-methodology on October 1, 2021.

Cator, K., Schneider, C., & Vander Ark, T. (2014, April). *Preparing teachers for deeper learning: Competency-based teacher preparation and development.* Accessed at https://gettingsmart.com/wp-content/uploads/2014/01/FINAL-Preparing-Teachers-for-Deeper-Learning-Paper.pdf on February 19, 2020.

Center for Inspired Teaching. (n.d.). *Inspired teaching youth.* Accessed at https://inspiredteaching.org/youth on October 3, 2021.

Center for Teaching Innovation. (n.d.). *Setting learning outcomes.* Accessed at https://teaching.cornell.edu/teaching-resources/designing-your-course/setting-learning-outcomes on February 4, 2021.

Center on Online Learning and Students with Disabilities. (2016). *Equity matters 2016: Digital & online learning for students with disabilities.* Lawrence, KS: Author. Accessed at http://dataserver.lrp.com/DATA/servlet/DataServlet?fname=EquityMatters2016Final.pdf on December 13, 2020.

Center on Positive Behavioral Interventions and Supports. (2020, March). *Creating a PBIS behavior teaching matrix for remote instruction.* Eugene, OR: University of Oregon. Accessed at https://assets-global.website-files.com/5d3725188825e071f1670246/5f6a5a02d2d6bf09474dd563_Creating%20a%20PBIS%20Behavior%20Teaching%20Matrix%20for%20Remote%20Instruction.pdf on December 14, 2020.

Chait, J. (2020, October 7). Remote learning is a catastrophe. Teachers unions share the blame. *Intelligencer.* Accessed at https://nymag.com/intelligencer/2020/10/remote-education-distance-learning-schools-teacher-unions-red-for-ed.html on September 23, 2021.

Chamberlain, P. (2020). Knowledge is not everything. *Design for Health, 4*(1), 1–3. Accessed at https://tandfonline.com/doi/full/10.1080/24735132.2020.1731203 on January 21, 2021.

ChanLin, L. J. (2008). Technology integration applied to project-based learning in science. *Innovations in Education and Teaching International, 45*(1), 55–65.

Chaplin, H. (2009, December 23). *Public media, public education, and the public good: An interview with Heather Chaplin (part two).* Accessed at https://civic.mit.edu/2009/12/23/public-media-public-education-and-the-public-good-an-interview-with-heather-chaplin-part-0 on September 28, 2021.

Chapman, J. R., & Rich, P. J. (2018). Does educational gamification improve students' motivation? If so, which game elements work best? *Journal of Education for Business, 93*(7), 315–322.

Charter Technology Solutions. (n.d.). *How to maintain students' motivation during remote learning.* Accessed at https://charterts.com/2020/student-motivation on September 25, 2020.

Chen, G. (2021, August 14). *Parental involvement is key to student success* [Blog post]. Accessed at https://publicschoolreview.com/blog/parental-involvement-is-key-to-student-success#:~:text=Parental%20involvement%20not%20only%20enhances,esteem%2C%20absenteeism%2C%20and%20motivation on February 19, 2021.

Chen, H.-L., & Wang, S. (2016). *Turning passive watching to active learning: Engaging online learners through interactive video assessment tools.* Paper presented at the annual Convention of the Association for Educational Communications and Technology, Las Vegas, NV.

Cheng, R. W., Lam, S., & Chan, J. C. (2008). When high achievers and low achievers work in the same group: The role of group heterogeneity and processes in project-based learning. *British Journal of Educational Psychology, 78*(2), 205–221.

Cheung, A. C. K., & Slavin, R. E. (2016). How methodological features affect effect sizes in education. *Educational Researcher, 45*(5), 283–292. Accessed at https://doi.org/10.3102/0013189X16656615 on September 29, 2021.

Chuong, C., & Mead, S. (2014, June). *A policy playbook for personalized learning: Ideas for state and local policymakers.* Washington, DC: Bellwether Education Partners. Accessed at https://bellwethereducation.org/sites/default/files/PolicyPlays_Final.pdf on September 22, 2021.

Churchill, D. (2017). *Digital resources for learning.* Singapore: Springer.

Churchill, D., King, M., Webster, B., & Fox, B. (2013). Integrating learning design, interactivity, and technology. In H. Carter, M. Gosper, & J. Hedberg (Eds.), *Electric dreams: Proceedings ascilite 2013 Sydney* (pp. 139–143). Tugun, Queensland, Australia: Australasian Society for Computers in Learning in Tertiary Education. Accessed at www.ascilite.org/conferences/sydney13/program/papers/Churchill.pdf on October 13, 2021.

Clark, D. (2020, October 9). *Engagement—most used yet most misunderstood word in learning?* [Blog post]. Accessed at http://donaldclarkplanb.blogspot.com/2020/10/engagement-most-used-yet-most.html on September 30, 2021.

Coccia, M. (2017). The fishbone diagram to identify, systematize and analyze the sources of general purpose technologies. *Journal of Social and Administrative Sciences, 4*(4). Accessed at http://kspjournals.org/index.php/JSAS/article/view/1518 on October 11, 2021.

Collaborative for Academic, Social, and Emotional Learning. (n.d.). *About CASEL*. Accessed at https://casel.org/about-us on October 3, 2021.

Collie, R. J., Martin, A. J., & Frydenberg, E. (2017). Social and emotional learning: A brief overview and issues relevant to Australia and the Asia-Pacific. In E. Frydenberg, A. J. Martin, & R. J. Collie (Eds.), *Social and emotional learning in Australia and the Asia-Pacific: Perspectives, programs and approaches* (pp. 1–13). Berlin, Germany: Springer Science + Business Media. Accessed at www.researchgate.net/publication/312468927 on October 1, 2021.

Committee for Children. (n.d.). *Leading the SEL revolution*. Accessed at www.cfchildren.org on October 3, 2021.

Compound Interest. (2015, July 30). *A simple guide to neurotransmitters*. Accessed at www.compoundchem.com/2015/07/30/neurotransmitters on August 12, 2020.

Condliffe, B. (2017). *Project-based learning: A literature review* (Working paper). New York: MDRC. Accessed at https://eric.ed.gov/?id=ED578933 on October 2, 2021.

Conzemius, A. E., & O'Neill, J. (2014). *The handbook for SMART school teams: Revitalizing best practices for collaboration* (2nd ed.). Bloomington, IN: Solution Tree Press.

Cooperative Learning Institute. (n.d.). *Roger and David Johnson*. Accessed at www.co-operation.org/rogeranddavid on October 1, 2021.

Counts, L. (2019, June 19). How information is like snacks, money, and drugs—to your brain. *BerkeleyHaas*. Accessed at https://newsroom.haas.berkeley.edu/how-information-is-like-snacks-money-and-drugs-to-your-brain on September 25, 2020.

Couros, G. (2018). *Using technology to humanize* [Blog post]. Accessed at https://georgecouros.ca/blog/archives/8660 on September 25, 2018.

Creighton, S., & Szymkowiak, A. (2014). The effects of cooperative and competitive games on classroom interaction frequencies. *Procedia—Social and Behavioral Sciences, 140*, 155–163. Accessed at https://doi.org/10.1016/j.sbspro.2014.04.402 on October 2, 2021.

CTS. (n.d.). *How to maintain students' motivation during remote learning*. Accessed at https://charterts.com/2020/student-motivation on September 25, 2020.

Cullotta, K. A. (2020, September 17). Remote learning, in school? Some suburban public schools closed by COVID-19 have reopened for e-learning supervision—at a price to taxpaying parents. *Chicago Tribune*. Accessed at https://chicagotribune.com/coronavirus/ct-covid-19-schools-remote-learning-supervision-20200917-jysvva4kczctlfwxfqy5rccj2q-story.html on September 17, 2020.

Curtis, C. (2020, October 13). Isolated students may struggle to stay mentally healthy. *Edutopia*. Accessed at www.edutopia.org/article/isolated-students-may-struggle-stay-mentally-healthy on September 29, 2021.

Dalgarno, B. (2014). Polysynchronous learning: A model for student interaction and engagement. In B. Hegarty, J. McDonald, & S.-K. Loke (Eds.), *Rhetoric and reality: Critical perspectives on educational technology* (pp. 673–677). Dunedin, New Zealand: Australasian Society for Computers in Learning in Tertiary Education.

Darby, F. (2019, April 17). *How to be a better online teacher: Advice guide* [Blog post]. Accessed at https://chronicle.com/article/how-to-be-a-better-online-teacher on April 21, 2021.

Darby, F. (2021, January 11). *Planning a great online class through roundabout design*. Accessed at www.facultyfocus.com/articles/online-education/online-course-design-and-preparation/planning-a-great-online-class-through-roundabout-design on October 2, 2021.

Darby, F., & Lang, J. M. (2019). *Small teaching online: Applying learning science in online classes*. San Francisco: Jossey-Bass.

Darling-Hammond, L., & Adamson, F. (2013). *Developing assessments of deeper learning: The costs and benefits of using tests that help students learn*. Stanford, CA: Stanford Center for Opportunity Policy in Education.

Darling-Hammond, L., & Oakes, J. (2019). *Preparing teachers for deeper learning*. Cambridge, MA: Harvard Education Press.

Darling-Hammond, S., Fronius, T. A., Sutherland, H., Guckenburg, S., Petrosino, A., & Hurley, N. (2020). Effectiveness of restorative justice in US K–12 schools: A review of quantitative research. *Contemporary School Psychology, 24*(3), 295–308.

Dashevsky, E. (2015, August 20). 10 surprising things technology will make obsolete by 2025. *PC Magazine*. Accessed at https://pcmag.com/news/10-surprising-things-technology-will-make-obsolete-by-2025 on January 30, 2021.

Data Quality Campaign. (2016). *Time to act: Making data work for students*. Accessed at https://dataqualitycampaign.org/wp-content/uploads/2016/04/Time-to-Act.pdf on October 3, 2021.

Davis, M. (2019, June 14). Will coding become a basic life skill? Yes and no, say experts. *Big Think*. Accessed at https://bigthink.com/the-future/coding-life-skill on September 23, 2021.

Dayan, Z. (2017, October 8). *3 reasons autistic children excel at computer coding* [Blog post]. Accessed at https://codemonkey.com/blog/3-reasons-autistic-children-excel-at-computer-programming on February 1, 2021.

Daylamani-Zad, D., Angelides, M. C., & Agius, H. (2014). Collaboration through gaming. In M. C. Angelides & H. Agius (Eds.), *Handbook of digital games* (pp. 235–273). Hoboken, NJ: Wiley. Accessed at www.researchgate.net/publication/263820048_Collaboration_through_Gaming/citation/download on October 2, 2021.

de Bono, E. (1985). *de Bono's thinking course*. New York: Facts on File.

Dede, C. (2014, December). *The role of digital technologies in deeper learning*. Boston: Jobs for the Future. Accessed at https://files.eric.ed.gov/fulltext/ED561254.pdf on September 22, 2021.

Dendy, K. (2020, August 4). Children with special needs face challenges in distance learning. *KEZI News*. Accessed at www.kezi.com/content/news/Parents-of-children-with-special-needs-speak-out-on-learning-challenges-572010551.html on February 4, 2021.

Deterding, S., Dixon, D., Khaled, R., & Nacke, L. (2011, September). From game design elements to gamefulness: Defining "gamification." In A. Lugmayr (Ed.), *Proceedings of the 15th International Academic MindTrek Conference: Envisioning Future Media Environments* (pp. 9–15). New York: Association for Computing Machinery.

Dewey, J. (1916). *Democracy and education: An introduction to the philosophy of education*. New York: Macmillan.

Dewey, J. (1933). *How we think: A restatement of the relation of reflective thinking to the educative process*. Boston: D. C. Heath & Co.

Deye, S. (2017). Promoting digital literacy and citizenship in school. *National Conference of State Legislatures, 25*(7). Accessed at www.ncsl.org/research/education/promoting-digital-literacy-and-citizenship-in-school.aspx on July 8, 2021.

Diallo, A. (2020, April 19). How to reach students without internet access at home? Schools get creative. *The Hechinger Report*. Accessed at https://hechingerreport.org/how-to-reach-students-without-internet-access-at-home-schools-get-creative on December 13, 2020.

Dichev, C., & Dicheva, D. (2017). Gamifying education: What is known, what is believed and what remains uncertain: A critical review. *International Journal of Educational Technology in Higher Education, 14*(9). Accessed at https://educationaltechnologyjournal.springeropen.com/articles/10.1186/s41239-017-0042-5 on September 25, 2020.

Dixson, M. D. (2010). Creating effective student engagement in online courses: What do students find engaging? *Journal of the Scholarship of Teaching and Learning, 10*(2), 1–13. Accessed at https://files.eric.ed.gov/fulltext/EJ890707.pdf on October 3, 2021.

Dixson, M. D. (2015). *Measuring student engagement in the online course: The Online Student Engagement Scale (OSE)*. Accessed at https://files.eric.ed.gov/fulltext/EJ1079585.pdf on April 27, 2021.

Dockterman, D. (2017, August 7). *Turning high expectations into success* [Blog post]. Accessed at https://gse.harvard.edu/news/uk/17/08/turning-high-expectations-success on May 8, 2021.

Dondi, M., Klier, J., Panier, F., & Schubert, J. (2021, June 25). *Defining the skills citizens will need in the future world of work*. Accessed at www.mckinsey.com/industries/public-and-social-sector/our-insights/defining-the-skills-citizens-will-need-in-the-future-world-of-work on September 28, 2021.

Doppelt, Y. (2003). Implementation and assessment of project-based learning in a flexible environment. *International Journal of Technology and Design Education, 13*(3), 255–272.

Dorn Charter School. (n.d.). *Remote learning.* Accessed at www.dorncharterschool.org/remote-learning on September 28, 2021.

Dorn, E., Hancock, B., Sarakatsannis, J., & Viruleg, E. (2020). *COVID-19 and learning loss—disparities grow and students need help.* Accessed at www.mckinsey.com/industries/public-and-social-sector/our-insights/covid-19-and-learning-loss-disparities-grow-and-students-need-help on November 8, 2021.

Drain, M. (2010). Justification of the dual-phase project-based pedagogical approach in a primary school technology unit. *Design and Technology Education: An International Journal, 15*(1), 7–14.

Drucker, P. F. (1954). *The practice of management.* New York: Harper & Row.

Dyer, K. (2021, August 24). *75 digital tools and apps teachers can use to support formative assessment in the classroom* [Blog post]. Accessed at www.nwea.org/blog/2019/75-digital-tools-apps-teachers-use-to-support-classroom-formative-assessment on September 24, 2021.

Ebner, R. J. (2020, September 2). *Tips for fostering students' self-regulated learning in asynchronous online learning environments.* Accessed at www.facultyfocus.com/articles/online-education/online-course-delivery-and-instruction/tips-for-fostering-students-self-regulated-learning-in-asynchronous-online-learning-environments on October 3, 2021.

EDpuzzle. (n.d.). *Obtaining parental consent (templates included).* Accessed at https://support.edpuzzle.com/hc/en-us/articles/360012390292-Obtaining-parental-consent-templates-included- on July 9, 2021.

Educational Leadership Staff. (2014, November 5). 10 inspiring quotes for teaching and engaging students in poverty. *ASCD.* Accessed at https://inservice.ascd.org/10-inspiring-quotes-for-teaching-and-engaging-students-in-poverty on September 20, 2021.

Ellerbeck, H. (n.d.) *Educating children remotely: A focus on social-emotional learning.* Accessed at https://steinhardt.nyu.edu/ihdsc/on-the-ground/educating-children-remotely on November 9, 2021.

Elola, I., & Oskoz, A. (2016). Supporting second language writing using multimodal feedback. *Foreign Language Annals, 49*(1), 58–74.

Elola, I., & Oskoz, A. (2017). Writing with 21st century social tools in the L2 classroom: New literacies, genres, and writing practices. *Journal of Second Language Writing, 36,* 52–60.

Ene, E., & Upton, T. A. (2018). Synchronous and asynchronous teacher electronic feedback and learner uptake in ESL composition. *Journal of Second Language Writing, 41,* 1–13 Accessed at https://sciencedirect.com/science/article/pii/S1060374317304393 on January 30, 2021.

English, K. (2007). *Nikki & Deja.* New York: Clarion Books.

Engzell, P., Frey, A., & Verhagen, M. D. (2021). Learning loss due to school closures during the COVID-19 pandemic. *Proceedings of the National Academy of Sciences of the United States of America, 118*(17). Accessed at https://doi.org/10.1073/pnas.2022376118 on October 3, 2021.

Eredics, N. (n.d.). *5 signs that a classroom is inclusive.* Accessed at www.readingrockets.org/article/5-signs-classroom-inclusive on April 23, 2021.

Ertmer, P. A., Richardson, J. C., Lehman, J. D., Newby, T. J., Cheng, X., Mong, C., et al. (2010). Peer feedback in a large undergraduate blended course: Perceptions of value and learning. *Journal of Educational Computing Research, 43*(1), 67–88. Accessed at https://doi.org/10.2190/EC.43.1.e on October 3, 2021.

European Commission. (2019). *The digital competence framework 2.0.* Accessed at https://ec.europa.eu/jrc/en/digcomp/digital-competence-framework on February 1, 2021.

Feldman, J. (2018). *School grading policies are failing children: A call to action for equitable grading.* Oakland, CA: Crescendo Education Group.

Fenton, W. (2018). *The best (LMS) learning management systems.* Accessed at www.pcmag.com/picks/the-best-lms-learning-management-systems on April 17, 2021.

Fernandes, S., Mesquita, D., Flores, M. A., & Lima, R. M. (2013). Engaging students in learning: Findings from a study of project-led education. *European Journal of Engineering Education, 39*(1), 55–67.

Fetters, A. (2020, November 11). Distance learning is straining parent-teacher relationships. *The Washington Post*. Accessed at https://washingtonpost.com/lifestyle/2020/11/12/parent-teacher-relationships-covid on February 4, 2021.

Feuerstein, R. (1980). *Instrumental enrichment: An intervention program for cognitive modifiability*. Baltimore, MD: University Park Press.

Feuerstein, R., & Lewin-Behnam, A. (2012). *What learning looks like: Mediated learning in theory and practice, K–6*. New York: Teachers College Press.

Feuerstein, R., Falik, L. H., & Feuerstein, R. S. (2015). *Changing minds and brains—the legacy of Reuven Feuerstein*. New York: Teachers College Press.

Feuerstein, R., Feuerstein, R. S., & Falik, L. H. (2010). *Beyond smarter: Mediated learning and the brain's capacity for change*. New York: Teachers College Press.

Feuerstein, R., & Lewin-Benham, A. (2012). *What learning looks like: Mediated learning in theory and practice, K–6*. New York: Teachers College Press.

Field, K. (2020). 10 tips to support students in a stressful shift to online learning. *The Chronicle of Higher Education*, 8–11 Accessed at https://success.camden.rutgers.edu/sites/studentSuccess/files/How%20Faculty%20%20Can%20Support%20Students%20in%20traumatic%20times.pdf on December 13, 2020.

Fiock. H., & Garcia. H. (n.d.). How to give your students better feedback with technology: Advice guide. *The Chronicle of Higher Education*. Accessed at https://chronicle.com/article/how-to-give-your-students-better-feedback-with-technology on September 20, 2021.

Fishman, B. (n.d.). *School is a game . . . but is it a good game?* Accessed at https://online.macomb.edu/courses/22139/pages/school-is-a-game-dot-dot-dot-but-is-it-a-good-game-fishman on February 5, 2021.

Fitzgerald, D. (2020, October 19). Teachers offer virtual learning tips for parents, students. *Government Technology*. Accessed at www.govtech.com/education/k-12/Teachers-Offer-Virtual-Learning-Tips-for-Parents-Students.html on February 4, 2020.

Fleming, N. (2020a, March 27). New strategies in special education as kids learn from home. *Edutopia*. Accessed at www.edutopia.org/article/new-strategies-special-education-kids-learn-home on May 31, 2021.

Fleming, N. (2020b, October 1). Seven ways to do formative assessments in your virtual classroom. *Edutopia*. Accessed at www.edutopia.org/article/7-ways-do-formative-assessments-your-virtual-classroom on December 13, 2020.

Fleming, N. (2020c, April 24). Why are some kids thriving during remote learning? *Edutopia*. Accessed at www.edutopia.org/article/why-are-some-kids-thriving-during-remote-learning on September 25, 2020.

Fletcher, J. (2019, February 14). Using art in assessments. *Edutopia*. Accessed at www.edutopia.org/article/using-art-assessments on October 11, 2021.

Florida Inclusion Network. (n.d.). *Tips for families in supporting their children with disabilities in virtual formats*. Accessed at https://floridainclusionnetwork.com/wp-content/uploads/2020/03/Parent-Virtual-Tips-SWD-Final-03.24.20.pdf on December 13, 2020.

Fonollosa, J., Neftci, E., & Rabinovich, M. (2015, November 19). Learning of chunking sequences in cognition and behavior. *PLOS Computational Biology*. Accessed at http://journals.plos.org/ploscompbiol/article?id=10.1371/journal.pcbi.1004592 on December 14, 2020.

Fowler, D. (2020, June 4). We need to get all Canadian students online quickly in the face of pandemic uncertainty. *CBC Radio-Canada*. Accessed at www.cbc.ca/news/opinion/opinion-children-students-internet-access-1.5583321 on September 14, 2021.

Freeman, S., Eddy, S. L., McDonough, M., Smith, M. K., Okoroafor, N., Jordt, H., et al. (2014). Active learning increases student performance in science, engineering, and mathematics. *Proceedings of the National Academy of Sciences of the United States of America*, *111*(23). Accessed at https://doi.org/10.1073/pnas.1319030111 on September 28, 2021.

Fronius, T., Darling-Hammond, S., Persson, H., Guckenburg, S., Hurley, N., & Petrosino, A. (2019, March). *Restorative justice in U. S. schools: An updated research review*. Accessed at www.wested.org/wp-content/uploads/2019/04/resource-restorative-justice-in-u-s-schools-an-updated-research-review.pdf on December 14, 2020.

Furman, C. (2021, February 1). *Getting to know the whole student in distance learning* [Blog post]. Accessed at https://edutopia.org/article/getting-know-whole-student-distance-learning on September 27, 2021.

Gallagher, H. A., & Cottingham, B. (2020, August). *Improving the quality of distance and blended learning* (Brief No. 8). Accessed at https://annenberg.brown.edu/sites/default/files/EdResearch_for_Recovery_Brief_8.pdf on December 13, 2020.

Gallagher, K. (2020). *How to promote student autonomy in online discussions.* Accessed at www.teachhub.com/teaching-strategies/2020/04/how-to-promote-student-autonomy-in-online-discussions on April 23, 2021.

Gallagher, K., Magid, L., & Pruitt, K. (n.d.). *The educator's guide to student data privacy.* Accessed at www.connectsafely.org/eduprivacy on April 28, 2021.

Gamification of learning. (2021, June 18). In *Wikipedia.* Accessed at https://en.wikipedia.org/wiki/Gamification_of_learning on September 20, 2021.

Ganimian, A. J., Vegas, E., & Hess, F. M. (2020). *Realizing the promise: How can education technology improve learning for all?* Washington, DC: Brookings Institution. Accessed at www.brookings.edu/essay/realizing-the-promise-how-can-education-technology-improve-learning-for-all on September 28, 2021.

Gardner, H. (1983). *Frames of mind: The theory of multiple intelligences.* New York: Basic Books.

Gee, J. P. (2005). Learning by design: Good video games as learning machines. *E-Learning and Digital Media, 2*(1), 5–16.

Ghandour, R. M., Sherman, L. J., Vladutiu, C. J., Ali, M. M., Lynch, S. E., Bitsko, R. H., et al. (2019). Prevalence and treatment of depression, anxiety, and conduct problems in US children. *The Journal Pediatrics, 206,* 256–267.

Giannakos, M. N., Krogstie, J., & Aalberg, T. (2016). Video-based learning ecosystem to support active learning: Application to an introductory computer science course. *Smart Learning Environments, 3*(11). Accessed at https://link.springer.com/article/10.1186/s40561-016-0036-0 on February 22, 2021.

Gilakjani, A. P., Leong, L.-M., & Ismail, H. (2013). Teachers' use of technology and constructivism. *International Journal of Modern Education and Computer Science, 5*(4), 49–63. Accessed at www.researchgate.net/publication/269651683_Teachers'_Use_of_Technology_and_Constructivism on October 2, 2021.

Gili. (2017, January 26). *What is a Hyperdoc and how do I use it???* [Blog post]. Accessed at http://msmshelpdesk.blogspot.com/2017/01/what-is-hyperdoc-and-how-do-i-use-it-by.html on June 13, 2021.

Gillies, R. M. (2016). Cooperative learning: Review of research and practice. *Australian Journal of Teacher Education, 41*(3). Accessed at http://dx.doi.org/10.14221/ajte.2016v41n3.3 on February 3, 2021.

Glossary of Education Reform. (2016). *Student engagement.* Accessed at https://edglossary.org/student-engagement on February 25, 2021.

Gobir, N. (2021). *How sketchnoting can help with "Zoom fatigue," student agency and building relationships.* Accessed at www.kqed.org/mindshift/57500/how-sketchnoting-can-help-with-zoom-fatigue-student-agency-and-building-relationships on March 20, 2021.

Goldberg, R. (2018, December 11). *Digital divide among school-age children narrows, but millions still lack internet connections* [Blog post]. Accessed at https://ntia.doc.gov/blog/2018/digital-divide-among-school-age-children-narrows-millions-still-lack-internet-connections on February 26, 2021.

Goldman, S., Carroll, M., & Royalty, A. (2010). *Destination, imagination & the fires within: Design thinking in a middle school classroom.* Accessed at https://stanford.edu/dept/SUSE/taking-design/proposals/Destination_Imagination_the_Fire_Within.pdf on February 2, 2021.

Golinkoff, R. M., & Halperin, M. (2020, June). *Children have insights on the benefits and challenges of remote learning: Just ask them* [Blog post]. Accessed at www.childandfamilyblog.com/child-development/remote-learning-for-children on September 25, 2020.

Goodman, M. J., Sands, A. M., & Coley, R. J. (2015, January). *America's skills challenge: Millennials and the future.* Princeton, NJ: Educational Testing Service. Accessed at https://ets.org/s/research/30079/asc-millennials-and-the-future.pdf on April 24, 2021.

Goodreads. (n.d.a). *Albert Einstein quotes.* Accessed at https://goodreads.com/quotes/253933-i-never-teach-my-pupils-i-only-attempt-to-provide on February 22, 2021.

Goodreads. (n.d.b). *Bill Gates quotes.* Accessed at https://goodreads.com/quotes/1432743-technology-is-just-a-tool-in-terms-of-getting-the on February 22, 2021.

Goodreads. (n.d.c). *David Amerland quotes.* Accessed at https://goodreads.com/quotes/1293450-we-are-hard-wired-to-engage-with-those-we-trust-and on February 25, 2021.

Goodreads. (n.d.d). *Dr. Seuss quotes.* Accessed at https://goodreads.com/quotes/22842-you-have-brains-in-your-head-you-have-feet-in on February 25, 2021.

Goodreads. (n.d.e). *Maya Angelou quotes.* Accessed at https://goodreads.com/quotes/153929-you-can-t-use-up-creativity-the-more-you-use-the on February 25, 2021.

Goodreads. (n.d.f). *Mihaly Csikszentmihalyi.* Accessed at https://goodreads.com/author/show/27446.Mihaly_Csikszentmihal on February 22, 2021.

Gordon, S. (2021, April 25). *The real-life effects of cyberbullying on children.* Accessed at www.verywellfamily.com/what-are-the-effects-of-cyberbullying-460558 on October 3, 2021.

GradePower Learning. (2018, September 13). *What is self study? The benefits for students.* Accessed at https://gradepowerlearning.com/what-is-self-study on October 3, 2021.

Grading in education. (n.d.). In *Wikipedia.* Accessed at https://en.wikipedia.org/wiki/Grading_in_education on September 27, 2021.

Graham, S. (2019). Changing how writing is taught. *Review of Research in Education, 43*(1), 277–303. Accessed at https://doi.org/10.3102/0091732X18821125 on September 28, 2021.

Gray, J. A., & DiLoreto, M. (2016). The effects of student engagement, student satisfaction, and perceived learning in online learning environments. *International Journal of Educational Leadership Preparation, 11*(1). Accessed at https://eric.ed.gov/?id=EJ1103654 on September 28, 2021.

Greater Good in Education. (2019a). *Encouraging prosocial actions in students.* Accessed at https://ggie.berkeley.edu/practice/encouraging-prosocial-actions-in-students on September 27, 2021.

Greater Good in Education. (2019b). *Prosocial teaching strategies.* Accessed at https://ggie.berkeley.edu/academic-instruction/prosocial-teaching-strategies/#tab on September 20, 2021.

Greater Good in Education. (2019c). *SEL lessons for online learning (middle school).* Accessed at https://ggie.berkeley.edu/collection/sel-lessons-for-online-learning-middle-school on September 27, 2021.

Greene, R. W. (2010). *The explosive child: A new approach for understanding and parenting easily frustrated, chronically inflexible children* (Rev. and updated edition). New York: Harper.

Greene, R. W. (2014). *Lost at school: Why our kids with behavioral challenges are falling through the cracks and how we can help them.* New York: Scribner.

Greene, R. W. (2016a). *Lost & found: Helping behaviorally challenging students (and, while you're at it, all the others).* San Francisco: Jossey-Bass.

Greene, R. W. (2016b). *Raising human beings: Creating a collaborative partnership with your child.* New York: Scribner.

Gregory, A., & Evans, K. R. (2020). *The starts and stumbles of restorative justice in education: Where do we go from here?* Accessed at http://nepc.colorado.edu/publication/restorative-justice on December 6, 2021.

Guglielmino, L. M., & Guglielmino, P. J. (1977). *Self-directed learning readiness scale.* Boca Raton, FL: Guglielmino and Associates.

Gurung, R. A. R., & Galardi, N. R. (2021, February 11). Syllabus tone, more than mental health statements, influence intentions to seek help. *Teaching of Psychology.* Accessed at https://journals.sagepub.com/doi/abs/10.1177/0098628321994632 on September 24, 2021.

Haiken, M. (2021, February 12). *Five ways to gamify your classroom* [Blog post]. Accessed at https://iste.org/explore/In-the-classroom/5-ways-to-gamify-your-classroom on February 23, 2021.

Hake, R. R. (1998). Interactive-engagement versus traditional methods: A six-thousand-student survey of mechanics test data for introductory physics courses. *American Journal of Physics, 66*(1), 64–74. Accessed at https://doi.org/10.1119/1.18809 on September 28, 2021.

Halvorsen, A. L., Duke, N. K., Brugar, K. A., Block, M. K., Strachan, S. L., Berka, M. B., et al. (2012). Narrowing the achievement gap in second-grade social studies and content area literacy: The promise of a project-based approach. *Theory and Research in Social Education, 40*(3), 198–229. Accessed at https://files.eric.ed.gov/fulltext/ED537157.pdf on April 24, 2021.

Hamadi, M., El-Den, J., Azam, S., & Sriratanaviriyakul, N. (2020). Integrating social media as cooperative learning tool in higher education classrooms: An empirical study. *Journal of King Saud University—Computer and Information Sciences.* Accessed at www.sciencedirect.com/science/article/pii/S1319157820305838 on October 1, 2021.

Harris, L. R., Brown, G. T. L., & Harnett, J. A. (2014). Understanding classroom feedback practices: A study of New Zealand student experiences, perceptions, and emotional responses. *Educational Assessment, Evaluation and Accountability, 26*, 107–133. Accessed at https://doi.org/10.1007/s11092-013-9187-5 on October 3, 2021.

Harris, M. (2018, June 26). *Personalized learning w/hyperdocs* [Blog post]. Accessed at www.learnersedge.com/blog/personalized-learning-with-hyperdocs on January 30, 2021.

Hartman, M. (2020). *This fall, back-to-school may block back-to-work for many parents* [Audio podcast transcript]. In *Marketplace*. Minnesota Public Radio. Accessed at https://marketplace.org/2020/08/18/back-to-school-may-block-back-to-work-for-many-parents on September 25, 2020.

Harvard University. (n.d.). *Pedagogical best practices: Residential, blended, and online.* Accessed at https://teachremotely.harvard.edu/best-practices on December 13, 2020.

Hasso Plattner Institute of Design at Stanford University. (2018). *Design thinking bootleg.* Accessed at https://static1.squarespace.com/static/57c6b79629687fde090a0fdd/t/5b19b2f2aa4a99e99b26b6bb/1528410876119/dschool_bootleg_deck_2018_final_sm+%282%29.pdf on December 3, 2020.

Hattie, J. (2009). *Visible learning: A synthesis of over 800 meta-analyses relating to achievement.* London: Routledge.

Hattie, J. (2012). *Visible learning for teachers: Maximizing impact on learning.* London: Routledge.

Hattie, J. (2016). *Hattie ranking: Backup of 138 effects related to student achievement.* Accessed at https://visible-learning.org/2016/04/hattie-ranking-backup-of-138-effects on October 3, 2021.

Hattie, J., & Jaeger, R. (1998). Assessment and classroom learning: A deductive approach. *Assessment in Education, 5*(1), 111–122. Accessed at http://dx.doi.org/10.1080/0969595980050107 on October 3, 2021.

Hattie, J., & Timperley, H. (2007). The power of feedback. *Review of Educational Research, 77*(1), 81–112.

Hattie, J., & Zierer, K. (2017). *10 mindframes for visible learning: Teaching for success.* New York. Routledge.

Hayat, M. U. (2020, August 27). Remote learning for students who don't have internet access in 2020. *eLearning Industry*. Accessed at https://elearningindustry.com/remote-learning-students-dont-have-internet-access-2020 on September 15, 2021.

He, Y. (2014). Universal Design for Learning in an online teacher education course: Enhancing learners' confidence to teach online. *MERLOT Journal of Online Learning and Teaching, 10*(2), 283–298.

Heerwegh, D. (2005). Effects of personal salutations in email invitations to participate in a web survey. *Public Opinion Quarterly, 69*(4), 588–598. Accessed at www.jstor.org/stable/3521523 on October 3, 2021.

Heick, T. (n.d.). *Five levels of student engagement: A continuum for teaching.* Accessed at www.teachthought.com/pedagogy/levels-of-student-engagement-continuum on February 5, 2021.

Heim, J., & Strauss, V. (2020, September 15). School discipline enters new realm with online learning. *The Washington Post*. Accessed at www.washingtonpost.com/education/school-discipline-enters-new-realm-with-online-learning/2020/09/14/e19a395e-f393-11ea-999c-67ff7bf6a9d2_story.html on April 25, 2021.

Heller, R., & Wolfe, R. E. (2015, December). *Effective schools for deeper learning: An exploratory study.* Boston: Jobs for the Future. Accessed at https://jfforg-prod-new.s3.amazonaws.com/media/documents/Effective-Schools-for-Deeper-Learning-010416.pdf on February 26, 2021.

Higgins, S., Katsipataki, M., Kokotsaki, D., Coleman, R., Major, L. E., & Coe, R. (2013). *The Sutton Trust: Education Endowment Foundation teaching and learning toolkit—manual.* London: Education Endowment Foundation. Accessed at https://dro.dur.ac.uk/11453 on October 3, 2021.

Higley, M. (2018). *Reasons why collaborative online learning activities are effective*. Accessed at https://elearningindustry.com/collaborative-online-learning-activities-reasons-effective on April 20, 2021.

Hill, J. (2020, September 22). *High-fidelity, professional-grade audio on Zoom* [Blog post]. Accessed at https://blog.zoom.us/high-fidelity-music-mode-professional-audio-on-zoom on April 17, 2021.

Hill, N., & Gayle, L. (2020, September). *Engaging parents and families to support the recovery of districts and schools* (Brief No. 12). Accessed at https://annenberg.brown.edu/sites/default/files/EdResearch_for_Recovery_Brief_12.pdf on December 13, 2020.

Hill, P. (2020). *Reasons for skepticism in K–12 student learning report*. Accessed at https://philonedtech.com/reasons-for-skepticism-in-k-12-student-learning-report on February 23, 2021.

Hilton, M. (2008). *Research on future skill demands: A workshop summary*. Washington, DC: National Academies Press.

Hiltz, S. R., & Wellman, B. (1997, September). *Asynchronous learning networks as a virtual classroom*. Accessed at https://researchgate.net/profile/Starr_Hiltz2/publication/220426232_Asynchronous_Learning_Networks_as_a_Virtual_Classroom/links/5469f55a0cf2397f782fcee3.pdf on January 30, 2021.

Hoffman, N. (2015, February). *Let's get real: Deeper learning and the power of the workplace* (Policy bulletin). Boston: Jobs for the Future. Accessed at https://files.eric.ed.gov/fulltext/ED561285.pdf on February 25, 2021.

Holland, B. (2016, February 25). *Design thinking and PBL* [Blog post]. Accessed at www.edutopia.org/blog/design-thinking-and-pbl-beth-holland on October 1, 2021.

Holmes, M. M., & Pillo, C. (2000). *A terrible thing happened*. Washington, DC: Magination Press.

Honig, M. I., & Rainey, L. R. (2015, October). *How school districts can support deeper learning: The need for performance alignment*. Boston: Jobs for the Future. Accessed at https://files.eric.ed.gov/fulltext/ED560756.pdf on February 26, 2021.

Hopkinson, A. (2017, April 12). High schools turning to student portfolios to assess academic progress. *EdSource*. Accessed at https://edsource.org/2017/high-schools-turning-to-student-portfolios-to-assess-academic-progress/580147 on September 25, 2020.

Hough, H., Witte, J., Wang, C., & Calhoun, D. (2021, February). *Evidence-based practices for assessing students' social and emotional well-being* (Brief No. 13). Accessed at https://annenberg.brown.edu/sites/default/files/EdResearch_for_Recovery_Brief_13.pdf on September 27, 2021.

Hoy, W. K., & Tschannen-Moran, M. (1999). Five faces of trust: An empirical confirmation in urban elementary schools. *Journal of School Leadership, 9*(3), 184–208.

Huh, J.-S. (2021). *Juggling "roomers" and "Zoomers"? How teachers make hybrid learning work*. Accessed at www.edsurge.com/news/2021-03-17-juggling-roomers-and-zoomers-how-teachers-make-hybrid-learning-work on April 23, 2021.

Hung, D. (2015). *4 unsung environmental benefits of online education*. Accessed at www.triplepundit.com/story/2015/4-unsung-environmental-benefits-online-education/35151 on April 16, 2021.

Hung, W. (2008). Enhancing systems-thinking skills with modelling. *British Journal of Educational Technology, 39*(6), 1099–1120. Accessed at https://doi.org/10.1111/j.1467-8535.2007.00791.x on October 2, 2021.

Hunt, B. (Writer), & Delaney, M. (Director). (2020, October 2). The hope that kills you (Season 1, Episode 10) [TV series episode]. In J. Ingold & L. Katzer (Executive Producers), *Ted Lasso*. Ruby's Tuna; Doozer; Warner Bros. Television.

Hurley, K. (2018, September 26). *Short term and long term effects of bullying*. Accessed at www.psycom.net/effects-of-bullying on October 3, 2021.

HyperDocs Admin. (2020, April 17). *HyperDocs templates for getting started* [Blog post]. Accessed at https://hyperdocs.co/blog/posts/hyperdocs-templates-for-getting-started on February 25, 2021.

Illinois State Board of Education. (n.d.). *Social-emotional learning standards*. Accessed at www.isbe.net/Pages/Social-Emotional-Learning-Standards.aspx on October 3, 2021.

Internal Displacement Monitoring Centre. (2020, April). *Global report on internal displacement: Summary*. Accessed at www.internal-displacement.org/sites/default/files/publications/documents/2020-IDMC-GRID-executive-summary.pdf on April 15, 2021.

International Institute for Restorative Practices. (2006). *Restorative justice and practices*. Accessed at https://4.files.edl.io/d097/06/25/18/174144-1c4b6e52-c7a5-43d1-b70c-d1ca5e9a32e0.pdf on December 13, 2020.

International Society for Technology in Education. (n.d.). *ISTE standards for students*. Accessed at www.iste.org/standards/for-students on February 26, 2021.

Ion, G., Barrera-Corominas, A., & Tomàs-Folch, M. (2016). Written peer-feedback to enhance students' current and future learning. *International Journal of Educational Technology in Higher Education, 13*(15). Accessed at https://link.springer.com/article/10.1186/s41239-016-0017-y on February 18, 2020.

Jacobs, G. M., & Ivone, F. M. (2020). Infusing cooperative learning in distance education. *The Electronic Journal for English as a Second Language, 24*(1), 1–15. Accessed at www.tesl-ej.org/pdf/ej93/a1.pdf on October 2, 2021.

Jacob, R., & Parkinson, J. (2015). The potential for school-based interventions that target executive function to improve academic achievement: A review. *Review of Educational Research, 85*(4), 512–552.

Jacobson, L. (2018). Texting tool gives schools a platform to get parent feedback. *K–12 Dive*. Accessed at www.k12dive.com/news/texting-tool-gives-schools-a-platform-to-get-parent-feedback/539603 on July 6, 2021.

Jalli, N. (2020, March 17). Lack of internet access in Southeast Asia poses challenges for students to study online amid COVID-19 pandemic. *The Conversation*. Accessed at https://theconversation.com/lack-of-internet-access-in-southeast-asia-poses-challenges-for-students-to-study-online-amid-covid-19-pandemic-133787 on December 8, 2020.

James, M. (2020). *The impact of game-based learning in a special education classroom* [Master's thesis, Northwestern College]. NWCommons. Accessed at https://nwcommons.nwciowa.edu/education_masters/244 on October 3, 2021.

Jamso. (2018). *Ten top quotes about gamification* [Blog post]. Accessed at www.jamsovaluesmarter.com/blog/top-gamification-quotes on September 25, 2020.

Jian, Q. (2019). Effects of digital flipped classroom teaching method integrated cooperative learning model on learning motivation and outcome. *The Electronic Library, 37*(5), 842–859. Accessed at https://doi.org/10.1108/EL-02-2019-0024 on January 20, 2021.

Johnson, D. W., & Johnson, R. T. (1974). Instructional goal structure: Cooperative, competitive, or individualistic. *Review of Educational Research, 44*, 213–240.

Johnson, D. W., & Johnson, R. T. (1989). *Cooperation and competition: Theory and research*. Edina, MN: Interaction Books.

Johnson, D. W., & Johnson, R. T. (2002). Learning together and alone: Overview and meta-analysis. *Asia Pacific Journal of Education, 22*(1), 95–105.

Johnson, D. W., & Johnson, R. T. (2004). *Assessing students in groups: Promoting group responsibility and individual accountability*. Thousand Oaks, CA: Corwin Press.

Johnson, D. W., & Johnson, R. T. (2016). Energizing learning: The instructional power of conflict. *Educational Researcher, 38*(1), 37–51. Accessed at https://doi.org/10.3102/0013189X08330540 on September 23, 2020.

Johnson, D. W., & Johnson, R. T. (2017). *Cooperative learning*. Accessed at https://2017.congresoinnovacion.educa.aragon.es/documents/48/David_Johnson.pdf on January 20, 2021.

Johnston, O., Wildy, H., & Shand, J. (2019). A decade of teacher expectations research 2008–2018: Historical foundations, new developments, and future pathways. *Australian Journal of Education, 63*(1), 44–73. Accessed at https://sage.altmetric.com/details/58317803 on October 3, 2021.

Jones, B., & Gerzon, N. (2021, May 21). *Developing student agency during online learning*. Accessed at https://csaa.wested.org/formative-insight/developing-student-agency-during-online-learning on October 3, 2021.

Kabat-Zinn, J. (2003). Mindfulness-based interventions in context: Past, present, and future. *Clinical Psychology: Science and Practice, 10*(2), 144–156.

Kamenetz, A. (2020). Survey shows big remote learning gaps for low-income and special n3eeds children [Audio transcript]. NPR. Accessed at https://npr.org/sections/coronavirus-live-updates/2020/05/27/862705225/survey-shows-big-remote-learning-gaps-for-low-income-and-special-needs-children on September 27, 2021.

Kamenetz, A. (2021). New data highlight disparities in students learning in person [Audio broadcast transcript]. *Morning Edition*. Accessed at www.npr.org/2021/03/24/980592512/new-data-highlight-disparities-in-students-learning-in-person on April 16, 2021.

Kehrwald, B. (2008). Understanding learner experiences with learner support and technology-mediated social processes. *Distance Education, 29*(1), 89–106.

Kelly, D., Xie, H., Nord, C. W., Jenkins, F., Chan, J. Y., & Kastberg, D. (2013). *Performance of U.S. 15-year-old students in mathematics, science, and reading literacy in an international context: First look at PISA 2012* (NCES 2014-024). Washington, DC: National Center for Education Statistics.

Killian, S. (n.d.). *Top 10 evidence-based teaching strategies for those who care about student results*. Accessed at https://newsroom.unl.edu/announce/csmce/5272/29630 on January 30, 2021.

Kirschenbaum, H., Napier, R., & Simon, S. B. (2021). *Wad-ja-get?: The grading game in American education* (50th anniversary ed.). Ann Arbor, MI: Michigan Publishing Services.

Klang, N., Olsson, I., Wilder, J., Lindqvist, G., Fohlin, N., & Nilholm, C. (2020). A cooperative learning intervention to promote social inclusion in heterogeneous classrooms. *Frontiers in Psychology, 11*. Accessed at www.frontiersin.org/article/10.3389/fpsyg.2020.586489 on September 28, 2021.

Klein, A. (2020, January 13). Yes, college admissions officers do look at applicants' social media, survey finds. *Education week*. Accessed www.edweek.org/leadership/yes-college-admissions-officers-do-look-at-applicants-social-media-survey-finds/2020/01 on September 27, 2021.

Knight, J. K., & Wood, W. B. (2005). Teaching more by lecturing less. *Cell Biology Education, 4*(4), 298–310. Accessed at https://doi.org/10.1187/05-06-0082 on October 1, 2021.

Kokotsaki, D., Menzies, V., & Wiggins, A. (2016). Project-based learning: A review of the literature. *Improving Schools, 19*(3), 267–277.

Koohang, A., Paliszkiewicz, J., Klein, D., & Nord, J. H. (2016). The importance of active learning elements in the design of online courses. *Online Journal of Applied Knowledge Management, 4*(2), 17–28.

Koran, M. (2020, June 3). *"Every day looks absolutely wild": The chaos of teaching during a pandemic*. Accessed at https://theguardian.com/world/2020/jun/03/teaching-during-coronavirus-pandemic-california on February 25, 2021.

Kraft, M. A., & Rogers, T. (2014, October). *The underutilized potential of teacher-to-parent communication: Evidence from a field experiment* (RWP14-049). Accessed at https://scholar.harvard.edu/files/mkraft/files/kraft_rogers_teacher-parent_communication_hks_working_paper.pdf on December 13, 2020.

Kraft, M., Schueler, B., Loeb, S., & Robinson, C. (2021, February). Accelerating student learning with high-dosage tutoring. *EdResearch for Recovery: Design Principles Series*. Accessed at https://annenberg.brown.edu/sites/default/files/EdResearch_for_Recovery_Design_Principles_1.pdf on September 20, 2021.

Krutka, D. G., & Carano, K. T. (2016). Videoconferencing for global citizenship education: Wise practices for social studies educators. *Journal of Social Studies Education Research, 7*(2), 109–136. Accessed at https://files.eric.ed.gov/fulltext/EJ1121636.pdf on February 23, 2021.

Kukulska-Hulme, A. (2002). Cognitive, ergonomic and affective aspects of PDA use for learning. In *European Workshop on Mobile and Contextual Learning (mLearn 2002), 20–21 Jun 2002, Birmingham, University of Birmingham*. Accessed at http://oro.open.ac.uk/49020/2/kukulska-hulme%20-%20mlearn2002.pdf on September 29, 2021.

Kupczynski, L., Mundy, M. A., Goswami, J., & Meling, V. (2012). Cooperative learning in distance learning: A mixed methods study. *International Journal of Instruction, 5*(2), 81–90. Accessed at https://files.eric.ed.gov/fulltext/ED533785.pdf on February 22, 2021.

Kuzmanović, D., Pavlović, Z., Popadić, D., & Milosevic, T. (2019). *Internet and digital technology use among children and youth in Serbia: EU kids online survey results, 2018*. Belgrade, Serbia: Institute of Psychology, Faculty of Philosophy. Accessed at https://papers.ssrn.com/sol3/papers.cfm?abstract_id=3514191 on September 28, 2021.

LaBarre, S. (2020, September 3). *Zoom is failing teachers: Here's how they would redesign it*. Accessed at www.fastcompany.com/90542917/zoom-is-failing-teachers-heres-how-they-would-redesign-it on September 25, 2020.

Landers, R. N., Auer, E. M., Collmus, A. B., & Armstrong, M. B. (2018). Gamification science, its history and future: Definitions and a research agenda. *Simulation & Gaming, 49*(3), 315–337.

Lavallee, C. (2020, October 1). *Four strategies for taking the performing arts online.* Accessed at https://globalonlineacademy.org/insights/articles/four-strategies-for-taking-the-performing-arts-online on December 13, 2020.

Lee, C. (2020, March 28). *Real learning in a virtual classroom is difficult.* Accessed at https://arstechnica.com/staff/2020/03/a-crash-course-in-virtual-teaching-real-learning-achieved on November 2, 2020.

Lee, J., & Hammer, J. (2011). Gamification in education: What, how, why bother? *Academic Exchange Quarterly, 15*(2), 1–5.

Lee, J., Song, H.-D., Hong, A. J. (2019). Exploring factors, and indicators of measuring students' sustainable engagement in e-learning. *Sustainability, 11*, 985. Accessed at https://doi.org/10.3390/su11040985 on September 23, 2021.

Leigh, V. (2020, March 20). Distance learning: Parents worry their special needs kids will lose skills. *News Center Maine.* Accessed at www.newscentermaine.com/article/news/health/coronavirus/distance-learning-parents-worry-their-special-needs-kids-will-lose-skills/97-fa29c16c-c1b7-4022-9bd3-98803c32f0c2 on January 20, 2021.

Lei, H., Cui, Y., & Zhou, W. (2018), Relationships between student engagement and academic achievement: A meta-analysis. *Social Behavior and Personality, 46*(3), 517–528. Accessed at https://proquest.com/openview/2802734d3528ae64843257f2c8f8db0f/1?pq-origsite=gscholar&cbl=47863 on September 23, 2021.

Levine, P., & Kawashima-Ginsberg, K. (2015, February). *Civic education and deeper learning.* Boston: Jobs for the Future. Accessed at https://files.eric.ed.gov/fulltext/ED559676.pdf on February 26, 2021.

Lewis, K. R. (2016, October 3). Rethinking child discipline. *The Atlantic.* Accessed at www.theatlantic.com/education/archive/2016/10/rethinking-child-discipline/502667 on December 14, 2020.

Lewis, S., Whiteside, A. L., & Dikkers, A. G. (2014). Autonomy and responsibility: Online learning as a solution for at-risk high school students. *International Journal of E-Learning and Distance Education, 29*(2), 1–11.

Lexico. (n.d.). *Community.* Accessed at https://lexico.com/en/definition/community on September 27, 2021.

Lobdell, M. (2015). *Study less, study smart: A guide to effective study techniques and enhanced learning.* North Charleston, SC: CreateSpace.

Lockee, B. B. (2021). Online education in the post-COVID era. *Nature Electronics, 4*(1), 5–6. Accessed at https://doi.org/10.1038/s41928-020-00534-0 on September 29, 2021.

Lodge, J. M., & Harrison, W. J. (2019). The role of attention in learning in the digital age. *Yale Journal of Biology and Medicine, 92*(1), 21–28. Accessed at www.ncbi.nlm.nih.gov/pmc/articles/PMC6430174 on October 1, 2021.

Loeb, S. (2020, March 20). *How effective is online learning? What the research does and doesn't tell us* [Blog post]. Accessed at www.edweek.org/ew/articles/2020/03/23/how-effective-is-online-learning-what-the.html on September 25, 2020.

Los Angeles Unified School District. (2020, March 30). *Los Angeles unified "at-home learning" partnership with California PBS stations now has over 30 states with local stations using the model.* Accessed at https://achieve.lausd.net/site/default.aspx?PageType=3&DomainID=4&ModuleInstanceID=4466&ViewID=6446EE88-D30C-497E-9316-3F8874B3E108&RenderLoc=0&FlexDataID=87338&PageID=1 on September 15, 2021.

Loughlin-Presnal, J., & Bierman, K. L. (2017). How do parent expectations promote child academic achievement in early elementary school? A test of three mediators. *Developmental Psychology, 53*(9), 1694–1708. Accessed at https://doi.org/10.1037/dev0000369 on October 3, 2021.

Lueth, K. L. (2014, December 19). Why the internet of things is called internet of things: Definition, history, disambiguation. *IOT Analytics.* Accessed at https://iot-analytics.com/internet-of-things-definition on January 21, 2021.

Maclean-Bristol, C. (2017, July 28). *What is a playbook and do you need one?* Accessed at www.b-c-training.com/bulletin/what-is-a-playbook-and-do-you-need-one on October 3, 2021.

Mahoney, J. L., Durlak, J. A., & Weissberg, R. P. (2018). *An update on social and emotional learning outcome research*. Accessed at https://kappanonline.org/social-emotional-learning-outcome-research-mahoney-durlak-weissberg on April 30, 2021.

Mahoney, J. L., & Hall, C. (2017). Using technology to differentiate and accommodate students with disabilities. *E-Learning and Digital Media*, *14*(5), 291–303. Accessed at https://journals.sagepub.com/doi/full/10.1177/2042753017751517 on September 28, 2021.

Major, A. (2020, March 24). *14 tips for helping students with limited internet have distance learning*. Accessed at https://kqed.org/mindshift/55608/14-tips-for-helping-students-with-limited-internet-have-distance-learning on April 23, 2021.

Markauskaite, L., & Goodyear, P. (2014). Tapping into the mental resources of teachers' working knowledge: Insights into the generative power of intuitive pedagogy. *Learning, Culture and Social Interaction*, *3*(4), 237–251. Accessed at www.researchgate.net/publication/260008348_Tapping_into_the_mental_resources_of_teachers'_working_knowledge_Insights_into_the_generative_power_of_intuitive_pedagogy/citation/download on September 28, 2021.

Martin, F., Budhrani, K., Kumar, S., & Ritzhaupt, A. (2019). Award-winning faculty online teaching practices: Roles and competencies. *Online Learning*, *23*(1), 184–205. Accessed at https://files.eric.ed.gov/fulltext/EJ1211042.pdf on December 12, 2020.

Martin, F., & Parker, M. A. (2014). Use of synchronous virtual classrooms: Why, who, and how? *MERLOT Journal of Online Learning and Teaching*, *10*(2), 192–210. Accessed at https://webpages.uncc.edu/fmartin3/site2018/publications/JournalArticles/30_JOLT2014_UseSynchronousVirtualClassrooms.pdf on February 23, 2021.

Martin, J. (2019). Building relationships and increasing engagement in the virtual classroom: Practical tools for the online instructor. *Journal of Educators Online*, *16*(1). Accessed at https://files.eric.ed.gov/fulltext/EJ1204379.pdf on February 3, 2021.

Marzano, R. J. (2017). *The new art and science of teaching*. Bloomington, IN: Solution Tree Press.

Marzano, R. J., Pickering, D. J., & Pollack, J. E. (2001). *Classroom instruction that works: Research-based strategies for increasing student achievement*. Alexandria, VA: Association for Supervision and Curriculum Development.

Mason, J. (2020, August 24). *10 ideas for using virtual breakout rooms during distance learning* [Blog post]. Accessed at https://weareteachers.com/virtual-breakout-rooms/ on February 23, 2021.

Mathewson, T. G. (2019, March 27). How to unlock students' internal drive for learning. New York: Hechinger Report. Accessed at https://hechingerreport.org/intrinsic-motivation-is-key-to-student-achievement-but-schools-kill-it on October 3, 2021.

Matusek, S. (2021, March 16). *The pandemic's remote learning legacy: A lot worth keeping*. Accessed at www.csmonitor.com/USA/Education/2021/0316/The-pandemic-s-remote-learning-legacy-A-lot-worth-keeping on April 16, 2021.

Mayo Clinic Staff. (2019, June 20). *Screen time and children: How to guide your child*. Accessed at www.mayoclinic.org/healthy-lifestyle/childrens-health/in-depth/screen-time/art-20047952 on October 1, 2021.

McCarthy, J. (2016). Reflections on a flipped classroom in first year higher education. *Issues in Educational Research*, *26*(2), 332–350. Accessed at www.semanticscholar.org/paper/Reflections-on-a-flipped-classroom-in-first-year-McCarthy/9cd444f08c92344000c3dd8cfaf8ae5575088dec on September 28, 2021.

McCutcheon, J. (2020, August 27). Internet at home not available to 26pc of children living in remote New South Wales. *ABC News*. Accessed at www.abc.net.au/news/2020-08-28/internet-access-for-students-in-the-bush-unequal-to-city-kids/12601120 on December 8, 2020.

McGonigal, J. (2011). *Reality is broken: Why games make us better and how they can change the world*. New York. Penguin Press.

McLeod, S. (2019, July 6). *9 questions that help get at student agency and personalization* [Blog post]. Accessed at http://dangerouslyirrelevant.org/2019/07/9-questions-that-help-get-at-student-agency-and-personalization.html?utm_source=feedburner&utm_medium=feed&utm_campaign=Feed%3A+dangerouslyirrelevant+%28Dangerously+Irrelevant%29 on February 23, 2021.

McLuhan, M. (1964). *Understanding media: The extensions of man*. New York: McGraw-Hill.

McTighe, J., & Willis, J. (2019). *Upgrade your teaching: Understanding by Design meets neuroscience*. Alexandria, VA: Association for Supervision and Curriculum Development.

Means, B., Toyama, Y., Murphy, R., Bakia, M., & Jones, K. (2010). *Evaluation of evidence-based practices in online learning: A meta-analysis and review of online learning studies*. Washington, DC: U.S. Department of Education. Accessed at www2.ed.gov/rschstat/eval/tech/evidence-based-practices/finalreport.pdf on September 25, 2020.

Mehta, J., & Fine, S. (2015, December). *The why, what, where, and how of deeper learning in American secondary schools*. Boston: Jobs for the Future. Accessed at https://edre.uark.edu/_resources/pdf/whywhatwheremehta.pdf on February 26, 2021.

Mentzer, B., Black, E. L., & Spohn, T. R. (2015). An analysis of supports for persistence for the military student population. *Online Learning*, *19*(1), 31–47. Accessed at https://files.eric.ed.gov/fulltext/EJ1061486.pdf on September 28, 2021.

Meyer, H. (2004). Novice and expert teachers' conceptions of learners' prior knowledge. *Science Education*, *88*(6), 970–983. Accessed at https://doi.org/10.1002/sce.20006 on October 3, 2021.

Michael, J. (2006). Where's the evidence that active learning works? *Advances in Physiology Education*, *30*(4), 159–167. Accessed at https://doi.org/10.1152/advan.00053.2006 on October 1, 2021.

Micklethwait, L. (2004). *I spy shapes in art*. New York: Greenwillow Books.

Miller, E. C., & Krajcik, J. S. (2019). *Promoting deep learning through project-based learning: A design problem* [Position paper]. Accessed at https://diser.springeropen.com/track/pdf/10.1186/s43031-019-0009-6.pdf on February 26, 2021.

Miller, K. (2018, October 25). *Microteaching reflection* [Blog post]. Accessed at https://blogs.lt.vt.edu/ken7jgm/2018/10/25/microteaching-reflection on October 3, 2021.

Mills, M. (2020, September 9). *Why tech troubles are the bane of parents' existence during distance learning*. Accessed at https://www.parents.com/kids/education/back-to-school/why-tech-troubles-are-the-bane-of-parents-existence-during-distance-learning on September 28, 2021.

Moravec, M., Williams, A., Aguilar-Roca, N., & O'Dowd, D. K. (2010). Learn before lecture: A strategy that improves learning outcomes in a large introductory biology class. *CBE: Life Sciences Education*, *9*(4), 473–481.

Morgan, D. L. (2007). Paradigms lost and pragmatism regained: Methodological implications of combining qualitative and quantitative methods. *Journal of Mixed Methods Research*, *1*(1), 48–76. Accessed at https://journals.sagepub.com/doi/abs/10.1177/2345678906292462?journalCode=mmra on September 28, 2021.

Morin, A. (n.d.). 5 reasons students aren't engaging in distance learning. *Understood for All*. Accessed at https://understood.org/en/school-learning/for-educators/empathy/5-reasons-students-arent-engaging-in-distance-learning on January 20, 2021.

Murphy, S. (2001). *Captain Invincible and the space shapes*. New York: HarperCollins.

Myers, H. (2020, October 6). *27 tech tools teachers can use to inspire classroom creativity* [Blog post]. Accessed at https://ozobot.com/blog/27-tech-tools-teachers-can-use-to-inspire-classroom-creativity on February 5, 2021.

National Center for Learning Disabilities. (2020). *Significant disproportionality in special education: Current trends and actions for impact*. Washington, DC: Author. Accessed at www.ncld.org/wp-content/uploads/2020/10/2020-NCLD-Disproportionality_Trends-and-Actions-for-Impact_FINAL-1.pdf on October 3, 2021.

National Governors Association Center for Best Practices & Council of Chief State School Officers. (2010a). *Common Core state standards for English language arts and literacy in history/social studies, science, and technical subjects*. Washington, DC: Authors. Accessed at www.corestandards.org/assets/CCSSI_ELA%20Standards.pdf on May 28, 2019.

National Governors Association Center for Best Practices & Council of Chief State School Officers. (2010b). *Common Core state standards for mathematics*. Washington, DC: Authors. Accessed at www.corestandards.org/assets/CCSSI_Math%20Standards.pdf on April 1, 2020.

National Institute on Drug Abuse. (n.d.). *Trends and statistics*. Accessed at www.drugabuse.gov/drug-topics/trends-statistics on October 3, 2021.

National Institute on Drug Abuse. (2018). *Comorbidity: Substance use disorders and other mental illnesses*. Accessed at www.drugabuse.gov/publications/drugfacts/comorbidity-substance-use-disorders-other-mental-illnesses on December 6, 2021.

National School Reform Faculty. (n.d.). *Four "A"s text protocol*. Accessed at www.nsrfharmony.org/wp-content/uploads/2017/10/4_a_text_0.pdf on April 20, 2021.

National University. (n.d.). *7 social emotional learning strategies for remote teaching*. Accessed at www.nu.edu/resources/7-social-emotional-learning-strategies-for-remote-teaching on October 3, 2021.

Nelson, H. (2020, August 11). Special education resources for teachers to use during distance learning. *Azusa Pacific University*. Accessed at www.apu.edu/articles/special-education-resources-to-use-during-distance-learning on June 12, 2021.

NGSS Lead States. (2013). *Next Generation Science Standards: For states, by states*. Washington, DC: National Academies Press.

Nichols, H. (2020, October 8). Getting set up for collaboration in online PBL units. *Edutopia*. Accessed at www.edutopia.org/article/getting-set-collaboration-online-pbl-units on April 16, 2021.

Nickelsen, L., & Dickson, M. (2019). *Teaching with the instructional cha-chas: 4 steps to make learning stick*. Bloomington, IN: Solution Tree Press.

Noguera, P., Darling-Hammond, L., & Friedlaender, D. (2015, October). *Equal opportunity for deeper learning*. Boston: Jobs for the Future. Accessed at https://files.eric.ed.gov/fulltext/ED560802.pdf on February 26, 2021.

Nordengren, C. (2019, July 15). *Goal-setting practices that support a learning culture*. Accessed at https://kappanonline.org/goal-setting-practices-support-learning-culture-nordengren on April 23, 2021.

Nurjanah, Dahlan, J. A., & Wibisono, Y. (2021). The effect of hands-on and computer-based learning activities on conceptual understanding and mathematical reasoning. *International Journal of Instruction, 14*(1), 143–160. Accessed at www.e-iji.net/dosyalar/iji_2021_1_9.pdf on February 5, 2021.

NYC Outward Bound Schools. (n.d.). *Best practices for virtual project-based learning*. Accessed at www.nycoutwardbound.org/resources-covid-19-response/resources-for-staff-teachers/best-practices-for-virtual-project-based-learning on April 20, 2021.

Ogle, D. (1986). K-W-L: A teaching model that develops active reading of expository text. *The Reading Teacher, 39*, 564–570.

Olesova, L. A., Richardson, J. C., Weasenforth, D., & Meloni, C. (2011). Using asynchronous instructional audio feedback in online environments: A mixed methods study. *MERLOT Journal of Online Teaching and Learning, 7*(1).

O'Dowd D. K., Aguilar-Roca N. (2009). *Garage demos: Using physical models to illustrate dynamic aspects of microscopic biological processes*. Accessed at www.lifescied.org/doi/10.1187/cbe.09-01-0001 on December 6, 2021.

O'Neill, J., & Conzemius, A. (2006). *The power of SMART goals: Using goals to improve student learning*. Bloomington, IN: Solution Tree Press.

Palmer, K. (2021, June 30). *Black and Brown students are more likely to receive harsher and more frequent punishment than White students. The solution isn't just about teachers*. Accessed at www.businessinsider.com/black-brown-students-punished-more-white-school-how-to-solve-2021-6 on October 3, 2021.

Panadero, E., & Jönsson, A. (2013). The use of scoring rubrics for formative assessment purposes revisited: A review. *Educational Research Review, 9*, 129–144. Accessed at www.researchgate.net/publication/234169756_The_Use_of_Scoring_Rubrics_for_Formative_Assessment_Purposes_Revisited_A_Review/citation/download on October 3, 2021.

Panke, S. (2019). *Design thinking in education: Perspectives, opportunities and challenges* [Review article]. Accessed at https://degruyter.com/document/doi/10.1515/edu-2019-0022/html on February 24, 2021.

Pappas, C. (2016, May 6). *7 tips to create visually appealing eLearning courses*. Accessed at https://elearningindustry.com/7-tips-create-visually-appealing-elearning-courses on April 17, 2021.

Parcak, S. (2019). *Archaeology from space: How the future shapes our past*. New York: Holt.

Paris, S. G., & Ayres, L. R. (1994). Becoming reflective students and teachers with portfolios and authentic assessment. *American Psychological Association*. Accessed at https://doi.org/10.1037/10158-000 on September 25, 2020.

Parr, K. (2020, September 29). *How to log in to Edmentum Exact Path* [Video file]. Accessed at www.youtube.com/watch?v=59krrT3UvtE on October 3, 2021.

Pearson Online & Blended Learning. (2020). *Teaching with impact: Developing meaningful teacher-student connections*. Accessed at https://pearsoned.com/teaching-impact-developing-meaningful-teacher-student-connections on February 4, 2021.

Pellegrino, J. W., & Hilton, M. L. (Eds.). (2012). *Education for life and work: Developing transferable knowledge and skills in the 21st century*. Washington, DC: National Academies Press.

Perper, R. (2020, April 12). New York City public school teachers describe being unprepared and overwhelmed as the coronavirus forces schools to shut down. *Insider*. Accessed at www.businessinsider.com/new-york-city-teachers-overwhelmed-unprepared-for-school-shutdowns-2020-4 on September 25, 2020.

Phusavat, K., Hidayanto, A. N., Kess, P., & Kantola, J. (2018). *Integrating design thinking into peer-learning community: Impacts on professional development and learning* [Abstract]. Accessed at https://eric.ed.gov/?id=EJ1211088 on April 19, 2021.

Pitler, H., Hubbell, E. R., & Kuhn, M. (2012). *Using technology with classroom instruction that works* (2nd ed.). Alexandria, VA: Association for Supervision and Curriculum Development.

Plitnichenko, L. (2020, May 30). *5 main roles of artificial intelligence in education* [Blog post]. Accessed at https://elearningindustry.com/5-main-roles-artificial-intelligence-in-education on January 21, 2021.

Poth, R. D. (n.d.). *Powerful learning through PBL* [Blog post]. Accessed at https://blog.definedlearning.com/learning-through-pbl on February 26, 2021.

Prensky, M. (2001). Digital natives, digital immigrants part 1. *On the Horizon, 9*(5), 1–6.

Prettyman, A., & Sass, T. R. (2020, July). *The efficacy of virtual instruction in K–12 education: A review of the literature*. Accessed at https://gpl.gsu.edu/download/virtual-learning-in-k-12-education-literature-review/?wpdmdl=1952&refresh=602b1b845b5dc1613437828 on December 13, 2020.

Quotery. (n.d.). *John Trainer quote*. Accessed at https://quotery.com/quotes/children-not-distraction-important-work on February 25, 2021.

Ralston-Berg, P., Buckenmeyer, J., Barczyk, C., & Hixon, E. (2015). Students' perceptions of online course quality: How do they measure up to the research? *Internet Learning Journal, 4*(1).

Ramachandran, V. (2021). *Stanford researchers identify four causes for "Zoom fatigue" and their simple fixes*. Accessed at https://news.stanford.edu/2021/02/23/four-causes-zoom-fatigue-solutions on April 17, 2021.

Rashid, T., & Asghar, H. M. (2016). Technology use, self-directed learning, student engagement and academic performance: Examining the interrelations. *Computers in Human Behavior, 63*, 604–612.

Reeve, J. (2016). Autonomy-supportive teaching: What it is, how to do it. In W. C. Liu, J. C. K. Wang, & R. M. Ryan (Eds.) *Building autonomous learners: Perspectives from research and practice using self-determination theory* (pp. 129–152). New York: Springer.

Reilly, K. M. (n.d.). How parents can help with homework (without taking over). *Scholastic*. Accessed at www.scholastic.com/parents/family-life/parent-child/homework-help-parents.html on February 4, 2020.

Reinen, B. (n.d.). *Bevin's blog* [Blog post]. Accessed at http://teachtrainlove.com/virtual-learning-13-tips-for-zoom-breakout-rooms on January 20, 2021.

Responsive Classroom. (n.d.). *What is Responsive Classroom?* Accessed at https://www.responsiveclassroom.org on October 3, 2021.

Riddle, T., & Sinclair, S. (2019). Racial disparities in school-based disciplinary actions are associated with county-level rates of racial bias. *Proceedings of the National Academy of Sciences of the United States of America, 116*(17). Accessed at https://doi.org/10.1073/pnas.1808307116 on October 3, 2021.

Rizga, K. (2020, April 13). What teachers need to make remote schooling work. *The Atlantic*. Accessed at https://theatlantic.com/education/archive/2020/04/how-remote-school-can-work-covid-19-pandemic/609895 on November 2, 2020.

Robertson, K. (2014, October 14). *Supporting ELLs in the mainstream classroom: 12 strategies for language instruction*. Accessed at www.colorincolorado.org/article/supporting-ells-mainstream-classroom-12-strategies-language-instruction on October 3, 2021.

Robertson. K. (2020). Distance learning for ELLs: Planning instruction. *Colorín Colorado*. Accessed at https://colorincolorado.org/article/distance-learning-ells-instruction on September 20, 2021.

Roblyer, M. D., & Wiencke, W. R. (2003). Design and use of a rubric to assess and encourage interactive qualities in distance courses. *American Journal of Distance Education, 17*(2), 77–98. Accessed at https://doi.org/10.1207/S15389286AJDE1702_2 on October 3, 2021.

Rockin Resources. (n.d.). *Top 10 things teachers need to know for distance learning* [Blog post]. Accessed at https://rockinresources.com/2020/05/top-10-things-teachers-needs-to-know-for-distance-learning.html on February 25, 2021.

Rogers Behavioral Health. (n.d.). *What toll is social media taking on today's teens?* Accessed at https://rogersbh.org/resources/what-toll-social-media-taking-todays-teens on October 3, 2021.

Rose, D. H., Harbour, W. S., Johnston, C. S., Daley, S. G., & Abarbanell, L. (2008). Universal design for learning in postsecondary education: Reflections on principles and their application. In S. E. Burgstahler & R. C. Cory (Eds.), *Universal design in higher education: From principles to practice* (pp. 45–59). Cambridge, MA: Harvard Education Press.

Rothschild, M. (2014, October). Interview with Constance Steinkuehler. *Focus on Technology in the Classroom*, 4–6. Accessed at https://wida.wisc.edu/sites/default/files/resource/FocusOn-Technology-in-the-Classroom.pdf on October 2, 2021.

Rudolph, K. D., Hammen, C., Burge, D., Lindberg, N., Herzberg, D., & Daley, S. E. (2000). Toward an interpersonal life-stress model of depression: The developmental context of stress generation. *Development and Psychopathology, 12*(2), 215–234. Accessed at https://doi.org/10.1017/S0954579400002066 on October 3, 2021.

Sabia, R., Bowman, J., Thurlow, M. L., & Lazarus, S. S. (2020). *Providing meaningful general education curriculum access to students with significant cognitive disabilities* (TIES Center Brief No. 4). Minneapolis, MN: TIES Center, University of Minnesota. Accessed at https://ici.umn.edu/products/gG7qNWe1TuyhWVtRg6igIg on October 2, 2021.

Sadaf, A., Martin, F., & Ahlgrim-Delzell, L. (2019). *Student perceptions of the impact of quality matters-certified online courses on their learning and engagement*. Accessed at www.researchgate.net/publication/337679226_Student_Perceptions_of_the_Impact_of_Quality_Matters-Certified_Online_Courses_on_Their_Learning_and_Engagement on November 9, 2021.

Sailer, M., & Homner, L. (2020). The gamification of learning: A meta-analysis. *Educational Psychology Review, 32*(1), 77–112. Accessed at https://doi.org/10.1007/s10648-019-09498-w on February 24, 2021.

School Reform Initiative. (n.d.). *The descriptive review of a child*. Accessed at www.schoolreforminitiative.org/doc/descriptive_review_child.pdf on September 27, 2021.

Schwartz, H. L., Grant, D., Diliberti, M., Hunter, G. P., & Setodji, C. M. (2020). *Remote learning is here to stay: Results from the First American School District panel survey*. Accessed at https://rand.org/content/dam/rand/pubs/research_reports/RRA900/RRA956-1/RAND_RRA956-1.pdf on September 23, 2021.

Schwartz, H., & Hill, P. (2021). *Analysis: Survey of district leaders shows online learning is here to stay. Some ways of making it work for students beyond the pandemic*. Accessed at www.the74million.org/article/analysis-survey-of-district-leaders-shows-online-learning-is-here-to-stay-some-ways-of-making-it-work-for-students-beyond-the-pandemic on April 15, 2021.

Scott, S. G. (2009). Enhancing reflection skills through learning portfolios: An empirical test. *Journal of Management Education, 34*(3), 430–457. Accessed at https://doi.org/10.1177/1052562909351144 on October 3, 2021.

Seale, C. (2020, May 19). Parent involvement has always mattered. Will the COVID-19 pandemic finally make this the new normal in K–12 education? *Forbes*. Accessed at https://forbes.com/sites/colinseale/2020/05/19/parent-involvement-has-always-mattered-will-the-covid-19-pandemic-finally-make-this-the-new-normal-in-k-12-education/?sh=600d82485e46 on January 21, 2021.

Section 504 of the Rehabilitation Act of 1973, Pub. L. No. 93-112, 87 Stat. 394, codified at 29 U.S.C. § 701. (1973).

Sessums, C. (Moderator). (2020). *Competency-based learning network: CBL/CBE programs status—Fall 2020* [Webinar]. Accessed at www.d2l.com/resources/webinars/cbl-cbe-programs-status-fall-2020 on October 3, 2021.

Setiana, D. S., Ili, L., Rumasoreng, M. I., & Prabowo, A. (2020). Relationship between cooperative learning method and students' mathematics learning achievement: A meta-analysis correlation. *Al-Jabar: Jurnal Pendidikan Matematika, 11*(1), 145–158. Accessed at www.researchgate.net/publication/346752113 on September 28, 2021.

Sewanee. (n.d.). *Equity, inclusion, and remote teaching.* Accessed at https://new.sewanee.edu/technology/remote-teaching/pedagogy-best-practices-for-teaching-remotely/equity-inclusion-and-remote-teaching on December 13, 2020.

Shakespeare, W. (1998). *As you like it.* A. Gilman (Ed.). New York: Penguin Books. (Original work published 1623)

Shakespeare, W. (2004). *The tempest.* P. Hulme & W. H. Sherman (Eds.). London: Norton. (Original work published 1623)

Shi, W., & Han, L. (2019). *Promoting learner autonomy through cooperative learning.* Accessed at https://files.eric.ed.gov/fulltext/EJ1221280.pdf on April 20, 2021.

Shin, M.-H. (2018). Effects of project-based learning on students' motivation and self-efficacy. *English Teaching, 73*(1), 95–114. Accessed at www.ccusd93.org/cms/lib/AZ02204140/Centricity/Domain/124/Student-Centered%20Learning%20and%20PBL.pdf on October 3, 2021.

Silverman, S. M., Iseman, J. S., & Jeweler, S. (2009). *School success for kids with ADHD.* Waco, TX: Prufrock Press.

Simon, S. B., Howe, L. W., & Kirschenbaum, H. (1972). *Values clarification: A handbook of practical strategies for teachers and students.* New York: Hart.

Simpson, O. (2012). *Supporting students for success in online and distance education* (3rd ed.). New York: Routledge.

Sklar, J. (2020, April 24). "Zoom fatigue" is taxing the brain. Here's why that happens. *National Geographic.* Accessed at www.nationalgeographic.com/science/2020/04/coronavirus-zoom-fatigue-is-taxing-the-brain-here-is-why-that-happens/#close on December 13, 2020.

Smiderle, R., Rigo, S. J., Marques, L. B., Coelho, J. A. P. M., & Jaques, P. A. (2020). The impact of gamification on students' learning, engagement and behavior based on their personality traits. *Smart Learning Environments, 7*(3). Accessed at https://slejournal.springeropen.com/articles/10.1186/s40561-019-0098-x on February 25, 2021.

Smith, D., Fisher, D., & Frey, N. (2015). *Better than carrots or sticks: Restorative practices for positive classroom management.* Alexandria, VA: Association for Supervision and Curriculum Development.

Speziale, K. (n.d.). *Study confirms project based learning has a positive impact on how students learn science and math* [Blog post]. Accessed at https://blog.definedlearning.com/blog/project-based-learning-research on February 4, 2021.

Speziale, M., Speziale, K., McCook, B., & Letwinsky, K. (2016, November 1). *Our research shows that when students work on projects, they learn more.* Accessed at www.eschoolnews.com/2016/11/01/our-research-shows-that-when-students-work-on-projects-they-learn-more on October 3, 2021.

Stewart, R. A. (2007). Investigating the link between self directed learning readiness and project-based learning outcomes: The case of international Masters students in an engineering management course. *European Journal of Engineering Education, 32*(4), 453–465.

Strieb, L. (Ed.). (2011, Winter). *Prospect's descriptive processes: The child, the art of teaching, and the classroom and school* (Rev. ed.). North Bennington, VT: Prospect Archives and Center for Education and Research. Accessed at https://cdi.uvm.edu/sites/default/files/ProspectDescriptiveProcessesRevEd.pdf on September 27, 2021.

Strobel, J., & van Barneveld, A. (2009). When is PBL more effective? A meta-synthesis of meta-analyses comparing PBL to conventional classrooms. *Interdisciplinary Journal of Problem-Based Learning, 3*(1), 44–58. Accessed at https://doi.org/10.7771/1541-5015.1046 on October 2, 2021.

Teacher Tapp. (n.d.). *Lockdown 2.0: What do we know so far?* Accessed at https://teachertapp.co.uk/lockdown-2-0-what-do-we-know-so-far on October 1, 2021.

Teo, T., Tan, S. C., Lee, C. B., Chai, C. S., Koh, J. H. L., Chen, W. L., et al. (2010). *The self-directed learning with technology scale (SDLTS) for young students: An initial development and validation.* Accessed at https://academia.edu/4502039 on February 5, 2021.

Terada, Y. (2018, March 8). Research-tested benefits of breaks. *Edutopia.* Accessed at www.edutopia.org/article/research-tested-benefits-breaks on April 17, 2021.

Terada, Y. (2020, June 23). Covid-19's impact on students' academic and mental well-being. *Edutopia.* Accessed at www.edutopia.org/article/covid-19s-impact-students-academic-and-mental-well-being on September 28, 2021.

Terada, Y., & Merrill, S. (2020, December 4). The 10 most significant education studies of 2020. *Edutopia.* Accessed at www.edutopia.org/article/10-most-significant-education-studies-2020 on December 14, 2020.

Thakare, R. (2018, June 7). *Flipped classrooms: The tool you need to create an elearning ecosystem.* Accessed at https://elearningindustry.com/flipped-classrooms-the-tool-you-need-to-create-an-elearning-ecosystem on September 28, 2021.

Thompson, K. (2017, August 21). The neuroscience of what makes Game Based Learning (GBL) effective. *Business Simulations.* Accessed at https://businesssimulations.com/articles/the-neuroscience-of-what-makes-game-based-learning-gbl-effective on August 15, 2020.

Timms, M., DeVelle, S., & Lay, D. (2016). Towards a model of how learners process feedback: A deeper look at learning. *Australian Journal of Education, 60*(2), 128–145.

Tiwari, R., Arya, R. K., & Bansal, M. (2017). Motivating students for project-based learning for application of research methodology skills. *International Journal of Applied and Basic Medical Research, 7*(5), 4–7.

Todor, O. (2015). Research on the usefulness of Feuerstein method in educating the sociability of children aged between 3 and 7 (preschool children). *Procedia—Social and Behavioral Sciences, 180,* 1692–1697.

Top Hat Staff. (2021, May 13). *20 pros and cons of technology in the classroom in 2021* [Blog post]. Accessed at https://tophat.com/blog/technology-in-the-classroom-pros-and-cons on September 28, 2021.

Torres, K. (2020, April 14). This working mom unapologetically took her first-grade son out of virtual learning and it started a very important Twitter thread. *BuzzFeed.* Accessed at www.buzzfeed.com/kristatorres/survival-and-protecting-his-well-being-come-first on August 15, 2020.

Transforming School Discipline Collaborative. (2020). *Toolkit for transforming school discipline in remote and blended learning during COVID-19: A component of the TSDC toolkit for school transformation.* Accessed at https://static1.squarespace.com/static/5871061e6b8f5b2a8ede8ff5/t/5f29cd58672fd139aebe5eba/1596575066019/2020+TSDC+Toolkit+for+Discipline+in+Remote+and+Blended+Learning.pdf on April 25, 2021.

Truity. (n.d.). *Photo career quiz.* Accessed at https://truity.com/test/photo-career-quiz on January 30, 2021.

Turnali, K. (2016, August 25). Innovation with design thinking demands critical thinking. *Forbes.* Accessed at www.forbes.com/sites/sap/2016/08/25/innovation-with-design-thinking-demands-critical-thinking/?sh=162ed3746908 on October 1, 2021.

Tuttle, M. (2017). *Flipped classroom curriculum proposal for university English language course.* Accessed at https://www.researchgate.net/publication/320107456_Flipped_Classroom_Curriculum_Proposal_for_University_English_Language_Course/citation/download on October 2, 2021.

Tyre, P. (2010, November 27). A's for good behavior. *The New York Times.* Accessed at www.nytimes.com/2010/11/28/weekinreview/28tyre.html on October 3, 2021.

UNICEF. (2020, November 30). *Two thirds of the world's school-age children have no internet access at home, new UNICEF-ITU report says* [Press release]. Accessed at www.unicef.org/press-releases/two-thirds-worlds-school-age-children-have-no-internet-access-home-new-unicef-itu on December 8, 2020.

University of Nevada, Reno. (n.d.). *Active learning spaces.* Accessed at www.unr.edu/tlt/instructional-design/active-learning-spaces on January 20, 2021.

University of New South Wales Sydney. (n.d.). *The RASE pedagogical model for integrating technology*. In *Introduction to educational design in higher education* [Online course]. Accessed at www.futurelearn.com/info/courses/educational-design/0/steps/26421 on October 3, 2021.

University of Waterloo. (n.d.). *Self-directed learning: Learning contracts*. Accessed at https://uwaterloo.ca/centre-for-teaching-excellence/teaching-resources/teaching-tips/tips-students/self-directed-learning/self-directed-learning-learning-contracts on February 4, 2021.

USA Facts. (2020). *4.4 million households with children don't have consistent access to computers for online learning during the pandemic*. Accessed at https://usafacts.org/articles/internet-access-students-at-home on December 8, 2020.

U.S. Bureau of Labor Statistics. (2021, April 21). *Employment characteristics of families summary* [Press release]. Accessed at www.bls.gov/news.release/famee.nr0.htm on February 25, 2021.

U.S. Department of Education. (n.d.). *Transforming teaching and leading*. Accessed at www.ed.gov/teaching on September 28, 2021.

U.S. Department of Education. (2009). *Teacher's guide to international collaboration on the internet*. Accessed at www2.ed.gov/teachers/how/tech/international/index.html on September 23, 2021.

U.S. Department of Education. (2020). *Family Educational Rights and Privacy Act (FERPA)*. Accessed at www2.ed.gov/policy/gen/guid/fpco/ferpa/index.html on February 25, 2021.

Valderas, J. M., Starfield, B., Sibbald, B., Salisbury, C., & Roland, M. (2009). Defining comorbidity: implications for understanding health and health services. *The Annals of Family Medicine*, *7*(4), 357–363. Accessed at https://doi.org/10.1370/afm.983 on February 5, 2021.

van Alten, D. C. D., Phielix, C., Janssen, J., & Kester, L. (2019). Effects of flipping the classroom on learning outcomes and satisfaction: A meta-analysis. *Educational Research Review*, *28*, 1–18. Accessed at www.researchgate.net/publication/333548679_Effects_of_Flipping_the_Classroom_on_Learning_Outcomes_and_Satisfaction_a_Meta-Analysis on October 2, 2021.

Vargová, L., Zibrínová, L., & Baník, G. (2020). The way of making choices: Maximizing and satisficing and its relationship to well-being, personality, and self-rumination. *Judgment and Decision Making*, *15*(5), 798–806. Accessed at www.decisionsciencenews.com/sjdm/journal.sjdm.org/20/200616/jdm200616.pdf on September 28, 2021.

Vaughn, S., Danielson, L., Zumeta, R., & Holdheide, L. (2015, August). *Deeper learning for students with disabilities*. Boston: Jobs for the Future. Accessed at https://files.eric.ed.gov/fulltext/ED560790.pdf on February 26, 2021.

Vernon, J. (2010, July 8). *E-portfolio quotes and definitions* [Blog post]. Accessed at https://mindbursts.com/2010/07/08/e-portfolio-quotes-and-definitions on September 25, 2020.

VocoVision. (n.d.). *Speech therapy archives*. Accessed at www.vocovision.com/topic/speech-therapy on October 3, 2021.

Vonderwell, S., & Savory, J. (2002). Online learning: Student role and readiness. *The Turkish Online Journal of Educational Technology*, *3*(2), 38–42. Accessed at https://files.eric.ed.gov/fulltext/EJ1101894.pdf on January 20, 2021.

von Frank, V. (2011). Leadership teams set the course for school improvement. *The Learning Principal*, *7*(1), 3–5. Accessed at www.spps.org/site/handlers/filedownload.ashx?moduleinstanceid=59054&dataid=37547&FileName=leadership_teams_set_the_course_for_improvement_2.pdf on October 3, 2021.

Vossen, H. G. M., Koutamanis, M., & Walther, J. B. (2017). An experimental test on the effects of online and face-to-face feedback on self-esteem. *Cyberpsychology: Journal of Psychosocial Research on Cyberspace*, *11*(4). Accessed at https://cyberpsychology.eu/article/view/8738/8145 on September 27, 2021.

Vuorikari, R., Punie, Y., Carretero, S., & Van den Brande, L. (2016). *DigComp 2.0: The digital competence framework for citizens—Update phase 1: The conceptual reference model*. Accessed at https://bit.ly/3na8mpb on September 23, 2021.

Walker, A., & Leary, H. (2009). A problem based learning meta analysis: Differences across problem types, implementation types, disciplines, and assessment levels. *Interdisciplinary Journal of Problem-Based Learning*, *3*(1), 12–43. Accessed at https://doi.org/10.7771/1541-5015.1061 on October 2, 2021.

Walma, A. (2020, May 19). *How to engage students in remote learning, part 1* [Blog post]. Accessed at https://kentisdbulletin.wordpress.com/2020/05/19/how-to-engage-students-in-remote-learning on February 5, 2021.

Walsh, K. (2010). *Motivating students to read through project based learning.* [Master's thesis]. St. John Fisher College, Rochester, NY.

Wardlow, L. (2016, April 28). *How technology can boost student engagement* [Blog post]. Accessed at www.pearsoned.com/technology-can-boost-student-engagement on January 30, 2021.

Wayne LEADS. (n.d.). *S.M.A.R.T. objectives.* Accessed at https://hr.wayne.edu/leads/phase1/smart-objectives on September 25, 2021.

Welbers, K., Konijn, E. A., Burgers, C., Bij de Vaate, A., Eden, A., & Brugman, B. C. (2019). Gamification as a tool for engaging student learning: A field experiment with a gamified app. *E-Learning and Digital Media, 16*(2), 92–109. Accessed at https://doi.org/10.1177/2042753018818342 on February 4, 2021.

Welcomer, J. (2020, June 22). *Getting to 100% student engagement in distance learning* [Blog post]. Accessed at https://edsource.org/2020/getting-to-100-student-engagement-in-distance-learning /634282 on January 21, 2021.

Weslake, A., & Christian, B. J. (2015). Brain breaks: Help or hindrance? *TEACH Collection of Christian Education, 1*(1), 38–46. Accessed at https://research.avondale.edu.au/teachcollection/vol1/iss1/4 on October 1, 2021.

White, A. (2003). *The application of Sinclair and Coulthard's IRF structure to a classroom lesson: Analysis and discussion.* Birmingham, England: University of Birmingham. Accessed at www.birmingham.ac.uk/documents/college-artslaw/cels/essays/csdp/awhite4.pdf on October 3, 2021.

Whitener, S. (2017, July 27). *How to understand the difference between goals and outcomes* [Blog post]. Accessed at https://forbes.com/sites/forbescoachescouncil/2017/07/27/how-to-understand-the-difference-between-goals-and-outcomes on November 2, 2020.

Wide Open School. (n.d.). *English-language learners: Resources for grades 3–5.* Accessed at https://wideopenschool.org/student-activities/english-language-learners/grades-3-5/#all on January 15, 2021.

Wiggins, G. (2012). Seven keys to effective feedback. *Educational Leadership, 70*(1), 10–16. Accessed at http://csl.sd79.bc.ca/wp-content/uploads/sites/148/2018/11/Seven-Keys-to-Effective-Feedback-Educational-Leadership.pdf on February 4, 2021.

Wilder, S. (2014). Effects of parental involvement on academic achievement: A meta-synthesis. *Educational Review, 66*(3), 377–397.

William and Flora Hewlett Foundation. (2013). *Deeper learning defined.* Accessed at www.hewlett.org/library/hewlett-foundation-publication/deeper-learning-defined on February 25, 2021.

Willingham, A. J. (2020, September 8). Parents' biggest frustration with distance learning. *CNN.* Accessed at www.cnn.com/2020/09/08/us/distance-learning-problems-parents-trnd/index.html on September 25, 2020.

Wilson, K., & Korn, J. H. (2007). Attention during lectures: Beyond ten minutes. *Teaching of Psychology, 34*(2), 85–89.

Wisniewski, B., Zierer, K., & Hattie, J. (2020, January 22). The power of feedback revisited: A meta-analysis of educational feedback research. *Frontiers in Psychology.* Accessed at www.frontiersin.org/articles/10.3389/fpsyg.2019.03087/full on February 25, 2021.

Wolper-Gawron, H. (2015, February 24). *Kids speak out on student engagement* [Blog post]. Accessed at https://edutopia.org/blog/student-engagement-stories-heather-wolpert-gawron#:~:text=Kids Speak Out on Student Engagement ,last thing... 5 Student choice. More on February 25, 2021.

Worldometer. (n.d.). *World population projections.* Accessed at https://worldometers.info/world-population/world-population-projections on February 23, 2021.

Wright, J. (2011). *All4Ed releases new dropout study on class of 2010.* Accessed at www.economicmodelling.ca/2011/03/23/all4ed-releases-new-dropout-study-on-class-of-2010/ on February 4, 2021.

Wright, R. D. (Ed.). (2015). *Student-teacher interaction in online learning environments.* Hershey, PA: Information Science Reference.

Wuetherick, B., & Dickinson, J. (2015). Why ePortfolios? Student perceptions of ePortfolio use in continuing education learning environments. *International Journal of ePortfolio, 5*(1), 39–53. Accessed at http://theijep.com/pdf/IJEP135.pdf on May 5, 2021.

Xie, X., Xue, Q., Zhou, Y., Zhu, K., Liu, Q., Zhang, J., et al. (2020). Mental health status among children in home confinement during the coronavirus disease 2019 outbreak in Hubei Province, China. *JAMA Pediatrics, 174*(9), 898–900.

Xu, J., Zhang, J., Harvey, T., & Young, J. (2008). A survey of asynchronous collaboration tools. *Information Technology Journal, 7*(8), 1182–1187.

Yahoo! Finance. (2021, April 13). *Frost and Sullivan reveals the 50 game-changing technologies transforming the future.* Accessed at https://finance.yahoo.com/finance/news/frost-sullivan-reveals-50-game-071400443.html on September 29, 2021.

Yildirim, I. (2017). The effects of gamification-based teaching practices on student achievement and students' attitudes toward lessons. *The Internet and Higher Education, 33,* 86–92.

Yogev, A., & Ronen, R. (2014). Cross-age tutoring: Effects on tutors' attributes. *The Journal of Educational Research, 75*(5), 261–268. Accessed at https://tandfonline.com/doi/abs/10.1080/00220671.1982.10885392 on September 20, 2021.

Zeiser, K. (2016, August 31). *Three studies show impact of deeper learning* [Blog post]. Accessed at https://air.org/resource/blog-post/three-studies-show-impact-deeper-learning on February 26, 2021.

Zeiser, K. (2019a). *Spotlight on deeper learning.* Accessed at https://air.org/resource/spotlight-deeper-learning on January 5, 2021.

Zeiser, K. (2019b). *Study of deeper learning: Opportunities and outcomes.* American Institute for Research. Accessed at www.air.org/project/study-deeper-learning-opportunities-and-outcomes on October 2, 2021.

Zeiser, K., de los Reyes, I. B., & Yang, R. (2020, June). *Equitable access to the interpersonal and intrapersonal benefits of deeper learning.* Washington, DC: American Institutes for Research. Accessed at https://air.org/sites/default/files/Deeper%20Learning-Equity-Interpersonal-Intrapersonal-Benefits-508-June-2020.pdf on February 26, 2021.

Zeiser, K., Scholz, C., & Cirks, V. (2018). *Maximizing student agency: Implementing and measuring student-centered learning practices.* Washington, DC: American Institutes for Research. Accessed at https://eric.ed.gov/?id=ED592084 on October 3, 2021.

Zhang, L., Basham, J. D., & Yang, S. (2020, December). Understanding the implementation of personalized learning: A research synthesis. *Educational Research Review, 31.*

Zhu, E., Kaplan, M., Dershimer, R. C., & Bergom, I. (2011). *Use of laptops in the classroom: Research and best practices* (CRLT Occasional Paper No. 30). Ann Arbor, MI: Center for Research on Learning and Teaching. Accessed at https://eric.ed.gov/?q=source%3A%22Center+for+Research+on+Learning+and+Teaching%22&id=ED573973 on October 3, 2021.

Zingaro, D. (2012). *Student moderators in asynchronous online discussion: A question of questions* [Doctoral dissertation]. University of Toronto, Toronto, Canada. Accessed at www.danielzingaro.com/jolt.pdf on April 20, 2021.

Zoom. (2021, September 9). *Requesting or giving remote control.* Accessed at https://support.zoom.us/hc/en-us/articles/201362673-Request-or-Give-Remote-Control on September 23, 2021.

Zydney, J. M., deNoyelles, A. & Seo, K. K.-J. (2012). *Creating a community of inquiry in online environments: An exploratory study on the effect of a protocol on interactions within asynchronous discussions* [Abstract]. Accessed at www.learntechlib.org/p/50700 on April 20, 2021.

INDEX

A

Aberdeen School District, South Dakota, 38
academic mindset, 48
access issues, 6, 36–38
    communicating with parents about, 208–209
    with digital documents, 85
    e-portfolios and, 97–99
accessibility, 84
accommodations, 158
activities, in instructional design, 46
affective engagement, 51–62
agency, 63, 65, 86
agreements, failure to adhere to, 152–154
ALARMS acronym, 109
Americans With Disabilities Act, 197, 203
Amerland, D., 19
analytical thinking, 97
Anderson, M., 154, 156
Angelou, M., 41
anxiety, 6, 154–158
    prevalence of, 154
    signs of, 157
    strategies for, 158
Apple Dictation, 37
apps, 23, 24
    parent instructions for, 212
    podcast-making, 84
artifacts, 32
    definition of, 87
    DIY, 83–84
    instructions for late, 89
assessment, 32, 181–195
    abandoning, 187
    cheating and, 187
    of cooperative learning, 188–192
    definition of, 182
    of engagement, 193–194
    e-portfolio, 90, 92, 93
    of feedback, 161
    feedback and, 167
    how to, 186–187
    of instructional design, 76–79
    learning management systems in, 19
    of needs, 201
    parent/guardian role in, 213–215
    peer, 188–190
    of project-based deeper learning, 192–193
    self-, 168
    team rubrics for, 190–192
    technology in enhancing, 182–185
assumptions, 146
asynchronous learning, 8, 213, 214
    in breakout rooms, 22–23
asynchronous meetings, 54
at-risk students, autonomy and support for, 105–106
attachments, 37
attention span, 33, 213
audio, 203
authentic learning, 67
autonomy
    engagement and, 105–106
    guiding rubrics for, 106, 107–108
    reflection and, 117
    sketchnoting and, 110
    social-emotional learning and, 145–146

B

backward-transfer prompts, 122
Bailenson, J. N., 26
Barrett, H. C., 86–87
basic stems, 120–121
Bautista, K., 199
Bellanca, J. A., 35
benevolence, 163
Bentley, J., 4
Best Buddies, 202
best practices
    for English learners, 73
    for feedback, 166–170, 178
    for online instruction, 4–5
    for project-based deeper learning, 67–68
Bitsko, R. H., 154

blogs, 211
bots, 23, 24
Brain Balance Achievement Centers, 213
brain-based instruction, 8
brainstorming, 44, 45
Brainstorming Chart reproducible, 18
Breakout EDU, 71
breakout monitors, 45
breakout rooms, 22–23
    cooperative learning with, 54
    for elementary students, 58
    scheduling, 58, 60–61
    student instructions for, 56–57
breaks, 27, 31, 56, 200
    parent instructions for, 213
bullying, 134, 148

C

Canva, 88
Canvas, 22
Cardoza, K., 154, 156
care and comfort minutes, 200
career interest interviews, 199
categorization, 97
celebrations, 145
charter management organizations, 216–217
charts, 203
chat backs, 172
chat messages, 54, 129
    engagement in, 130
chat rooms, 22, 62–63
cheating, 187
cheerleaders, 44, 45
Chen, G., 205
Children's Online Privacy Protection Act (COPPA), 90, 216
chunking, 55, 63
clarifying questions, 62
class newsletters, 114
Classcraft, 71
cognitive engagement, 51–62
collaboration, 45
    cooperative learning and, 51–53
    for document organization, 85
    feedback and, 167
    gamification and, 68, 71
    measurable skills for, 53–54
    rules/norms for, 116–117
    technology and, 47

collaborative and proactive solutions model, 151, 152
collaborative discussions, 62–65
Collaborative for Academic, Social, and Emotional Learning (CASEL), 133
collaborative learning, 20
comics, collaborative, 59
communication, 45. *See also* feedback
    collaboration and, 53
    collaborative discussions, 62–65
    community building and, 112–113
    competency in, 48
    digital documents and, 81–101
    email, 37, 117, 152–153
    introductory, 27
    measurable skills for, 53–54
    with parents and guardians, 205–218
    phone and text, 36
    simultaneous online, 48
    stress, anxiety, depression, and, 158
    tools, instruction on, 58
    in VCSs, 32
community, 105, 110–117
    definition of, 110
    getting to know students and, 144
    in hybrid classes, 128–131
    internet access and, 38
    reflection on teamwork in, 124–128
    restorative practices for, 133
comorbidities, 198
competence, 7
compliance rules, 216–217
confidentiality, 90, 100, 163, 210
    breaking, 148
conflict, 130
Connecting Dots Between Experience and Inexperience reproducible, 12, 16–17
ConnectSafely, 90
Consortium for School Networking, 216–217
content expertise, 48
contingency plans, 32, 35–36, 74–75
contracts, restorative, 151
cool feedback, 32, 164
cooperative learning, 42
    assessment of, 188–192
    autonomy and, 105–106
    cognitive and affective engagement and, 51–53
    collaboration and, 45
    community building and, 111–112, 126
    groups for, 52–53

how it looks online, 54
key learning elements in, 55
social-emotional learning and, 134
Cottingham, B., 161
COVID-19 pandemic, 1–2, 5
community building during, 124–126
loss of community in, 110
mental health check-ins during, 134–135
parental involvement during, 206
research on virtual learning in, 46–47
students with special needs during, 200
crashes, 35–36, 73–74
creative thinking, 43–44
critical thinking, 45, 48
cultural considerations, 3
cyberbullying, 148

D

Darby, F., 31, 51, 187
Data Quality Campaign, 216–217
de Bono, E., 121
decision making
creative, 45
mindfulness and, 118
social-emotional learning and, 133
Deeper Learning Hub, 48
deeper learning lessons, 49–50
deeper learning projects, 49–50
depression, 6, 154–158
prevalence of, 154
signs of, 157
strategies for, 158
design thinking, 41–42
adapting curriculum using, 42–45
cycle in, 42–43
roles in, 44–45
Dewey, J., 119
differentiated instruction, 8, 202–203
Digital Competence Framework for Citizens, 34, 215
digital documents, 81–101
creating, 81–84
e-portfolios, 85–100
on expectations, 141, 142–145
organizing, 84–85
protection of, 217–218
students with special needs and, 203
for workflow organization, 81–84
digital skills, 8
digital tool needs assessment, 31

Dikkers, A. G., 105–106
directed reading thinking activities (DRTAs), 3
discipline, 146, 153
discussion forums, 32
discussion threads, 62–63
discussions, collaborative, 62–65
in hybrid classes, 129–130
distractions, 103, 133, 159
behavior causing, 147–152
Dixson, M. D., 193
Dorn, E., 7
DOVE guidelines, 45, 130, 192
Dragon by Nuance, 37
Dropbox DIY, 88
DRTAs. *See* directed reading thinking activities (DRTAs)
Dulin, J., 124–126
dysfunctional behaviors, 147–154
dyslexia, 199

E

Earl, L., 161, 194
Edublogs, 87
Education Endowment Foundation, 161
"The Educator's Guide to Student Data Privacy" (Gallagher, Magid, & Pruitt), 90
EdWordle, 71, 176
Einstein, A., 106
Elk Grove Unified School District, California, 4
email, 37, 117, 152–153
empathy, 43, 157
encouragers, 44, 45
engagement, 7
assessing student feelings about, 130–131
assessment of, 193–194
autonomy and, 105–106
community building and, 110–117
definition of, 103
digital tools and, 106
of English learners, 72–73
e-portfolios and, 86
evidence-based methods promoting, 51–62
in fieldwork, 68
gamification and, 68, 72
goal setting and, 105, 106, 109–110
in instructional design, 43
mindful, 103–131
in peer-to-peer feedback, 174–177
in prosocial behavior, 139–147

responsibility rosters and, 52–53
stimulating online reflections and, 117–128
teaching strategies for, 104
technology and, 47
using VCSs, 32–34
English learners, 6
engaging with online instruction, 72–73
gamification and, 68, 72
e-portfolios, 85–86
common contents of, 93
enriching entries in, 87, 89
grade-level organization of, 94–97
managing, 90–97
organizing, 94–97
pacing charts for, 97–99
privacy and, 90, 100
proficiency checking, 94
schedules in, 137
shutting down, 218
students without technology for, 97–99
systems for, 86–87, 88
teacher, 100–101
equity
assessment and, 183
hybrid classes and, 128–131
major dysfunctional behavior and, 153–154
restorative justice and, 147, 149
students with special needs and, 197–204
European Union Digital Competence Framework for Citizens, 34, 215
evidence, explicit, 46
evidence-based practices, 11
for cognitive and affective engagement, 51–62
in instructional design, 46–48
exclusionary discipline, 153
expectations, 109
clarity of, 167
communicating, 144–146, 206–211
positive, 141
for prosocial behavior, 139–144

F

facilitators, 44–45
fact finding questions, 62
Family Educational Rights and Privacy Act (FERPA), 90, 216
far-transfer prompts, 122
fatigue, 26, 27

feedback, 32, 161–179
after lessons, 173–174
anxiety, depression, and, 158
audio, 167
best practices for, 166–170
in chat discussions, 130
cool, 32, 164
on e-portfolios, 93
formal, 162–163, 170–172, 176–177
guiding rubrics for, 167–170
hard, 164
importance of, 161–162
informal, 162
during lessons, 172–173
model for, 162
to parents, 213–214
peer-to-peer, 172–177
prosocial norms and, 139, 140, 141
seeking student, 41
social-emotional learning and, 146
from students, 170–172
technology tools for, 165–166
tracking correspondence in, 177–178
two-way communication, 163–164, 165
warm, 32, 93, 130, 164, 192
what it looks like, 162–166
field trips, virtual, 33–34
fieldwork, 68
fillable forms, 81–82, 84
Fiock, H., 186
Fisher, B., 173
Fishman-Weaver, K., 199
Fleming, N., 197
Fletcher, J., 172–173
Fletcher, M., 129
Flipgrid, 173–174
flipped classrooms, 8, 42, 71
forward-transfer prompts, 122
Francis Slocum Elementary School, Indiana, 3
Free and Appropriate Public Education for Students With Disabilities, 202
friendlies for all, 177

G

Gallagher, H. A., 161
game-based learning
designing, 68–72
English learners and, 72, 73
playbook for implementing, 68, 69
resources and platforms for, 69, 71

games, 42
Gamification of Learning, 68
Garcia, H., 186
Gates, B., 103
Gayle, L., 137
Ghandour, R. M., 154
Ginopolis, M., 133
Glossary of Education Reform, 103, 181
goal setting, 105, 106, 109–110
    social-emotional learning and, 137
Gobir, N., 110
Google Docs, 36, 37, 88
Google Hangouts, 26
Google Workspace for Education, 36–37
grade reports, 163
gradebook apps, 90
GradeCraft, 88
grading, 182
grading rubrics, 83, 168
Grandin, Temple, 199
graphic organizers, 82, 119
graphics, 203
Graphite, 69
Greene, R. W., 152
grit goals, 74
groups
    for cooperative learning, 52–53
    heterogeneous, 55
    home, 200
    hybrid classes and, 128–129
    study, 54
guest speakers, 33
Guiding Questions reproducible, 15–16
guiding questions/comments, 62–63, 72, 121
guiding rubrics, 83
    for autonomy, 106, 107–108
    cooperative learning, 190–191
    for e-portfolios, 91–92
    for feedback, 167–170, 178
    for reflection on teamwork, 127, 128
    for students with special needs, 201–202

H

Hancock, B., 7
handwriting, 48
hard feedback, 164
Hattie, J., 139, 162, 166, 178
Hawking, S., 200

health considerations, 26
Hechinger Report, 131
Heim, J., 139
Hill, N., 137
Hill, P., 2–3
Hines, T., 173
Holmes and Watson, 59
home groups, 200
homelessness, 6
Hong, A. J., 104
hotspots, 37
Hoy, W. K., 163
Huh, J.-S., 128–129
hybrid classes, community building in, 128–131
HyperDocs, 203
hyperlinks, 203

I

icebreakers, 113–114
ideation, 44
IEPs. *See* individualized education plans (IEPs)
images, 203
impulse control, 201
includer role, 129
individualized education plans (IEPs), 156, 197, 198–199, 201
inquiry, 67
Instruction Idea Gathering reproducible, 15, 34
instructional design, 41–79
    balance in, 46
    for cognitive and affective engagement, 51–62
    for collaborative discussions, 62–65
    deeper learning outcomes and, 48–50
    design thinking for, 41–45
    for engagement, 104–105
    for English learners, 72–73
    flipped classrooms and, 71
    for game-based learning, 68–72
    planning and assessment for, 76–79
    research-based practices for, 46–48
    roles in, 44–45
instructions, 48
    for breakout rooms, 56–57
    for e-portfolios, 87, 89
    for parents, 213
Internal Displacement Monitoring Centre, 2
International Society for Technology in Education (ISTE) standards, 11
    internet access, 6, 73–74

surveys on, 208–209
Internet Essentials from Comcast, 38
internet safety, 148
interventions, 54
isolation, 6, 48, 87

J

jigsaw strategy, 56, 63
Johnson, D. W., 51
Johnson, R. T., 51
Johnson, V., 137
journals
    for feedback, 173
    goal, 110

K

Kahler, S., 110
Kahoot!, 69, 71, 128
Katherine Smith Elementary School, San Jose, California, 32
Kehrwald, B., 134
keyboarding, 177
    handwriting and, 48
Khan Academy, 24, 72
Kidblog, 87
Knows–Needs to Know–Learned (KNtKL) graphic organizers, 171, 172
Knows–Wants to Know–Learned (K-W-L), 171
KNtKL. *See* Knows–Needs to Know–Learned (KNtKL) graphic organizers
Koutamanis, M., 134
Kyer, K., 165–166

L

Lard, G., 32–33
late deliverables, 89
Lawrence-Lightfoot, S., 205
laws
    parents and, 215–218
    privacy, 90
    students with special needs and, 202, 203
leaders, in design thinking, 44–45
learning management systems (LMS), 19–20
    document organization for, 84–85
    e-portfolio alignment with, 90
    key function preview of, 84
learning packets, 75
learning plans for digital skills, 34–35

Lee, J., 104
Lewis, S., 105–106
LMS. *See* learning management systems (LMS)
Loeb, S., 5
Lucas Education Research, 66

M

MacArthur Foundation, 68
makeup workshops, 74–75
making-my-own (MMO) audio, 84
managers, in collaboration, 117
Martin, J., 166–167
Masie, E., 1
Matusek, S., 134–135
Mayo Clinic, 26–28, 156
Mazorowski, A., 1
meetings. *See also* breakout rooms; chat messages
    brainstorming in, 44
    IEP, 199
    morning and end-of-day, 128–129
    with parents, 208, 209, 212, 215
    recording, 33
    roles in, 44–45, 55
    small-group, 130
    team, 71
    whole-class, 114, 128
meetups, small-group, 200
mental health check-ins, 134–135
Merrill, S., 48, 81
metacognition, 6, 118
Microsoft Teams, 26
Microsoft Word DIY, 88
Miller, A., 58
Miller, B., 137
mindful engagement, 104. *See also* engagement
mindfulness, 118
modeling, 119
moderator skills, 64
motivation, 182
museumhack.com, 111

N

National Center for Learning Disabilities, 202
National Geographic Kids, 4
National School Reform Faculty, 63, 65
natural disasters, 2
Nearpod, 187
near-transfer prompts, 122

needs assessments, 201
needs-to-know
    prior knowledge relevance, 50
    SEL workshops, 129
    workshops, 74–75
Nelson, H., 200
newsletters, 114
Nordengren, C., 109
"Normal Attention Span Expectations by Age" (Brain Balance Achievement Centers), 213
norms, 32, 139
    prosocial behavior, 139, 140

O

Ogle, D., 171
online learning
    attention span and, 33
    benefits of, 5, 7–8, 46–47
    best practices for, 4–5
    COVID-19 pandemic, 1–2
    criticisms of, 5–6
    instructional design for, 41–79
    internet access and, 6
    losses in, making up for, 73–75
    prevalence of, 2–3
    research-based practices for, 46–48
    what teachers want to know for, 8
Online Self-Regulated Learning Questionnaire, 135, 136
outcomes
    engagement and, 103
    feedback and, 178
    of project-based deeper learning, 66
    setting expectations for, 140
    social-emotional learning and, 135

P

pacing charts, 32, 58, 60–61
    for e-portfolios, 97–99
    in e-portfolios, 91
    for social-emotional learning, 138
paired partners, 202
Palestine Independent School District, Texas, 38
Parcak, S., 1
parental consent, 215–218
parents and guardians, 1
    in assessment, 213–215
    communication with, 205–218
    e-portfolio privacy and, 100
    expectations communication for, 206–209
    failure to adhere to agreements and, 152–154
    partnership with, 205
    phone calls to, 112
    of primary-grade learners, 215
    in restorative procedures, 151–152
    struggles of in COVID-19 pandemic, 2
    student depression, anxiety, and, 158
    supporting, 212–213
passwords, 100, 218
Paul, A., 52
PBDL. *See* project-based deeper learning (PBDL)
PBS TV stations, 38
PDFs, creating, 31
peer-learning activities, 114–117
performance rubrics, 176
permissions passwords, 100
personal relevance, 50
personalization, 4
Personalized Deeper Learning: Blueprints for Teaching Complex Cognitive, Social-Emotional, and Digital Skills (Bellanca), 35
Peters, R., 65–66
PhET, 24
photos, converting into PDFs, 31
physical drop box strategy, 38
Pillars, W., 110
plagiarism, 148
playbooks, 3, 35–37, 82
    for assessment, 185
    on assessment, 185
    for breakout startups, 56–57
    for e-portfolios, 90, 92
    for fieldwork, 68
    for game-based learning, 68, 69, 70
    for guiding rubrics, 83
    instructional design and, 64–66
    on norms, 140
    responsibility roster, 52, 53
    for restorative justice, 154, 155
    student, 82
    teacher, 82
    for two-way feedback, 175, 176, 182
    "What if?," 74
Playful Learning, 72
playlists, 82–83, 184
plus-minus-interesting tactic, 121
podcasts, 84, 211
poll-group-repoll, 121

polling judges, 45
polls, 114, 121, 210
polysynchronous learning, 8
portfolios, 32
predicting questions, 62
printing documents, 84, 85
privacy, 90, 100
    compliance practices, 217–218
    parents and, 215–218
problem solving, 158
    gamification and, 68
procedures, 28, 30–32. *See also* playbooks
    for prosocial norms, 141
product rubrics, 176
project-based deeper learning (PBDL), 7
    assessment of, 192–193
    benefits of, 66–67
    cons of, overcoming, 67–68
    instructional design for, 65–68
project-based learning, 7, 42
    instructional design for deeper, 65–68
prompts, for reflection, 120–122
prosocial skills, 133
Protection of Pupil Rights Amendment (PPRA), 90
protocols, 63, 65
punishment, 146

Q

questions
    feedback and, 161, 167
    guiding, 72
    types of, 62

R

RAND Corporation, 8
rapport, 166–167
RASE acronym, 46
RASE model, 206
read-it teams, 59
real-life relevance, 50
reciprocal teaching, 59
recorders, 44, 45
recording classes, 33
reflection, 86
    engagement and, 105
    on e-portfolios, 97
    example of deeper, 122–124
    example of quick, 122, 123
    goal setting and, 110
    grade-level strategies for, 119–120
    modeling, 119
    prompts for, 120–122
    self-managed, 118–119
    stimulating mindful online, 117–128
    teacher-initiated, 120
    on teamwork in community, 124–128
registration, 21
Rehabilitation Act of 1973, 202
relationship skills, 133
relationships
    community and, 110–117
    sketchnoting and, 110
relevance, 50
reliability, 163
remote learning. *See* online learning
report cards, 182
reporters, 117
research, 11
    on cooperative learning, 51
    on self-direction, 131
research skills, 8
resources, 8
    for communicating expectations, 206–209
    e-portfolio systems, 86–87, 88
    for game-based learning, 69, 71
    for instructional design, 42
    in instructional design, 46
    for social-emotional learning, 134
respect, 146–147
responsibility rosters, 52–53
Responsive Classroom, 86
restorative contracts, 151
restorative justice, 146–147, 152–154, 158
    template for, 154, 155
restorative practices, 133
Robertson, K., 73
Robinson, L. O., 149
Rothschild, M., 68
round-robins, 119, 129
routines, 109, 145

S

Sarakatsannis, J., 7
say-it-with-love go-rounds, 177
scheduling, 56

for e-portfolios, 97–99
pacing charts for, 58, 60–61
self-management preparation, 58
for social-emotional learning, 158
social-emotional learning and, 135, 137, 145
teacher availability, 112, 113
school climate, 153
School Reform Initiative, 65
Schoology, 88
Schwartz, H., 2–3
screen grids, 129
screen sharing, 21
Seale, C., 215
SEL. *See* social-emotional learning (SEL)
self-assessment, 168
self-awareness, 133, 135, 158
self-directed learning, 47, 48, 131
self-esteem, 134
self-management, 86, 133
    autonomy and, 105–106
    reflection and, 118–119
    social-emotional learning and, 135, 136
    technology and, 47
self-reflection, 86
self-reliance, 52
"75 Digital Tools and Apps Teachers Can Use to Support Formative Assessment in the Classroom" (Dyer), 165
sexting, 149
Sherman, L. J., 154
sketchnoting, 110, 111
Skype, 26, 125
slow learners, 7
SMART outcomes, 49–50, 109
social awareness, 133
social media, 100
    anxiety, depression, and, 156
    distraction from, 103
    mindfulness and, 118
social-emotional learning
    communicating expectations and, 144–146
    distractive/dysfunctional behaviors and, 147–152
    failure to adhere to agreements and, 152–154
    getting to know your students and, 144
    infractions and, 146–147
    prosocial behavior and, 139–147
    restorative justice and, 146–147
    strategies for, 134–135
    student stress, anxiety, depression, and, 154–158
    for students with special needs, 197, 200
social-emotional learning (SEL), 6, 133–159
    community building and, 111–112
    core competencies for, 133
    definition of, 133
    engagement and, 105
    explicitly teaching, 51
    gamification and, 68
    sketchnoting and, 110
    skill development for, 134–138
Socrative, 186–187
Song, H.-D., 104
spammer alarms, 100
special needs, students with, 6, 197–204
    challenges in teaching, 197–200
    differentiated instruction for, 202–203
    gamification and, 72
    transferable skills for, 201–202
Speech Texter, 37
speech-to-text, 37
Spreaker Studio, 84
standards
    cooperative goals and, 54
    grading based on, 182–183
    reflection aligned to, 123, 124
    social-emotional skills, 134
sticky notes, 171
story telling, 59
Strauss, V., 139
stress, 154–158
student playbooks, 82
student response systems, 202
students
    agency of, 63, 65
    digital skills for, 34–35
    getting to know, 144
    leadership of, 63
    preparing for their future, 6–7
    struggles of in COVID-19 pandemic, 2
Students' Digital Skills reproducible, 40
students with disabilities, 6
study groups, 54
subject-matter achievement, 8
suicidal thoughts, 158
summaries, weekly, 211
summarizing, questions for, 62
support, 6, 46
SurveyMonkey, 128, 207
Sutton Trust, 161

synchronous learning, 8, 22
system crashes, 35–36, 73–74

T

tables, 203
T-charts, 54, 56
teacher playbooks, 82, 83
teacher portfolios, 100–101
teachers and teaching
    availability documents, 112, 113
    in COVID-19 pandemic, 1–2
    evidence-based practices for, 4
    importance of, 3
    introduction videos by, 112
    peer teams of for design thinking, 42–43
    reciprocal, 59
    self-assessment for, 183–185
    technology skills of, 6
    what teachers want to know for, 8
    workstations for, 26–27, 28
teams, 32
    community building with, 111
    feedback in, 167
    gamification and, 71
    introducing students in, 57
    procedures for building, 51–52
    read-it, 59
    reflection on teamwork in community, 124–128
    tech genius, 74
tech geniuses, 32, 74
technology, 3–9, 19–40. *See also specific types of technology*
    access to, 6
    accommodations for, 36–38
    correct usage of, 8
    crashes with, 35–36, 73–74
    effects of on student learning, 8
    in enhancing assessment, 182–185
    for feedback, 165–166
    inquiry using, 67
    internet access and, 36–38
    introducing students to your, 28–32
    learning management systems, 19–20
    peer help with, 32
    preparing students for, 6–7
    student engagement and, 32–34
    student skills for, 34–35
    video conference systems, 20–28
Ted Lasso (TV show), 44

templates
    responsibility roster, 52–53
    restorative discussion, 154, 155
    for restorative justice, 150
    self-regulation questionnaire, 135, 136
Terada, Y., 48, 81
text design, 203
text readers, 85
"That's a Good Idea" strategy, 129–130
thinking, 48
    allowing time for, 56
    analytical, 97
    complex, 7
    creative, 43–44
    critical, 45
    design, 41–45
    reflective, 117–128
Thinking Like a Lawyer: A Framework for Teaching Critical Thinking to All Students (Seale), 215
three statements feedback, 177
three-write-share feedback, 171–172
time management, 213, 214
timekeepers, 116
Timperley, H., 166
Torres, K., 1
Trainer, J., 197
transfer prompts, 122
transitions, 145
truancy, 149
Truity, 199
trust, 146–147, 163, 164
Tschannen-Moran, M., 163
turn taking, 56
tutoring, 7, 37–38, 202
    making up for online losses with, 74–75

U

UNICEF, 6
Universal Design for Learning (UDL), 85
University of California Berkeley, Greater Good in Education, 134

V

VCS. *See* video conference systems
video conference systems (VCSs), 20–28, 203
    apps and bots, 23, 24
    breakout rooms, 22–23
    chat rooms, 22
    communication using, 32

crashes with, 35–36
feedback in, 170
introducing students to, 28–32
joining class checklist for, 28, 30
popular, 26
registration, 21
screen sharing, 21
selecting, 25–26
skills for, 34–35
student engagement and, 32–34
waiting rooms, 21
workspace setup for, 26–28, 29
video transcripts, 85
virtual field trips, 33–34
Viruleg, E., 7
Visible Learning (Hattie), 139
Vladutiu, C. J., 154
Vossen, H. G. M., 134

W

waiting rooms, 21
Walther, J. B., 134
warm feedback, 32, 93, 130, 164, 192, 213–214
warm word hugs, 176

we agree feedback, 177
websites, 23–25
parent instructions for, 212
welcome letters, 207–208
Wellstone, Paul, 81–101
"What if?" student playbooks, 74
WhatsApp, 37, 173
Whiteside, A. L., 105–106
Who's on First?, 121–122
Wilder, S., 205
Wisconsin Center for Educational Research, 68, 72
word clouds, 114
workflow, organizing, 81–84
workspace setup for, 26–28
workstations, 26–28, 29
student, 212
touring others', 31–32

Z

Zingaro, D., 63
Zipkes, S., 33–34, 67
Zoom, 26
Zoom fatigue, 26, 27

Personalized Deeper Learning
James A. Bellanca

Foster deeper learning with two templates—one for students, the other for teachers—that increase student agency and learning transfer within critical skill sets. Any teacher—regardless of grade, existing curriculum, or student load—can adapt, scale, and sustain these powerful personalized learning plans. Chapters include driving questions, concrete strategies, helpful tool examples, playlists, sample rubrics, and more.
BKF975

Capturing the Classroom
Ellen I. Linnihan

Harness the power of video to cultivate equity, create stability, and reach students any time. With *Capturing the Classroom*, you will explore doable ways to establish, organize, share, and maintain a video archive to support any content area or curriculum. Learn how to capture lectures, labs, classroom discussions, tutorials, review sessions, and more. Whether you have access to high-end video equipment or simply a smartphone, you've got this.
BKF998

Mindsets and Skill Sets for Learning
Bill Zima

Cultivate confident thinkers who have a strong sense of agency over their lives. In *Mindsets and Skill Sets for Learning*, author Bill Zima clearly outlines what student agency looks and sounds like in the classroom. Rely on the book's framework to help you develop a learner-centered classroom culture, establish well-defined learning targets, deliberately plan and structure lessons, and more.
BKL051

Creating the Anywhere, Anytime Classroom
Casey Reason, Lisa Reason, and Crystal Guiler

Discover how to enhance student learning in online and blended classrooms. This user-friendly resource offers direct guidance on the steps K–12 educators must take to facilitate online learning and maximize student growth using digital tools. Each chapter includes suggestions, tips, and examples tied to pedagogical practices associated with learning online, so you can confidently engage in the best practices with your students.
BKF772

Virtual PLCs at Work®
Paul C. Farmer and Dennis King

Virtual teaming and virtual learning have been practiced for decades but never to the level required today. As the educational landscape continues to evolve, ensure your PLC evolves right along with it. With this resource as your guide, you'll explore an abundance of tools and tips for maintaining your PLC structures and proven best practices to help instruction and learning thrive beyond the four walls of your school.
BKG028

Solution Tree | Press

Visit solution-tree.com or call 800.733.6786 to order.

Wait! Your professional development journey doesn't have to end with the last pages of this book.

We realize improving student learning doesn't happen overnight. And your school or district shouldn't be left to puzzle out all the details of this process alone.

No matter where you are on the journey, we're committed to helping you get to the next stage.

Take advantage of everything from **custom workshops** to **keynote presentations** and **interactive web and video conferencing**. We can even help you develop an action plan tailored to fit your specific needs.

Let's get the conversation started.

Call 888.763.9045 today.

SolutionTree.com